Stanley W. Lore
1972

ANXIETY AND EGO FORMATION IN INFANCY

Sylvia Brody and Sidney Axelrad

INTERNATIONAL UNIVERSITIES PRESS, Inc.

New York   New York

Copyright 1970, International Universities Press, Inc.

Library of Congress Catalog Card Number: 74-141660

Manufactured in the United States of America

CONTENTS

FOREWORD

A number of years ago we began work on the theoretical aspects of this book, prompted by a dissatisfaction with the state of psychoanalytic ego psychology, which was based upon propositions about the mental life of the infant without recourse to direct observation of infants. Although hypotheses about early psychic development may emerge from psychoanalytic reconstruction, a theory of psychic development should explicate a series of logically interconnected relationships about direct observations. This position was reinforced when, during the work of the Infant Development Research Project, we began to see systematic connections between the behavior of mothers and their infants which, to the best of our knowledge, could not be articulated retrospectively by the clinical method of psychoanalytic reconstruction; and when we realized that our observations of infants in the first year of life could not be fitted into the framework of what is commonly referred to as ego psychology. We have tried to set forth a theory of some aspects of early ego formation that is within the structure of classic psychoanalysis and that is confirmed by our observations and, of course, by observations of many others in the fields of psychoanalysis, developmental psychology, and ethology.

The core of this book consists of material about the mothers and infants studied in the Infant Development Research Project. These data were not gathered to test our theory. If they had been, we would have filled one of the gaps in our material of which we are aware. For example, data for the intervals in between the four ages at which we observed the infants derive

v

only from interviews. The Project originally was designed to find out whether the typology of maternal behavior described in *Patterns of Mothering* could be replicated in an urban environment, with a much larger sample, studied longitudinally through the first year of the infants' lives. Collection of information about the growth of the infants was inherent in the plan of procedures; so at the end of the study there was at hand a body of material about emotional and cognitive development of infants which could be related to types of mothering they had received. The same material could serve as an empirical test of the theory previously developed, and as raw data for its refinement.

This presentation is intended primarily for the psychoanalytically oriented clinician. The method of the study was naturalistic, not experimental, except as the tests which yield developmental quotients are little experiments. Basically, we have quantified and tested clinical judgments and observations by means of appropriate statistical measures.

The research was supported by The National Institute of Mental Health (Grant 1429) between 1963 and 1967. The writing of this book was greatly encouraged by the decision of The Grant Foundation to support a further longitudinal study of the mothers and infants, in which we are engaged. We feel immense gratitude to Caroline Chandler, M.D., then of The National Institute of Mental Health, to Eli Ginzberg, Hepburn Professor of Economics at Columbia University, and to Adele Whitney Morrison, of The Grant Foundation, for their deep interest in our work.

The investigation was made possible by the support of Dr. Hugh R. K. Barber, Chief of Obstetrics in the hospital where we worked. Dr. Irwin P. Sobel, Chief of Pediatrics, helped us with enthusiasm in the planning stages of the research, and was a constant source of encouragement and assistance during the conduct of the study, when we were members of the Department of Pediatrics. Without him this study would not have been possible. The work was carried out with the help, during various periods, of Deborah B. Beck, Susan W. Coates, Yale Kramer, M.D., the late Rose Coleman Lipton, M.D., Suzanne W. Todd, and the late Aimee Wiggers, M.D. Dorothy C. Krugman, as psychological consultant, generously made available to us her extensive knowledge of infant testing procedures and evaluation. Edward T. Meyer assisted as statistical and programming consultant. Special thanks are due to Stanley Kahn for his help as administrative assistant, and to Suzanne W. Todd for her unfailing tact in dealing with mothers; and to both for their steadfast identification with the aims of the Project.

We are indebted to Salomea Isákower, M.D., and to Margaret Mahler, M.D., for having read and commented upon an early version of a part of the manuscript; to Professor Leo Zippin of the Department of Mathematics of Queens College of the City University of New York, for having read a section of the final manuscript and examined a part of the statistical analysis; to Professor Paul Neurath of the Department of Sociology, and Professor Emma Spaney of the Department of Psychology, of Queens College of the City University of New York, who helped us substantially as statistical consultants in various phases of the work; to Professor Seymour Goodman, Director of the Computer Center of Queens College of the City University of New York, who helped us more than he would be willing to say. Dean Marvin Taylor of Queens College of the City University of New York read the entire manuscript and reviewed the statistical procedures.

We are very grateful to Marsha Moroh, statistician of the Child Development Research Project, for her thoughtfulness and patience while she helped us in the final phase of presenting our findings; to Elisabeth R. Jenks, M.D., who cheerfully answered many medical questions that arose in the course of the work and the data analysis; and we owe many thanks to the staff of the Office of the Division of Graduate Studies of Queens College of the City University of New York, who performed a remarkably cooperative and efficient task in preparing a very

complicated manuscript. The authors, of course, have the sole
responsibility for whatever errors are to be found in the book.

Sylvia Brody, Adjunct Professor of Psychology
Graduate Department of Psychology
Graduate Center, City University of New York

Sidney Axelrad, Dean of Graduate Studies
Queens College of the City University of New York
Co-Director, Child Development Research Project

September 1969

Part I
STRUCTURE AND EVENT IN EARLIEST EGO FORMATION

CHAPTER 1

Infantile Anxiety and Ego Formation

The emergence of the affect[1] of anxiety from a matrix of physiological and psychic interrelationships during infancy is a complex and significant issue. All of our genetic formulations regarding psychological health and illness, and many dynamic formulations regarding defenses, rest upon our understanding of the processes of this emergence. We should like to embark upon its study equipped with a knowledge of the reciprocal influences of cognition and primary process and of the nature of consciousness. We should like to have at hand some accepted classification and theory of affects. But in addition to our metapsychological theory and a great array of clinical reports, we have only a modest group of empirical findings, mainly about early evidence of ego function, to work with.

We shall present a synopsis of that part of the literature which has most heavily influenced our thinking. It is by no means complete. It does not review the enormous number of writings on the topic, nor does it provide a full description of

---

[1]*Affect* and *emotion* are used interchangeably here, and denote *awareness* of a stirred-up state of the organism. There are both maturational and developmental factors in the emergence of this awareness. Part of the burden of this book is to spell out these factors in particular. Before the development of the affect, the very young infant is subject to stirred-up states. The most obvious is the affectomotor storm. We assume that he responds to these states without mental awareness of them and that the same situation is true of pleasurable stirred-up states, as evidenced by the smiling of the four-week-old.

3

the works of the authors cited. We wish mainly to show the groundwork from which our ideas have come. Despite all of the advances of modern ego psychology, the ego itself still has to be understood, according to Freud's definition of 1923, as a coherent organization of mental processes, i.e., as a state of psychic organization which makes possible mediation between the demands made upon the organism by the instinctual drives, by reality, and by ethical values. We understand ego *formation*, then, as the development of the cumulative process by which the control of functions necessary for that intrapsychic mediation takes place. Since the quality of this control is highly variable within the individual, especially during periods of change and of heightened conflict, the quality of ego functioning in any person will depend upon the strength and maturity of specific organic structures as well.[2]

In recent times the ego has been said, more or less loosely, to be defined by its functions. The statement is useful for descriptive purposes, but it leads away from an understanding of processes involved in the development of the ego as a psychic entity. Perception, motility, memory, reality testing, abstract reasoning, are commonly stated to be functions of the ego. But if the ego is defined as if it were a series of behaviors, eventually one is left with a position closer to that of classic behaviorism, or to Allport's concept of functional autonomy. Once behavioral aspects are stressed, it becomes more parsimonious to deal with the black box than with the concept of psychic structure.

Our viewpoint is that forms of behavior are under the jurisdiction of the ego. We therefore suggest the conceptualization that the ego is a psychic structure linked to behavior through the control of behavior. Provisionally, we might describe ego formation as follows: Sensations have to register

---

[2]At any specific moment or period of time the quality will be governed according to the principle of multiple function (Waelder, 1936); the general level of efficacy and the general degree of stability of the ego in any person may best be indicated by statements describing the synthetic function (Nunberg, 1931).

upon an immature psyche, not yet organized into a psychic structure. When they are inwardly perceived, the capacity to observe begins. The development of a set of control functions is absolutely dependent upon the priority of this psychic act. The primary organization of primary observations, and the consequent control of functions, constitute essential mental processes that later will be absorbed by the ego.

There is common agreement that anxiety proper can be experienced only at a certain point of ego organization. This does not tell us even in a broad way what are the psychic conditions necessary for recognizing a danger and for recognizing affective experience as happening within a self—the precondition for anxiety proper. It does not clarify by what means the inner recognition takes place, nor what distribu-tions of energy may be needed for the affective and the cognitive experiences per se. An understanding of those distributions would involve prior insight into certain more elementary functions governed by the ego: object recognition, a vague body consciousness, vague awareness of sensory responsiveness and motility, and perhaps even some archaic and amorphous notions of cause and effect—some precursors of a secondary process. To a large extent, this book is devoted to an explication of these processes.

When in 1926 Freud stated that the ego was the seat of anxiety, he was revising his earlier theory of anxiety as transformed libidinal energy. He was attempting to make sharply clear that anxiety has a physiological base in excitations occurring within the birth process, and that later in infancy the same kinds of physiological responses are pressed into service to alert the organism to impending danger. Freud in that context was not especially concerned with the ways in which the transition from physiological to psychological anxiety came about. It was enough to postulate that the transition took place as a result of danger felt by the infant—essentially the danger of being alone and helpless—and that the felt experience was affective and so necessarily belonged to the psychic organization of the ego. Freud's statement implies that a rudimentary ego must have attained some stage of development for anxiety to occur. In recent years, various important considerations regarding this development have been expressed. Greenacre (1941, 1945) asked whether a predisposition to anxiety may not stem from constitutional factors, in particular from the intensity of reflex stimulations that are experienced in the fetal and perinatal periods and that are organized at birth or shortly after. The constitutional factors might mark the threshold at which danger—which may first be understood in the lack of familiarity—begins to be vaguely apprehended. Greenacre's position (1945) suggested that physiologically caused anxieties might be prerequisite to "a first dawn of psychic content." She was referring to a later predisposition to anxiety, to an anxiety-riddled ego, and was relating the later occurrence to infantile events. There is no contradiction between her viewpoint and ours; our concerns are with temporally different aspects of the same process.

Ribble (1945) dealt with physiological effects of tension states in early infancy. She proposed that excessive hunger for oxygen, food, stimulation, and other instinctual satisfactions constituted primary physiological dangers to which infants were most vulnerable in the first three months of life, and which promoted "pre-affect" anxiety. Ribble, however, was not concerned with the shaping of a psychic institution by anxiety. Spitz (1950) stated explicitly that the affect of anxiety arises from conflict between ego and id: accordingly, ego differentiation is prerequisite to the appearance of anxiety proper, which Spitz placed after the sixth month. The process of establishing the ego he placed between the third and the sixth month. Before that, he said, physiological tension states arise from conflict among the drives or between the infant's "whole system" and the environment. Spitz also distinguished between fear and anxiety in infancy: fear provoking flight from a consciously remembered and recognized threat, anxiety being a danger signal, its prototype the birth experience; he added that anxiety is aroused unconsciously by threat against the protective shield. Hoffer (1952) raised the question of what psychological events bring about cathexis of body and of objects. He suggested that as physiological stress becomes used for the anticipation of anxiety, active drives toward objects emerge and a partial id-ego differentiation takes place.

Bowlby (1960a, 1960b) considered several conceptualizations of anxiety and sought to explain its origin in the experiences of the infant. He distinguished between primary anxiety, which is very close to Freud's early theory of dammed-up libido; fright, which impels toward escape reactions; and expectant or anticipatory anxiety, which implies some foresight, and avoidance behavior. Primary anxiety occurs with physical separation from the mother, is "due simply to the rupture of the attachment" from her, and is an outcome of the nontermination of activated instinctual response systems: "Soon after birth ... conditions of isolation tend to activate crying and a little later tend to activate both clinging and following also; until [the infant] is in close proximity to-his familiar mother-figure these instinctual response systems do not cease motivating him. Pending this outcome, it is suggested, his subjective experience is that of primary anxiety; when he is close to her it is one of comfort" (Bowlby, 1960a, p. 93). Primary anxiety, at least in the beginning, is not to be construed as signal anxiety, although if it reaches a certain degree of intensity it is linked directly to the onset of defense mechanisms. Bowlby made these distinctions for the purpose of a discussion of separation anxiety, and was explicit about not dealing with anxiety arising from the threat of psychic disorganization. The latter threat is integral to our thinking, as we consider it to be a base of all anxiety proper.

Freud (1926) had written, "It very often happens that processes take place or begin to take place in the id which cause the ego to produce anxiety," and Brenner (1955), touching upon the problem of how the ego can do this, suggested that probably the perception of danger gives rise to a fantasy of a traumatic situation, and that it is the fantasy which causes signal anxiety. This suggestion borders on a proposition that we shall submit. The point of difference from our proposition, and it is a fundamental one, lies in our disinclination to think that signal anxiety can be touched off initially by a fantasy. It appears to us that the signal in infancy rather is composed of far more elementary phenomena. In the adult, some experience that is associatively linked to a fantasy does, of course, touch off neurotic signal anxiety. And finally, Benjamin (1961) asked, "When is the ego mature enough to experience anxiety?"

Certain questions which seem to us preliminary to an inquiry into the emergence of the affect of anxiety are thus foreshadowed. For example, we may ask: At what point of cortical development can tension states be perceived to reside in the body? At what point of either internal or external stimulation can perception create or release a signal that the body is in danger of disequilibrium? These questions oblige us to examine the significance of recent findings regarding earliest sensory responsiveness of human and lower organisms, and, where possible, to relate the findings to psychoanalytic postulates regarding psychic development.

This examination is intended to clarify our central propositions: that the emergence of the affect of anxiety and the beginning of ego formation take place in conjunction with one another, and that the two events flow out of a joint process. We suggest that physiological *arousals* promote the exercise of perceptual and motoric structures, and that perception of the tension states thus aroused is reacted to with affect. Cognition and affect continue, in concert, to promote normal development of ego functions. This set of propositions does not merely construe for infancy a situation analogous to phases of childhood, when anxiety is frequently a spur to ego development or to mastery of instinctual impulses.[3] The propositions are concerned rather with the inherent quality of anxiety, and with the distribution of cathectic energy which gives it prescience and truly seats it in the ego. A tentative summary

[3]This relationship is almost a paradigm for the role of anxiety in the analytic process.

description of these psychic events of early infancy would be: Anxiety is one of the principal affects with which the ego is ushered into being; as the infant organism perceives some dystonic condition in his own body and perceives as well his own immediate, involuntary response to the condition, the ego is born and exercises a primary function.[4]

[4]We shall not take up issues of primary ego autonomy and ego apparatuses, e.g., Hartmann (1950). Obviously, the capacity for ego development rests upon the presence of inborn structures. Problems inherent in the concept of primary autonomy have been dealt with elsewhere (Brody, 1956). "Ego apparatuses" seems to us an unwieldy term because it suggests, as indicated above, that the ego is composed of a group of functions or that the functions are part of an ego equipment, whereas it is more precise and economical to say that the ego controls the functions. It also appears to us simpler to think of organic *structures* that allow for the maturation of behavior, and ego *functions* that serve to organize small units of behavior, for purposes that may be rational or irrational. The term *apparatus* often dulls necessary distinctions between what is organic, what is behavioral, and what is functional. We have also not made use of the terminology of Piaget in these considerations, although our thesis does use some of Piaget's observations and some of his modes of conceptualization. The greatest difference between his formulations and ours probably lies in our explicit reference to memory traces. Piaget does, however, use such terms as "familiar," "accommodating," "assimilating," and "recognizing," and we submit that if one shifts the focus of attention from the activation of reflexes to the functions of affective residues in mental life, then for each of the latter concepts of Piaget some structural element of memory, i.e., a combination of an engram and an ability to recognize an already experienced object, is implicit.

CHAPTER 2

Sensorimotor Development

A number of psychoanalysts have transposed empirical findings from physiology and psychology about maturation and development during human infancy into a framework of psychoanalytic theory concerning, for example, ego-id differentiation, early object relations, and anxiety.[1] The psychoanalytic statements resulting from this transposition have been expressed globally, for the most part; some of them will be referred to below. But as more, and more findings relevant to psychoanalysis appear, because certain behavioral sciences have concentrated increasingly on aspects of early development, it behooves us to examine those that may have effects upon metapsychology, and to state the relationships in terms of psychoanalytic theory as specifically as possible.

Carmichael (1951) assembled and reviewed evidence showing that the responsiveness of the fetal organism changes with changing maturity. One same stimulus may evoke different though not necessarily maturer reactions at different points of development, but each response, when it occurs, is specific and not chance. Carmichael reports that an observed fetal reaction may, as a total pattern, be new, but it comprises specific units that are not new. It results from both the maturational state of the organism and the vestibular and proprioceptive stimuli

---

[1]E.g., Ambrose (1961, 1963b), Gifford (1960), Greenacre (1941, 1944, 1945), Kris (1951), Schur (1953, 1958), Spitz (1945, 1946a, 1951a, 1955, 1957).

momentarily affecting postural tonus. Thus, while an observed reaction is not focused and involves a general neuromuscular action, the conditions under which it is elicited directly alter its specificity. To complicate the assessment of the fetal reaction, there is the fact that during "refractory periods" responses may not appear at all. The "disappearance" of certain responses is readily observable in normal neonates, whose changing levels of consciousness and states of need or of alertness affect their immediate responsiveness. Carmichael states clearly that each response that does occur is specific, and is traceable to specific qualities in the stimulus and in the fetal organism; that at any point of growth the nonappearance of a particular response may indicate only a quiescence, not a nonexistence, of the related functions; that functional capacities may be demonstrated well before the given function can take a useful role; and that development of many kinds of response proceed with a varying rhythm.

Behavior is called 'spontaneous' when it is not easily traceable to specific stimulation. Thus, it is a name for ignorance. So-called spontaneous behavior may result from a number of antecedent conditions, such as an alteration in the internal environment of the organism. It may also result from hidden or unobserved stimulation of receptor mechanisms such as those in the muscles, tendons, joints, or the non-auditory labyrinth of the inner ear [1951, p. 293].

To state the existence of a relationship between individual behavior and specific elements in the total situation in which behavior occurs would appear to be a truism, especially when by total situation we include both internal and external environments. Applied to the behavior of an infant, this means that while an infant's response would be restricted to what he is so far capable of, organically and psychologically, the response is not to be considered random or inconsistent. It is very difficult to believe this if one makes only short or random or inconsistent observations of neonates, and it is extremely frustrating to measure responsiveness in a short trial. But an assumption of randomness in infant behavior would imply that determinism operates only after an initial developmental period, and that events of early infancy are as insignificant for later development as the events of childhood were long assumed to be. Nissen (1951) put the problem aptly in his comprehensive discussion of phylogenetic comparisons: where the situation is a relatively open one and provides opportunities for varied activity, the behavior may be called random, but it is never truly so, for always it is determined by environmental conditions plus the perception of them by the infant.

From Pratt's studies (1954), probably the most comprehensive ones yet available on the subject of neonatal development, we take one finding to be of main relevance here. It is that the greater the duration and intensity of an external stimulus, the more it may absorb the attention of the infant. While this may appear too obvious to be of special importance, it has major implications. These are: that a series of long-lasting and intense stimuli are likely to have significantly different effects than short and weak ones; that long-lasting and intense inner stimuli may at a certain point of duration and strength be sufficient to block out responses to outer stimuli, and vice versa; and that the whole balance of pressure from inner and outer sources is likely to be experienced with wide individual variation at successive stages, and especially at the earliest stages of greatest vulnerability to stimuli of any kind. An assessment of what constitutes long or short duration, with lesser or greater intensity of the stimulus, involves examination of patterns of individual capacities for discrete forms of activity, according to organic possibilities and according to the conditions under which various functions can be evoked. Evidence that confirms the findings of Pratt and Carmichael has been gathering rapidly.

The literature describing experimental observations of neonatal behavior has been flourishing, and we select for reference only those works most immediately relevant to our theme. The best examples differ from older literature in two main ways: they report experiments with more subtle and more complex stimuli, and they take greater account of something called *state*. The significance of state in evaluating neonatal responsiveness has been made explicit by a large group of investigators,[2] who have offered evidence that constitutional differences in state observable in the first days of life affect the neonate's freedom to distinguish external stimuli and to adapt to them.

Considerations of state present complex issues. The term appears to have different meanings, purposes, and assumptions in different contexts. Fries (1944), when she spoke of activity level, anticipated in behavioral terms the phenomenon referred to by most investigators as state, but she did not mean quite the same thing. If one uses state, or a series of states, in her sense of congenital activity type, or if one explicates a total set of conditions, possibly even including maturational level, as Escalona (1962) does, many more assumptions have to be made than if one uses the concept of state as we do, to describe the gestalt of the infant's physiological equilibrium at a given moment. The gestalt is most readily observable in the infant's degree of arousal at a specific time, or in the degree of tension that accompanies his responses to a specific stimulus at a specific time.

In studies of recent years in which state has been taken into account, infants have been observed to respond to external stimuli much earlier than had been supposed, with varying degrees and kinds of sensorimotor activity, and according to immediate conditions of hunger or satiation, sleepiness or wakefulness, as well as according to native strength and level of irritability. Wolff (1959), for example, noted this in his study of four neonates, who were observed for almost 18 hours a day during their first five days of life. He found that specific but characteristically different reactions appeared in regular and irregular sleep; that crying and kicking were not only greater

[2]Brazelton (1962), Brown (1964), Escalona (1962), Fish (1963), Gough (1962), Graham, Matarazzo, and Caldwell (1956), Paine (1965), Prechtl and Beintema (1964), Wolff (1959).

before meals than after meals but had a different quality; that auditory and visual pursuit of objects were elicited within the first 24 hours of life during periods of alert inactivity; and that spontaneous (reflex) smiles occurred after the first 24 hours in response to various stimulations, during or shortly after defecation or urination, and during periods of alert inactivity. Graham, Matarazzo, and Caldwell (1956) examined 176 normal and 81 traumatized neonates for behavioral differences, and found considerable unevenness of functioning in both groups. Ratings were made of each infant's pain threshold, general maturation, vision, irritability, and muscle tension. All intercorrelations were low, yet several are of particular interest. Irritability-pain and vision-maturation were positively correlated for both groups, but were statistically significant only for the normals. Irritability-tension were positively correlated in both, but significantly only among the traumatized infants. Irritability-vision were positively and significantly correlated for the traumatized, but negatively correlated for the normals. Vision-pain were negatively correlated in both groups. As might have been expected, among the traumatized infants there was also considerable individual variation in the length of time during which they maintained abnormal performances.

A study of autonomic functions in the neonate by Richmond and Lustman (1955; see also Lustman, 1956) describes the variable responsiveness of neonates to air pressure upon various body zones at three days of age. Richmond and Lipton (1959), in a related study, observed the effects of sensory stimuli and changes of balance upon autonomic activity of neonates and found that responsiveness varied with the state of the infant before, during, and after stimulation. Those authors emphasized that sensory stimulation or restriction in postnatal periods can modify developing structure in the central nervous system of the young organism. They concluded that under usual conditions the neonate probably responds to external stimuli much more than has been stated in the past.[3]

Birns et al. (1965), after exciting infants ranging from 36 to 96 hours old, found that the infants could be soothed by auditory stimulation. The most effective soothing stimulus was a low tone (150 c.p.s.), the next most effective a high tone (500 c.p.s.), and an intermittent low tone (150 c.p.s.). Four seconds on and one second off was more effective than no tone. This experiment permits the inference that neonates can differentiate among tones of varying intensity and between continuous and intermittent tones of the same frequency. Lipsitt (1966), and Siqueland and Lipsitt (1966) have demonstrated conclusively that reflexive learning takes place in the neonate. Fantz (1966), in a series of experiments in perception of very young infants, demonstrates that the neonate and the very young infant are capable of cortical activity.

Some of the sensory and neuromuscular responses of the neonate are reflexive and shortly disappear, but they cannot for that reason be assumed to have no effect upon the infant organism. Auditory response may be keen and does not diminish. Visual response is often present, does not get extinguished, and continues to improve. An increasing number of studies have shown that visual fixation and pursuit movements can be elicited in even the first days of life. Spitz (1965) disputes this with the argument that visual perception is not innate; that the very young infant is capable of only an undifferentiated awareness of a mass of body sensations, a coenesthetic perception, which is "extensive, primarily visceral and centered in the autonomic nervous system," present from birth, and manifested in the form of emotions. It precedes sensory perception. Spitz believes that the mouth is the

---

[3]It has been established that brain structure and composition are altered by various types of stimulation. In a series of experiments on rats, it was found that "rats given enriched experience develop, in comparison to restrained litter-mates, greater weight and thickness of cortical tissue and an increase in total acetylcholinesterase activity of the cortex" (Bennett, Diamond, Krech, and Rosenzweig, 1964).

central perceptual organ in earliest infancy, and that it facilitates a transition from the primary inner *reception* (coenesthetic) to outer *perception* (diacritic). While it is possible that the mouth is the first erogenous zone that serves perception, the concept of coenesthesis (which derives from vitalism and refers to a general feeling arising from the sum of bodily sensations as distinct from specific sensations) does not clarify the oral component in perception. It also underestimates visual components of early perception which in the last decade have been verified experimentally. Spitz argues that the neonatal ability visually to distinguish differences does not mean that the neonate perceives patterns, as seeing has nothing to do with mentation. He supports this position by a quite untenable comparison of visual learning in the once-blind (Von Senden, 1960) with the visual responsiveness of the newborn.[4] Schur (1966) follows Spitz in emphasizing that the oral component in earliest perception is primary, over and above perception in other modalities. Oral responsiveness is more visible than auditory or visual responsiveness and can more obviously reflect tension reduction, but this fact does not necessarily imply that the latter are less immediate or less efficient perceptual avenues to external stimuli.

Major investigation of innate visual form perception has been carried out by Fantz (1958, 1961, 1963, 1964, 1966, 1967) and Fantz and Nevis (1967a, 1967b), who have provided evidence that human infants, from the neonatal period on, can see and discriminate patterns; that patterns elicit more visual attention from birth than do color or brightness alone; that by the third month attention to familiar patterns decreases and attention to novel patterns increases; that from birth on, what is attended to and perceived has a direct influence on action and on what is learned from past actions. "There is no known study which has failed to give evidence

---

[4]Spitz's (1965) position, as expressed in *The First Year of Life*, has been reviewed elsewhere (Brody, 1966).

for selective attention to form or pattern in early infancy" (Fantz, 1966). Fantz, Ordy, and Udelf (1962) tested visual acuity for black and white striped patterns, as against plain gray, in three separate groups of normal infants under six months of age (some from the fourth day, some from the first month, and some from two months), a total of 126 infants, and found them increasingly capable, according to maturation, of discerning the visual patterns.

Numerous other investigators have observed visual capacities of the newborn. We have already referred to the findings of Wolff (1959) regarding visual pursuit in the first 24 hours. Dayton and Jones (1963) found good visual acuity in 18 of 39 newborns, and both fixation and conjugate pursuit in 17 of 43 newborns. Greenman (1963) reported that visual response could be elicited in 95 percent of 127 neonates within their first 96 hours, many within 20 minutes after birth. Wertheimer (1961) observed one newborn at the age of three minutes: she was crying, with eyes closed. At the sound of a click in her ear she stopped crying, turned her eyes in the direction of the click, and did so for a significant number of repeated clicks at each ear, showing a rough discrimination of a stimulus and a coordinated visual and auditory response in the first 10 minutes of life. Hershenson (1964) found a significant preference for a stimulus of intermediate intensity rather than for dim or bright stimuli, and found that preference for the bright stimulus was also greater than chance. According to Haynes, White, and Held (1965) as well, there is evidence that the alert neonate is capable of focusing his eyes, i.e., he has accommodative capacity. In the neonate, the focusing is on targets at a specific distance (18 cm.). As the infant matures, the range of flexible accommodation increases, and by the fourth month it approximates the ability of the adult. Korner and Grobstein (1966) found that crying neonates, when taken out of their cribs and held up to the shoulder, not only stop crying (a common observation) but scan the environment in a state of visual alertness.

TABLE 1

VISUAL RESPONSE AT THREE DAYS[a]

N = 134

			N	%	Cumulative %
Credit 0:	No fixation or pursuit *and* one of the following abnormal features observed: a. wandering, uncoordinated movements b. immobilization or staring c. pinpoint pupils		5	3.7	
Item	1:	No fixation or pursuit but none of above abnormalities	34	25.3	29.1
Item	2:	Fixation brief or obtained with difficulty	37	27.6	56.7
Item	3:	Fixation clearly present and easily elicited, i.e., occurs in a majority of trials	8	5.9	62.6
Item	4:	Horizontal pursuit questionably present	5	3.7	66.4
Item	5:	Horizontal pursuit movements through an arc of 30° obtained with difficulty	8	5.9	72.3
Item	6:	Horizontal pursuit movements through an arc of 30° easily obtained	5	3.7	76.1
Item	7:	Vertical pursuit movements obtained	9[b]	6.7	82.8
Item	8:	Horizontal pursuit movements through an arc of 90° obtained	5	3.7	86.5
Item	9:	Vertical pursuit movements through an arc of more than 30° obtained	15[b]	11.1	97.7
Item	10:	Horizontal pursuit movements through an arc of more than 90° obtained	3	2.2	100.

[a] The Visual Scale is taken from Graham, Matarazzo, and Caldwell (1956) and is used here with permission of the American Psychological Association. Their stimulus object was the examiner's hand, a bell, or a metal tape measure. They made no effort to standardize the stimulus because they were attempting to determine whether visual capacity was present under the most favorable conditions. Our stimulus was either the red ring used in the Gesell Schedules or a flashlight covered with red paper, and responses were credited to either stimulus.

[b] A small number of infants achieved credit for items 7 and 9 but failed to do so for items 6 and 8. A few others achieved credit for item 8 but not for item 7.

Paine (1965) presents evidence of the cerebral activity of neonates and young infants, indicating that interaction, particularly visual interaction, of the neonate with the environment takes place earlier and in a much more patterned manner than previously had been thought to be true. H. Thomas (1965), using two groups of infants, one ranging in age from two to 14 weeks, the other from 15 to 26 weeks, has shown that the older group preferred more complex visual stimuli than the younger, although there was some preference for the more complex stimuli in the younger group. Brazelton, Scholl, and Robey (1966) selected 96 neonates for their alert appearance and tested their visual fixation and pursuit responses in the first weeks of life. At age one 87 of the infants were deemed to be normal, and nine "abnormal or suspect." Of the normal infants, 50 had been able to pursue the test object as neonates, whereas none of the infants later considered abnormal or suspect did so. The authors consider that the ability of the neonate to respond appropriately to a visual stimulus is good evidence of an intact central nervous system. To judge from the number of recent studies of human visual development, and of relationships between stimulation and early development (Kagan, 1969; Lewis, Kagan, and Kalafat, 1966; Moss, 1967; White and Held, 1963), we can expect many more such pertinent findings to appear in the next years and to bear significantly upon our knowledge of earliest object cathexis.

Comparable observations of visual responsiveness of neonates between 72 and 96 hours of life, made in the course of the Infant Development Research Project, to be described below, are shown in Table 1 (p. 18), which summarizes data concerning visual fixation and pursuit movements of 134 neonates.[5]

Our observations of increased attentiveness in many infants *during* testing of visual and other sensory responsive-

---

[5]One hundred forty-four neonates were examined, but 10 could not be kept awake long enough for adequate evaluation. (Of the 144 infants, 122 remained in the final sample.)

ness, and of absence of consequent irritability,[6] have led us to consider that particular intensities of sensory stimulation may augment anticipation of a perceptual excitation and may in turn affect the infant's perceptual threshold.

The gradual appearance of the smiling response has been observed by Wolff (1963) in eight infants from birth through the third month. During the first week of life, it was most dependent on the infant's state of alertness and upon auditory stimuli. By the third week it appeared while visual pursuit movements were observable. By the fourth week the smile was elicited in three of his infants by visual presentation of the face, and it invariably followed inspection of the facial contours until eye-to-eye contact was achieved—then came the smile. Beginning with the fourth week, the smile was a predictable and selective response to a number of specific stimuli.

When close scrutiny is applied to infant responsiveness, we find that broad descriptions of their behavior as "diffuse," "nondifferentiated," or as merely "tension-reducing," or "pleasure-seeking," all turn out to be too-hasty generalizations. The foregoing findings, derived from empirical studies of early infant responsiveness, may be summarized: (1) Fetal and neonatal responses are never merely random; they always have pattern and direction and effect. (2) The greater the duration and intensity of the stimulus, the more it may absorb the attention of the infant. (3) Specific interindividual and intraindividual variations of sensorimotor responses, in a number of modalities, are observable from the first days of life. (4) Patterns of sleep in which neurophysiological discharge occurs rhythmically begin in the neonatal period and appear to occur less frequently as life proceeds; but the occurrence per

[6]On repeated trials, a considerable number of neonates reacted to the shining red light with a sneeze. The exact number is not known because at first the reaction was assumed to be merely accidental. We did not ascertain whether the sneeze occurred more regularly with or without fixation. This may have been a standard photophobic response, well-known in adults but hitherto not reported among infants.

se must be accounted for in evaluating the effects—possibly reciprocal effects—upon internal arousals of the neonate. States of alertness and drowsiness are well-known to merge and interchange in the first weeks of life. It has seemed to us reasonable, especially in view of many recent and current experimental and clinical findings such as have been exemplified here, to consider that the original, transient sensations of the infant of this age, and specifically the first occurrences of the sights and sounds that follow birth, are sharp physiological "experiences." Even though the capacity to respond to separable elements of these "experiences" may be traced back to fetal life, they impinge upon the organism under absolutely unfamiliar conditions. What often has been referred to as the "diffuse" or "undifferentiated" responsive activity of the neonate probably indicates the presence of beginning discharge patterns closely related to those that have been observed in the neonate during sleep (Fisher, 1964; Roffwarg, Muzio, and Dement, 1963; Wolff, 1966). We are tempted to regard these early discharge patterns occurring during sleep— the rapid eye movements, the accelerated respiration, the myoclonic twitches, the grimaces and erections, and other observable phenomena—as marking the start of drive differentiation in the postnatal period. Fisher (1964) has suggested that while the physiological processes may not be employed for visual dreaming until three to six months of age, dreaming in other sensory modalities may occur earlier; that although dreaming in the neonate is not possible, the processes observed during the neonatal REM periods may form a substrate for later instinctual discharge.

Our observations of responsiveness in neonates and in very young infants suggest that it may be helpful to retain the idea that the earliest discharge patterns observable in the postnatal period, or in the first days of life, may indeed be directly related to dreaming. Perhaps their presence should be taken as a sign that memory traces are in the process of being laid down, and that these traces, deriving from the several sensory modalities, are already beginning to serve in the formation of dream-process phenomena. This would mean that an impulsion toward discharge of tension can occur from the moment of birth, if not during birth. Consequently the fragmentary memory traces, and so the fragmentary mental representations, might immediately develop to an intensity sufficient for hallucinatory purposes in the first hours of life.

We assume that the most important function of the dream is to discharge instinctual drive energies that would otherwise disturb sleep, and we recognize that the instinctual drive can operate only after a structural development takes place. That is, primary biological energies, or "drive elements," form paths for subsequent instinctual drive discharge. The central question here appears to be how early in life the biological drive "element" ushers in a structural development.

The data and findings cited above strengthen the possibility that discrete sensory responsiveness may be elicited in the neonatal period, and may at once begin to subserve autoerotic discharge. The rapid build-up of tension and the diffuse discharge observable in the first days of life may already indicate the presence of hallucinatory processes. It may be that the earliest mental representations find a composition and a formal content only after primitive biological energy has been channelized through repetition into elements of recognizable experiences, via memory traces. Memory traces, we might say, may be "reproduced" at first through a primary process, probably in configurations of minute duration, and organized solely in having a sequence according to adventitious experiences. Secondly, the memory traces may be reproduced through the secondary process, overtly evidenced by the infant's capacity to make signs, and later to verbalize. A fault in our thinking may arise from an implicit but persistent assumption, despite our knowledge of primary processes, that dreaming must take some consensual form or have some discernible or discrete content. We are disposed rather to think of the neonatal REM periods, which have a higher frequency than those of adults, as measures of spontaneous discharge of autoerotic tensions of a nonspecific kind, generated internally and built up during regular sleep.[7] The autoerotic quality would be most expected to be present in inverse proportion to the degree of psychic development, and therefore most naturally to be anticipated in the neonate. This would help to explain the presence of REM periods in animals, even those that have been decorticated or are anencephalic. The manifestations of such autoerotic discharge would be the startles, the twitches, the fanning of fingers and toes, and certain reflex facial movements of the neonate. It may well be that the gradual diminution of the generalized discharge patterns lead to more and more specific pregenital patterns, along with other forms of gross discharge. One might view the total spontaneous activity of the neonate as prone to be more highly sexual or instinctual than elements of the same activities at later phases of development. Thus Freud's conception of infantile sexuality appears to be palpably confirmed: sexuality is indeed infantile, and infants are indeed sexual. To become an adult, psychologically speaking, requires the localization of sexual excitement and discharge at the genital zone. In waking life, it requires the move from autoerotism to genital object cathexis.

A few of the comments of Nissen (1951), from his studies of comparative development, about the role of exploratory behavior in perceptual organization are relevant here. Nissen indicates that in some animals, and to an increasing extent among the higher primates, there are constant movements of the body and sense organs whose aim is to keep the animal in touch with what is going on in his environment, and these occur even without external stimulation.

> Always accompanying gross exploratory behavior and often occurring independently of locomotion, are adjustments of the sense organs and their accessory apparatus. The eyes (and/or the head) are turned and focussed; the tongue, and lips, and the fingers explore the object tactually; other activities are suspended. Gross exploration has no meaning except as it 'exposes' the environment to the sense organism, making perception possible.

[7]*Autoerotic* is used here in the original sense of Freud (1914).

... The sensitizing component determining this [exploratory] behavior, it would appear, is almost constantly active; its directing incentive comprises all incoming sensory data, and its consummatory response is to make sense of those data—to identify them with inborn or previously established patterns, to relate their parts into an organized whole, and to analyze the whole into its constituent parts ... Almost nothing is thrown into the discard as irrelevant, and this appears to be especially true of younger individuals [pp. 357–378].

Our observations of human neonates show an abundance of such "adjustments of the sensory organs and their accessory apparatus," even when the infants are in relatively quiet states. Typically, before feeding one sees little turns of the head toward a part of clothing or bedclothing that can be touched; or sucking of fingers or fist; or opening and closing of eyes; or heightened facial responsiveness to touch, in the form of grimaces, frowns, pouts, and tonguing. All such manifestations of low threshold for external stimulations are conspicuously increased if the infant is uncovered. One of the difficulties encountered by Fisher and one of us (S.B.), when we attempted to observe the occurrence and duration of erections of male infants during sleep, was that however gently the infants were uncovered they usually awoke, curled up or squirmed restlessly, and often became mildly irritable as well; they did not cry, but they showed continuous sensorimotor "adjustments" until they were re-covered. In a contented postprandial state, many infants show increased set mainly for sensory explorations. Naturally, as they advance in physiological development and as available sensorimotor experiences are increased, a higher organization of mental processes connecting them to the environment is expected to follow.

The conclusion follows that there are structures available to the very young infant for the recognition of sensations, for the assimilation of sensations into perceptions, and for the organization of percepts in engrams. All of the latter processes would bear gradually upon the infant's ultimate capacity to bind and to organize the continuing flow of tension mobilized in growth and development. Psychic determinism can be demonstrated from the moment of birth.

The gaps in our present knowledge about the beginnings of psychic structure make it premature, we think, to assume that elements of an entity which later on we call psychic structure do not exist in the first days of life. We really do not know the duration of a totally undifferentiated phase.

While the capacity to dream a coherent train of mental representations cannot be reported prior to the acquisition of language, and so during infancy, no more than ego nuclei and no more than fleeting states of consciousness may need to be present in the organism for elements of a dream process to set in. And this process, however fleetingly and formlessly it begins or makes itself manifest in diffuse activity during REM states, may itself instigate structural differentiation, from the time of birth. Our conclusion is that it is reasonable to deduce that the larval elements of an archaic form of mentation are present in the neonate and young infant. These would be the elements requiring the smallest degree of inhibition of energy. They may be conceived of as forming the prestages of primary process. They are far distant from the kind of mentation present in even the older infant of six months; but they constitute the precursors of psychic structure. They are stimulus bound, hence internally uncontrolled, but later they enter into the control system.

A degree of tension is obviously necessary to motivate any behavior. An infant who has experienced optimal degrees of tension, sufficient to motivate activity through which tension may be discharged economically and pleasurably, may be expected to have optimal amounts of energy at his disposal for sensorimotor explorations, for the attainment of gratification from his alertness, and for the development of his curiosities. In contrast, an infant who has experienced unusual stress, with hypercathexis of pain, sensory discomforts, or sensory confusion, may be expected to be left with a reduced readiness to perceive external stimuli and to organize perceptions. We should not be surprised to find an inverse relationship between cumulative physiological stress and the capacity for object perception leading to object cathexis.

The understanding of early perceptions of sensation and of the ways they serve and are served by ego formation calls for the acquisition of data about variations, among normal infants, of responsiveness to the rise and fall of comforts and discomforts of many kinds, over continuous periods of time, and especially during periods in which new adaptations are being required of the infant. Even a little reflection about the kinds of variations that may occur in different behavioral modalities brings numerous questions to mind. For example: Are the temporary disappearances of function described by Carmichael (1946)—and also the later fluctuations in growth described by Gesell (1954)—concomitant with advances in different modes of functioning, i.e., are the "disappearances" coordinated in time with alterations of cathexis in separate activities? How varied a set of responses to one stimulus can be elicited at a given age or under changing conditions? Are there plateaus of perceptual development? Under what conditions do responses at any period of growth become stable or fixed? What maturational effects result from increased stimulation of reflex responses either to soothing or to irritating stimuli? To what extent can pleasing external stimuli interfere with an infant's attention to visceral sensations? What relationships may there be between quality of sleep and quality of waking behavior? How long do memories of any experience at varying points of growth and development last?

But for the present we are limited to dealing with one question: the conditions under which sensations in the infant's body, arising internally or aroused by external stimuli, begin to be perceived and to leave memory traces that may affect the immediate progress of his general psychic development, and his anxiety potential.

CHAPTER 3

Imprinting

A number of experiments in imprinting carried out during the last decade touch upon specific connections between sensory and emotional arousal and adaptive behavior in animal infancy. While we anticipate only indirect analogies and comparisons between animal and human infant development or behavior, not alone because of the obviously complex differences between species, but also because of the additionally complex variables in the imprinting response itself,[1] a number of findings are considered because they suggest comparable processes of socialization among human infants.

The phenomenon of imprinting has been studied in birds and animals whose young are mobile almost immediately after birth. It has usually been measured by the responses following the first stimulus, usually visual or visual and auditory, to which the subject is exposed, and by the subject's usually retaining this attachment permanently. Among the salient studies are those of Hess (1959a, 1959c) who, like Lorenz, distinguished imprinting from later learning in that it can occur only during a physiologically critical period in early life, and in that it is acquired through an innate releasing mechanism rather than through training. Hess describes it (1959a) as a rigid form of learning of the rough, generalized characteristics of the imprinting object;

[1]Some of the different findings even in subspecies, and with even slight experimental variations, have been discussed by Fuller and Waller (1962), Polt and Hess (1964), and Sluckin (1965).

it differs from association learning, which occurs immediately after the peak of imprintability and takes in the specific details of the imprinting object. Several of Hess's findings are significant here: He found (1959c) that punishment did not retard the imprinting process, and (1959a) that the strength of imprinting depended upon the degree of effort exerted by the duckling subjects he used (i.e., the distance they had to cover, the hurdles they had to overcome) during the imprinting period, rather than the duration of the period itself. From the latter he deduced (1959a, 1959b) a Law of Effort: the strength of imprinting equals the logarithm of the effort expended by the animal during infancy. Later he found (1960) that the strength of imprinting was negatively affected by the lowering of stress through the use of drugs, which added confirmation of the Law of Effort. But of first significance in this context is Hess's conclusion (1959a, 1959b) that the onset of fear ends the critical age for imprinting.

Many related experiments on the effects of heightened stress upon the imprinting response have appeared. A pertinent one is that of Pitz and Ross (1961), who found that exposure of chicks to sudden and intense auditory stimuli enhanced imprinting. They saw imprinting as a function of a degree of arousal, and defined arousal as the total amount of stimuli impinging upon the organism. In view of the fact that the period of heightened arousal was momentary, Pitz and Ross suggest that maximal imprinting, like other kinds of learning, requires an optimal level of arousal beyond which performance declines; and that in addition to the expenditure of energy which according to Hess facilitates imprinting, something more general is necessary, such as a certain amount of central nervous system activation. We anticipate that the same condition holds for an imprinting process that takes place in human infants, as we shall discuss below.

Certain studies that deal with the larger process of socialization among animals and with the primary appearance of fear reactions, which end imprinting, bear directly upon the hypotheses we shall submit regarding affective and perceptual developments in human infancy.

Guiton (1961) noted that chicks who followed the stimulus model in a group were less strongly imprinted than those exposed alone, and he attributed this to greater fear shown by the single chicks. An alternative explanation is that in a group the attention is spread between the other chicks and the imprinting object, whereas the hypercathexis of the isolated chicks would seem more likely to flow only to the imprinting object.

Bernstein (1957) found that discrimination learning among rats was improved by gentle handling after 20 days (after the weaning period) and up to 60 days, that interrupted relationships to the human handlers produced more errors than did a minimal relationship; and that extra-handled rats learned more, and more quickly. Bernstein's tentative explanation for the permanent effects of handling upon learning has seemed to us useful. He suggests that extra handling results in the animal's acquiring an expectancy, or a preparatory set, which creates tension as the time for being handled approaches. The tension is resolved by the actual handling that ensues and then begins to mount again, and so on. One would like to be able to demonstrate that the tension is at first evident physiologically, and subsequently is experienced psychologically, i.e., with cognition and affect. Obviously, the optimal degree of handling seems to affect the emergence of psychological structure. The better the type of handling, the earlier is the emergence and functioning of the inborn structure required for cognition and affect. Below we will present findings about the capacity for frustration tolerance, a capacity which requires psychological structure and some degree of secondary process.

Denenberg and Karas (1960) found that rats who were unhandled and rats who were handled for the first 20 days of life both performed poorly on tests of avoidance learning, the former because they were too emotional, the latter, too calm. The best learning was accomplished by animals handled in the first 10 days. The authors suggested that there are two critical periods for the effect of stimulation which have to be evaluated together: one which extends up to 16 days and is based on physiological processes, and in which there is development of adrenal-cortical stress mechanisms; the other which extends from 17 to 30 days and is based on psychological processes, and in which fear is reduced by familiarity.

Freedman, King, and Elliot (1961) found that the socialization period for dogs was two to 14 weeks, the seventh week being the critical age. In that week, when socialization receptiveness was highest, the dogs showed the highest activity level and the most tail-wagging and vocal behavior. After that they increasingly avoided or resisted humans. It appeared that motor and perceptual development reach maturity, but the motivation to flee from a strange species is not yet strong in the full critical period. Those authors suggest that a balance of the two factors, motor and perceptual maturity plus low flight motivation, is characteristic of the period critical for the formation of primary social relationships. Elliot and Scott (1961) also found that pups isolated from the bitch in strange pens for successive periods during the critical period for socialization showed distress most in the seventh week; Scott, Deshaies, and Morris (1961) reported that similar isolation for 20 hours per day produced strong emotional reactions, and speeded up the process of socialization.

A study by Moltz, Rosenblum, and Halikas (1959) may be said to cut across many of the findings so far described. Its intention was to test Hess's Law of Effort, but we think it may be construed helpfully to us, as linking physiological and psychological tensions involved first in imprinting and then in socialization. Moltz et al. attempted to test Hess's Law by preventing ducklings from following the imprinting object, i.e., by increasing the degree of effort to be expended. (It is probably not relevant here that their procedures and the subspecies of ducklings used were somewhat different from those used by Hess.) Contrary to Hess, they found no significant differences in the strength of imprinting between ducklings that had been restrained from actively making effort to pursue the stimulus object, and ducklings that had been permitted to follow the object freely. They saw no relation between the amount of activity exhibited during the period of restraint and during the subsequent following; indeed, some of the restrained ducks sat quietly during the confinement period and followed vigorously when given opportunity to pursue the object. To us it seems likely, however, that during the confinement period the ducks experienced a cumulative stress that propelled the subsequent vigorous following; while their sitting quietly showed no visible expenditure of energy, it may nevertheless be implied that their inner excitation and the pressure they felt toward discharge increased during the period of restraint. Tension not observable to the eye could have excited energy comparable to that of the freely moving ducklings, especially visual energy, and resulted in a comparable spending of energy.[2] The issue is important because of its possible application to physical inactivity of human infants. Physical quietness or retarded physical responsiveness need not be equated with absence of tension or of effort expenditure, or with lowered cathexis of sensorimotor discharge processes. Klopfer and Hailman (1964) have also seen a contradiction to Hess's Law of Effort in their finding that perceptual responses of chicks have greater primacy than motor responses in imprinting. H. James (1959) and Gray (1960) have in fact reported that imprinting can occur without any locomotor following. Collins (1965) corroborated that imprinting occurred whether chicks were allowed actually to follow and make contact, to follow but not make contact, or simply to observe.

If the degree of tension in an animal perceiving the im-

[2]The proposition that the delayed opportunity to expend energy in the following of the imprinting object had no significant effect upon the strength of the imprinting is reminiscent of similar propositions regarding nonsignificant effects of restraint, or lack of exercise of perceptual and motor functions, among human infants (Brody, 1956).

printing object but restrained from touching or following it were measured, it might very well be greater than the tension aroused by overcoming obstacles in order to reach a moving decoy. The studies we have seen make no reference to degrees of tension or excitement in the restrained animals. The human infant, because of his primitive physical development, can follow only visually. Imprinting could only occur actively through visual means, passively through accommodation to the mother's handling. The degree of tension present in the infant that might correspond to effort can also be measured. We assume that tension is aroused in the human counterpart of the imprinting process, and that the discharge of such tension consummates earliest libidinal cathexis of an object.

Imprinting is of obvious survival value for the species as well as for the individual. It makes mothering possible in species where the infant organism must take an active role in being mothered. It also sets one of the conditions for the choice of a sexual partner. The fact that extraspecies objects can be imprinted does not speak against the survival value of imprinting. And the fact that there is a learned aspect to imprinting does not speak against its biological function, for statistically, during the critical period and in a state of nature, the imprinting object will belong to the animals' own species. As various observers have noted, there is no reason to believe that the human species should be exempt from this kind of process. Sackett, Porter, and Holmes (1965) have reported upon an imprintinglike phenomenon, and have suggested the existence of a critical period of several months' duration, in monkeys.

CHAPTER 4

Critical Periods in Human Infancy

W e shall try to show that a number of events believed to be part of the unique ontogenetic development of the human are actually phylogenetic. Imprinting, socialization, and critical periods provide the clearest link.

Gray (1958) has defined imprinting as "an innate disposition to learn the parent or parent-surrogate," and has proposed that the smiling response is the motor equivalent of the following response that occurs below the level of the infrahuman primates. He places the critical period for human imprinting from about six weeks to about six months, beginning with the onset of learning, continuing with the smiling response, and ending with stranger discrimination. Ambrose (1963a) differs, probably correctly, with Gray's reasoning, but agrees that smiling may be a human form of imprinting, and he equates following with smiling. According to Ambrose, the infant's smile, along with the mother's loving maternal behavior, make for greater closeness between mother and infant. He suggests that the smile is dependent upon the ability to fixate upon the face of the mother. Earlier, Ambrose (1961) had found that the critical period for the primacy of fixation upon the mother's eyes begins at approximately the fifth week of life, and ends (with the onset of stranger discrimination) at about 12 weeks for family-reared infants, and at about 18 weeks for institutionally reared infants. This span of weeks appears to Ambrose to be one of many sensitive periods for the development of social responsiveness in the human species.

33

If, as seems likely, an imprintinglike phenomenon exists among human infants, the infant's smile appears to us to be too mature a response to be regarded as that phenomenon. Our hypothesis would rather be that there are two major critical periods of socialization among human infants. The first, in which there is imprinting to the human species in general, may be signified by the ability to fixate, visually or auditorily, as observed by sharp increases or decreases of body movement (limbs, head, facial features) or of activity level, and by visual pursuit of the human object. The ability to fixate is prerequisite to the ability to smile. The appearance of the smile may be a result of a kind of practice or work, i.e., an expenditure of effort for an end other than the activity itself; or an end result of some instinctual discharge. If so, it would be experienced by the infant as a relief of tension. The relief would lie in the achievement of familiarity of a percept: it occurs when no further effort is necessary to attain the percept. It effects a habituation to the hitherto unfamiliar. It is as if the organization of the hitherto amorphous world into patterns and *Gestalten* permits an easy and pleasurable discharge of tension. The course of smiling is from attention to a mechanically patterned object to a discriminatory response to more and more specific stimuli, i.e., from taking in the most general configuration of the human facial features to recognizing the face of the specific mother.

According to G. W. Bronson (1968a), fear of novelty (novel percepts) begins when the familiar percept, such as the mother's face, is encoded. One determinant of the pleasure upon sighting the mother would then be expected to arise from relief at being spared the pain (fear) of dealing with the unfamiliar. This may help to explain why the unfamiliar is better tolerated by the infant when the mother is present (G. W. Bronson, 1968b).

The second critical period, in which there is imprinting to the mother or her surrogate, may be signified by the ability to discriminate the mother or her surrogate from other human objects. It would be shown by the immediacy of the smiling response to her above others. It is relevant that Bayley (1932) and Levy (1960) found that, typically, crying at sight of or during handling by strangers hardly ever occurs up to the age of two months, but becomes highly significant between six and 10 months. According to the Gesell Developmental Schedules, discrimination of the mother is normative at 24 weeks, whereas the social smile is normative at eight weeks.

We now refer back to the phenomenon of imprinting. As we propose, and as we shall later elaborate, the first phase of imprinting for the human species in general is likely to be as swift and irreversible as Scott (1963) reports it to be for birds. We suggest that visual fixation upon the human face presented at very close range and especially when reinforced by the human voice, plus visual pursuit movements, may be the human equivalent of following among animals. Human infants do have only sensory means of locomotion in the first weeks of life. Among older infants, the second phase of imprinting, marked by recognition of and smiling approach toward the mother, may indicate a process far more complex. A six-week to six-month period of primary socialization, as suggested by Scott (1963), seems too gross. It is in accordance with our observations to divide the primary socialization period into at least the two major phases we have alluded to, the first beginning with fixation[1] and pursuit movements, the second beginning with discrimination of the mother qua mother.[2] Many mothers have reported the latter as occurring in the fourth month.

[1] It seems conceivable that some psychotic infants have a defective releasing mechanism, which causes the first imprinting object to be an inanimate one rather than the mother or her surrogate. Witness the early and persistent preoccupation of psychotic children with objects that turn and whirl or that provide repetitive sounds. Might a similar kind of "defective imprinting" take place in the phenomenon of the "placer sheep" (Guthrie-Smith, 1926), in the permanent impairment of their capacity to herd and to breed, or in the failure of the cloth-reared monkeys (Harlow and Zimmerman, 1959) to socialize and to mate?

[2] Scott in fact intimated, in an earlier publication (1958), the probability of the existence of two critical periods of socialization in all highly social animals.

The observation that stranger discrimination, i.e., withdrawal from strangers, ends the critical period of socialization in humans is in harmony with the findings of Hess (1959a, 1959b, 1959c), Scott (1962, 1963), and others, regarding the end of imprinting in animals with the onset of fear and of escape reactions. Hess states (1959a) that at birth animals do not show fear but that the amount of fear toward imprinting stimuli increases steadily from the first hours of life and mounts until it causes avoidance, and the end of imprinting. Fear responses then prevent the animal from engaging in the social behavior necessary for imprinting to take place. The curve of fear increase was in Hess's findings paralleled by the curve of increase of motor ability (necessary for following), and both curves followed the curve of the critical period for imprinting. Hess submits that the same relationship may hold true for the human infant: that since the onset of fear has been placed in the sixth month (Spitz, 1946b), that age may signify the limit of a maximal imprinting among human infants. According to our formulations, a level of socialization in this period would be qualified by the essential characteristics of perceptual rather than motoric development. It is a fact that among human infants, locomotor ability to withdraw from feared objects rises sharply at about that age, when the capacity to change body positions increases markedly. According to Scott (1962), various findings indicate that any sort of strong emotion (pain, fear, hunger, loneliness) that is experienced at critical periods will speed up socialization among animals; but that the developing ability, for example in the puppy, to associate fear responses with particular stimuli arouses an escape reaction which contributes to the closing off of the critical period of socialization.

It follows from these considerations that imprinting or its counterpart in the human species is a special form of learning and may involve a hypercathexis of primary percepts, that is, a perception of objects as not yet apart from the self, and a perception which succumbs to a truer object cathexis at a later point of maturation, when objects come to be recognized as separate from the self and as "interfering" with the object-self unity. Imprinting in the human would thus be seen as a form of object cathexis, perhaps the simplest kind of affective bond, first to the species and then to the mother, subsequently to other parental objects. The "interference" of percepts of external objects, the rise of secondary narcissism, might be viewed in relation to the onset of anxiety arousal and early conflict, in some ways analogous to the onset of fear and the ending of imprinting in lower species.

Our purpose in construing these links is to make as discrete as possible the relationships that may inhere among the earliest forms of object cathexis, the dystonic affect of anxiety, and the development of the ego.

CHAPTER 5

Anxiety Preparedness and the Protective Shield

Before presenting a set of hypotheses concerning the origins of infantile anxiety, it is necessary to review the standard metapsychological formulations.

Freud changed his conception of anxiety in 1926. We shall have to turn repeatedly to the formulations of that time, in which he traced the source of anxiety to the biological alterations of the state at birth. He stated that physiological stresses in the infant are induced by hunger, pain, or other irritants. As libidinal desires to suck, to be kept warm, and in safe balance are satisfied, parts and then the whole person of the satisfying mother are perceived. Recognition of a unit of being that is separate from the infant but necessary to his comfort appears, and brings with it the connection between being alone and being helpless. The awareness that the intensely cathected object can be needed, but missing, arouses in the infant a sense of impending danger, a feeling reproduced from the period of its physiological parallel in the birth process, when the organism experienced increased excitation against which it was helpless. At birth the excitations chiefly affect cardiac and respiratory functions. Later on, the excitations recur as an accompaniment to the perception of impending danger, and they add to it painful feelings called anxiety. Pain is the reaction to the loss of the object. Anxiety is the reaction to the danger which that loss entails, and it is further displaced to the danger of the loss of the object itself. The quality of pain arises as an intense longing is set up for the lost object, and because the cathexis is continuous and mounting. In short, when psychic pain in reaction to the loss of external object is added to the physiological reaction of anxiety we have the psychological affect of anxiety. Subsequently, the ego organization responds to threat with more or less appropriate signals of the anxiety.

We have here a remarkable set of propositions, for while experimental data to confirm them are still wanting, the propositions appear to be clinically verified at least insofar as infantile experiences have been reconstructed by psychoanalytic method and by psychoanalytic observers of infant behavior.

Freud (1926) did not enlarge upon the "certain preparedness for anxiety" which he said was undoubtedly present in the infant, and which becomes manifest as development proceeds through childhood in the continued longing for the intensely cathected mother. He also did not refer to any specific phase of infancy or childhood when he stated that "This anxiety has all the appearance of being an expression of the child's feeling at its wits' end, as though in its still very undeveloped state it did not know how better to cope with the cathexis of longing" (p. 137). The point or points at which the preparedness for anxiety becomes an affective experience were not made evident. That understanding requires hypotheses by means of which to assess the intensity of an infant's cathexis of the mother or her surrogate, and his threshold for stress when alone and when in need. And it is toward this end, toward an understanding of the elements of anxiety preparedness, that our discussion has been proceeding.

On the basis of the afore-mentioned psychological findings about neonatal response, we may describe the neonate, still recovering from the birth experience, as a bundle of sensations affected by the activity of reflexes, autonomic functions, stirrings of instinctual drives that attach to vital functions, and external stimuli impinging upon his sensorium. But we cannot, from these data, describe how the transition from physiological stress to the psychological affect of anxiety takes place.

By common psychoanalytic definition it would appear that the affect could only emerge when object perception exists, as only then can a sense of danger from object loss be experienced. Now if the development of object perception follows other developmental lines or other forms of behavior, then it lacks stability in the period of its initial development in infancy, and for varying periods during infancy. We know how far beyond early childhood the images of self and object shift, separate, and merge again, in processes noted by A. Freud (1953) and Jacobson (1954). The two discrete percepts may lose their separate unitary qualities under conditions of stress or conflict; it seems to us, however, that it may be possible to discern bare elements of the process of self-object differentiation in observations of the rise and fall of sensorimotor behavior of neonates. Either in the infant's own spontaneous or reactive behavior or through the observable medium of the maternal activity, the infant may be observed to increase or to diminish many kinds of activity. Sometimes his movements are arrested entirely, sometimes accelerated, sometimes they are in prolonged flux. At unknown points in the continuum of early experience, differentiations between sensations registered from inside and from outside, vague feelings of the source of stimuli, must begin to occur. The totally satisfied infant, if we can conceive of such a one, would have little need to perceive "reality," and little need to develop mental discrimination between states of tension and states of rest.

Survival itself is insured through the exercise of vital functions and the corollary anaclitic pleasures. It is from the latter that the instinctual impulses which comprise the id are derived. If the vital functions were satisfied automatically, and anaclitic pleasures followed automatically, without any output of energy, why would there be any need for a development of ego functions other than those which would insure the continuation of pleasure? Why would any perception of an outer world occur? Primary narcissism, or the so-called oceanic feeling, could prevail and could remain unpenetrated by displeasure.

Freud (1911) referred to the function of attention as instituted to search the external world, and as meeting the sense impressions halfway,[1] and in a footnote he considered the infant's reactivity to distress as signs of the infant's move from the pleasure principle to the reality principle. We should say that an unconscious cathexis of particular sensations, and a laying down of earliest memory traces, might therefore come to serve as instigators of more and more differentiated perceptions, of more and more specific motor discharges, and of the capacity for delay. Ideally, the dosage of displeasure that induces self-object differentiation would be received in minimal steps. The differentiating perceptions would at the same time allow, as Freud indicated, for the further revival of the original gratifying sensations, and the temporary withdrawal from the stimuli of reality.

We are aware of the positions of Hartmann (see fn. 4, Chapter 1) and of Schur (1966), who follow a cryptic remark of Freud (1940) about an undifferentiated phase preceding the formation of the id and the ego. Recent experimental findings, described above, which contradict the usefulness of this conceptualization in showing that perception exists in the neonate, pose questions regarding the duration of an undifferentiated phase. Schur's picture of the formation of psychic structure appears to be as follows: at birth there are reflexes; these give rise to tension; the experience of satisfaction which then takes place through tension reduction results in the formation of a wish (instinctual drive), a functional prototype of the id. All events that occur before the formation of the wish belong to the undifferentiated phase. The "experience of satisfaction" (Freud, 1900) thus gives rise to the id; the pri-

---

[1]Loeb (1945) commented similarly on the illusions that remain throughout our lives about what in our feelings and thoughts derives from outside and what from inside, and about our own individual constancy and continuity. "Sense impressions stand on the borderline between inner and outer world, and they, with our thoughts, represent a combination of environment and inner organismal factors. It is by means of sense impressions that we construct both worlds and connect the two" (p. 628).

mary experiences of satisfaction are oral, and are increased gradually by a range of sensorimotor perceptions and an enlarging network of percepts and memory traces. As Schur relies upon Freud's remark (1940) that the id has its own world of perception, he prefers to limit the term *perception* to a capacity to organize sensory data. He speaks of *responsiveness* in the newborn, but implies that perception proper comes into being in a spiraling development of id and ego out of an undifferentiated phase. Accordingly, the very young infant cannot be said to experience perception, i.e., he does not have the capacity to organize sensory data.

To state the difference between our position and that of Schur most sharply: we regard perception as behavior based upon innate structures, and, in accordance with recent empirical and experimental findings we construe that the innate structure becomes operative as soon after birth as it is triggered by an appropriate stimulus. We regard not perception itself, but the control and organization of perception, as functions of the ego. The series of psychic events outlined by Schur is based upon a series of assumptions which seem to us not to clarify available data. The data make it more plausible to assume that the arousal of instinctual needs constitutes a part of the process of birth, and that their mental representations, although unorganized, are instantaneous.

And so we arrive at Freud's concept of the protective shield (1920). With the increase of interest in the early development of perception, this concept has been referred to more and more frequently, and is therefore relevant to considerations regarding the rise of the affect of anxiety during infancy. According to Freud's surmise, as a result of the ceaseless impact of external stimuli upon the living organism, a surface or protective shield is gradually formed upon the organism. This surface, or vesicle, develops a permanent and unchangeable crust through which to receive external stimuli in small quantities by means of the sensory organs, and through which to be protected at the same time from too great an impact of external stimuli. Freud considered this shield to be effective in relation to outer stimuli only. In consequence, inner sensations of pleasure and unpleasure are predominant in the organism. A psychic tendency arises, then, to treat the unpleasurable inner excitations as if their sources were external, thus to have the protective shield serve against them as well as it serves against outer excitations.

Let us assume for the present that endocrine, histological, and neurological structures compose such a shield; that observable withdrawal reactions of the neonate give evidence of impact upon the shield and of the exercise of the shield's protective function; and that attentive or approach reactions of the neonate give evidence of smooth penetration of the shield and of the exercise of its receptive function.

Freud indicated that the protective function was almost more important than the receptive function. As far as we can tell, considerations of the existence of such a shield have referred almost exclusively to the protective function. In part, this may be a consequence of an earlier translation of "shield" as "barrier." The protective function may indeed be the more important one for survival, and especially from a clinical point of view. We have no clear basis, however, for assuming that it is consistently more important for survival at consecutive stages of growth, nor even that it is consistently the first of the two functions to be effective. The fact that infants make distress known through evident sounds and movements does dramatize the innate striving of the organism to protect itself from disagreeable sensations from any source. The other innate striving, to receive, to keep, or to increase a given comfort, or to restore a missing one, is less noisy in the young infant and much harder to observe. The passing sensations that may be assumed to be registered in memory traces from feelings of warmth, of being snug, of hearing a variety of gentle, pleasing sounds, or of being able to imbibe something that augments general bodily well-being—any of these should be and may be no less important for the normal strengthening of the infant's attentiveness. The registration of these "good" events upon the memory would appear to demonstrate a disposition to absorb agreeable sensations. Such "registrations" are likely to be scant and difficult to discern.[2] We hardly expect a young infant to show conspicuous evidence of either *mild* pleasure or *mild* irritability; nevertheless those sensations may be present. Many neonates, before feeding, appear to be in mild stress. They do not utter a sound or even open their eyes, but they do squirm, and often "cry" soundlessly—they go through all the motions characteristic of intense crying as if in a pantomime, though often at the end they break into a wail. A contented infant, for example after feeding, may respond to sounds by startling, or only by freezing, and he may respond to tactile or visual stimuli only with heightened attentiveness. On two occasions, what seemed to be a vocal expression in an infant on the fourth day of life has been observed fortuitously, in the hospital nursery. In the first instance, as the infant lay alert and inactive, after a comfortable feeding by his mother, and during the gentle presentation of test objects by the examiner, the infant several times expressed a soft sound, which may best be described as a brief exhaling of breath, and may be imitated by the "mm-mm" sound made with lips apart. The experienced infant nurse who was stationed in the nursery described the sound as being somehow like the purring of a kitten; it was a definite sound, and she had heard it "every so often" in the nursery, not while attending an infant in his crib, but while holding him in arms, after he had taken some water and remained alert. While these are

[2]Fantz, whose investigations of visual perception in infancy are probably the most exacting and extensive, prefers to speak of learning as an empirical process of acquiring knowledge through the sense organs, rather than as a process of response and reinforcement. His findings have affirmed an emphasis on the neonate's *capacity to receive*, attend to, and discriminate stimuli. He sees learning as a taking in of rather than reacting to stimuli. "The significance of the visual preference studies is in the proof that infants from birth have the capacity to receive and discriminate patterned stimulation, that they do attend selectively to parts of the environment, and that therefore the *acquisition of knowledge about the environment begins at the first look* " (Fantz and Nevis, 1967a, p. 218).

fragmentary observations, particularly difficult to confirm without instrumentation, they indicate a need for systematic, minute observations of early stages of responsive behavior.

It may be that discrete stimuli to which the very young infant can respond, those which his sensorium can receive and which sustain or increase states of comfort, should from his point of view be regarded as positive stimuli. The nipple can be sucked, the finger or rattle can be grasped, the sound can be turned toward, the firm wrapping can be relaxed into. Receptivity to stimuli in various modalities thus may pilot cognitive functions from the time of birth, and may facilitate the conversion of physiological to psychological anxiety. Klatskin et al. (1966) found that visual alertness and scanning appeared when displeasure stopped. Stimuli to which the infant cannot respond with equanimity, those which are likely to disrupt or diminish states of comfort, may from his point of view be regarded as negative stimuli: cold, hunger, loss of equilibrium, sounds that jar. To receive these without disturbance the infant needs some kind of protective assistance. Flight movements may be insufficient for "escape," yet not random; for when the infant is placed in a prone position the "swimming" efforts toward a change of bodily position, even in the first weeks of life, may propel him into a snug corner of his crib, where he can nestle with his head against the boundary, and sleep.

Initially, receptive experiences may bring a coalescence of self and outer world, and a brief plateau of withdrawal of any effort toward differentiation. The elasticity of the receptive function would make for a normal capacity for elastic distinctions between self and outer world. It is conceivable that an excessive receptivity would lead to states in which the organism would be overwhelmed and confused by the impact of incoming stimuli, and may later be represented in psychotic states.[3] Reception of negative stimuli which are disruptive,

[3]Does the normal hallucinatory gratification hypothesized by Freud as occurring in infancy signify the presence of a normative gap

and concomitant effort to ward them off, may be considered as "preparing" the organism for psychological anxiety.

In view of its postulated survival value, the shield would surely not be supposed to operate against vital functions or against unconditioned reflexes such as sucking or grasping. The vital functions might in fact be facilitated by the shield's receptive capacity. We do not know either how massive or how frequent a stimulus must be to break through the protective shield, or how gentle a stimulus must be to be received through it. Except for infants in states of extremely low or high excitement, the degree of response is a function of the (internal or external) stimuli to which the infant is exposed, either at a given moment or cumulatively. This "dependence" may provide the essential meaning of "stimulus bound." Perhaps the concept of the protective shield can be most useful when we think of it as encompassing the whole sensory organization, with the integument as the first and main medium for the discrimination of external stimuli that are to be shied away from *or* absorbed, according to the physiological and maturational capacity of the infant.[4]

Benjamin (1965) saw the protective shield as both a biological given and as a product of development. He proposed that at birth a "passive barrier" is present "due to lack of functioning connections." Having found that at the age of three to four weeks normal infants show a marked increase of sensitivity to external and internal stimulation, an increase

---

in the early form of the protective shield? And does this "gap" form a psychic state to which the organism returns in a psychotic regression? To speculate further: Is it conceivable that hypnagogic phenomena such as are re-experienced in psychoanalytic treatment (Isakower, 1938; Brody, 1964) also represent a temporary regressive coalescence before a new, dynamic alteration occurs in a progressive move toward differentiation at a higher level of maturation? Can the dream screen and the Isakower phenomenon be regarded as mental representations of the protective shield?

[4]The sensory importance of the skin for communication has been cogently presented by Geldard (1960).

corroborated by EEG changes, he concluded that it indicated the waning of the "passive barrier." He further proposed that an "active barrier" develops as early as eight to 10 weeks and matures rapidly thereafter, making it possible for the older infant and young child to protect themselves from excessive stimulation by active efforts. He regarded the period between three to four weeks and eight to 10 weeks as one of heightened vulnerability, when the infant is in special need of maternal protection against stimuli. Benjamin advanced the hypothesis that the maternal failure adequately to manage this need might contribute to a heightened predisposition to anxiety.[5]

Ideally, it would seem, the efficacy of the shield would be such as to allow the organism to experience neither oversharp nor oversudden alterations of homeostasis; to grow aware, even as momentary excitations are aroused, of gradations of comfort or discomfort, and of their sources; and to facilitate the release of energy for sensorimotor responses which would be likely to maintain or to increase comfort, and to get rid of discomfort. Freud (1915) described the detection of qualitative differences between inner and outer stimuli through muscular activity as a "first discrimination and a first orientation" of an infant organism. In view of the endless dovetailing of inner and outer excitations proceeding from the onset of postnatal life, we should expect that the sensory confusion of the infant would be immense before any discrete percepts or discrete memory traces are formed, and that the accomplishment of the "first discrimination" and the "first orientation" would be impressive kinds of infant work. So we should expect that the quality and quantity of the infant's perceptual work leads him toward the psychological experience of being a unit and being alone, and toward the realization that an object that has only recently become cathected is missing. This realization

---

[5]Our observations of infants at six weeks did show differences among those who were more or less adequately protected by their mothers from stimuli, as will be shown below.

would presumably be thoroughly intertwined with the development of anxiety preparedness. Freud (1926) indicated that there can be no mental content about danger in the fetus:

> It can only be aware of some vast disturbance in the economy of its narcissistic libido. Large sums of excitation crowd in upon it, giving rise to new kinds of feelings of unpleasure, and *some organs acquire an increased cathexis, thus foreshadowing the object-cathexis which will soon set in* [p. 135; italics supplied].

Should this be true of the fetus, we suggest that for the very young infant, increased cathexis within the organism may be linked with the receptive function of the protective shield, for when the larger quantities of excitation press upon the infant and sensations give rise to motility, some of the excitations—the internal ones—will be inescapable, at least until help comes from an external source. Pleasurable stimuli require no search for an outer world because they occur with no disturbing discontinuity of experience—the shield is not breached. Dystonic stimuli break through the shield, arouse more and disrupt more, and appear to call for a greater output of energy. Observation of the neonate in quiet states certainly suggests that the wish to be rid of dystonic stimuli is greater than the wish to repeat pleasurable stimuli. The best example of the dystonic stimulus is pain. When Freud (1923) referred to the intimate relation between the two kinds of stimuli, internal and external, he drew attention to pain as an intermediate perception, which acts like an internal one even when its source is external.

During his terminal illness Jones (1957) was able objectively to consider the psychological effects of pain. He described how at the peak of intense pain, localization of its source gets lost and the entire body is filled with nothing but pain. At that point, the dread of a surprise breakthrough in the "defensive barrier" at once rouses up strong defensive reactions such as breath holding and body stiffening. These reactions are not helpful; nevertheless it appeared to Jones that they occurred in proportion to the depth of felt anxiety. Considering such readiness of an adult organism in severe physical stress to lose the perception of inner boundaries, and to summon all available energies for physiological defense reactions, we imagine that something very similar may happen to a young infant who is not yet clearly aware of what sensations derive from inside his own body—though with different sequelae, of course. The infant is incomparably less able to locate or to relieve pain when he feels it, and he has not yet developed a psychological attitude toward it. He may be all the more readily overwhelmed by internal sensations, and all the more ready for his energies to be drawn away from perception of the margins between external and internal stimuli.

To the extent that adequate and timely rescues from painful experiences do come, and to the extent that external excitations impinge at a rate that allows for gradually increased cathexis of bodily organs, the protective shield could serve a harmonious adaptation to stress. We observe that some infants are readily irritated to the point of restlessness, squirming, and fretting, and some accept with too little protest the handling to which they are necessarily subjected. We might say metaphorically that in the former the shield is not solid enough or has defects, and that in the latter the shield is too impenetrable and leaves the infant wanting in capacity to receive stimuli and to adapt to them at a moderate pace. The concept of a too-thin or a too-thick "protective barrier" (as it was called in the translation then available) was proposed by Bergman and Escalona (1949), but solely with reference to over- or underprotection *against* stimuli.[6] Over and above a general degree of solidity in this hypothesized shield, no doubt there would be significant individual variability, structurally and functionally, particularly in sensorimotor areas, making for an individual infant's kind or degree of vulnerability, as might be

[6]Although Bergman and Escalona discussed the relevance of the protective barrier for earliest infantile experience, it should be noted that the age of the youngest child they described was 2.8 months; the other four children were 24 months, 25 months, six years, and seven years old.

deduced from the observations of Graham, Matarazzo, and Caldwell (1956) cited above.

The essential points, in this context, seems to us to be not whether the shield can be pierced by stimuli of a certain intensity—that is a matter of neurophysiological responsiveness. We are concerned, rather, with the psychological integration and organization of the manifold stimuli which impinge upon the organs—an active, integrative process rather than a mechanical registration: a process advanced by *both* the protective and receptive functions of the protective shield. Hypercathexis, which is an active phenomenon but one that cannot be achieved by rudimentary structures, is the key to this process. That is, postponement of action may be linked to the receptive function of the protective shield, and so may be prerequisite for the onset of the secondary process.

Freud (1900, 1923), and after him Spitz (1950), Schur (1966), and others have taken up the point that the first stage of psychic functioning is represented by an unpleasurable accumulation of excitation. Yet there seems to be no reason why pleasure cannot be "received" or experienced without prior unpleasure or displeasure, why one affect of pleasure cannot follow another, or why it cannot follow a neutral state of no pleasure. The model of pleasure following dystonic states certainly would appear to be correct for the experience of the neonate, for whom the moment of birth must bring exquisite displeasure. But this model need not hold for the infant generally. The anaclitic nature of nonnutritional oral gratification shows that one pleasurable affect can follow swiftly upon the other, as in the infant who immediately after satiation brings thumb to mouth. Both pleasure and displeasure must have adaptational value; for if vital functions were not pleasurable, those that are voluntary would not be performed.[7] From the standpoint of survival, of mobilization of

[7]The anaclitic pleasurable affects tend to be passive, and for that reason may be experienced regressively. This may be of clinical significance in connection with children who "get along" with exces-

the organism against danger, particularly in the case of an organism as helpless as the human infant, displeasure may impel more toward activity, toward (more visible forms of) adaptation.[8] Let us assume that consciousness, an inborn quality, has an adaptational function. Pleasurable affects in the very young organism would seem to have the quality of autoerotic satisfaction, and in the early life of the individual probably would seem to be attributed chiefly to an internal source (though in reality the source is the mother). Displeasure would occur when the automatic satisfaction (attributed by the infant to himself) is missing. An appeal to the external world is made. In accordance with this reasoning, anxiety, the combined perception of the breakthrough of dystonic stimuli plus the outcry for relief, would be the first *conscious* affect.

These considerations lead us to propose that where *either* internal or external stimuli are too exclusive in their impact upon a young infant, and the protective shield is *either* organically unsound or for dynamic reasons fails in *either* its receptive or its protective functions, there will be an impairment in the infant's ability to differentiate between inner and outer excitations, and in his capacity to experience a balance of passive and active accommodation to stimuli. Consequently, confusion of both sensation and response would aggravate the pain or stress invoked by tension, would increase narcissistic cathexes, would reduce the infant's anxiety preparedness, and would eventually block a fluid cathexis of external objects. These propositions only apply to early infancy. Freud (1920) stated regarding the mental conditions that precipitate a traumatic neurosis:

> It [the traumatic neurosis] is caused by lack of any preparedness for anxiety, including lack of hypercathexis of the systems that

---

sive gratification but do not adapt to reality tasks and have low levels of aspiration.

[8]Pleasure insures the survival of the human species; anxiety, that of the individual.

would be the first to receive the stimulus. Owing to their low cathexis those systems are not in a good position for binding the inflowing amounts of excitation and the consequences of the breach in the protective shield follow all the more easily. It will be seen, then, that *preparedness for anxiety and the hypercathexis of the receptive systems constitute the last line of defence of the shield against stimuli.* ... the difference between systems that are unprepared and systems that are well prepared through being hypercathected may be a decisive factor in determining the outcome ... [pp. 31–32; italics supplied].[9]

So far we have tried to trace psychic paths by which stimuli may affect the infant and may reinforce either states of comfortable alertness or states of discomfort and stress. A consciousness of danger impending from any stress could only result from some disruption or from some noticeable change in the ideal efficacy of the protective shield—when too many discomforts or too few comforts are received. An enlarging consciousness of undiminishing physiological stress (conceivably lasting only fractions of a minute) can be observed to arouse something akin to psychic pain as we know it, i.e., a dystonic sensing of object loss or, more precisely, comfort loss. Full consciousness of the organismic danger entailed by the loss of comfort would presumably be achieved in very many small steps, deriving from minimal perceptual cues and gradually giving rise to an affect of anxiety. We should assume that this affect would in turn remain *in statu nascendi* for many weeks. Seen thus, the affect of anxiety comes at the end of a process of a multitude of increases and decreases of stress, and a multitude of perceptions, recognitions, and reactions, all of these psychophysiological experiences becoming crystallized in a capacity to experience signal anxiety.

[9]This statement provides the theoretical reason for the psychological preparation of the surgical patient. It indicates the importance of the patient's prior knowledge of what is going to happen to him, of his having a chance to hypercathect and to master the expectable danger by small and appropriately timed doses of anxiety in advance of the event. Given that preparation, he can, so to speak, hypercathect the memory trace of a future event. The danger has been rehearsed and so evokes less fear.

There would seem to be a direct relationship between the preparedness to deal with physiological stress and the capacity for object perception and reality testing. The longer or more frequently the infant's needs remain unsatisfied, the more intense will the cathexis of inner sensations become. The less physiological tolerance the infant has for stress, the more he may be impelled to fend off new perceptions and to remember instead, although with a vague *mélange* of sensory images, the earlier wish fulfillments.[10] Similar propositions have been brought forward by others. For example, Greenacre (1941) suggested that the existence of an anxiety pattern might precede birth, probably would be augmented in the birth process, and would lead to a predisposition to anxiety. The physiological basis for an anxiety response seemed present in intrauterine life, in reflexes which may become organized at birth and which probably are manifest at first in an irritable responsiveness. Greenacre suggested that variations in the birth process, or in discomforting situations arising in the earliest postnatal weeks, might increase organic anxiety reactions and anxiety potential. Others have emphasized the relation between diminishing organismic stress and the rise of object cathexis. For example, Hoffer (1952) alludes to the cumulative influence of infantile states of helpless-

---

[10]"As a result of the link that has thus been established [i.e., between the mnemic image of apperception and the memory trace of the excitation produced by the need], next time this need arises a psychical impulse will at once emerge which will seek to re-cathect the mnemic image of the perception and to re-evoke the perception itself, that is to say, to re-establish the situation of the original satisfaction. An impulse of this kind is what we call a wish; the reappearance of the perception is the fulfilment of the wish; and the shortest path to the fulfilment of the wish is a path leading direct from the excitation produced by the need to a complete cathexis of the perception. Nothing prevents us from assuming that there was a primitive state of the psychical apparatus in which this path was actually traversed, that is, in which wishing ended in hallucinating. Thus the aim of this first psychical activity was to produce a 'perceptual identity'—a repetition of the perception which was linked with the satisfaction of the need." [Freud, 1900, pp. 565–566].

ness upon anxiety preparedness, and the consequent active drives toward external objects. Mahler (1952) speaks of the progressive displacement of energy from inside to the peripheral body rind, and the gradual responsiveness to the external world. But for our purposes the development of anxiety potential requires a deeper investigation, especially in regard to the accruing "substance" of ego rudiments.

As the signal of anxiety is triggered by affect, the triggering is a function of the ego. The fact that anxiety is a felt response of the ego generally has been construed to mean that a nascent ego, or ego precursors, must exist *before* the affect of anxiety can be experienced.[11] This would seem to be correct if by the *affect* of anxiety we restrict ourselves to the idea of a full-fledged *emotion,* which we have defined as an *awareness* of a stirred-up state of the organism. Our construction is that a process of anxiety *development* takes place, in which stages in the development of the protective shield and of preparedness for anxiety lead through physiological paths to a concomitant emergence of rudimentary ego functioning and of an affect—an emotion—of anxiety.

We should expect that the more primitive, restricted, or labile the observable affect of an infant, the more would it be inappropriate or inappropriately controlled at the time of observation. A fundamental question would be whether such infants would be those insufficiently able to transform physiological to psychological anxiety at necessary points of development, and whether such insufficiency might be detected subsequent to its effects. At present we do not know if the transformation is itself observable, either at the moments of its occurrence or cumulatively.

It is conceivable that where the psychic apparatus has been flooded by physiological anxiety or insufficiently aroused by it, freedom to experience other affects would be diminished. Where the degree of physiological anxiety has

[11] Arlow (1963), Greenacre (1945), Brenner (1953), Kubie (1941), Schur (1953), Spitz (1950), and others.

noxious effects (obviously dependent on individual biology) upon the tiny organism, other subsequent and derivative affects would be warded off, and normal affective positions would be skewed. Or one might say that if physiological anxiety is too generalized (at either extreme) so may the other affects which represent the discharge, mainly of aggressive impulses (aroused primarily by frustration), tend to find expression too diffusely; to overwhelm the organism and impel the infant toward excessive activity or inactivity in any expressive modality.

CHAPTER 6

Anxiety Preparedness: Patterns

So far we have been dealing with phenomena which in the human are hardly observable. Our argument began with Freud's concepts of anxiety preparedness and the protective shield. We have tried to show that evidence exists, from a variety of psychological disciplines, indicating that these concepts were not merely assumptions but concise theoretical descriptions of complex physiological data. We have stressed the receptive function of the protective shield, a function whose study appears to us to have been neglected. For the human infant, our basic hypothesis is that a capacity to discriminate between inner and outer excitations is a prerequisite for the appropriate hypercathexis of the receptive function of the protective shield.

We see anxiety preparedness as an adaptive reaction to penetration of the shield, by both active and passive accommodation to stimuli (not necessarily observable), and by an emerging tendency to appeal for help (signal anxiety) operative when stimuli become excessive. Concomitantly, the first conscious affect aroused, in appropriate instances, in efforts to turn away from or to blunt stimuli perceived to be noxious, or in pursuit of comforting stimuli, is anxiety. From an early period of infancy on, this anxiety can be a rudimentary form of signal anxiety which, turned outward, is an undifferentiated cry for the mother; turned inward, it is a silent summoning of a prototypical defense.

Our data provide no direct observations of infants between

the ages of three days and six weeks. At the latter age, the first for which we have systematic material about infant development and maternal behavior, our data show a continuum of early infantile states and behaviors. It encompasses infants who maintain quiescent states with little interruption and who appear to seek no relief from somatic stress, infants who seek relief from inner excitations and are arousable by external stimuli in varying degrees, infants who are predominantly irritated by inner excitations, and infants who are mainly reactive to external excitations which they seek to prolong.

We do not have material, as indeed no investigators have had for a normal sample, on constitutional or inherited factors as they may relate to anxiety preparedness. However, we can present clinical examples of infantile experiences that appear to promote an infant's capacity, in the first six weeks, to discriminate sensations emanating from the outer world from those emanating from inside himself; to diminish discomforts from inner and from outer sources; to advance a positive cathexis of external stimuli. These examples are meant only to touch upon vicissitudes of anxiety preparedness which may become more and more adequate, or more and more inadequate, at least partly as a function of differential handling in the environment (trauma excluded).

The six illustrative examples include, at age three days: brief notes about the neonate's appearance, activity, muscle tone, and turgor; the balance observed between relaxation, tension, and irritability; mouthing; sensorimotor responses to auditory, visual, and tactile stimuli; and adequacy of feeding. At age six weeks, the examples include: the infant's appearance and facial expression; physical postures and activity; accommodation to holding; degrees of tension; sensorimotor responses; smiling; vocalizations; mouthing; and adequacy of feeding and sleeping. At six weeks, notes are added about each mother's general expressive behavior; her observed and reported modes of infant handling and stimulation, her attitudes toward his development; and her emotional freedom to be aware of and to try to satisfy his changing needs.

Where we call attention to certain similarities or differences between conditions of the infants at three days and six weeks, we do not mean to indicate that definitive changes in development have occurred, or that stabilities have been clearly maintained. The psychological examination of the infant at age three days was included in the research design so that the medical impression of normal status could be reinforced, and so that a decision could be made about including the infant subject in the research sample. Obviously, while observation of a specific response at age three days made clear the infant's capacity for it, absence of that response was not a sign that the capacity was absent. The infant's failure to respond at the time of observation might indicate only that in his immediate state the stimulus failed to evoke the expected response; it still allowed for the possibility that the response might have been evoked at a different hour or on a different neonatal day. Thus the single set of neonatal observations, compared with those at the later age, provide only a partial glimpse of continuity or change in the individual infant's overt behavior. For the total sample of infants, no significant patterns were found to persist between the two ages. The stability or change in specific forms of responsiveness among individual infants are still clinically noteworthy.

CASE 1

Roslyn: Age 3 Days

This infant was physically quiet, though the degree of her activity and her alertness were in the normal range. Her movements were moderately smooth and not tense. Muscle tone and skin turgor were very adequate. When pulled to sitting she held her head erect briefly. No irritability was seen, and mouthing was moderate. Auditory reactions were very good, as persistent listening to the rattle was obtained.[1] Visual fixation was brief

[1]Auditory reactions were rated on a five-point scale devised by Graham, Matarazzo, and Caldwell (1956), as follows: a. Response to bell (startle, blink). b. Response to rattle (as above). c. Listening to rattle

and obtained with difficulty.[2] Tactile response was especially good, as to the touch of gauze upon her mouth and nose she reacted with coordinated movements of head, mouth, and arms.[3] The persistence and vigor of all these responses were moderate.

Roslyn's hunger cry was loud but sporadic, and was relieved by much loud fist sucking. She needed urging to grasp the nipple and to suck, took two ounces well (breast), with moderate but variable eagerness, and shortly after the nipple was withdrawn she fell asleep.

Roslyn: Age 6.6 Weeks

Roslyn was chubby, firm, and healthy-looking. Her large eyes lent expressiveness to an otherwise almost immobile face. During most of the time she was observed she lay in a TNR position, with limb movements minimal and small in range. Coordination was adequate and muscle tone good. Symmetrical positions were attained only very occasionally and very briefly. When brought to a sitting position she held her head well and a mild grimace appeared, but her body tension hardly increased. When held in arms by the examiner she was quite limp, except shortly after her feeding; at that time she also was observed to be especially relaxed in the supine, with her limbs loosely extended and her fists open. Physical vigor was seen only when, in prone, she lifted her head to Zone 1

(opening eyes, decreased movement, head turning). d. Persistent listening to rattle (three or four presentations), or listening also to bell. e. Both persistent listening to rattle and listening to bell.

[2]For full scale, see Graham, Matarazzo, and Caldwell (1956, p. 519).

[3]Tactile response to cotton gauze placed on the baby's mouth and nose was rated on a four-point scale, from the same examination of Graham et al. (1956), as follows: a. Any movement within 2″. b. Specific movements of either head or mouth (back-and-forth movements or sustained head retraction or movements of mouth in direction of stimulus). c. Both specific head and mouth movements present more than 50 percent of the time. d. Head, mouth, and coordinated arm movements all present.

and strained to turn it from side to side. Now and then she licked at the mattress and peered at it under her face.

Responses to test objects were very considerably delayed, and poor. At the sound of the bell she became still but did not turn her head; when the rattle was shaken she only fluttered her eyes. All attempts to arouse visual fixation were in vain. When her fist was touched with the rattle she failed to react, but when with difficulty it was put into her hand she held it tight. Her main appropriate response was to show irritability when the diaper was placed on her face. At best, her attention to external stimuli was fleeting, except when given something to mouth. There were no signs of fatigue or restlessness. She showed no awareness of her mother or of the examiner, and no scanning of the environment. No smile could be elicited. The only sign of emotion appeared when she seemed to be on the verge of a frown or a grimace, after her feeding and when pulled to sitting. Vocalizations were frequent but weak. Except for her loud sucking on the pacifier, she was almost entirely still.

Roslyn was reported to suck her thumb with intensity before falling asleep, and would do so at other times as well, but the mother preferred to give her the pacifier. The baby would fret when, turning her head in the prone position, she lost the pacifier; often her cry went unheard because it was, as the mother said, a strange squeaky sound, like a series of sharp intakes of breath. As observed, the cry was most like a strong, high-pitched whimper. Roslyn was also reported to suck her wrists so hard that they often showed large blue bruises.

Breast feeding was adequate but somewhat sluggish, very like the feeding seen at three days. Sleep was entirely satisfactory, except during a brief period of change in the family's routines.

The Mother

Mrs. R, a multipara, was a pert, talkative, gracious woman. She moved and spoke with a freedom that soon appeared excessive. She gave the impression of straining to show delight in all aspects of the baby's care. Nevertheless she admitted, quite spontaneously, a recurring disappointment about her own insecurity as a mother. She had made a few observations about the baby's behavior, and spoke much of her relief that Roslyn was so undemanding, and had "no wakeful periods." Although she described glowingly how much Roslyn loved to be held, and could curl up happily in her arms, Mrs. R explained that she did not pick the baby up much. She felt that there should be definite "holding periods" but had not yet decided when they should be. Mr. R did not pick Roslyn up much, either—he was afraid to. Sometimes the older siblings talked to the baby.

Mrs. R talked gaily and volubly about Roslyn, but rarely talked to her. She was attentive and very tender to the baby, but related far more directly to the interviewer, even while she was breastfeeding. She offered very little physical contact to the baby except during the feeding, and treated her kittenishly. She showed overt conflict between her wish to be playful with the baby and her feeling of obligation to be educative, and oscillated between excessive activity and failure to note an excessive lethargy in the infant.

Roslyn, Comment

Since the neonatal period, Roslyn's activity level appears to have decreased. Tension also appears to be too low for adequate responsiveness to external stimuli; only tactile sensitivity remains prominent. Vigorous sucking now is her most engrossing activity. Mrs. R is very satisfied with the baby's absence of stress, and makes no effort to stir the baby to a higher level of reactivity. Mrs. R's own vivacity may prevent her from noting the contrasting inertia of the baby, or from considering that the baby's alertness and well-being might be enhanced by some form of sensory arousal. Mother and infant appear thus to cooperate in protecting Roslyn from encounters with new stimuli. As Roslyn experiences "learning" gratifications mainly of an oral nature, preparedness for anxiety appears to be still dormant in her.

CASE 2

Sally: Age 3 Days

Sally was a moderately alert, minimally active infant. Muscle tone and turgor were good, and her movements had a relaxed quality, but when pulled to sitting she arched and resisted. A mild irritability seemed to be relieved by finger-sucking. Mild mouthing was also seen. No crying at all was heard. On hearing the bell and rattle, she startled and blinked her eyes but did not turn her head or decrease activity. Visual fixation was brief and obtained with difficulty. To the tactile stimulus she reacted with mild movements of head and mouth. In general, her responses were moderate in strength and not persistent.

Before her feeding she was peaceful, and apparently because of sleepiness she had a slight difficulty in grasping the nipple and in sucking steadily. She took one-and-a-half ounces of milk (breast) and fell asleep.

Sally: Age 5.1 Weeks

Sally was a small, well-formed baby, active and alert-looking, but with a tense facial expression that reduced her attractiveness. When she lay unattended in the crib her movements were frequent and extensive but often jerky. Rigidity and tightness characterized her body in most positions, possibly least in the prone. Head turning occurred mainly when she was prone. In the supine she looked about while sucking very hard on her hand. When pulled to sitting and when held in arms she held her head well, but felt heavy and did not relax. At times she pouted and frowned.

Sally seemed easily irritated by test stimuli, yet as the testing proceeded the fretting diminished, as if she was being distracted from some inner discomfort. Auditory responses were moderately smooth, as she listened to the bell at once with decrease of activity and facial response, but not for long. Similarly, visual responses were adequate, stronger for persons than for the dangling ring, but neither strong nor lasting. Her response to the diaper on her face was immediate and frantic, with many aversive movements of head and limbs. She could not be induced to hold the rattle.

Smiling was difficult to elicit until after feeding and a nap, and only after much effort on the part of the examiner. Sally did then respond to facial movements by the examiner and uttered a few vowel sounds which the mother said she had not often heard. The only other vocalizations heard during waking states were breath sounds and loud wailing. Finger-sucking and tonguing were prominent activities. Several times Sally put four fingers at a time into her mouth, keeping her mouth very wide open at the same time.

The Mother

Mrs. S, a primipara, had expected Sally to sleep longer than she did, but when Sally awoke and began to fret Mrs. S remained in her seat, saying the feeding could wait. Sally fussed for about 15 minutes, then cried loudly for more than half an hour, until she fell asleep again. During sleep, restless head movements and little sounds were frequent. On waking again, she whimpered and fretted, but Mrs. S still delayed picking her up until a full hour later than she had said she would feed; and during the (breast) feeding, she continuously and almost inaudibly chided Sally for just playing and not sucking. Actually the feeding seemed smooth except for frequent pauses by the baby, apparently a result of fatigue or sleepiness. Mrs. S had for several weeks been having difficulty in establishing a regular feeding schedule. The baby's sleep was variable. Sometimes she fell asleep readily, sometimes cried for a long time and suddenly fell asleep. The only sure way to have her fall asleep was to put her outdoors (this was in June). Sleep itself was reported to be restful, unlike that which was observed during the prefeeding period.

Mrs. S was young and inexperienced, and frankly irritated by the baby's discontent. At home, she said, Sally could be quiet for short periods when alone, looking about and sucking on her hand, but sometimes she cried for a very long time because she had "learned the trick of crying to be picked up." Mrs. S did not hold her because she believed that babies should learn that there are definite play periods. She had provided some crib toys to which Sally had so far paid no attention. Mr. S, after giving Sally her evening bottle, usually held her very briefly as he, too, feared spoiling her.

Sally, Comment

Sally shows good capacity to react favorably to gentle but persistent stimulation. She is alert, but irritability and tension have increased sharply since her neonatal days. She appears to derive little or no satisfaction from any stimuli, and her capacity be be comforted is decreased. Interest in feeding appears to be moderate, but this is hard to evaluate because the feeding was delayed, and agitation may have interfered with her appetite.

Mrs. S is troubled by Sally's crying yet is severely inhibited in her capacity to offer solace or distraction to the baby. She expressed no enjoyment of Sally, no pride, and no optimism about future adjustments, and she never showed any playfulness toward her. The only intimacy observed was in the whispering and in a rote patting of the baby's body during feeding. Mrs. S's fear of being too indulgent leads her to behave austerely, the baby's tension and discomfort are unrelieved, and mutual dissatisfaction may be rising. In Sally, preparedness for anxiety seems poor. She is not being helped to accommodate either to welcome or to unwelcome arousals, and her principal reactions to them are unrest and flight movements. She is daily and frequently overwhelmed by tension states, suggesting that narcissistic cathexis is being augmented, that her development of object cathexis is being attenuated, and that anxiety is not on the way to being reduced to a signal.

Case 3

Tina: Age 3 Days

Tina was an extremely relaxed infant. Her activity was minimal though all movements were smooth. Muscle tone was somewhat low, turgor was only moderate, and her motor activity "lacked drive." When pulled to sitting she remained limp, and her head drooped. She was unusually tolerant of handling, showed no irritability, and did not cry at all. Little mouthing was observed. She was hard to keep awake at first, but became remarkably alert during testing. Auditory response to the sounds of rattle and bell consisted only of startling and blinking. Visual responsiveness was superior: horizontal pursuit movements through an arc of 30° were obtained, though with difficulty. To the touch of the diaper on her face she reacted with head and mouth movements only. In general, the persistence and vigor of her responses were poor.

She was quiet before feeding, grasped the nipple at once, sucked with only moderate vigor and rhythm, but with an alert facial appearance. After taking two ounces (bottle), she seemed to lose interest in the feeding and fell asleep.

Tina: Age 4.6 Weeks

Tina was now a small, wiry, thin-skinned girl who at first glance looked quite fragile. A little contact with her soon dispelled this impression. Her body had good muscle tone, her facial expression was very lively. Her movements were small in range, fairly smooth, and comfortably intermittent. Although she moved about comparatively little, all of the movements had a quality of sureness and control. Awake, she lay in a TNR position a good deal of the time, keeping her head to one or the other side easily; occasionally her positions were symmetrical. In the prone she could also turn her head smoothly from one side to the other, though she lifted it only to Zone 1. When pulled to sitting, she held her head well. When held in arms she accommodated excellently, and her body felt strong. At all times she was amenable and very easy to handle.

Her responses to auditory stimuli were very strong and prolonged: she listened with a definite change of facial expression. Visual fixation to the dangling ring was good, after slight delay, but she lost sight of it almost at once in favor of intense and persistent regard of the examiner. The tactile stimulus on her face was omitted, in error, but judging from Tina's other responses to touch, it seemed reasonable to assume that she probably would have responded smoothly, with appropriate irritation. It took considerable effort to pry open her fist, but once she grasped the rattle she held it exceedingly tight.

Throughout the visit Tina maintained a readiness to smile at her mother or the examiner at the slightest provocation. Her one-sided grins were accompanied by gentle movements, soft cooing sounds, and were most appealing. Her social responsiveness never flagged, and her attentiveness was matched by an inner repose. She licked her hand, poked around her mouth with her fingers, tongued, but did not suck her fingers. She had been offered a pacifier a few weeks earlier but had rejected it.

Before her feeding Tina was quiet. As she began to suck, her extremities at first looked tense. She took five ounces without delay, sucked rhythmically and strongly, and gradually her body was relaxed. After being burped, easily, she made soft, seemingly contented sounds. The feeding procedures were fairly quick and thoroughly easy. Tina was reported already to have taken fruits and cereals well, and to sleep a good deal and soundly between feedings. She had begun to sleep through 12 hours a night. During the day, she sometimes stayed quietly awake for as long as two hours.

The Mother

Mrs. T, a multipara, was a light, compact young woman, clearly confident about and pleased with her maternal tasks. Her expressive behavior was consistently moderate. She moved and spoke appropriately, with directness and economy. She was friendly but never forward. Toward Tina she was kindly and tender but made no particular effort to win the baby's attention. She reported that at home she played with Tina a good deal, and she spoke with pride of Tina's alertness, good mood, responsiveness, and good feeding and sleeping. With similar pleasure she described the family's interest in Tina, and their common eagerness to hold, play with, and feed her. Mrs. T showed an excellent balance of ability to anticipate the baby's needs and to allow for some natural delay in ministering to them. Everything she did seemed effortless, and Tina seemed to be entirely contented and well cared for.

Tina, Comment

At almost five weeks, Tina is again found to be remarkably alert and unirritable. Mildness of activity is still present but her movements have acquired sureness, strength, and persistence. Visual responsiveness is still most mature, and other responses have become stronger and more varied. Mouthing is still not conspicuous. Feeding and sleeping retain their satisfactory character. All in all, Tina appears to be having ample practice in assimilating new and varied sensorimotor experiences, with no undue somatic interference. The maturity of her physical movements, her responsiveness, and her socialization suggest that she has already had good practice in accommodating to the rise and fall of tension states. It could be surmised that she might soon arrive at a capacity to experience an early form of signal anxiety, that is, to begin to recognize the mother as a source of relief in moments of felt danger.

CASE 4

Urwin: Age 3 Days

Urwin was a physically quiet but very alert-looking neonate. His movements were few but smooth. Muscle tone appeared to be low but adequate, and turgor was good. Only when pulled to sitting did he become limp, and his head drooped. Auditory responses were very good: at the sounds of the rattle and the bell his activity decreased, he turned his head to the sounds, and listened persistently to both. Visual responsiveness was excellent: fixation on the red light was easily elicited, horizontal pursuit movements through an arc of 30° were easily obtained, and vertical pursuit movements were also obtained. Tactile responses were also excellent: head and mouth movements occurred more than 50 percent of the time. The vigor and persistence of these reactions were, in general, moderate.

The only time Urwin was at all irritable was before feeding. He sucked spontaneously and well, and lay alert and relaxed after taking three ounces of milk (bottle). No mouthing or finger-sucking was seen.

Urwin: Age 6.1 Weeks

Urwin was now a large, fat, sober, yet alert-looking infant. Although he stayed fully awake during the two-and-a-half hours of the visit, he lay supine with limbs loosely flexed, and was practically inert for all of the time except when held for feeding, when placed in a chair, or when tested. Mainly he lay with his head turned sharply to one side, and it could be turned to the mid-position only with a good deal of force. His movements, mainly of the lower limbs, were symmetrical, somewhat jerky, and small in range. He resisted being pulled to sitting, arching stiffly and putting all of his weight on his feet. Upon the mother's suggestion he was pulled up by his hands, gently, and then he did sit with his head adequately erect. When held by the examiner he became rigid, arched his back, and dropped his head backward until it became impossible to hold him. When the mother propped him in the big armchair, and sometimes when she held him, he slumped heavily. In contrast to his poor bodily accommodation, his facial expressions varied appropriately. Although he often stared vacantly into space, he did also frown, grimace, smile strongly, pout with lower lip turned down, look tense and ready to cry. Mild irritability appeared only when the mother stimulated him in her arms or propped him in the big armchair.

All sensorimotor responses were delayed. Auditory responses were evident mainly in dilation of his eyes. Visual fixation on the dangling ring was very difficult to elicit, and he did not move his head beyond the mid-line in pursuit. He did not focus on the examiner's face but did so very well on the mother's face whenever she came close to him. In fact, he smiled broadly when she talked to him excitedly, holding her face extremely close to his and bringing her nose into his mouth. Tactile response to the diaper on his face showed mainly in mild head and mouth movements. He was slow to grasp the rattle but did hold it, and this turned out to be his most persistent response. This baby's degree of arousal and his attention span were often hard to gauge, because he showed so little variation of behavior before, during, and after testing. Neither fatigue nor restlessness appeared at any point, nor was any alteration of state observed. When unattended in the crib, his gaze often had a blank quality.

For almost all of the time that he was in his mother's arms, but not always in the crib, he sucked the pacifier with remarkable strength and rhythm. When it was removed before feeding, his fists flew to his mouth, and the mother had to wrest them away to insert the nipple. She said that often he had taken his fist, and more recently his thumb, into his mouth, but she had removed it in favor of the pacifier. To make sure he did not lose the pacifier she often pressed it into his mouth and held it there with her own finger; but usually she propped it on a diaper when he lay with his head turned to one side. She was observed to stop his fussing in just this way for a long time before feeding him. Spontaneous mouthing or finger-sucking were thus precluded from observation.

Urwin's vocalizations were clear and strong, especially loud while he sucked on the pacifier but at other times as well. According to report, his feeding was entirely satisfactory, as he was taking fruit juices and cereal eagerly. His sleep was also very good except when disturbed, a few nights a week, by colic.

The Mother

Mrs. U, a primipara, reported that Urwin's day had no regular pattern. She and her husband enjoyed handling all of his routines interchangeably and without any regard for schedules. One has to experiment to keep a baby happy, she said; one should feed him when he is hungry, let him sleep when he is sleepy, and let him play when he feels like playing. Both parents indulged in a great deal of lusty physical play with the baby, talked and sang to him, were demonstratively affectionate, and offered him many toys with visual and aural appeal. Mrs. U added, however, that she could always keep him in a good mood anywhere, anytime, with the pacifier.

This hearty mother dominated the infant almost incessantly. She watched him when not holding him and when he was in her lap she moved her hands or her mouth on parts of his body continuously. Her necessary physical contacts with him were also protracted by considerable ineptness. She addressed him with lavish praise, excitement, and sometimes annoyance, and she attributed many emotions to him, such as boredom, aggravation, and a desire to push her away. Even her expressions of tenderness to him had a fierce quality.

Urwin, Comment

In Urwin one sees an unusual maintenance of a state of alertness combined with a dearth of spontaneous activity and a sluggish reactivity. Although apparently capable of good sensorimotor responsiveness, only visual response to the mother and tactile responses are distinct at six weeks. Physical handling arouses either strong tension and avoidance movements, or a contrasting limpness. Expressive behavior is strongest in facial nuances, in vocalizations, and in sucking—that is, in reactions emanating from the head and face—and is in marked contrast to insufficient accommodation to physical handling. His behavior in many respects is strikingly different from what was seen at age three days, when muscle tone was adequate, movements were smooth, mouthing was not observed, and sensorimotor responses were consistently high in all areas. At six weeks, alertness, low irritability, and good appetite are still present, but he also has colic.

Mrs. U seems unable to take time to recognize the baby's states or his need for anything but placation. Although she speaks of a baby's need to do what pleases him, she grants herself no time to discover what might please Urwin. Her reports suggest such excessive, erratic, and indiscriminate arousal of and response to his momentary needs and moods that spontaneous activity or reactivity on his part appear almost to be stifled. Anxiety preparedness in this infant would appear to be excessive, or very uneven. For while he receives certain visual and oral stimulations with ease, he appears able neither to accept nor to protect himself adequately from most inner or outer stimuli. He either freezes or melts; that is, he makes an effort to avoid the stimuli by physical rigidity or by surrendering totally with physical flaccidity.

CASE 5

Victor: Age 3 Days

This infant had an appearance of robustness, looked alert, and was normally active. Tension was rated normal, turgor and muscle tone good. He pulled to sitting with adequate tension and mild head lag. No irritability, crying, or mouthing were observed before his feeding. His face had a few scratches. Auditory reactions were excellent, in that he listened to the rattle persistently. Visual fixation was brief and obtained with difficulty. Tactile responsiveness was superior in that both specific head and mouth movements occurred more than 50 percent of the time. His head movements, in the prone, were strong.

He fed (bottle) rapidly, vigorously, and alertly, but after taking three ounces he gagged and regurgitated a moderate amount. Bringing his fingers to his mouth, he groped about his lips with them but did not get them into his mouth. He grew restless, squirmed, and cried. It was hard to estimate whether his discontent was due to remaining hunger or to a wish to continue sucking; the nipple through which he had sucked was found to have a very large hole. The attending nurse said that aside from being irritable early in the mornings, Victor slept most of the day between feedings.

Victor: Age 5.4 Weeks

Victor was now a big, heavy baby, and his face was pallid, sickly-looking, and not alert. His nasal passages were congested, his breathing labored and rapid. His movements were narrow in range and jerky, his coordination poor. For major periods of observation his body was tense and tight. When pulled to sitting he became floppy, whimpered, and trembled. When he was pulled to standing, the sounds of protest stopped but he was not able to support any weight on his feet, which collapsed beneath him. In the prone position he seemed comfortable and lay quietly, with his head turned to one side. Several times, when awake, he coughed, gagged, and cried without any overt cause or any build-up of distress.

At the sound of the rattle he opened his eyes a bit wider, grimaced, and appeared to listen; this was his clearest response. Visual responsiveness was slightly delayed, until the examiner jiggled the dangling ring, which Victor then pursued to about 90° without moving his head at all. He did not at first react at all to the diaper on his face, and then only turned his head aside. He was not able to grasp the rattle in his left hand, was helped to do so in the right, but soon dropped it. No smile could be elicited, and no direct regard of persons. No mouthing or hand-to-mouth activity was seen, nor had the mother noted any. She had recently offered Victor a pacifier because she thought he might need more sucking, but he had rejected it. Vocalizations were slight and immature.

The mother reported that she customarily fed Victor only after he let her know, by screaming, that he was hungry. However, despite his screaming after a very late arrival, she kept him waiting for a long time past his expected feeding time. He was observed to move from a state of sleep to being awake with a few tiny noises and then a burst of vociferous crying in about 10 seconds, presumably at the time he was hungry. During the crying, he gagged, coughed, wheezed, and trembled, and jerked and flailed all of his limbs. During the feeding of cereal, fruit, and milk, which was rapid and disruptive, there was more jerky leg-kicking, fanning of toes, and clenching of both fists. As at the end of the feeding he was still irritable, the mother gave him water in a propped bottle so he could content himself with sucking. Again he coughed and gagged and spat up a good deal of mucus.

The mother explained that he could fall asleep after feeding only with a nipple attached to a bottle. He slept well, except that often he was startled when the family dog stood by his crib and barked. She added that he hated being moved or interrupted during sleep; could not bear being turned to the prone position while asleep; became annoyed (in sleep) if moved even to be dressed, or if he lost his propped bottle. At these times he screamed, stiffened his body, held his breath, flushed, and was very hard to comfort. He was not played with much. The mother talked to him mainly at night, when the other children were asleep; sometimes her husband held him, and sometimes his eldest sibling talked to him. Otherwise, when awake and unattended, Victor was most likely to look around a bit, and if he didn't get what he wanted—food, usually—he "got into one of his fits." Usually, unless he was being fed when awake, he screamed, and had been seen to squeeze his cheeks with both fists, in vexation.

The Mother

Mrs. V was a smiling, chatty, shy young multipara. Often she was bemused and distant, and usually she was indifferent to the baby's emotional states. Affectlessly, she called attention to his difficult breathing and to an infection in his navel, showed more worried interest in his "nervousness," but obviously regarded his crying as inevitable. She handled him as little as possible and made no effort to communicate with him in any way. Nevertheless she appeared to feel affection for him. There was something appealing about her naïveté and her childlike looking to the interviewer for approval of her care of the baby.

Victor, Comment

Since the neonatal period Victor has lost his appearance of health. Irritability is high and tension has markedly increased. Visual responsiveness is adequate but other sensory reactions are interfered with by somatic stress, and he does not accommodate to social stimulation. Feeding patterns have remained unsatisfactory. Only nonnutritive sucking gives him peace, and without it he cannot fall asleep. In waking states he experiences few comforts, he is chronically overwhelmed by massive arousal of need, and has few periods of content alertness in which to receive sensory gratification, or to differentiate between inner and outer excitations, or to seek comforts for himself. His anxiety preparedness would seem to be pathogenically low.

CASE 6

Ward: Age 3 Days

Ward was a small, very relaxed, normally active infant. His movements were unusually smooth and coordinated, and leg movements were notably rhythmic. He pulled to sitting with good muscle tone and no head lag. Turgor was good. He had a few scratches on his cheeks. No irritability and no crying were observed. A fair amount of finger-sucking occurred, and he vocalized softly during feeding and during testing.

Sensorimotor responsiveness was superior in all areas. He listened to both rattle and bell persistently. Visual pursuit movements through a horizontal arc of 30° were easily obtained, and vertical pursuit movements were also obtained. In response to the diaper on his face he moved head and mouth more than 50 percent of the time and at the same time showed gentle coordinated arm movements. Persistence and vigor of all of these responses were good.

Before feeding he was entirely content. Although his eyes were closed while he fed he sucked spontaneously, eagerly, and vigorously. After taking two ounces (breast) he coughed once, regurgitated a trifle, relaxed, and fell asleep. A few minutes later he opened his eyes, and looked alert and peaceful.

Ward: Age 5.5 Weeks

Ward had become large, chubby, and placid. His movements were small in range and fairly smooth, neither vigorous nor frequent, but well directed. Gradual movements of his head from side to side were more prominent than body or limb movements. It seemed possible that his physical quietness was related to his being dressed in a great deal of clothing, which could have hampered his activity. Mainly he lay relaxed in either supine or prone, and attained symmetrical positions frequently. He was reported to have raised his head to Zone 2, often resting his upper weight on his forearms, but this was not observed. When pulled to sitting he held his head adequately. When held in arms by the examiner, he rested easily against her shoulder and held his head sturdily erect.

Auditory responses were most sustained: he stopped moving and appeared to listen well. Visual response, though somewhat sluggish, was very adequate, and stronger for persons than for test objects. Tactile response was delayed and gentle: after about 30 seconds he merely opened his mouth. His grasp was weak: he held the rattle only when it was put into his hand and then only for a few seconds. His mood was equable throughout, and he showed no fatigue.

He was unusually unirritable except when hungry, but then his cries grew to screams which persisted until he was fed. He took five ounces (bottle) eagerly but cried and strained while doing so, which the mother attributed to gas pains, explaining that typically he sucked rapidly and defecated at the same time. During this period of his distress she dandled his body, tickled his feet, and talked to him, in vain. He seemed lethargic and difficult to distract from his crying until his feeding was resumed. His mother was clearly proud of his appetite, and was so ready and eager to feed him at every opportunity that feeding and sleeping nearly punctuated each other during the visit. The baby was reported to fall asleep easily and to sleep soundly almost from the end of one feeding to the beginning of the next.

At times when he was awake all members of the family played with him and offered him toys. When unattended, he was said to stare about quietly, and sometimes he had seemed to be listening to music. The mother described how he laughed and made throaty sounds when held and kissed, especially when held upright (this was observed), and how he smiled to everyone at home.

The Mother

Mrs. W was a small, sturdy, active woman, full of smiles. Often she spoke with a barely contained excitement, showing high pleasure in all aspects of Ward's care. She seemed to relish everything she could do for him, and her efficiency was obvious. She made allusions to all of his activities, kept glancing at him happily and then shyly looking at the interviewer as if to share her joy.

Ward, Comment

The relaxed, contented state, and the very adequate physical activity observed in Ward at three days have been maintained, but sensorimotor responsiveness has become less vigorous and less definite. The sudden rise of distress before and during feeding is also in striking contrast to the states of quiet alertness. The cry during feeding may be due to gastric distress. It is also possible that this infant has become habituated to a sequence of waking, crying, and food accommodation in too quick succession by Mrs. W's eagerness to feed at the slightest sign of appetite, in which case the infant's tension tolerance may have become unduly lowered. The insurance of low tension might also account for the quietness when not feeding. Thus in Ward there appear to be indications of high anxiety preparedness, in his capacity to receive stimuli during inactive alert states, and in his ready capacity to react to changing somatic states, but low preparedness in a possibly insufficient tolerance of hunger tension, or insufficient capacity for delay.

The sum of the mothers' differences toward their particular infants may be considered as a partial index of maternal skill in sustaining the infants' biological capacity for anxiety preparedness, and in furthering the infants' early socialization to the mother qua species member. Another way to describe the early socialization is to consider that, normally, it allows for a symbiotic imprinting to the mother. She becomes a specific type of need-gratifying object. We believe that later on the infant's capacity to feel signal anxiety and to develop positive cathexes of other objects will reflect the forms and intensities of need gratification that the mother has made available.[4]

[4]For the infant ages of six months and one year, we shall present below statistical material indicating relationships between maternal behavior, degrees of infantile anxiety, and ego development.

CHAPTER 7

Anxiety and Socialization

The proposition that there are discrete stages of preparedness for anxiety and that there is a joint emergence of the affect of anxiety and of ego must be stated in verifiable terms if it is to have more than speculative significance. The developmental steps toward this joint emergence may be encompassed in the two phases of socialization which, as suggested above, influence and are influenced by the preparedness for anxiety.

We hypothesize the psychological events occurring in the two phases of socialization as follows:

PHASE 1

The first phase begins with the sensory awakening of the neonate during the first six weeks of life, and is marked by the imprinting of the mother as a species-specific object in the fourth month. It is imaginable that during his earliest weeks an infant has felt, more or less regularly, alternations of comfort and discomfort; cold, warm; wet, dry; loud, quiet; hard, soft; light, dark; cramped, falling; snug, loose. To take a commonly observed sequence, let us say that shortly after hunger contractions begin, milk comes into the infant's mouth to be sucked in. A day later he may note something more: the milk does not come into his mouth the moment he feels hunger, but briefly he senses instead the presence of a hovering moving object, and hears a soft and pleasing sound very close to his face. That is, after the onset of the hunger contractions but before the onset of sucking, a sensorimotor pleasure has intervened, in the form of a tiny social adventure with some comforting object. The infant has been tided over the first wave of hunger without food, and has meanwhile received pleasure from another source. If subsequent experiences inform him with fair consistency that painful sensations of hunger are usually soon followed by sensorimotor pleasures as well as by milk, we may suppose that his waiting for the milk will in later hunger states arouse a perceptual search for the source of the intervening or accompanying pleasure. Then the infant will not only be alerted to the visual and auditory social stimuli, but will also be impelled to exercise physical responses in turning toward the pleasing stimulus. He will practice head turning if he is supine, head turning and head lifting in the prone; all his limbs may be thrown into a kind of centrifugal activity; tongue, lips, fingers, and fists may be particularly excited. These intervening responses, practiced from day to day, provide experiences in the positive aspects of delay, increase of the infant's anticipation of sensory satisfactions, and generally afford him a quantity of sensorimotor tensions, which in themselves provide satisfactions and stem the inner tension of hunger until milk comes.

We can observe that where the infant's attention to environmental arousals is thus gradual and pleasing, there are corresponding pleasing arrests, or suspensions, of the infant's motor activity, suspensions that are like little latencies of the impulse life, during which perceptual activity grows apace, and immediately after which motor activity may be spontaneously resumed—producing a rhythm of sensory and motor activities. These activities, for example, reflex sucking or grasping, depend on the infant's neurophysiological readiness to receive and to be excited by external stimuli. They obviously require no consciousness of stimulation or response, and they are elicited by many kinds of objects. In the first days of life, auditory response can quite regularly be elicited. We have already referred to recent studies which show that visual fixation and visual pursuit movements occur in the first days, and can be regularly elicited by the fourth or fifth week.

Table 2 presents the visual response scores of 130 infants in the second month, as observed during the Infant Development Research Project. For both four-week and eight-week items, the frequency of the social response is greater than the frequency of the response to inanimate objects, except for the single reverse situation in items 4 and 5. The higher frequency of the social response is, of course, of adaptational value; a higher frequency of response to inanimate objects, which cannot provide relief in case of need, would be pathological.

TABLE 2

VISUAL RESPONSE AT SIX WEEKS

N = 130.[a] MEAN AGE: 6.143 WEEKS

	N	%
[b]1. Expression: impassive face	127	97.6
[b]2. Expression: vague, indirect regard	125	96.1
[b]3. Supine: stares indefinitely at surroundings	124	95.3
[b]4. Dangling Ring, Rattle: regards line vision only	118	90.7
[b]5. Social: regards examiner's face, activity diminishes	108	83.0
6. Expression: alert expression	104	80.0
[b]7. Dangling Ring: follows to mid-line	98	75.3
8. Expression: direct, definite regard	90	69.2
9. Supine: regards examiner	81	62.3
10. Social: follows moving person	74	56.9
11. Expression: smiles (social)	71	54.6
12. Social: facial social response	71	54.6
13. Dangling Ring: follows past mid-line	70	53.8
14. Dangling Ring: delayed mid-line regard	58	44.6
15. Dangling Ring: regards examiner's hand	57	43.8

[a]One infant could not be tested at six weeks.
[b]Normative at four weeks. All other items normative at eight weeks. All items selected from Gesell Developmental Schedules (Gesell and Amatruda, 1949).

The intensity with which visual pursuit is practiced by any normal infant in the next months is easy to observe. By the third month he spontaneously turns his head to gaze at more distant objects, notices when objects close by are removed, and, as may be of supreme importance for object discrimination, he begins to keep visual attention upon his own hands and seems able to attend to the sound of his own voice. The visible increase of intentional visual searching, inspecting, watching, coordinated with hand and hand-to-mouth movements, suggests that it is during the third and fourth months of life that consciousness is attained, and that the first phase of socialization, marked by visual fixation, form perception, and pursuit of the human object qua species, comes to an end.

A hypercathexis or consciousness of satisfaction or of its absence, during these rhythmic alternations of sensation, perception, and response, would appear to constitute the greatest single psychological moment in mental development. It seems reasonable to consider that this hypercathexis of sensations and perceptions leads directly to an awareness of a difference between self and object, to object cathexis, even at a most primitive level. Consciousness belongs to the perceptual system, and the proposition that consciousness arises instead of a memory trace (Freud, 1923, 1925) still provides our clearest understanding of the emergence of an awareness of sensation.

PHASE 2

The second phase of socialization may, we think, be marked by the infant's discrimination of the mother as an individual, rather than as a member of the species: the mother is the specific imprinting object. Although high social responsiveness may easily be extended to other persons as well, the mother is sought out by eye, ear, hand, and voice, and is desired as the infant's primary companion. The ready response to the mother is most observable in the smiling response to her overtures. The smile as a predictable response to the mother may indicate the onset of a process of discrimination between her and others, a process often evident in an infant's notable curiosity about nonmothers, new persons. Attention to all human objects may constitute prime positive evidence that specific affects are taking shape; that the overwhelmingly negative responses are receding, and that hitherto less conspicuous positive responses are emerging more definitely or more frequently. Consciousness of sensation, of affect, of self, and of object may at this time be attained.

Early in this second phase of socialization, which we may estimate to set in as the fourth month approaches, and to be completed in the seventh month, some capacity for anticipation and delay has already appeared: it has become observable in the rise or the quickening of attention to sources of gratification. The infant now seems able to differentiate quickly and sharply between comforting and discomforting stimuli, and he shows a "proud" urge for sensorimotor explorations. He does not mind brief disappearances of his mother as long as he finds that he can retrieve her "at will," much as he can retrieve the sight of other objects that disappear temporarily— his own hands, or familiar inanimate objects in his environment. Clearly he does not prefer to be alone. Even a most contented infant of about five months will be reported to cry when his mother, after being pleasantly attentive, puts him down in his bed and walks away. He can be comforted by others, but he functions most smoothly in the care of his most familiar mother.

Empirical evidence that infants increase attention to nonfamiliar visual percepts during the first six months (Fantz, 1964; Hershenson, 1964) supports the idea of a hypercathexis of the mother qua individual toward the close of that period.

It is usually beginning in his fifth and sixth months that the infant recognizes his mother as the chief object through which gratifications are provided and stresses are relieved. He becomes increasingly eager to play with her. He loves turning to or away from her freely, reaching to her, bouncing on her lap, grasping her hair, nose, eyeglasses, anything in the area of her exciting face. He happily takes the initiative in social contacts with her, forcing her to respond by his grunts, sighs,

squeals, and noisy bubble-blowing. He is engaged in the reciprocal "dialogue" described by Spitz (1963). Even a relatively
harsh mother appears to acquire the infant's intense emotional
investment and to receive his most immediate shows of delight, anger, protest, joy. And, in general, the infant of this age
who is adequately stimulated by the mother is also more likely
to show eagerness in reaching toward inanimate objects and
exploring them visually, manually, and orally, as will be indicated in findings presented below. He may easily become
stimulus bound, enthralled by life, so to speak, and noisily and
physically responsive to it. Moreover, he has become aware
that objects have functions—they can be banged, shaken,
pushed, held tight; and as the cathexis of inanimate objects
increases, the infant is likely to find himself less threatened by
the mother's absence. Now her voice alone, coming from another room, may content him for short periods, because he can
attend to other objects or events while he waits for her.

And now other objects, nonmothers, threaten by their
very appearance to come between infant and mother: they are
now to be regarded with a new kind of caution before they
can be accepted. At this point, in which socialization to the
mother as an individual has taken place, and in which the
danger of loss of comfort may be perceived consciously, the
preparedness for anxiety may reach a first peak of maturity.
Infants of this age, from about six months on, do not necessarily show fear of strangers. Often they stare with a fixed
attentiveness at a stranger, or at a familiar person dressed or
groomed unfamiliarly, and either may have to undergo a sort
of "customs inspection" before being admitted to the infants'
social domain. We have found that new persons are more
likely to pass inspection and to be responded to positively
by infants experienced in social communication with their
mothers.

Table 3 presents the relationship between very high and
very low degrees of social stimulation by the mother, of infants up to six months of age, and the social responsiveness of
infants to both the mother and the unfamiliar adult in unfamil-

iar surroundings, during the approximately three-hour period of their visit to the research quarters. The data are drawn from interviews and observations of 122 infants studied in the Infant Development Research Project.[1] Only those cases have been used in which the mother's report was adequate for rating and appeared to be reliable, contained no contradictions, and could be supported by our own observations. Cases in which the maternal stimulation was considered moderate were also excluded, as the effects of moderate stimulation were most likely to be influenced in either direction by paternal or sibling stimulation, and the latter was difficult to confirm even during several home visits. This left an N of 77.

Statistical significance for Table 3 (p. 85) was not calculable because of the low frequency in several cells; therefore we grouped the data and calculated the chi squares and significance in Tables 3A and 3B (p. 86). Table 3A combines the entries for high and moderate responsiveness, and Table 3B combines the entries for moderate and low responsiveness.

Of 35 infants who at six months were indicated to have had abundant stimulation by their mothers, 31 reacted to the unfamiliar person in the observational setting with high degrees of responsiveness. Two whose responsiveness was moderate had mothers who were overactive and dominating in their stimulation; and two whose responsiveness was low both had mothers who overwhelmed them with continuous childish physical play (Table 3B). Of the 42 infants who were stimulated little or not at all by their mothers, 32 showed little or no social responsiveness (Table 3A). Four infants in this group of 42 were highly responsive: all four received high stimulation from the father, siblings, or other adults. Of the remaining six whose responsiveness was moderate, five received considerable attention from siblings or adults.

---

[1] All findings here and below refer to 122 infants, a number that excludes nine cases dropped from the sample population because of abnormalities that became evident during the year.

TABLE 3

MATERNAL STIMULATION AND INFANT RESPONSIVENESS AT SIX MONTHS

| | Responsiveness | | |
	High	Moderate	Low
High Stimulation	31	2	2
Low Stimulation	4	6	32

Maternal Stimulation:

High: Mother reports generally high attentiveness during day, with frequent vocal, tactile, and kinesthetic stimulation; and a great deal of play, rough or gentle, occurring independently of routine care.

Low: Mother reports attentiveness mainly for routine care; few or no attempts to play with or communicate with infant; infant left alone while awake for long periods, held rarely and only in limited situations, e.g., while mother watches television.

Infant Responsiveness:

High: Infant initiates smiling or smiles easily and often, and shows visual and vocal interest in both mother and observer.

Moderate: No initiation or ease of smiling; mild or sporadic vocal communication, but both can be elicited by mother or observer.

Low: No initiation or ease of smiling, and little or no reciprocal smiling at or vocalization to mother or observer.

It is clear that there is a significant relationship between high and low degrees of social stimulation by the mother and social responsiveness of the infant at six months.

These findings are only suggestive as to the complexity of perceptual developments in early infancy. Nevertheless it is reasonable to apply them to our propositions regarding the significance of visual perception for the socialization process. We know that under two months, and approximately before the social smile appears regularly, the infant may fixate upon the human face and also upon other familiar inanimate stimuli.

TABLE 3A

MATERNAL STIMULATION AND INFANT
RESPONSIVENESS AT SIX MONTHS

	Responsiveness	
	High and Moderate	Low
High Stimulation	33	2
Low Stimulation	10	32

Chi square = 38.8
Significant at .001 level.

TABLE 3B

MATERNAL STIMULATION AND INFANT
RESPONSIVENESS AT SIX MONTHS

	Responsiveness	
	High	Moderate and Low
High Stimulation	31	4
Low Stimulation	4	38

Chi square = 48.1
Significant at .001 level.

At about two months, the facial movements of the smile consists of present a novel aspect to the infant's perception, and may facilitate an imprinting response to the species; for in the ensuing three or four months the smile configuration that was first responded to in the mother or her surrogate grows more and more familiar, and the smile of nonmothers comes to be imbued with the attractive aspect of novelty. So human faces are responded to during the three-to-six-month period liberally, generally, and without differentiation. All friendly

overtures are welcomed by the infant, and he may work hard
to elicit attention from persons who are slow to pay him court.
The capacity for such reciprocal responsiveness might be said
to consolidate the first phase of the socialization process, as
we have outlined it.

At about six months, the infant discriminates the mother
from other persons. If now he prefers her and grows more
wary of others, it might be because now a new variety of
maternal attributes or features, those that are visually more
complex, are better perceived and attended to. The six-to-
nine-month period, approximately, is that in which the infant
is quick to grab at the mother's hair, to poke his fingers into
her mouth, to slap at her face, as noted above. He is excited,
we might say, by those aspects of her figure that heretofore he
has seemingly neglected. And this vivid response to the
mother as an individual, to the mother as a specific imprinting
object, would consolidate the second phase of the socialization
process. One is tempted to imagine a continuous, spiraling
process of socialization and learning, according to levels of
curiosity, activity, and gratification achieved in the course of
infancy.

The phases of socialization that we have hypothesized
overlap to some extent Mahler's (1963, 1965, 1966, 1967) suggested normal phases of the normal separation-individuation
process. According to her propositions, a normal symbiotic
phase attains a peak at five or six months of age. For the same
age period (when most infants are able to discriminate the
mother), we have stipulated that imprinting to the mother as
an individual rather than as a member of the species may take
place. During the next four or five months Mahler observed a
process of differentiation of infant from mother: bodily dependence is decreased, the visual field broadens, and increases
are visible in locomotor functions, in hand-mouth-eye coordination, in active pleasure in the use of the entire body, in
manipulation of objects, and in strivings toward external
stimuli. Mahler emphasizes that these advances emerge and
are expressed in close proximity to the mother, and that "the

infant's interest in his own body as well as in that of the mother seems definitely to take precedence over all activities."

A continuum appears to exist, extending from a formless perception of the most constant moving figure to a vividly clear perception of specific objects, animate and inanimate, by the end of the first year.

According to our view of the development of anxiety, a failure to maximize the infant's cathexis of the mother, and so of the external world attaching to her presence and behavior, by the latter part of the first year, would be expected to heighten the threat of object loss. Infants most threatened, and probably mostly those who live under institutional conditions, may indeed show clear signs of anxiety. But infants living under more normal conditions may show only a heightened anxiety potential or a heightened susceptibility to distress, observable in longer periods of freezing, whimpering, restlessness, and the like.

The foregoing formulations have taken for granted, as a theoretical example, an infant who achieves a preparedness for anxiety through optimal degrees of experience in pleasure and unpleasure. The balance that any infant can achieve in such experiences may be regarded as a significant determinant of the degree of arousal and the duration of physiological stress, and of the further arousals of perceptions. Consciousness of the experiences may set into motion the development of rudimentary ego functions,[2] may inaugurate or literally sub-

---

[2]"One thing there was which pleased him: when he lay listening to the beating of his heart—his corporeal organ—so plainly audible in the ordered silence of the rest period, throbbing loud and peremptorily, as it had done almost ever since he came, the sound no longer annoyed him. For now he need not feel that it so beat of its own accord, without sense or reason or any reference to his non-corporeal part. He could say, without stretching the truth, that such a connexion now existed, or was easily induced: he was aware that he felt an emotion to correspond with the action of his heart. He need only to think of Madame Chauchat—and he did think of her—and so, he felt

stantiate anxiety preparedness, and may prepare the transition from the first to the second phase of socialization. It would follow that subsequent to infancy, the degrees to which the anxiety preparedness is augmented or diminished will directly affect the actual ego functioning. One might think of the presence of this preparedness for anxiety metaphorically, as an organism's being poised for flight yet not necessarily taking flight.

Two kinds of sensory arousal, one dominant in each of the two phases of socialization, may occur. The first would be that which is automatic, close to a conditioned reflex, and which touches an innate releasing mechanism. It promotes the onset of the critical period for the first imprinting and strengthens the imprinting response to the species. It would be reinforced by successive experiences that are gradually perceived as occurring within the organism itself. The second arousal would occur at a point of stimulus satiation, a perception of inner tension and of motor capacities to discharge tension or to summon relief from tension. It would promote the critical period for the second phase of imprinting, and for the perceptual consciousness of the mother. It would also set in motion the beginnings of association learning: within the second phase of socialization. An essential quality of the cathexis for the mother would include awareness of the possibility of her absence, and a normal preparedness for comfort loss and the affect of anxiety. As a result, the infant might respond actively to felt danger by an impulse to take flight, and this impulse and its discharge would be consciously experienced. It would follow that subsequent to infancy, the degrees to which the preparedness for anxiety is augmented or diminished directly affects perceptual consciousness and ego functioning.

This hypothetical description implies that ego rudiments are formed in a course of alternating processes or rhythms,

---

within himself the emotion proper to the heart-beats."—Thomas Mann, *The Magic Mountain*.

oscillating at first between irritability and reflex response, later between physiological stress reactions and fragmentary sensory arousals, and, still later, between psychological reactions or dawning affect and perceptual consciousness; the full first cycle is attained in approximately the first six weeks of life, and prepares for anxiety—a preparedness which remains necessary for survival and reaches maturity in approximately the first six months of life.

One may conceptualize a comparability between the fear which in the infancy of animals arrests imprintability (the fear being the sign that imprinting to an object has occurred; it precludes intense attachment to new objects) and that level of anxiety in human infants in which purely physiological stress narrows to a psychological stress, i.e., to a recognition of objects who can be expected regularly to provide comforts and to relieve discomforts. As association learning sets in with the end of imprinting in animals, so it may be that perceptual consciousness in human infants sets in when physiological stress is superseded by consciousness of unpleasure and of an object who can relieve it. Needless to say, the object may be a part object and may not be recognized as a separate unit of being. The important fact in this context is that the imprinting is a rigid form of learning which proceeds according to laws quite unlike those of association learning.

Scott's afore-mentioned statement about the socialization of animals is exactly in accord with our proposition about the socialization of infants. Scott suggests that the socialization process may be divided into two parts, or two critical periods. The primary one occurs relatively early though not necessarily at birth, and determines the group of animals to which an individual will become attached, usually one of the same species. It tends to be self-limiting. A secondary socialization to other animals and groups may occur later, e.g., a sexual relationship, but it is still limited strictly by the kind of primary socialization that has preceded it:

Most species seem to have behavioral mechanisms which make it difficult to form attachments to dissimilar individuals once primary socialization has taken place. These mechanisms differ from species to species. In some, primary socialization must take place within a few hours, and with others, it may take place over a period a years. There is also evidence that much hereditary variability affecting primary socialization can occur within a single species [Scott, 1958, p.184].

One would expect that among human infants the increasing exercise of perception, responsiveness, and memory would build into the psychic organization strivings toward the further advancement of ego functions, beyond the function of providing signal anxiety. The initial emergence of anxiety as a response to danger would itself be a precipitate of combined cognitive and affective processes, developing hand in hand, and at no point being discrete or separable. Among these processes we should include the capacity for pursuit movements of head, mouth, eye, ear, and hand; of the limbs en masse and eventually of one hand; of the vocal apparatus; of the responsive smile. Possibly the opportunity to direct a broad range of pursuit movements toward a single object is involved in the basic trust that Erikson (1950) has discussed. And it may be that the attainment of each kind of pursuit movement, each body-ego maturity deriving therefrom, constitutes one of a long series of the psychic organizers to which Spitz (1959) has referred.

It would harmonize with this description of the relation between anxiety and ego formation to suggest that the prototypes of normal defense reactions (Greenacre, 1958; Hartmann, 1952; Spitz, 1961) enter into ego functioning in similar ways. Scott (1958) has described the ease with which fear responses in the dog are aroused by sudden noises or by any large moving object; once the fear reaction has been established as a habit, it is extremely long-lasting, but it can easily be overcome during the time when the puppy cannot escape and is dependent upon others for its food. As the animal grows older, it is more and more difficult for the trainer to overcome the escape reaction and to establish positive social relationships with the animal. These formulations also agree with those of Benjamin (1963), who has distinguished between an earlier-appearing stranger anxiety and a later-appearing separation anxiety.

The readiness for both stranger and separation anxiety may be formed in infantile phases of preparedness; i.e., the infant gradually becomes capable of psychological concomitants of stress, first relevant to the absence of the mother qua person, later to the absence of the mother qua mother. Normally, he retains this capacity to feel a signal that an anxiety-provoking experience is impending, and at best he will develop an increasing capacity to halt the full access of anxiety. The degree to which he attains the capacity in later infancy to receive a signal and to act accordingly will then be determined by a long complementary series of experiences on every psychic level. And the degree and form which the anxiety takes in any infant in the later part of the second phase of socialization, as we have described it, will vary in manifold ways, for example, according to whether the infant has felt sufficiently or insufficiently gratified by the mother prior to the access of full anxiety proper.

It will have become evident that we regard the ego rudiments and the affect of anxiety as prerequisite to and part of the process of socialization, and as taking form in developmental steps which may be stated, in highly abbreviated form, in the following propositions:

We submit that for *a first phase of socialization*, during the first three months of life:

1. Sensorimotor responses of a larval nature build recognitions of sensations.

2. Consciousness of body functions begins with an awareness of the sensations, the recognitions, the sensorimotor responses, that are taking place and that from time to time may be executed intentionally. The attempt to make intentional movement arouses an element of the capacity for anticipation and delay, and impels the infant toward further sensorimotor explorations.

3. Advance and control of sensorimotor skills are encouraged by positive stimuli which afford pleasurable affect, and by negative stimuli which bring unpleasure and optimally intensify attempts toward mastery. Both kinds of stimuli thus serve the pleasure principle and serve as well the broadening of awareness that sets a base for reality testing.

4. Imprinting to the mother as species-object is achieved.

For a second phase of socialization, which may begin as early as the third month, and lasts approximately until the seventh month, we submit that:

1. Rises in physiological tension provide the most visible interferences with the maintenance of pleasure, and also promote the most visible struggle (optimally, a productive struggle) with real stimuli.

2. The central attempt to maximize pleasure and minimize pain brings together an awareness of comfort loss (object loss), and efforts toward autonomous control of sensorimotor skills (partial ego functions, or ego rudiments). In this manner, advancement of ego functions proceeds in coordination with, and is inaugurated with, the formation of the affect of anxiety.

3. Imprinting to the mother as the specific object of instinctual cathexis is achieved.

Critical periods of development can without doubt be marked off in numerous ways, according to neurophysiological maturation, according to instinctual drive development and affect derivatives, or with respect to object relationships or other advances. We have chosen to consider the ways in which ego structure and socialization are linked by the development of the preparedness for anxiety. Anxiety in all its forms is bound up inevitably with psychic structure, and its development throws light on the primary phases of that structuring.

Part II
MATERNAL BEHAVIOR AND INFANT DEVELOPMENT

CHAPTER 8

The Infant Development Research Project

The foregoing theory was elaborated prior to the investigation of mother-infant interaction to be described. As indicated at the outset, we have focused upon the problem of the joint emergence of, and the reciprocal influences of, the affect of anxiety and the emergence of the ego during approximately the first seven months of life. The Infant Development Research Project, organized primarily for a further study of types of maternal behavior, naturally furnished data about the infants. The data collected about the mothers, and about their infants at the ages of six weeks, six months, and one year, made possible a testing of the hypotheses that have been formulated, and provided additional material encompassing other aspects of emotional and cognitive development through the first year of life.

THE PROBLEM

From Sparta to our own culture, methods of child rearing have been believed to have a profound influence upon the kind of adult the child becomes, and every society has had preferred modes of infant and child care. Nevertheless, replicable methods of studying the details of infant rearing, and hard evidence that there are indeed varying effects of preferred modes of early care, have been lacking (Axelrad, 1962).

We have addressed ourselves to two essential problems in this area: (1) whether and how the behavior of a mother with

97

her infant in our culture could be studied; specifically, whether types of mothering behavior could be isolated during the first year of the infant's life, through replicable methods; and (2) whether and how the type of mothering (in a nonlethal setting) could be shown to affect the development of the infant. Central to this investigation was the question whether the type of maternal behavior would remain constant throughout the first year of the infant's life, so that relatively constant and cumulative effects of her behavior and her related attitudes could be studied.

Related Studies

The state of scientific opinion and evidence concerning these phenomena are mixed. The most dramatic studies are of infants who have been institutionalized or separated from their mothers. The best-known study by Spitz (1945, 1946a) indicated that sufficient physical care but insufficient social and emotional contact between mother or caretaker and infant resulted in failure of the infant to thrive, in hospitalism, and in a high rate of infant mortality. A related study of infants institutionalized with their mothers (Spitz and Wolf, 1946) showed that the temporary disappearance of the mother during the second half of the first year of life of the infant brought about a sharp drop in the infant's Developmental Quotient and, in most infants, the appearance of anaclitic depression. Although the DQ climbed up again sharply upon the mother's return, it later dropped to a level lower than it had been before the mother's disappearance. The negative effects of institutional care on early personality formation was found to increase steadily after nine months of age (Flint, 1959). Adequate physical care but inadequate emotional and social stimulation of infants were found to result in their failure to develop adequately in the social and perceptual spheres, and in a blunting of the development of cognitive faculties (Provence and Lipton, 1962).

Bowlby's (1951) statements about the harm done by

mother-infant separation have been reassessed by Ainsworth (1962b) and others. Nonetheless, all accept the view that serious consequences, positive and negative, follow from the quality and quantity of mother-infant interaction. It is therefore interesting that Caldwell's review (1964) of the literature on effects of infant care shows that most studies have dealt not with the latter interaction but with general practices. A study of the effects of monomatric and polymatric handling of infants in the first year (Caldwell et al, 1963) indicated some differences among the children, and personality differences among the mothers who did or did not share their infant care, which antedated the birth of the child.

Rheingold (1961) investigated effects of environmental stimulation upon responsiveness to persons and objects among three-month-old infants in an institution, and others reared in own homes of high economic status, and found the former to be more attentive and more responsive. Her main and tentative explanation was that they received stimulation by more caretakers in more varied ways, and had learned more ways to hold the attention of an observer; this implied that the quantity and variety of institutional care might be regarded as providing an adequate alternative to home care by the mother, at least up to the age studied. Rheingold's findings are surprising only if one takes for granted that mothers' care of their infants at home is generally superior to that of the institutional caretakers, and if the quicker and more active responsiveness of the institutionalized infants is assumed to insure continued advances in social development, with no skewing of other aspects of development. A. Freud and Burlingham (1944) had earlier observed that up to the age of five months, infants in wartime residential nurseries achieved better general development than infants reared in the average household, but that during the remainder of the first year, the social, emotional, and cognitive development of the home infants was greater. Subsequently, motor gains were also earlier among the young children in the nursery, but speech development and habit training were superior among those at home. In sum, the child reared in the nursery had advantages in areas of development less related to his emotional life; for the child reared at home, the reverse appeared to be true.

Predictive statements about development were made by Escalona and Heider (1959) on the basis of observations of 31 children between the ages of four and six who had been originally observed at one point between four and 32 weeks of age. Only 68 percent of the predictions were correct, and only 53 percent of the specific predictions. No allowances were made for psychic events occurring in the period between infancy and the time for which the predictions were made. However, the predictions based upon environmental factors alone were better than those based upon continuity of behavior alone.

Thomas et al. (1964), in a longitudinal study of development in the first two years of life, used interviews with parents of 80 children as their primary data, on the assumption that the absence of parental objectivity, as commonly reported, is the result of too much distance in time between parental observation and reporting, and of too inexact methods of interviewing. To circumvent these faults, they interrogated parents for the first time when the infant was three months old, at three-month intervals for the rest of the first year, and at six-month intervals in the second year. The interview data were scored and analyzed according to nine criteria: activity, rhythmicity, adaptability, approach, threshold, intensity, mood, distractibility, and persistence. These authors conclude that, by and large, individual patterns of reactivity are observable in infancy and persist through later periods of life, and that environmental influences upon the child's behavior are of much less consequence than are primary patterns. They are led to endorse a popular rationalization of personality differences: "A striking variety of practices seems to have been assimilated equally well by children of different periods, cultures and classes" (p. 87). In stating that "Whatever the child care practice, the children [in the study] would, as a whole, be capable of adapting as long as the particular modes of handling the child were compatible with life" (p. 87), they also express a nihilistic attitude toward the usefulness of parent education, and they overestimate the psychological plasticity of the infant and child. The fact that the first interview with the parents occurred when the infant was about three months old may be assumed to have obscured a wealth of data from the earliest period in which patterns of mutual adaptation or maladaptation can have taken shape. As a general rule, interviewing should be relied upon only when direct observation is not possible. Although Thomas et al. discuss certain maladaptations resulting from "caricature" of a premorbid pattern, they do not touch upon the question of what makes for such caricature, and how early; nor upon what complex crosscurrents of caricature may occur in any child in any specific phase of infancy or childhood; nor upon which caricatures, if any, may be reversible. They conclude by stating that the child's primary behavior patterns influence parental behavior, rather than the other way around.

W. C. Bronson (1966) investigated the antecedents of emotional expressiveness and reactivity control in a group drawn from the Berkeley Guidance Study, in which the subjects were seen from 21 to 36 months of age through adolescence, and found a number of relationships between behavior problems in the first 21 months, socioeconomic status, and emotional characteristics of the father. Information regarding the mother-child pair during infancy was derived solely from interview material. In a study of the same group at age 30, Bronson (1967) found that the earlier styles of behavior persisted, although the meaning of the styles might have undergone change. Her findings strongly suggest that the origins of major factors of adult emotionality stem from the earliest years of childhood.

Ainsworth (1967) observed 26 mothers with 28 infants in Uganda over a period of nine months, using a combination of short-term longitudinal and cross-sectional approaches and observations of varying frequency. Part of her material is based upon direct observation, the bulk of it upon retrospective interviews conducted with the help of an interpreter. The infants ranged in age from two days to two years, and the most adequate data were about those in the age range of three to 13 months. The Uganda infants were found to be more developed in sensorimotor areas than infants of similar ages in Western culture, i.e., their sitting, crawling, walking, and toilet training were accomplished much earlier, and Ainsworth attributed this to the Uganda mother's greater training of, stimulation of, and interaction with the infant. The degree of the infant's emotional attachment to the mother appeared to be founded upon and to grow out of his own behavior toward her, strengthened (or weakened) by the kind of response she made to his behavior. A number were tested by a modified Gesell Schedule shortly after the field work was completed. The infantile DQs were much higher than those measured in early childhood. The drop is attributed to sharply reduced interaction with the mother after the birth of the next sibling, a loss of stimulation not compensated for by the environment. A main behavior pattern studied was the manner of infant feeding, mainly scheduled versus demand feeding. Ainsworth relates demand feeding to greater activity on the part of the infant, who crawls to the mother's breast at will, and scheduled feedings to greater passivity of the infant and reduced interaction between infant and mother.

Caudill and Weinstein (1969) studied 60 American and Japanese mothers taking care of their infants of three to four months, and found that even at this infant age a great deal of cultural learning had taken place. Those authors carefully adduced findings of other investigators to support their contention that the behavioral difference between the two samples of infants were learned rather than genetic or maturational.

The first systematic observations in the field of mother-infant interaction were carried out by Brody (1956) in a study designed to test whether maternal feeding behavior with infants represented the general maternal behavior with and attitudes toward those infants better than did any other single maternal activity. Among 32 mothers with infants at four, 12, 20, and 28 weeks of age, each pair observed at one of the given age levels, four types of maternal behavior were distinguished.

A classification of mother-infant interaction in feeding in the first three months (Ainsworth and Bell, 1970) describes maternal behavior encompassed in the above typology and in the one to be described below. Ratings used to assess other aspects of the interaction showed clear association between a mother's feeding methods, her perception of the infant, and her responsiveness to him. A subsequent analysis of maternal behavior (Ainsworth, 1969) according to four dimensions (sensitivity, cooperation, accessibility, acceptance) indicated that the basic dimension was sensitivity. This parallels the criterion of sensitivity used in our earlier study (Brody, 1956), and is closely connected to one of our present criteria, empathy, described below.

The research to be described here was planned to replicate the earlier investigation (Brody, 1956) with a larger sample, longitudinally rather than cross-sectionally, and in an urban setting. The procedures were not experimental. It was not considered possible to instruct mothers on modes of infant and child rearing and then to test for effects upon their subsequent behavior.

The Population

With the help of the Prenatal Clinic nurses and the obstetrical records, all pregnant women who were white, native-born, in good health, married and living with the fathers of their prospective infants, and expecting to deliver the infants in the hospital where the research was conducted, were identified and invited by the social worker of the Project to participate in a study of normal infant development. They were told that the aim of the Project was to learn about effects of environment upon early development; that their participation would require bringing the baby to the Project offices in the hospital three times during the baby's first year, allowing us to take films of his feeding, and to test him; we would also wish to ask the mother many questions about his development. About 70 percent of the mothers accepted the invitation. The mothers in the final sample ($N=122$) consist of a self-selected group of primiparae and multiparae, from all socioeconomic classes, and of the infants born to them at a large metropolitan hospital in New York City between the end of 1963 and the beginning of 1966. Distribution of the cases by social class, using the Hollingshead two-factor index of social position (1957), was approximately normal (Table 4).

TABLE 4

SOCIAL CLASS

Class	Number of Cases
I	16
II	26
III	33
IV	26
V	17

To be included in the sample the neonates had to be of normal, full-term, spontaneous birth, with Apgar scores not lower than 6 after one minute. By error, one infant with a score of 5 after one minute was included; this fact was not discovered until he was several months old. As he was then in good health and well developed, it seemed reasonable to keep him in the sample. The Apgar ratings were made routinely by the attending obstetrician and recorded by him or by the obstetrical nurse, along with the complete medical record of labor and delivery. It would have been desirable to have a member of the Project staff trained to make the Apgar ratings and present during each delivery of a prospective subject. Practical difficulties of staff availability and hospital regulations made it necessary, however, to rely upon the medical staff for a judgment of the infant's normality. As a result, scores were not recorded in some cases. In each of these, the infant's perinatal and postnatal condition was found to be normal by both the obstetrician and the pediatrician (the latter required by the hospital), and the infant was retained in the sample.

We wished our sample to be composed of infants assumed by usual clinical evaluations to be normal. Since we had no opportunity to estimate the presence or the significance of soft neurological signs of impairment in the neonate, we preferred to make use of a common run of mothers and infants, with the obvious exclusion of those who showed any detectable biological or psychological abnormality. Table 5 shows the Apgar scores for the 122 infants retained in the final sample.

TABLE 5

APGAR SCORES AT ONE MINUTE AND
FIVE MINUTES AFTER BIRTH[a]

Rating	After One Minute	After Five Minutes
5	1	—
6	2	—
7	5	—
8	18	2
9	32	3
10	51	109
	109	114

[a]No ratings were recorded for 13 infants at one minute, and for eight infants at five minutes.

During the main two-year period of recruitment of subjects, cases were dropped postnatally for a variety of reasons: medical complications in the postnatal period; severe eczema in the first weeks; the mother's decision to assign almost complete care of the infant to a nurse; clinical impressions of psychiatric disturbance in the mother; repeated failure of the mother to keep initial appointments.

To be retained in the final sample the infants had to be in normal physical condition during their first year. Seven infants were dropped during the year for the following reasons: cardiac defect; strabismus; congenital metatarsus varus; abnormally poor general development (by neurological examination).

To determine the total constitutional endowment of the infants would have been a separate task and, at this time, one involving insurmountable difficulties. The variables to be studied have not yet been explicated, nor the methods delineated. The absence of facts regarding constitution has not prevented the existence of opinions ranging from the judgment that it is the state of the infant that brings the mother to act as she does with him, to the judgment that we are all born alike and environment makes us what we are. We prefer a middle position: that at one extreme are infants so hypersensitive, and with so low a threshold for both inner and outer stimuli, that no kind of mothering can affect their behavior patterns in a basic way; and at the other extreme are infants born with such stability and so high a stimulus threshold that they are immune to almost all but lethal types of mothering. In the middle are the great mass who are significantly molded by the type of environmental experience they have, which during the first year of life is primarily at the hands of the mother or her surrogate.

PROCEDURES

Mothers were interviewed prenatally and during confinement, and were interviewed and observed at three subsequent times during their infants' first year of life. Infants were tested and observed in the postnatal period, and subsequently at the same three times when the mother was interviewed and observed. Finally, mothers and fathers were invited to confer with the Project director about the infants' development as soon after the first birthday as they wished.

1.   The Prenatal Interview

The plan was to carry out the first interview in the third trimester of pregnancy. Information was to be gathered regarding the mother's and her husband's social histories, and her child-rearing opinions and attitudes. For reasons governed by hospital procedures, a number of mothers could be interviewed only *post partum*. In those cases inquiry into the mother's knowledge, attitudes, and opinions about infant care was made before the end of the confinement period and as soon as possible after the infant's birth; the social history was sought on the same day, but a home visit was frequently required to complete it (see Appendix 3).

2.   Medical Record

All data describing the mother's medical condition during pregnancy, labor, and delivery, and the condition of the neonate, were copied from the hospital record (see Appendices 2 and 4).

3.   Confinement Visit

The mother was interviewed briefly during confinement, usually by the social worker who had originally recruited her participation, to inquire about her reactions to delivery, the hospital experience, and the infant, and about her attitudes toward going home (see Appendix 5).

4.   Neonatal Observation

The purpose of the first infant examination was to note any patent differences of sensorimotor reactivity and of physical and affective states, before, during, and after a feeding (by the mother whenever possible, or by a hospital nurse) among infants judged to be normal by accepted obstetric and pediatric standards. All mothers and infants left the hospital on the fifth day after delivery, and some left on the fourth day. As hospital routine and staff time usually allowed for only one examination of the infant by the Project psychologist or psychiatrist, the examination was carried out on the infant's fourth day, between 72 and 96 hours after birth, although it was understood that the neonatal condition might still be unstable (see Appendix 6).

5. Observations and Interviews During the First Year

At each of the infant ages of six, 26, and 52 weeks, the mother came to the Project offices with her baby, bringing with her whatever food she wished to feed him. When recruited, she had agreed that during these visits she would allow the baby to be filmed during an entire feeding by her, to be given a test of development, and would herself try to answer our questions about the baby and her experiences with him since the previous talk with her.

The visits of mother and infant were from two-and-a-half to four-and-a-half hours in duration, and usually were longer as the infant became older. The time of day was arranged to suit the mother's convenience. Funds were available to pay for her transportation to and from the Project offices and for baby-sitters at home, when necessary. On a very few occasions, mothers felt it necessary to bring older siblings along. The latter were then supervised by other staff members in separate rooms, sometimes with brief visits to the mother. A few times the maternal grandmother of the infant wished to be present but accepted exclusion. Fathers, too, occasionally accompanied the mothers and wished to be present for the entire visit. It was considered tactless to exclude them, and in fact with only one exception the fathers did strictly maintain the position of observers and in no way interfered with procedures.

Upon their arrival mother and infant were made comfortable. A variety of infant furniture was available. The mother was then informed by the staff member assigned to conduct the session[1] that we wished to film the baby's feeding, to observe his reactions to some test materials, and to talk with her about how he was getting along. We asked her to decide the order of these events according to whatever she felt would keep the baby most comfortable throughout the visit. Her

---

[1]Six staff members shared the assignments. The same person conducted the interview, tested the infant, and recorded all the events that occurred in the session.

decision usually was made in relation to when she expected the baby to be hungry or sleepy. Unless she wanted to feed the baby right away, as often happened with six-week-olds, the mother was encouraged to place the baby where she wished, or to hold him in her lap, and usually the interview then proceeded. The mother was reminded that she was free to interrupt at any time to do anything she might feel necessary for the baby, and that our procedures were secondary to her care of him.

Before the formal interview began, the interviewer recorded all spontaneous comments by the mother, and all information provided by her initial responses to questions about the general health and progress of the baby that were asked as a natural part of greeting her. When the baby was settled and questioning of the mother began, she was offered coffee, and cookies or a sandwich.

We tried to influence the order of events during the visit only with regard to administering the infant test items. If the mother wished the testing to be carried out shortly after her arrival, or when the baby was sleepy or hungry or in an upset state, we explained that babies usually respond better to the test materials when they are in a good mood, and somewhat familiar with the unusual setting, and the mothers were always then willing to postpone the testing.

When the mother decided to feed the baby, we offered to help with any necessary food preparation, and inquired about the usual way he was fed, i.e., in her lap, or in a high chair, etc., so that we could arrange for her to feed him in a way he was accustomed to. Once the furniture was arranged in the filming area of the room, we switched on the special lights and explained that because we would be observing the baby very carefully and writing down many details of his behavior, we would not be free to speak with her while the baby was being fed. We asked her to tell us when the feeding was over, as we would then switch off the camera. The camera was turned on in the moments before she sat down and prepared to feed.

After the feeding the mother was again invited to make herself and the baby comfortable. Typically, with six-week-olds, feeding was followed by sleep, and testing occurred when the infant was rested and alert. With the infants of 26 weeks there was considerable variation in the order of events. Many infants were tested after feeding but before sleep; some slept first, then were fed, and then tested. At 52 weeks, many infants played about the room or at their mothers' knees for extended periods, and were then fed or tested, according to their appetites or fatigability. Only a few slept during the visit. At the age of one year it was most important to have the infants accustomed to the room and the interviewer before testing.

The interview was completed between feeding and testing or after both (see Appendices 7, 8, 9).

THE PHYSICAL SETTING

The observation room was 18 by 16 feet, air-conditioned and soundproof. False windows were covered with Venetian blinds and brightly colored draperies. The floor was of cork tile, for extra soundproofing. The ceiling was equipped with fluorescent lights to provide maximum light and minimum heat, and arranged to maintain an over-all light of 160 foot candles. A one-way mirror, two by three feet, was set into the front wall, approximately four feet from the floor. Behind the mirror, in the camera room, two Auricon Cine Voice II Sound-on-Film cameras (16 mm.) were set on a table and heads which allowed for a complete horizontal and vertical sweep of the room in a 180° arc. The cameras were automatically timed so that both reels of film could be run without interruption for a total of 100 minutes. They were adapted to 16 frames per second instead of 24, so that the magazines in both cameras might cover a very long feeding sequence without reloading, and in order to save expense and storage space. High-speed, fine-grain film was used because the one-way mirror cut out approximately 60 percent of the light. In addition, two spotlights were used for the filming area, to give the illusion of greater depth to the subject matter. The optical sound on the film was backed up by simultaneous sound on tape, as a precaution against defects in the sound recorded directly on film. The cameras were set in operation by a remote-control switch placed inconspicuously at the side of the interviewer's desk in the observation room; a switch in the camera room allowed for operating the cameras from there as well. Another remote-control signal was placed in the secretarial office, to inform camera personnel when the camera was turned on (to check on focusing, reloading, lighting, and camera operation).

The entrance to the observation room was at the lower end of the left wall. Equipment and furniture were arranged as follows:

At the left wall: a straight chair; a baby-tenda; a portable platform that fitted over the baby-tenda and was used for a testing table; a sink; a small cabinet with kitchen utensils, an electric bottle-warmer, etc., in it, and a two-burner hot plate above it; and a small table used for setting food during feeding or as a base for the infant seat;

at the rear wall: a refrigerator in which mothers could place food until it was time to feed, and in which raw film was stored; a folded playpen; a small chest of drawers with test materials; and a crib;

at the right wall: a rocker; a high chair; a chest of drawers containing crib linens, diapers, bibs, etc.; an infant seat; and the interviewer's desk and chair;

at the center of the room, in the filming area: an easy chair; a console constructed like a step table, the larger rear section containing a microphone. On the face of the console was a clock, placed in easy view of the camera but at an angle outside the range of the mother's vision during filming. About two feet behind the easy chair, a shade, eight feet wide, was attached to the ceiling and drawn to the floor as a backdrop during filming;

at the front of the room: below the one-way mirror, a wooden toidy-seat with a lid (required by a few mothers for one-year-olds); and a small child's table and chair. In the same front area of the room the playpen, if desired, could be placed.

Except for the desk, cabinet, chests, and refrigerator, all of the furniture was movable, so that it could be easily arranged in any way the mother chose to feed her baby. She was free to sit in the armchair or the rocker or the straight chair or the swivel desk chair; and to hold the baby in her lap, or to place him in the infant seat, in the crib, in the baby-tenda, or in the high chair. One mother placed her baby on the toidy-seat, and one used the toidy-seat perched on top of the baby-tenda.

Maternal behavior with infants does not easily fall into discrete patterns. Analysis of its parts, however, has made possible a discrimination of types of maternal behavior, as represented in a mother's manner of handling and feeding her infant. Prior to the study reported here, it was established on the basis of a small sample of 32 (eight infants at each of four ages) that the mother's physical handling of her infant was the best single index of her total relationship to him at the age of four weeks, and that her manner of feeding him was the best single index of her total relationship to him at the ages of 12, 20, and 28 weeks (Brody, 1956). Here we present our empirical findings about a series of relationships between a more adequate typology of maternal behavior, again derived from direct observations of the mother's handling and feeding behavior, but spanning the whole first year of life, and the development of the infants belonging to each of the maternal types.[2] The findings indicate that a significant contribution to an infant's capacity to experience signal anxiety, and in turn to achieve control of earliest ego functions, is the type of maternal behavior to which he has been exposed. Obviously, maternal behavior is to be understood as the behavior of the

[2]Relationships between the previous typology and this one will be presented elsewhere.

adult who has main charge of the totality of the infant's experience in his environment. We prefer not to use the term "caretaker," which is now frequent in the literature, because of the neutrality which it implies.

Our interest has lain in processes and effects of mother-infant interaction, and not in a general distribution of types. It was assumed that there would be enough similarity in a series of 122 mother-infant pairs, in a given geographical area and a specific period of time, to permit a study of types and effects of mothering during the first year of an infant's life. Extrapolation to the general population of the percentages of types that were found is not warranted.

CHAPTER 9

Data Analysis

Statistical analysis of the clinical ratings of the mothers' handling and feeding of their infants distinguished seven types of maternal behavior among 118 mother-infant pairs. Each type remained stable throughout the infants' first year. An eighth group consisted of four unclassified cases.

A. The Clinical Data

Each film of an entire feeding of each infant was studied by repeated slow-motion projection, and rated on a five-point scale for three *qualities*, Empathy, Control, and Efficiency, and for the Consistency with which each of the three qualities was maintained. The ratings were: 1 = High, 2 = High Moderate, 3 = Moderate, 4 = Moderate-Low, 5 = Low. They were applied to liquid and semisolid or solid foods separately, for each film taken at six weeks, then for each film taken at 26 weeks, and finally for each film taken at 52 weeks.

The film ratings were done by one of us (S.B.), and were subsequently used in the statistical classification of the mothers. The reliability of the ratings has not been established for reasons of time and expense, and chiefly because we were unable to add to the research staff film raters with the necessary knowledge of both maternal behavior and infant development. We found that the process of training for evaluation of the 366 films, which ranged in duration from approximately 10 to 150 minutes, would have constituted a separate reliability study far greater in length than the study here described.

114

The fact that the maternal types were statistically differentiable according to behavioral measures, as described below, at the infant age of six weeks does not compensate for the lack of reliability in the clinical ratings. The behavioral classification at six weeks is, however, such a striking confirmation of the typology derived from the clinical ratings that it may permit us, for the present, to waive the question of reliability. We should like to emphasize that the film rater did not classify the mother as a type. She assigned ratings, according to the criteria that follow. These data were then turned over to the statistician, who independently performed the combinatorial analysis which yielded types.

The three qualitative variables are defined as follows:

Empathy

The optimal rating is *high*. Empathy is here defined as a form of behavior observed in the mother's efforts to communicate with her infant visually, vocally, or physically in a manner that can be expected to advance the infant's satisfaction with the food and the feeding process; in the freedom she allows him to move all or parts of his body without disturbing his body security; in her steady watchfulness of his immediate needs, and her capacity to respond selectively, appropriately, and with sensitive awareness of how her responses in turn affect the infant's state from moment to moment.

It is not assumed that a mother's smiling, touching, kissing, or playing with the baby, especially if these behaviors occur mainly at nonfeeding times or just after the actual feeding ends, reflect empathy, as many mothers feel free to engage their babies socially only when the feeding, or a part of it, is over, i.e., when the baby is no longer in a state of need; otherwise they are emotionally remote from the infants. Similarly, a mother's failure to smile at or to caress her baby or to engage in social play with him during feeding has not been construed as in itself a lack of empathy; her quietness may reflect thoughtfulness or reserve, and need not exclude a strong emotional investment in the infant.

Empathic behavior is considered *moderate* when the mother is just adequately attentive to the infant's states and needs, and her efforts to communicate with him or to make the feeding a social experience are occasional and short-lived. It is considered *low* when the mother is largely inattentive, makes little or no effort to communicate, and appears to take no note of the infant's reactions during the feeding process; her glance or smile at the infant is automatic and brief, or comes and goes in an abrupt or mechanical way.

Control

The optimal rating is *moderate*. Controlling behavior is assumed to range from active domination of the infant and the feeding procedures to passive detachment from him. Optimally, the mother takes responsibility for the infant's physical comfort and security, and at the same time sustains his interest in the feeding with some supportive measures (touching him gently, offering him a spoon) that do not distract him unduly from the feeding itself and help him to complete the feeding in good time, with adequate interest in the food and, depending upon his age, in the feeding process as well. The degree to which she dominates the infant vocally and socially, as well as physically, or allows him to exercise initiative, or neglects to encourage his feeding efforts, becomes more obvious as a help or a hindrance as the infant grows older, but it is clearly discernible even at six weeks. At all ages of the infant, the mother's controlling behavior is most readily observable in her physical nearness, her physical support, in the timing of her acts, and in the economy of her own movements and her movements of the infant.

Control is considered *high* when the mother acts in response to her own wishes rather than to the observable needs of the infant; when she overwhelms him with excessive stimulations (handling, talking, cleaning) or with the food itself, or when she interrupts, hurries, forces, or urges food upon him in spite of his obvious loss of appetite or his emotional or physical stress, and makes his feeding dissatisfying. Control is considered *low* when the mother fails to notice or to respond to the infant's obvious need for physical comfort or relief, and allows food intake to become awkward or unsatisfying.

Efficiency

The optimal rating is *high*. Efficiency is judged by the adequacy of the mother's feeding procedures, as seen in the kinds of equipment and utensils she uses, in the amount of food taken in proportion to the duration of each feeding, and in the degree to which the tension of both mother and infant are gradually lowered as the feeding proceeds.

Efficiency is considered *high* when mother and infant succeed smoothly in the feeding task, the infant's hunger abates gradually, with rising pleasure in the feeding as a social experience, and when it ends in mutual satisfaction for both partners. It is considered *moderate* when the mother's procedures and the infant's intake are adequate but the feeding is carried out mechanically or perfunctorily, without pleasure or displeasure notable on either side, and without excessive delays or interruptions. It is considered *low* when the mother's procedures are awkward or inappropriate; when the infant's physical discomfort makes the feeding difficult or unpleasant; intake is poor; foods are alternated too slowly, too rapidly, or are forced; when the mother does not make an effort to feed enough; when she delays or interrupts excessively, or when her main efforts are devoted to entertaining the infant, with or without toys, in order to feed at all.

Consistency of Empathy, Control, and Efficiency is defined as the degree of stability that is maintained in each of the behavioral variables during the course of an entire feeding.

Except in those cases where Consistency was patently high (where the mother was unfailing in sensitivity or supportiveness or competence, or, at the other extreme, where she was unremitting in her harshness, domination, or inefficiency), the judgment involved in this rating was necessarily more subjective and more difficult than that involved in the qualitative rating. It was not uncommon to see maternal behavior change, for better or worse, as the infant's appetite waxed or waned, or when he grew more or less restless or sleepy, playful or resistant. When infants were not accommodating, some mothers grew visibly anxious or restive, or withdrew; others made special efforts to engage their infants in positive social interchange, or set aside a disliked food. Some were quick to obey the infant's demands, and some were adamant in refusing to take account of them. And in some mothers these behaviors oscillated considerably during the course of a feeding. Thus, mothers who were empathic but insecure were not well able to be empathic consistently, whereas mothers who were generally unempathic sometimes had moments of emotional freedom, like bursts of sunshine, in which they became smiling and cordial to their babies. Or: Some mothers were consistently controlling when they fed liquids but lax when they fed semisolids. Or: Some were consistently competent in helping the infant to drink from a cup but interfered awkwardly when he tried to handle a spoon. Alterations of tempo, of physical and social communication, of offering or withdrawing toys or feeding utensils, and elements of elation or boredom affected Consistency of behavior.

The *quality* of Empathy, Control, and Efficiency refers to the degree of these behaviors that was characteristic during a feeding. The *Consistency* of the three variables refers to the evenness with which the characteristic behaviors were judged to prevail. In statistical terms, Consistency would be represented by a Standard Deviation.

Blind ratings were found to be misleading. The films were therefore rated with knowledge of such related facts as the mother's remarks about the baby's usual appetite for the meal he was being given; whether the mother delayed the feeding unduly; the specific food being given; the similarity of the observed feeding to the usual feeding situation at home; and the explanation for her method of burping and for other procedures (e.g., diaper changing in the midst of feeding) that were not self-explanatory. Films have obvious advantages over written records for analysis of data of direct observation,[1] but handicaps as well. Black-and-white film does not tell the contents of an opaque plastic bottle or a deep dish, does not allow cereal to be distinguished from meat; nor does it reveal why the mother silently sets aside one bottle and takes another, or hides while the baby takes his bottle, or ends the feeding abruptly while the baby is sucking actively. The importance of these details became evident many times. For more specific examples: A mother bottle feeds her six-week-old attentively and seems to be very patient, though her smile looks a bit forced, but the baby has bursts of restlessness, cries, and hardly sucks. The cause of distress is puzzling until the written record reveals that the mother had decided it was too much bother to bring milk with her, made no request for it (some mothers did), and felt sure that it was enough to give the baby warm water until she got home. Or: A mother holds a hungry six-month-old in a well-supported position and offers the bottle without delay, but the little girl frets, grimaces, and shortly gives way to repeated, angry, and severe bouts of crying. The record mentions that the mother has been adding cereal to the milk so that the baby will not get hungry before suppertime; the mother realizes that the nipple gets clogged, but offers the mixture nonetheless.

Mothers were asked routinely if the feeding in our office was typical of feedings at home. The accuracy of a mother's reply could not be taken for granted. In general, her statement that the observed feeding was typical or not appeared to signify her comfort or discomfort with it. Most often the question was answered in terms of quantity of food taken, and variations in intake usually were attributed to the baby's being more or less tired, the time of day, or the absence of siblings; they were much less often attributed to the unfamiliar setting.

---

[1]Not only for careful scrutiny and repeated analysis. It was a not uncommon experience for the observer to evaluate the mother's feeding behavior more positively in her presence, but more objectively when studying the film.

Remarks about the mother's own state being different from the usual one at home referred mainly to her being less preoccupied with other cares and more free to devote her full attention to the baby in the Project office.

In summary, each film of feeding by each mother was rated on a five-point scale for quality of Empathy, Control, and Efficiency, and for degree of Consistency in each of the qualities (six variables); for feeding liquids, and separately again for feeding semisolids or solids (12 variables); at each of the three infant age levels (a total of 36 variables). At any of the three levels, the number of variables was diminished by half if the mother chose to feed only liquids or only solids.

All of the clinical ratings made for 122 mothers at the infant ages of six weeks, 26 weeks, and 52 weeks, were subjected to Profile Analysis, as follows:

1. Each mother was compared to every other mother on the basis of the six clinical ratings, at all of the age/food combinations (six-week liquid feedings, six-week solid feedings, etc.). All pairs of mothers for whom at least one set of the six ratings at each age showed no less than four ratings with no more than one scale point of difference on a five-point scale (1 = High, 2 = High-Moderate, 3 = Moderate, 4 = Moderate-Low, 5 = Low) were denoted as similar.

2. The mothers were ranked in order of the number of other mothers similarly rated. Starting with the mother who had the greatest number of agreements, symmetrical matrices of agreement were constructed for all of the mothers agreeing with or similar to the first.

3. Mothers were deleted from the matrices one by one until those remaining constituted a homogeneous group with respect to the similarities defined in 1, above. Thus the dimensionality of any such matrix was reduced to the number of mothers who were all similar to one another. This procedure was continued until two of the matrices were reduced to a dimensionality of three. In this way seven homogeneous groups were formed, accounting for 68 of the 99 mothers who were subjects of the first phase of the research.

4. Analysis of Variance and Duncan's Multiple Range Tests in cases of a significant F ratio were performed for the seven groups on each of the six clinical variables at every age/food combination. This procedure having ascertained statistical discriminability among the groups on certain of the variables, assignments of the remaining 31 mothers to groups were made.

5. The assignment procedure involved the ranking of the groups at each age/food combination on the basis of the sum of the squared deviations of their means on the six variables from the comparable ratings for the mother to be assigned. A ranking was also done on the basis of the data for the entire year. The subject was then assigned to the group having the lowest sum of ranks. Thirty of the 31 unassigned mothers were assigned on the first run. One mother had tied rank sums for two groups. Group means and standard deviations were then recomputed and the tests of significance performed again. It was found that the chosen method of assignment had resulted in a *greater ability to* discriminate among seven of the groups. It was decided at this point to drop the eighth, and smallest, group, consisting of four mothers, because the large standard deviations and the failure of the group to differentiate statistically from any of the other seven, on any variable at any age/food combination, indicated that this in fact was not a group in the same sense as were the others, but rather a collection of idiosyncratic mothers.

6. Finally, the mother who had remained unassigned during the first run clearly fell into one of the two groups for which she had been tied, and was assigned on the second run. Test values were recomputed and all previously noted differences remained.

7. An additional 23 mothers, subjects of the second phase of the research, were then assigned to the seven groups on the basis of two sets of clinical variables. The first was the complete set of 36 variables[2] that had been used to make the

[2]Three parameters, each scored for Quality and Consistency (6); for liquids and for solids (12); at three ages (36).

initial assignments of maternal type. The second was a subset of the first, consisting of the 22 variables that had provided at least one statistically significant distinction among two maternal groups found in the original population of 99. The assignments resulting from the use of these two sets of variables were highly similar, with only one mother capable of being assigned to two different groups. She was therefore assigned to one of them on the basis of better clinical fitness.

Seven types of maternal behavior, embracing 118 of the 122 mothers, were discriminated. Tables 6–11 indicate, for the three ages, all direct intergroup discriminations, broken down for liquid and solid foods, although at any age it is considered sufficient to be able to discriminate within either of these categories in order to make the statement that a significant distinction can be made between any two groups at that age. The numerical entries in the cells of the tables refer to the clinical variables on which the two groups indicated by that cell differ significantly. The variables are:

1. Quality of Empathy
2. Quality of Control
3. Quality of Efficiency
4. Consistency of Empathy
5. Consistency of Control
6. Consistency of Efficiency

As shown in Tables 6 through 11, all groups, or types, as they are referred to henceforward, are statistically differentiable from one another, at each of the three ages of observation, on at least one of the six clinical variables describing liquid or solid feedings; which also means that the mothers within each type remain similar to one another at all age/food combinations. Furthermore, each of the seven types retains its identity as a type at all three ages. Table 12 summarizes the clinical ratings identifying each of the types. The characteristics of a particular type may change for the different age/food combinations, but the behavior of the mothers in each type will remain sufficiently similar, as not to change in type. Summary descriptions of the maternal behavior and attitudes of each of the types follow.

TABLE 6[a]

CLINICAL DISCRIMINATIONS OF TYPES OF
MATERNAL FEEDING BEHAVIOR

SIX WEEKS: FEEDING OF LIQUIDS

	I	II	III	IV	V	VI	VII
I		1,3,6	1,3,5	1,3	1,3	1	1,3,6
II			1,3	1,6	1	1	1
III				6	1,3,5	1,3,5	1
IV					1,3	1,3	1,6
V						1,3	1
VI							3

[a]Unless otherwise indicated, all tables presented are significant at the .05 level.

TABLE 7

CLINICAL DISCRIMINATIONS OF TYPES OF
MATERNAL FEEDING BEHAVIOR

SIX WEEKS: FEEDING OF SOLIDS

	I	II	III	IV	V	VI	VII
I		1,2,3,4,5,6	1,3	1,3		1,3,4,6	
II			1,2,4,5,6	2,5,6	1,2,3,4,5,6	1,2,5,6	1,2,3,4,5,6
III					1,3	4	
IV					1,3,5,6		1,3
V						1,3,4,6	
VI							4

TABLE 8

CLINICAL DISCRIMINATIONS OF TYPES OF MATERNAL FEEDING BEHAVIOR

SIX MONTHS: FEEDING OF LIQUIDS

	I	II	III	IV	V	VI	VII
I		1,3,4,5	1,3,5	1,3	1,3	1,3	3
II			4	2	1,5	1	1
III				2	1,3,5	1,2,3	1,3
IV					2,3	3	1
V							1
VI							1

TABLE 9

CLINICAL DISCRIMINATIONS OF TYPES OF MATERNAL FEEDING BEHAVIOR

SIX MONTHS: FEEDING OF SOLIDS

	I	II	III	IV	V	VI	VII
I		1,3,5	1,3,5	1,3	1,3	1	6
II			3	3	1	1,3	6
III					1,3	1,3	1,3,6
IV					1,3	1,3	1,3
V							1,6
VI							1,6

Table 10

Clinical Discriminations of Types of Maternal Feeding Behavior

One Year: Feeding of Liquids

	I	II	III	IV	V	VI	VII
I		1,2,3	1,3	1,3	1,3,4,5	2	
II			2	2	2	1,2,3,4,5	1,2,3
III					4	1,2,3	1,3
IV						1,3	1,3
V						1,2,3,4,5,6	1,3,4,6
VI							

Table 11

Clinical Discriminations of Types of Maternal Feeding Behavior

One Year: Feeding of Solids

	I	II	III	IV	V	VI	VII
I		1,3,4,5	1,3,5	1,2,3	1,3,5	1,2	3,5
II			1,3,4	1,2,3,4	1	1,3	1,2
III				2,5	1,3	1,3,5	1,3
IV					1,2,3	1,2,3	1,2,3,5
V						1,3	1
VI							1,2,5

TABLE 12[a]

SEVEN TYPES OF MATERNAL BEHAVIOR
IN THE FIRST YEAR OF LIFE

CLINICAL CHARACTERISTICS DURING INFANT FEEDING

TYPE	1 Quality of Empathy	2 Quality of Control	3 Quality of Efficiency	4 Consistency of Empathy	5 Consistency of Control	6 Consistency of Efficiency
I	high	moderate	high	high	moderate to high	high
II	low	variable	moderate but variable	moderate to high	moderate but variable	moderate but variable
III	low	variable	low	high	highly variable	moderate to high
IV	low	variable	moderate to low	high	variable	high
V	low to moderate	moderate to low	moderate but variable	high	moderate to high	moderate to high
VI	variable	moderate to high	moderate to high	moderate to high	moderate to high	moderate to high
VII	high but variable	moderate	highly variable	high but variable	moderate	moderate to high

[a]This table was constructed independently of the clinical descriptions which follow. It was based solely upon the numerical ratings assigned for the six clinical variables to each mother at each age/food combination. It is not directly comparable to Tables 6-11, as it comprehends the entire first year.

B. Behavioral Data

Six observers, excluding the clinical rater, made frequency counts for five measures of maternal feeding behavior, in interchanging teams of two at a time. With the use of a slow-motion Kodak Analyst Projector, it was possible to reach the necessary agreement on the frequencies with ease.

The behavioral measures were:

1. Each of the mother's acts of *feeding* liquids or solids, i.e., her offering of nipple, spoon, or cup: called *F*. At six weeks, and with few exceptions at six months, the number of introductions of these utensils into the baby's mouth was counted. At age one year, many infants fed themselves; for those infants, only the mother's presentations of the bottle, cup or spoon, or food into the baby's hands, or her setting them on the table before him, were counted. However, if she re-presented the food or utensils, helping him, urging him, or interfering with his self-feeding, the additional presentations were counted as well.

2. Each of the mother's *movements* of the infant's body during actual feeding, excluding intervals of rest: called *M*. A movement was defined as a postural change of the infant's body. It included changes of equilibrium and gross stimulations. Movements of a continuous nature, such as rocking, bouncing, or a series of position shifts, were counted by slow-motion analysis of the discrete elements.

3. The number and duration, in seconds, of *feeding episodes* during the entire feeding: called *FE*. A feeding episode was defined as a feeding of either liquid or solid foods for an uninterrupted period. For age six weeks, a pause in the feeding for any reason, lasting more than 15 seconds, was considered an interruption and marked the end of an episode; for ages six months and one year, a pause lasting more than 30 seconds was so considered. A shift from liquid to solid foods, or vice versa, always marked the end of an episode and the beginning of another, however brief the nonfeeding interim. When long periods of time intervened between feedings,

ranging, for example, from half-an-hour to two hours, the interim nonfeeding time was not counted, but the beginning of the latter feeding marked a new episode.

4. The total feeding time: called *TFT*. This referred to the total time from the beginning of the first feeding episode, including all of the interim nonfeeding periods, and all of the feeding episodes, until the complete ending of the feeding. It did not include feeding preparation or play after the end of the feeding.

5. The total feeding episode time for each age/food combination: called *TFET*. This referred to the actual time devoted to feeding, and excluded the time of the interim nonfeeding periods.

These five measures were used to generate the following ratios (see Tables 13 and 14):

6. Feedings/Feeding Episodes.
7. Movements/Feeding Episodes.
8. Movements/Feedings.
9. Total Feeding Time/Feedings.
10. Total Feeding Time/Movements.
11. Total Feeding Time/Feeding Episodes.
12. Total Feeding Episode Time/Feedings.
13. Total Feeding Episode Time/Movements.
14. Total Feeding Episode Time/Feeding Episodes.
15. Total Feeding Episode Time/Total Feeding Time.

The 15 measures were subjected to the same analytic techniques that were used for the differentiation of types according to the clinical variables. Some confirmation of the clinical data was obtained. As is not surprising in comparing such disparate realms, the confirmation is not a strict one-to-one relationship, but a large enough number of direct discriminations is possible on several of the behavioral variables to indicate that the clinically defined types tend to be characterized by certain behavioral patterns in the observed situation.

Tables 15 and 16 present the same information for the behavioral variables as is presented in Tables 6 and 7 for the clinical variables. Of 63 possible intergroup discriminations at all three ages, it was found that only 36 distinctions could be made directly, whereas 27 could not. It is of interest to note, however, that of those 27, six occurred at six weeks, six at 26 weeks, and 15 at 52 weeks. In other words, fewer distinctions could be made at the latest age.

At the age of six weeks, distinctions among all types can be made, although not all of them can be made directly. That is, for every two types, if we cannot discriminate directly between them for either liquid or solid feeding, then there is at least one other type from which they are both statistically differentiable on the basis of one or more different variables. For example, as shown in Table 14, it can be seen that for solids, types I and II are directly differentiable on 14 of the 15 behavioral variables, whereas types I and III are distinguishable because of their differentiation from type II with respect to variables 2 and 7 (differentiable between types I and II but not between types II and III).

TABLE 13

BEHAVIORAL VARIABLES OF SEVEN MATERNAL TYPES

SIX WEEKS: LIQUIDS

	Type I	Type II	Type III	Type IV	Type V	Type VI	Type VII
F	13.44[a]	20.89	19.47	18.50	9.76	12.73	16.60
M	41.37[a]	40.31	51.09	35.30	37.76	38.93	39.60
FE	5.37[a]	7.52	6.42	6.30	4.23	4.33	4.20
TFT	1275.22[b]	1064.84	1313.76	1166.70	1104.42	1137.46	946.20
TFET	888.70[b]	736.84	844.28	827.70	868.14	887.20	803.60

[a]Mean frequency.
[b]Mean number of seconds.

TABLE 14

BEHAVIORAL VARIABLES OF SEVEN MATERNAL TYPES

SIX WEEKS: SOLIDS

	Type I	Type II	Type III	Type IV	Type V	Type VI	Type VII
F	3.22[a]	28.47	7.00	9.60	1.95	14.93	0.00[c]
M	.85[a]	5.63	2.42	3.20	.33	6.60	0.00
FE	.37[a]	2.68	.42	1.40	.14	.86	0.00
TFT	59.48[b]	307.26	80.61	153.70	23.61	222.20	0.00
TFET	46.29[b]	268.78	70.14	133.60	19.38	155.40	0.00

[a] Mean frequency.
[b] Mean number of seconds.
[c] No mother in Type VII fed solids at six weeks.

TABLE 15

BEHAVIORAL DISCRIMINATIONS OF TYPES OF MATERNAL FEEDING BEHAVIOR

SIX WEEKS: FEEDING OF LIQUIDS

	I	II	III	IV	V	VI	VII
I		1,3			9,12		
II					1,3,9,12	3	
III					1,3,9,12, 15	12,15	
IV					9,12		
V							
VI							
VII							

TABLE 16

BEHAVIORAL DISCRIMINATIONS OF TYPES OF MATERNAL FEEDING BEHAVIOR

SIX WEEKS: FEEDING OF SOLIDS

	I	II	III	IV	V	VI	VII
I		1,2,3,4,5, 6,7,9,10,11, 12,13,14,15				1,2,4,5,6, 7,8,9,11, 12,14	
II			1,3,4,5,6, 9,10,11,12, 13,14,15	1,3,4, 5,6,15	1,2,3,4, 5,6,7,9, 10,11,12, 13,14,15	1,3,5,8, 10,13,15	1,3,4,5,6, 10,11,12,13, 14,15
III						4,7,8,9,11, 12	
IV					3,5,9, 12,15	7	15
V						1,2,4,5,6, 7,8,9,11, 12,14,15	
VI							4,5,7,8,9, 11

At the infant age of six months, and even more at age one year, it is no longer possible to distinguish all types clearly on the basis of the behavioral indices that were used. This is not in the least surprising when one recognizes that the variables that were considered are a direct reflection of maternal activity in feeding, and that by the infant age of one year this activity was found to be drastically reduced. In the great majority of the cases observed it became clear that few one-year-old infants are held in their mothers' laps during solid feedings; most take liquids, from either bottle or cup, by them-selves or with only partial maternal assistance; many feed themselves solids, either with fingers or spoons; and almost all exert considerable influence upon the methods and the dura-tion of their feedings. Because of the clinical differences among the infants of the several types of mothers, to be pre-sented below, we believe that the maternal typology is as valid at 52 weeks as at six weeks, although the appropriate behavioral variables have yet to be discerned.

Chi-square tests reveal no significant relationships be-tween either sex or parity of the infants and maternal type. The sample is not large enough to permit the use of the full Hollingshead (1957) scale of five classes, but when the Holl-ingshead index was collapsed to three classes, Upper, Middle, and Lower, chi-square analysis revealed that the classes were randomly distributed among the seven types. The same ran-dom distribution was found when the types were combined as types I, VI, and R, as described in Chapter 13.

CHAPTER 10

The Maternal Types

The following descriptions of the seven types of maternal behavior consist of very brief statements about the mothers' attitudes toward the interviewer and their conduct during interviews, their attitudes toward their maternal role and toward child rearing, the quality of their responsiveness to their infants, and their attitudes and opinions about the development and behavior of their infants. Material concerning all of these aspects of maternal behavior among all of the types will be presented elsewhere, in detail.

TYPE I: 24 MOTHERS, 27 INFANTS[1]

Mothers of type I take pleasure in observing and reporting about their infants, and give information agreeably and with appropriate affect. Many are able smoothly and confidently to divide their attention between infant and interviewer. They place little explicit emphasis upon standards of behavior for themselves or for their infants, or upon their competence as mothers, and they are open to influence regarding child rearing.

They are genuinely interested in the infants' moods and activities, and their physical care is considerate and economi-

[1] Ten mothers participated in the Project with two consecutive infants. Three of these were classified in type I twice. Comparisons of maternal behavior with consecutive infants will be presented elsewhere.

cal. Most are consistently free to initiate social or motor activities with the infants, to communicate by glance, voice, or
touch, and to respond to the infants' wishes for activity and
sociability. They show the infants much affection, and encourage and praise them. Usually their enjoyment of mothering
extends well beyond providing routine care.

Mothers of type I are the only ones whose ratings in all
three parameters reach adequate levels. Only nine of the 24,
however, attain optimal levels in all three, i.e., only nine respond sensitively to the needs of the infant and stimulate tactfully as well (Empathy), allow the infant to experience
tolerable degrees of tension or delay (Control), and carry out
routines efficiently (Efficiency). Of the other 15 mothers,
seven are so gentle that often they fall short of giving adequate stimulation, and show signs of becoming either too restrictive or too lenient. Five act with excitement or dominate
and show signs of promoting high levels of activity; these, like
the first nine mothers in the group, are most actively curious
about matters of infant development. Three are reluctant or
unable to dose frustration, and appear to encourage impulsiveness in their infants. Thus only a minority of mothers in type
I are considered to show maternal behavior free of adverse
potentials. This implies that while infants of type I mothers
are, regardless of biological endowment, in general more likely
to enjoy positive experiences with their mothers than infants
of other maternal types, they still may miss maternal assistance
in the development of optimal object cathexis and impulse
control, and of high levels of intellectual and social development.

TYPE II: 19 MOTHERS, 19 INFANTS

Type II mothers observe their infants casually and give
limited information about them. They are serious and attentive caretakers yet show little or no curiosity about matters of
child rearing. All but one are agreeable and cooperative toward the interviewer, but in all cases their manner is bland,

unaffected, or inhibited. Often they profess an assurance about mothering which is not convincing. Their emotional investment in the maternal role is subdued.

Their handling of the infants is dispassionate, restrictive, and impersonal. Occasionally it is both sensitive and careful; it is rarely grossly incompetent. These mothers seldom initiate social activity with the infants, and playfulness is markedly absent in the relationship. The mothers seem to take for granted their infants' development and capacity to conform to the mothers' attitudes or standards. They express little or no pleasure about the infants' behavior, but often stress early promotion of skills. One mother was exceptional in almost all of these respects, i.e., her emotional responses to her infant were consistently elated, her handling exciting, playful, and stimulating. She expressed extraordinary pleasure in every aspect of her infant's behavior, and stressed social graces rather than intellect or skills.

TYPE III: 21 MOTHERS, 21 INFANTS

Type III mothers, with few exceptions, are unwilling observers and poor reporters. They barely show interest in their infants' development and have almost no curiosity about child-rearing methods. Their overt cooperation varies: many are grimly restricted, many are emotionally shallow and do not take the interview seriously, and a few show artificial elation. Gentle emotions seem to embarrass these mothers. Only one expresses any lack of confidence as a mother; most declare an overweening confidence.

Most of these mothers show a capacity to handle their infants adequately or adeptly, but mainly their actions are mechanical, rough, or abrupt. They are peremptory and impatient, often condescending and critical. Tenderness is manifested only briefly or sporadically. Attitudes that at first appear to be permissive shortly are seen to reflect the mothers' disposition to ignore or to neglect the infants' passing needs or states; and a contrasting sharpness, visible in scolding, teasing, threatening, and dominating behavior, is common. These mothers seldom encourage their infants to experience age-appropriate curiosities or activities. A few mothers show pride in isolated aspects of their infants' performance. Pleasure in contact with the infants is rare or very short-lived.

Type IV: 10 Mothers, 10 Infants

Type IV mothers are exceedingly poor and unwilling observers. Their reports are vague, evasive, self-centered, and suffused with denials. Cooperation with the interviewer is superficial and often marred by irritability and negativism. These mothers are either tense, dissatisfied, and angry, or they are flippant and make a show of being nonchalant in the maternal role. All assert disinterest in learning more about infant care, and all refer to their infants' behavior critically, sarcastically, or with open hostility. Eight of the 10 mothers in this group appear to be overconcerned with their appearance: five show a distinctly masculine manner, three are overdressed and put on feminine airs. Although a few mothers in other groups, mainly in type III, also exaggerate feminine or masculine qualities of behavior, conspicuous masculinity appears only in mothers of type IV. No mother in this group shows interest in increasing her maternal competence or confidence.

These mothers respond to their infants very mechanically and as little as possible. They carry out bare routines with remarkable absence of sensitivity to the infants' feelings. The interaction they do provide is almost always impatient, delayed, begrudging, or condescending. They commonly deny the infants' visible distress, and speak to the infants abusively, complain about them, ignore them, or punish them. While they all show exaggerated affection at times, some especially in the form of kissing, all seem devoid of genuine tenderness toward the infants. With one exception, all express maternal pleasure only in regard to the infants' being undemanding. Either their positive or negative involvement with the infant is exaggerated, or their behavior is neutral and joyless. No natural intimacies between mother and infant are to be seen.

TYPE V: 21 MOTHERS, 21 INFANTS

Type V mothers are, with two possible exceptions, poor or superficial observers, and are uneasy when questioned. Their reports contain many clichés and generalizations. Insight into the needs of their infants is meager, apparently as a result of inhibition or chronically subdued affect, and methods of infant care interest only a few. Some show apathy or defensiveness or petulance, most are emotionally detached, and rapport is difficult to achieve. These mothers lack spirit and confidence and, except for the two noted above, show neither strong positive nor strong negative involvement in the maternal role.

With the infants they are cautious and apprehensive. They are slow to respond, or may do so impersonally, or may be quite unmoved by obvious needs of the infants. They are usually passive and aloof, and offer little stimulation of any kind. Several explicitly say that they expected to be bored by their babies. They take pleasure in telling how the infants are easy to care for, but hardly comment upon the infants' behavior or personalities. With one exception noted above, the relationship is characterized mainly by routine care, and the mother-infant relationship is impoverished.

TYPE VI: 14 MOTHERS, 15 INFANTS[2]

Type VI mothers vary considerably in their capacities to observe and report and in their interest in methods of child rearing, but all see their maternal position as important. They

[2]One mother was classified in type VI twice. See footnote 1, this Chapter.

relate thoughtfully to the interviewer. Most express high confidence in their mothering abilities or aim to achieve it. They handle their infants carefully, properly, with a visible degree of composure, but they lack sensitivity to the infants' changing states. They are steadily in charge, with variable degrees of animation, communication, and pleasure. In almost all cases the mother appears to be the dominant partner in the interaction. In other ways, these mothers fall into three groups.

Five, who are the least adequate observers, show more concern with the proper conduct of the interview than with accommodation to the infants' needs. Unless they have specific duties to perform they leave the infants alone and communicate with them minimally or not at all. They show little overt pleasure in mothering, are imperturbable, rarely stimulate their infants, and in general lack spontaneity.

Five who observe and report well are also well organized and often didactic to the interviewer. Their efficiency is rote or rigid, or subtly restrictive. Communication with the infants is almost entirely of a corrective nature. They do not seem to enjoy mothering but they do express pride in the infants' accomplishments.

Four are talkative and so exuberant that their observing and reporting suffer. Their enthusiasm leads them to be excessively playful and dominating. They are sincere and voluble in expressing pride and pleasure in their infants.

TYPE VII: 5 MOTHERS, 5 INFANTS

Type VII mothers believe themselves to be, and are, inadequate observers and reporters. They are highly amenable, friendly, responsive to the interests of the interviewer, and most eager to learn about infant care. They are fearful of taking action and sometimes wait for the interviewer to direct their maternal activities.

All try to be competent in handling the infants, but are often awkward or timid. They are self-conscious and insecure both in recognizing and in responding to the infants' needs.

They blossom when the infants respond to them, they can be very attentive and affectionate, yet are not often free to initiate communication or play, or to make demands upon the infants. Despite their obvious difficulties, they show strong positive involvement with the infants and enjoy their mothering.

TYPE VIII: 4 MOTHERS, 4 INFANTS[3]

The ratings of four mothers in the quality and consistency of behavior in the three parameters place them in none of the seven groups that have been differentiated nor in a group by themselves. Each shows maternal behavior that is very unusual in its childishness, ineptitude, or stereotypy.

The clinical types are not mutually exclusive. As a group, they form a continuum. The salience of the three qualitative variables did differ among the types, yet none of the three could be singled out as being the primary determinant of any one type. Each type consisted of a pattern of behavioral strengths and weaknesses. For example, it can be said that Empathy is related to Control more directly than to Efficiency; type VII mothers, often empathic to the point of leniency, practically never were overcontrolling, but all their good will did not render them efficient. Control is related to both Empathy and Efficiency, as mothers who can moderate the intensity of their actions are usually able to make appropriate judgments of the infants' states: but mothers with rigid Control, as in type IV, who act mainly according to their private assumptions about infants, have little freedom to be either sensitive to the needs of their infants or efficient. Efficiency works in more than one direction: It appears to allow for an ease of (empathic) response and an avoidance of domination, as in type I, or for excessive domination, as in type VI; but it can also harden a mother toward excessive or uneven domination, as in types III and IV.

[3]The data describing the four infants of Type VIII mothers, whose maternal behavior remained unclassified, are excluded from calculations of significance, below.

In general, mothers of types I and VII were the most empathic, those in types I and II were the most moderate in their control, and those in types I and VI were the most efficient. Mothers of types II and V were the most obviously inhibited. Those in type V were often withdrawn as well, and their withdrawal was reflected in low Empathy, low Control, and low Efficiency. Mothers of types III and IV were the most directly aggressive toward their infants; their Empathy and Efficiency were low or erratic, while their Control was high or harsh.

It will have become evident that, in general, mothers of types I and VI showed the most adequate maternal behavior, and those of types II, III, IV, V, and VII showed maternal behavior that was inadequate in assorted ways. Clinically, it may be said that as judged by the six criteria of their activities during feeding, mothers of types I and VI showed more consistently appropriate maternal behavior, while those of all other types showed higher degrees of ambivalence.[4] The overlapping characteristics of adequacy and inadequacy among the latter types resemble overlapping features found in any nosological classification. Where a neurosis exists, we do not expect its elements to be unique to a single diagnostic category, but rather that similar and related elements may inhere in a variety of syndromes.

[4]Relationships between this ambivalence and beating fantasies have been discussed in other contexts (Brody, 1956, 1970).

Part III
EFFECTS OF DIFFERENCES IN MOTHERING

CHAPTER 11

Developmental Quotients

Construction of the typology of maternal behavior enabled us to proceed with the study of whether relationships might be found between typical modes of maternal behavior and the levels of developmental quotient in the infant, and between the maternal behavior and the quality of ego development of the infants in the first year of life.

THE GESELL DEVELOPMENTAL SCHEDULES

Gesell Developmental Schedules were administered to the infants at six weeks, six months, and one year, and Developmental Quotients (DQs) were calculated according to a Binet type of scale.[1] Application of the same analytic techniques described above (analysis of variance and Duncan's multiple range test) indicated that at six weeks no developmental differences among infants of the various maternal types were apparent from DQs. At six months, seven of 21 comparisons, and at one year five of the comparisons, proved to be significantly different. These are shown in Table 17. The mean DQs and their associated standard deviations are shown in Table 18.

[1] At six months and one year, several items from the Cattell Infant Intelligence Scale and from the Buhler-Hetzer Infant Tests were used in addition, but excluded from calculation of the DQs. Reference to the infants' performance on these items will be made elsewhere.

143

TABLE 17

INTERTYPE DQ DISCRIMINATIONS

Maternal Type	Six Weeks	Six Months	One Year
I		VII	III, IV, V
II		VII	III
III		VI, VII	VI
IV		VI	
V		VII	
VI		VII	
VII			

An examination of the figures reveals that the growth of significant differences with age is reflective not of an increasing divergence of means but rather of sharply curtailed variances. (Table 18). These results may be interpreted as an indication of equipotentiality for development within each group of infants (of each maternal type) at six weeks,[2] and a regression over time toward some group mean, as indicated by the decreasing standard deviations, apparently as a function of maternal type. Thus one begins to form a

[2]At age three days there were no significant differences among the infants later classified as belonging to any one of the seven maternal types. The insignificance of differences at both three days and six weeks may of course be explained by the instability of behavior at these ages and by insufficient measures of development.

picture of seven maternal types providing greater or lesser enhancement of their infants' potential for development. Chi-square analysis of the relationship between social class, using the collapsed form of the Hollingshead scale, as de-

TABLE 18

MEANS AND STANDARD DEVIATIONS OF DQS

Maternal Type	N	Six Weeks	Infants at Six Months	One Year
I	27	Mean — 114.29	Mean — 111.66	Mean — 115.11
		S.D. — 33.32	S.D. — 12.95	S.D. — 10.24
II	19	Mean — 110.42	Mean — 111.63	Mean — 109.73
		S.D. — 27.29	S.D. — 10.46	S.D. — 12.04
III	21	Mean — 102.80	Mean — 102.76	Mean — 95.66
		S.D. — 26.89	S.D. — 14.53	S.D. — 22.09
IV	10	Mean — 117.60	Mean — 99.10	Mean — 96.80
		S.D. — 30.34	S.D. — 18.77	S.D. — 8.77
V	21	Mean — 122.00	Mean — 107.00	Mean — 99.95
		S.D. — 33.60	S.D. — 16.08	S.D. — 24.85
VI	15	Mean — 121.93	Mean — 115.53	Mean — 110.46
		S.D. — 32.66	S.D. — 8.23	S.D. — 10.46
VII	5	Mean — 90.80	Mean — 84.00	Mean — 108.00
		S.D. — 24.07	S.D. — 39.39	S.D. — 6.51

scribed above, and the four sectors of the Gesell Schedules showed social class and sex[3] to be randomly distributed.

[3]The greatest difference between males and females was in the language sector, in which average scores for females were higher than those for boys, though not significantly so. Earlier language and social development in females has been found by other investigators. Among our infants, conspicuous inactivity in vocal behavior was significantly higher for males; crying during dressing was significantly lower for males; and high vocal activity was significantly higher for females. Taken all together, these data point to a hypothesis that there is heightened genital cathexis among males, possibly at the expense of lower oral cathexis; and heightened oral cathexis among females, possibly at the expense of genital cathexis.

CHAPTER 12

The Assessment of Infant Development

Evaluations of normal development have been made on the basis of tests of maturational achievements which fall into standard categories during infancy, such as motor skills, sensorimotor discriminations, specific social reactions, comprehension of gesture and language, perception of relationships between inanimate objects, and capacity to act with discrimination of object functions. Tests produce scores and developmental quotients, which are indices to the current level of general development (Escalona, 1950). But a quotient alone cannot in itself allow for inferences about the history of an infant's progress toward the level of development he has achieved so far, nor about his capacity for further progress. We wished to find out the psychic conditions which, constitutional factors aside, might underlie the quotient and the developmental pattern it reflected. Therefore we sought concrete information about the infant's usual activities, moods, and states, his responses to new experiences, to stimulations, and to frustrations, and his characteristic styles of performance, in order to test whether any of these might be related to the type of maternal behavior he experienced.

Gesell and Amatruda (1949) suggested that a variety of developmental disturbances of infancy could be attributed to emotional factors: inhibition, seclusiveness, excessive crying, tantrums, overactivity, failure of attention, head rolling and

147

head banging, poking instead of grasping, etc. Gesell's essential work in the establishment of developmental norms outstripped, however, his considerations of emotional disturbances of infancy and early childhood. The great impetus for their study came from the work of Spitz on hospitalism (1945, 1946a) and of Spitz and Wolf on anaclitic depression (1946). Later, Spitz (1951b) described eight "diseases" of infants: coma in the newborn, colic, neurodermatitis, fecal play, aggressive hyperthymia, hypermotility, anaclitic depression, and marasmus. These appeared to him to result from extreme rejection or deprivation by the mother, and from extreme maternal attitudes ranging from overpermissiveness to hostility. The small number and severity of the illnesses he classified as abnormal are no doubt explained by the fact that the great majority of his subjects were living in institutions. Nevertheless, four of the eight manifestations were found in our sample, as will be discussed below. Major advances in recognition of infantile trauma and of the effects of extreme deprivation are reflected in the monographs of Bowlby (1951), Ainsworth (1962b) and Yarrow (1962).

Flint (1959) set up a provisional Infant Security Scale, a diagnostic check list of items for the assessment of mental health during the first two years of life, divided into four six-month periods. Her criteria relate to categories of dependence, trust, and enjoyment of effort. Most of the items for the first six months refer to adaptation to physical needs or stresses, and to handling. Many are normative ("accepts changes of diaper," "clutches toys," "enjoys bath"). Limited as this scale may be, it is the only one that attempts to estimate a balance of mental health or illness during infancy. Anna Freud (1965) in her comprehensive analysis of normality and pathology in childhood, barely mentions disturbances of the first year. The Group for the Advancement of Psychiatry (1966) proposed 24 classifications of psychopathological disorders of childhood. Only one, by John Rose, lists disturbances specific to the first year, and those are mainly biological or physiological; an additional few relate to problems of orality, locomotion, socialization, irritability, and to deprivation syn-

dromes. Rose's list encompasses more problems of psychogenic origin than any other. Hoopes's (1967) Infant Rating
Scale considers only infants up to three months of age, and
was designed mainly for the diagnosis of organic damage or
abnormality.

It seemed to us that basic to all of the behavior and the
achievements of the infant was the level and quality of his
object relations, that is, his characteristic balance of investments of psychic energy in internal processes, in persons, and
in things. Object relations of the very young infant are difficult to study, for they are silent or are accompaniments of the
satisfaction of vital functions like eating, or of sensorimotor
responses to stimulations of various kinds. But by six months
and after, the infant is often in command of enough expressive
behavior, and is sufficiently engaged in activities other than
those involving vital needs, for a measure of his object relations to be discerned. Our aim has been to construe relationships between kinds of infantile experience mediated by the
mother and the level of ego development at three points in
time during the first year of life. We make two assumptions.
The first, which is organismic, is that there are critical periods,
and that there is an inborn preparedness for anxiety which
initially is physiologically observable. The second is that environmental events, meshing with the critical periods and the
anxiety preparedness, determine the level of ego development
during infancy for all but atypical infants.

To assess the quality of psychic development in infants
belonging to each of the maternal types, we examined all of
the written records gathered during the mothers' and infants'
visits to the research quarters, at the three infant ages, i.e.,
interviews reported in detail and observational reports of the
subjects' behavior. Film and test data were excluded from
these examinations, as were all behavioral data comprehended
by the developmental tests used in direct examination of the
infants.

One of the two clinical examiners (S.B.) of the written
data had carried out all 27 tests and interviews in nine cases,

and 18 percent of the other 339 tests and interviews. The other examiner (S.A.) had done no tests or interviews. The five additional staff members who had conducted interviews and administered tests had no knowledge of the Signs (see below), as they had terminated their connection with the Project before the clinical examinations were undertaken. *The identification and classification of the infants' behavior was completed approximately 18 months before the film analysis and the construction of the typology of maternal behavior.* All cases at six weeks were scored by the two examiners jointly for signs of adverse development or psychic disturbance, and the few differences between the examiners were adjusted. The same procedure was then carried out for all cases at 26 weeks, and again at 52 weeks. All statements indicating adverse behavior or development were scored for *Signs of Disturbance* (SDi) and eventually were grouped into 13 sets, according to various clinically related functions, behaviors, states, and conditions.

A sign of psychic disturbance in the first year of life has been defined as a present or incipient habitual reaction that indicates (a) physiological dysfunction, (b) poor ego function, (c) inappropriate instinctual discharge, or (d) prematurely defensive accommodation to internal or external stimuli.

A total of 118 SDi were organized in the 13 sets. Table 19 lists the sets and the number of SDi found applicable at each of the three ages.

The composition of the sets was in some cases arbitrary. For example, as shown in Table 21, (p. 158), *Refusal to swallow* (SDi 13) is placed in set 2 although it could as well have been listed in set 8. And certain overlaps in the referents were inevitable, for example, *Irritability or restlessness, frequent states of* (SDi 22) is listed in set 4, whereas *Chronic irritability upon waking* (SDi 44) is listed in set 6; the distinction between the two lies in the specificity of the behavior cited. Consistent care was taken to avoid duplication in scoring, and to avoid scoring loosely or generally.

Our concern was with existing behavioral and psychic

TABLE 19

SIGNS OF DISTURBANCE: NUMBER OF SIGNS IN EACH SET

Set	Six Weeks	Six Months	One Year
1: Physiological Functions	9	5	5
2: Vital Functions	7	7	8
3: Sensory Responsiveness	3	3	3
4: Affective Reactions	2	7	7
5: Object Relations	3	12	11
6: Characteristic States of Behavior	4	12	13
7: Character Traits	4	8	8
8: Negativistic States	3	8	7
9: Habits	1	10	20
10: Stereotypic Movements	0	5	5
11: Fears	0	9	10
12: Self-Destructive Behavior	0	0	5
13: Cognition	0	2	2
Totals	36	88	104

conditions, whether of brief or continuing nature. The possible causes of these conditions were not yet to be considered. Thus, at age six weeks, *Excessive Wakefulness* (SDi 15) might be related, in a specific case, to gross stimulations in a crowded household, or to bouts of gastric distress; in either instance, the salient fact in this context was that the infant was awake too much of the time. At six months, *Conspicuously inactive and unresponsive: motor behavior* (SDi 43) might be related in a specific case to recent illness, slow maturation, or familial neglect; in any of these instances, motor inactivity was among the infant's current experiences. At one year, *Conspicuously low function pleasure: fine motor* (SDi 38) might be related in a specific case to a contrasting high social responsiveness, to poverty of experience with toys, to general apathy, or to recent trauma; in any of these instances, the infant was currently not exercising fine motor functions with pleasure. We took into account the phenomena in themselves rather than their preconditions or antecedents.

The 13 sets of SDi omit a number of behaviors, events, and conditions that originally were considered to be clinically significant but were later dropped from statistical calculations for the following reasons:

1. Frequencies were so high among the infants of all maternal types that the behavior appeared to be normative; for example, *fear of loud noises* (at ages six months and one year); or *fear when swung high or tossed up in the air* (at age one year, during rough play).

2. Indefiniteness of maternal reports; for example, *intestinal gas or cramps* (15 cases at six weeks and five at six months), when guessed at but not corroborated by the physician; or *jealousy* (a few cases at age one), for lack of objective criteria or evidence.

3. Probable organic etiology; for example, *food allergies,* (seven cases at six months and four at one year, with two cases overlapping), reported to be manifest in a variety of symptoms: colds, loose stools, constipation, blisters, rashes, irritability, and wakefulness.

4. Indefiniteness of etiology; for example, *convulsions* (two cases), occurring in febrile states, at age 10 months, self-limiting and found to have no sequelae in subsequent medical examinations; *sphincter spasms* (one case) not definitely diagnosed as such.

5. Causes and effects ambiguous or mixed; for example, *accidents* (at age one year, several cases of burns and cuts); and *falls*, which, like accidents, sometimes seemed related to sibling aggression, or to awkward care by adults, or to maternal neglect, or to infant impulsiveness, or to a mixture of these causes. The frequency of falls was not low, however. One infant had two falls before six weeks; five had one fall, and 10 had several falls before six months; four had one fall, and 12 had several falls, before one year (of the 12, four are included in the count before six months).

All of the written records were examined a second time for statements indicating advanced behavior or development, and scored accordingly for *Signs of Favorable Development*

(SFD). A total of 48 SFD were then organized in nine sets. Table 20 lists the sets and the number of SFD found applicable at each of the three infant ages.

TABLE 20

SIGNS OF FAVORABLE DEVELOPMENT:
NUMBER OF SIGNS IN EACH SET

Set	Six Weeks	Six Months	One Year
1: Physiological and Vital Functions	4	8	6
2: Sensory Responsiveness	2	3	2
3: Affective Responsiveness	4	5	5
4: Object Relations	4	7	8
5: Characteristic States	5	6	6
6: Character Traits	2	6	6
7: Adaptation	0	4	7
8: Cognition	0	3	3
9: Miscellaneous	0	0	2
Totals	21	42	46

A sign of favorable development in the first year of life has been defined as a present habitual reaction that indicates (a) very smooth physiological functioning, (b) superior control of ego functions, (c) marked function pleasure, and (d) ease of adaptation to internal or external stressful stimuli.

Here again, as with the SDi, certain SFD could have been placed in different sets. For example, as shown in Table 27, *Ease of smiling* (SFD 13) is included in set 3, although it could have been placed in set 4. And certain overlaps occur; for example, *Sustained inspection of new objects, new environment* (SFD 10) is listed in set 2, and *Enjoyment, visual and manual exploration, new objects* (SFD 40) is listed in set 7. The former refers to a specific activity, the latter to modal behavior, and the two do not necessarily coincide. *Activity and responsiveness: social* (SFD 27) might appear to duplicate *High function pleasure: in activity with persons* (SFD 20), but the former refers to a characteristic or pervasive state of behavior toward human objects, the latter to intensity of a specific behavior in relation to human objects.

One item of behavior originally considered clinically significant of advanced development but dropped from statistical calculation was *Ability to feed self*, at six months by independent holding of the bottle, and at one year by independent manipulation of the cup. Scoring was not reliable, largely because of the technical variations among feeding devices. Bottles with built-in straws, which permit drinking without lifting the bottle at all, hardly require the bottle to be held by the six-month-old. The training cup, which is essentially a bottle-like cup with a small opening that can be taken directly into the mouth like an inverted funnel, sharply reduces the amount of skill necessary for its use by a one-year-old. In addition, feeding situations at age one were so varied, the utensils so different from infant to infant, and the role of the mother in some instances so compelling or so awkward, that we were forced to the conclusion that the item of self-feeding could be rated properly only on the basis of standard situations, e.g., with the use of an ordinary cup by every one-year-old.

As can be seen in Table 20, in most instances, the number of SFD increases with age, again in accordance with the normally enlarging repertoire of the infant's behavior during the first year of life.

In summary, both SDi and SFD were assessed solely from examination of the records of interviews and direct behavioral observations, and without recourse to the infants' developmental tests. This was not only to avoid duplication in scoring, as noted above, and to avoid the creation of halo or opposite "horn" effects, but to insure emphasis upon qualitative aspects of behavior rather than upon norms. The SDi and SFD have been used to estimate the balance of manifest physiological and psychological strengths and weaknesses that we presume to have influence upon ego formation during the first year of life. They constitute a heuristic device. We have made no attempt to construct an atlas of normal and abnormal emotional and cognitive development.

Both SDi and SFD were constructed before the clinical and behavioral ratings of the maternal behavior, before the statistical discrimination of the maternal types, and before the calculation of the infants' DQs. The clinical ratings of maternal behavior were done by one of the investigators who assessed the SDi and SFD, before any analysis of the distribution of the Signs.

After the case material was analyzed and the SDi and SFD tabulated, the significance of frequencies among infants of each of the seven maternal types were tested as follows:

1. Chi-square tests were performed for each SDi and each SFD at each of the three ages.

The frequencies of only one SDi, *Irritability or restlessness, frequent states of* (SDi 22), were found to be significantly associated with infants of type I mothers (low frequency) and of type II mothers (high frequency) at age six weeks.

The frequency of one SFD, *Adequate feeding patterns* (SFD 8), was significantly associated with infants of type I mothers (high frequency) at age six weeks.

The frequencies of four SFD, *Adequate feeding patterns* (SFD 8), *Comfort easily restored* (SFD 15), *Social expansiveness: spontaneous* (SFD 17), and *High and varied forms of intentional imitativeness* (SFD 23), were significantly different among infants of the seven maternal types at age one year.

That so few SDi and SFD achieved significance may be attributed to three factors: the large number of maternal types that were constructed, the relatively small number of infants in the total sample, and the relatively low frequencies of many of the Signs. These are discussed below.

2. Chi-square tests were performed on individual SDi and SFD to test for the validity of statistically discriminating the infants of type I and of type VI mothers from infants of the rest (R) of the mothers (Types II, III, IV, V, and VII) for more powerful results than could be yielded by consideration of infants of all seven maternal types with one another. This was done in the following manner:

For each Sign under consideration, frequencies among

the infants of maternal type I and R, of type VI and R, and of type I and type VI were tested. The expected frequencies for each test were calculated in two different ways: first, based on the entire sample, and second, based on the subset of each two groups being considered. We then ascertained which infants (of which maternal type) contributed to the statistical significance of individual SDi and SFD, of certain related SDi or related SFD, and of certain sets of SDi or SFD.

The infants of maternal types I and VI were chosen for these comparisons because type I mothers were the only ones who showed *adequate* (not optimal) behavior in all of the three parameters by which they were classified clinically, and because type VI mothers, although lacking in emotional freedom, were highly efficient, in some cases more than some mothers in type I. Efficiency implies an appropriate and steady quality of stimulation, one that is predictable according to the task at hand. For the infant with an efficient mother there are fewer unexpected or novel situations to cope with under pressure, fewer jarring sensations to arouse distress or to require excessive efforts toward assimilation.

3. The sets of SDi and SFD were reanalyzed, as in step 2: using chi square and measuring the frequencies of Signs included in each of the sets, for infants of type I mothers in comparison to those of all others (R) except type VI; for infants of type VI mothers in comparison to all others except those of type I; and, finally, for infants of type I mothers in comparison to those of type VI mothers.

Since many of the individual SDi and SFD, and thus major parts of sets, apply at specific ages, and since we are interested in the effects of varying kinds of mothering over time, the findings are presented according to the ages at which the infants were studied, i.e., six weeks, six months, and one year.

CHAPTER 13

The Signs of Disturbance and the Signs of Favorable Development

A. THE TABLES

To simplify the task of following the discussion of the quantitative material, and to permit the reader to refer easily to the data, we present the tables dealing with the Signs of Disturbance at each of the three infant ages (Tables 21–23); the sets found to be significant (Table 24); the Signs of Disturbance found to be significant when grouped according to infants of maternal type I, type VI, and R (Table 25); and sets of the latter found to be significant (Table 26). The same method of presentation then follows for the Signs of Favorable Development (Tables 27–32).

For certain SDi, *does not apply* (d.n.a.) is indicated either because the behavior was not visible at the cited age, for example, *Colic* (SDi 8) at six months or one year; or because the behavior was considered to fall within the normal range and not to be in itself pathogenic, for example, *Smiling, none or rare* (SDi 47) at age six weeks; or *Thumb-sucking* (SDi 72) or *Excessive mouthing* (SDi 73) at age six months; or *Poor accommodation to holding* (SDi 30) at age one year. SFD for which *does not apply* is indicated are regularly those whose appearance is either not to be expected at the cited age, for example, *Gross coordination* (SFD 3) at six weeks; or normally is no longer suggestive of advanced development at the cited age, for example, *Prompt sensory responsiveness* (SFD 9) at age one year.

157

TABLE 21

SIGNS OF DISTURBANCE: SIX WEEKS

Signs	Maternal Types						
	I (27)	II (19)	III (21)	IV (10)	V (21)	VI (15)	VII (5)
Set 1: Physiological Functions (1-9)							
1. Limb tremor (in noncrying states)	2	4	4	1	1	2	0
2. Chin tremor (in noncrying states)	2	4	5	3	4	2	1
3. Tension, general	3	5	2	1	4	3	2
4. Tension, head and limbs only	0	1	3	0	2	1	0
5. Flaccidity, general	0	2	1	0	0	2	1
6. Hypertonicity	3	4	2	4	3	2	1
7. Uneven development or activity, upper and lower limbs	0	0	0	0	0	0	1
8. Colic	2	1	3	1	3	0	1
9. Eczema	0	0	2	0	0	0	0
Set 2: Vital Functions (10-18)							
10. Irregular sucking	0	0	2	2	0	1	0
11. Chronic vomiting, gagging (or spitting, at six weeks)				d.n.a.			
12. Poor appetite; refusal liquids or solids	0	2	0	2	0	0	0
13. Refusal to swallow	0	1	0	1	2	0	0

Set 3: Sensory Responsiveness (19-21)

(continued from Set 2)

#	Item								
14.	Sleep fitful, restless (except in transient period, as in teething or illness)	3	5	1	0	1	1	2	2
15.	Excessive wakefulness during day	0	2	0	0	1	1	1	0
16.	Excessive sleep	3	4	4	d.n.a.	5	5	1	
17.	Difficulty falling asleep, day or night								
18.	Needs special comfort to fall asleep (pacifier, holding, rocking, bottle, blanket, etc.)	3	2	3	1	4	2	2	0

Set 3: Sensory Responsiveness (19-21)

#	Item								
19.	Marked sensitivity to sensory stimuli, as shown in restlessness, irritability; includes jerking, startling, or "jumping" in sleep	1	5	4	1	3	1	1	0
20.	Low frustration tolerance, wet or soiled diapers	2	2	1	0	1	0	0	
21.	Marked delay of response to most stimuli	0	3	6	0	1	1	2	1

Set 4: Affective Reactions (22-28)

#	Item								
22.	Irritability or restlessness, frequent states of	5	17	7	3	8	9	9	2
23.	Crying states of	6	14	14	5	12	9	9	2
24.	Angry screaming, states of				d.n.a.				
25.	Sudden, vehement, inexplicable crying, panic				d.n.a.				
26.	Proneness to being upset				d.n.a.				
27.	Temper				d.n.a.				
28.	Facial expression, sad, depressed, or unchangingly sober				d.n.a.				

Table 21 (continued)

Signs	I (27)	II (19)	III (21)	IV (10)	V (21)	VI (15)	VII (5)
Set 5: Object Relations (29-41)							
29. Marked sensitivity to being handled: general (strong fussing, crying)	2	1	5	2	3	3	1
30. Poor accommodation to holding: arching, stiffening, squirming	2	1	1	1	1	2	0
31. Poor accommodation to holding: limpness, flaccidity	0	0	1	0	0	1	0
32. Refusal to be fed by mother				d.n.a.			
33. Lack of approach toward mother				d.n.a.			
34. Withdrawal from mother				d.n.a.			
35. Conspicuous demand to be held (by mother or other)				d.n.a.			
36. Rejection of social overture or affectionate approach				d.n.a.			
37. Conspicuously low function pleasure—gross motor				d.n.a.			
38. Conspicuously low function pleasure—fine motor				d.n.a.			
39. Conspicuously low object cathexis—persons				d.n.a.			
40. Conspicuously low object cathexis—inanimate objects				d.n.a.			
41. Transitional object				d.n.a.			

Set 6: Characteristic States of Behavior (42-54)

42. Conspicuously inactive and unresponsive: *general* behavior	0	1	3	0	0	1	1
43. Conspicuously inactive and unresponsive: *motor* behavior				d.n.a.			
44. Chronic irritability on waking, day or night	1	1	0	0	1	0	0
45. Conspicuously inactive and unresponsive: *social* behavior				d.n.a.			
46. Conspicuously inactive and unresponsive: *vocal* behavior				d.n.a.			
47. Conspicuously inactive and unresponsive: *smiling* behavior (none or very rare)				d.n.a.			
48. Apathy, or marked listlessness				d.n.a.			
49. Discomfort difficult to relieve, observed	1	5	2	2	1	0	0
50. Crying during dressing or diaper changes	1	2	0	2	4	1	1
51. Hyperactivity, general				d.n.a.			
52. Restlessness				d.n.a.			
53. Motor inhibition				d.n.a.			
54. Extreme aggressive-destructive behavior				d.n.a.			
Set 7: Character Traits (55-62)							
55. Low frustration tolerance, general	0	2	1	0	1	0	0
56. Low frustration tolerance: hunger	0	3	1	0	5	1	1
57. Low frustration tolerance: being alone	0	1	0	0	1	0	0
58. Low frustration tolerance: object stimulation				d.n.a.			
59. Low frustration tolerance: object removal				d.n.a.			

Table 21 (continued)

Signs	Maternal Types						
	I (27)	II (19)	III (21)	IV (10)	V (21)	VI (15)	VII (5)
Set 7: Character Traits (55-62) (continued)							
60. Low frustration tolerance: object inaccessibility or loss	0	2	0	0	0	0	0
61. Conspicuously high demand for food (quantity or rapidity)				d.n.a.			
62. Conspicuous demandingness, general				d.n.a.			
Set 8: Negativistic States (63-70)							
63. Marked resistance to weaning, any				d.n.a.			
64. Intolerance of prone, supine, or sitting positions (severe protest)	0	0	0	0	0	0	1
65. Marked resistance to being changed, dressed	1	0	0	0	0	0	0
66. Marked physical resistance to routines (bath, bed, sitting for meals)				d.n.a.			
67. Marked resistance to being pulled to sitting or to placing weight on feet (becoming limp; flexing knees)							
68. Demand for night bottle	0	1	0	0	1	0	0
69. Resistance to demonstration (test)				d.n.a.			
70. Negativism, general				d.n.a.			

Set 9: Habits (71-90)

	1	1	1	0	3	2	1
71. Dependence on pacifier							
72. Thumb-sucking; finger- or fist-sucking, or finger-chewing (not merely associated with teething)				d.n.a.			1
73. Excessive mouthing of objects (not merely associated with teething)				d.n.a.			
74. Biting (persons)				d.n.a.			
75. Screaming (prolonged)				d.n.a.			
76. Throwing or tossing (not in play)				d.n.a.			
77. Food throwing, or bottle throwing				d.n.a.			
78. Grabbing				d.n.a.			
79. Chewing inappropriate object				d.n.a.			
80. Blanket holding, sucking, or rubbing				d.n.a.			
81. Breath-holding				d.n.a.			
82. Strange or unusual posture or means of ambulation (marine crawl; hopping on buttocks; rolling; on all fours, with knees locked)							
83. Tonguing				d.n.a.			
84. Hitting, pinching, scratching (others)				d.n.a.			
85. Spitting food				d.n.a.			
86. Smearing feces				d.n.a.			
87. Eating feces				d.n.a.			
88. Persistent digging of fingers into objects, e.g., mattress, doll's eyes (as a principal occupation)				d.n.a.			
89. Miscellaneous: limb-banging, object-licking, nose-wrinkling or picking, fingering or rubbing nose, ears, hair, blanket				d.n.a.			
90. Habits, other				d.n.a.			

Sets 10, 11, 12, and 13 do not apply.

TABLE 22

SIGNS OF DISTURBANCE: SIX MONTHS

Signs	Maternal Types						
	I (27)	II (19)	III (21)	IV (10)	V (21)	VI (15)	VII (5)
Set 1: Physiological Functions (1-9)							
1. Limb tremor (in noncrying states)				d.n.a.			
2. Chin tremor (in noncrying states)				d.n.a.			
3. Tension, general	2	6	4	1	2	2	1
4. Tension, head and limbs only				d.n.a.			
5. Flaccidity, general	2	2	2	0	1	2	1
6. Hypertonicity	0	0	0	0	0	0	0
7. Uneven development or activity, upper and lower limbs				1			
8. Colic	0	2	0	d.n.a.	0	0	0
9. Eczema	0	0	2	0	0	0	0
Set 2: Vital Functions (10-18)							
10. Irregular sucking				d.n.a.			
11. Chronic vomiting, gagging	2	3	2	2	1	1	2
12. Poor appetite; refusal liquids or solids	2	3	5	3	3	3	1
13. Refusal to swallow				d.n.a.			

Item							
14. Sleep fitful, restless (except in transient period, as in teething or illness)	3	4	4	1	4	2	2
15. Excessive wakefulness during day	1	3	2	1	1	0	1
16. Excessive sleep	0	0	0	0	0	0	0
17. Difficulty falling asleep, day or night	0	3	3	0	2	1	1
18. Needs special comfort to fall asleep (pacifier, holding, rocking, bottle, blanket, etc.)	0	3	3	2	3	2	0

Set 3: Sensory Responsiveness (19-21)

Item							
19. Marked sensitivity to sensory stimuli, as shown in restlessness, irritability; includes jerking, startling, or "jumping" in sleep	2	3	2	0	2	0	1
20. Low frustration tolerance, wet or soiled diapers	6	3	3	2	5	2	0
21. Marked delay of response to most stimuli	3	0	6	2	3	0	2

Set 4: Affective Reactions (22-28)

Item							
22. Irritability or restlessness, frequent states of	9	10	13	7	9	6	4
23. Crying states	5	7	12	6	8	6	4
24. Angry screaming, states of	0	2	1	0	3	3	0
25. Sudden, vehement, inexplicable crying, panic	1	1	0	0	1	0	0
26. Proneness to being upset	1	0	0	0	2	0	0
27. Temper	5	4	9	3	1	3	0
28. Facial expression, sad, depressed, or unchangingly sober	1	1	0	0	1	1	0

Table 22 (continued)

			Maternal Types				
Signs	I (27)	II (19)	III (21)	IV (10)	V (21)	VI (15)	VII (5)
Set 5: Object Relations (29-41)							
29. Marked sensitivity to being handled: general (strong fussing, crying)	2	2	0	0	0	3	1
30. Poor accommodation to holding: arching, stiffening, squirming	3	4	7	2	1	1	1
31. Poor accommodation to holding: limpness, flaccidity	2	0	1	1	1	0	0
32. Refusal to be fed by mother	0	1	0	0	1	0	0
33. Lack of approach toward mother	0	1	2	1	1	1	0
34. Withdrawal from mother	0	0	0	1	0	0	0
35. Conspicuous demand to be held (by mother or other)	0	0	0	0	0	0	0
36. Rejection of social overture or affectionate approach	0	0	0	0	0	0	0
37. Conspicuously low function pleasure—gross motor	2	1	1	0	3	1	1
38. Conspicuously low function pleasure—fine motor	1	2	2	0	4	3	0
39. Conspicuously low object cathexis—persons	3	1	6	5	2	1	0
40. Conspicuously low object cathexis—inanimate objects	3	4	8	6	11	0	3
41. Transitional object				d.n.a.			

Set 6: Characteristic States of Behavior (42-54)

42. Conspicuously inactive and unresponsive: *general* behavior	2	1	5	5	5	1	1
43. Conspicuously inactive and unresponsive: *motor* behavior	2	1	4	4	5	2	2
44. Chronic irritability on waking, day or night	0	2	2	0	1	0	2
45. Conspicuously inactive and unresponsive: *social* behavior	0	2	2	3	3	1	3
46. Conspicuously inactive and unresponsive: *vocal* behavior	0	4	6	4	7	2	2
47. Conspicuously inactive and unresponsive: *smiling* behavior (none or very rare)	1	1	5	4	4	1	2
48. Apathy, or marked listlessness	0	1	1	1	2	0	1
49. Discomfort difficult to relieve, observed	0	2	3	0	3	2	0
50. Crying during dressing or diaper changes	0	0	1	0	0	0	0
51. Hyperactivity, general	0	0	0	0	0	0	0
52. Restlessness	0	0	0	0	0	0	0
53. Motor inhibition				d.n.a.			
54. Extreme aggressive-destructive behavior	1	1	3	0	0	0	1

Set 7: Character Traits (55-62)

55. Low frustration tolerance, general	1	1	2	0	6	3	2
56. Low frustration tolerance: hunger	4	7	8	5	11	9	9
57. Low frustration tolerance: being alone	0	0	0	0	0	0	0
58. Low frustration tolerance: object stimulation	0	1	0	0	2	1	1
59. Low frustration tolerance: object removal	1	4	3	1	3	3	2

Table 22 (continued)

Signs	Maternal Types						
	I (27)	II (19)	III (21)	IV (10)	V (21)	VI (15)	VII (5)
Set 7: Character Traits (55-62) (continued)							
60. Low frustration tolerance: object inaccessibility or loss	3	2	5	1	4	2	2
61. Conspicuously high demand for food (quantity or rapidity)	0	0	0	0	0	0	0
62. Conspicuous demandingness, general	0	0	1	0	0	1	1
Set 8: Negativistic States (63-70)							
63. Resistance to weaning, any	0	0	1	0	0	0	0
64. Intolerance of prone, supine, or sitting positions (severe protest)	5	1	7	3	3	1	1
65. Marked resistance to being changed, dressed	0	0	0	0	0	0	0
66. Marked physical resistance to routines (bath, bed, sitting for meals)	0	1	0	0	0	0	1
67. Marked resistance to being pulled to sitting or to placing weight on feet (becoming limp; flexing knees)	2	2	3	0	6	1	0
68. Demand for night bottle	0	0	0	0	0	0	0
69. Resistance to demonstration (test)	1	0	1	0	0	0	0
70. Negativism, general	1	1	1	0	1	0	0

Set 9: Habits (71-90)

	4	3	2	2	3	2	2
71. Dependence on pacifier						2	2
72. Thumb-sucking, finger- or fist-sucking, or finger-chewing (not merely associated with teething)							
73. Excessive mouthing of objects (not merely associated with teething)				d.n.a.			
74. Biting (persons)	0	0	0	0	0	0	1
75. Screaming (prolonged)	0	2	3	1	1	1	1
76. Throwing or tossing (not in play)		1	0	d.n.a.			
77. Food throwing, or bottle throwing	2	2	1	d.n.a.			
78. Grabbing			2	d.n.a.			
79. Chewing inappropriate object	0	1	0	0	0	1	0
80. Blanket holding, sucking, or rubbing	2	2	1	0	2	1	0
81. Breath-holding	0	0	2	0	0	0	0
82. Strange or unusual posture or means of ambulation (marine crawl; hopping on buttocks; rolling; on all fours, with knees locked)				d.n.a.			
83. Tonguing	0	1	0	0	0	0	0
84. Hitting, pinching, scratching (others)	2	2	1	d.n.a.	1	3	0
85. Spitting food	2			2			
86. Smearing feces				d.n.a.			
87. Eating feces				d.n.a.			
88. Persistent digging of fingers into objects, e.g., mattress, doll's eyes (as a principal occupation)				d.n.a.			

Table 22 (continued)

Signs	Maternal Types						
	I (27)	II (19)	III (21)	IV (10)	V (21)	VI (15)	VII (5)
Set 9: Habits (71-90) (continued)							
89. Miscellaneous: limb-banging, object-licking, nose-wrinkling or picking, fingering or rubbing nose, ears, hair, blanket	2	2	2	1	0	2	0
90. Habits, other	0	1	0	0	0	0	0
Set 10: Stereotypic Movements (91-95)							
91. Head shaking, rolling	2	0	1	0	1	2	0
92. Body rocking, rolling	3	6	7	3	7	5	2
93. Head banging	0	0	0	0	1	0	0
94. Banging, tossing, thrusting of head or limbs, back, or abdomen; turning, slapping, drumming of hands	5	3	5	1	3	0	1
95. Teeth-grinding	1	0	1	0	1	1	0
Set 11: Fears (96-106)							
96. Separation anxiety; including need for direct physical contact with or proximity to M	1	1	5	0	1	0	1
97. Stranger anxiety	0	0	1	0	0	1	0
98. Stranger anxiety with *withdrawal reactions*				d.n.a.			
99. Stranger anxiety with crying reaction				d.n.a.			

100. Fear of familiar object with some change, i.e., glasses, hair curlers	0	0	0	0	0	0	0
101. Physician; men	0	0	0	0	0	0	0
102. Relative	0	0	0	0	0	0	0
103. Strange places	0	0	0	0	0	0	0
104. Animal	0	0	0	0	1	0	0
105. Miscellaneous: bath; toy animal; sudden movements; toilet; swings; new baby; etc. (any one)	4	1	4	1	4	3	2
106. Miscellaneous (additions to 105)	0	0	0	0	1	0	0
Set 12: (107-111) does not apply							
Set 13: Cognition (112-113)							
112. Poor concentration, short attention span	3	6	8	4	5	0	1
113. Poor or low interest, exploration of environment	2	2	3	2	3	0	2

TABLE 23

SIGNS OF DISTURBANCE: ONE YEAR

Signs	Maternal Types						
	I (27)	II (19)	III (21)	IV (10)	V (21)	VI (15)	VII (5)
Set 1: Physiological Functions (1-9)							
1. Limb tremor (in noncrying states)				d.n.a.			
2. Chin tremor (in noncrying states)				d.n.a.			
3. Tension, general	2	2	3	1	1	0	0
4. Tension, head and limbs only				d.n.a.			
5. Flaccidity, general	0	0	2	1	1	0	0
6. Hypertonicity	0	0	0	0	0	0	0
7. Uneven development or activity, upper and lower limbs	0	0	0	0	0	0	0
8. Colic				d.n.a.			
9. Eczema	0	0	2	1	0	0	0
Set 2: Vital Functions (10-18)							
10. Irregular sucking				d.n.a.			
11. Chronic vomiting, gagging	0	0	1	0	1	0	0
12. Poor appetite; refusal liquids or solids	2	6	9	4	2	3	1
13. Refusal to swallow	0	1	3	0	0	1	1

Item							
14. Sleep fitful, restless (except in transient period, as in teething or illness)	3	6	4	3	4	5	3
15. Excessive wakefulness during day	0	2	2	0	0	2	0
16. Excessive sleep	0	0	1	0	0	1	0
17. Difficulty falling asleep, day or night	0	0	2	2	0	2	2
18. Needs special comfort to fall asleep (pacifier, holding, rocking, bottle, blanket, etc.)	4	5	4	1	4	6	1

Set 3: Sensory Responsiveness (19-21)

Item							
19. Marked sensitivity to sensory stimuli, as shown in restlessness, irritability; includes jerking, startling, or "jumping" in sleep	0	0	0	0	0	0	0
20. Low frustration tolerance, wet or soiled diapers	2	3	7	2	3	2	0
21. Marked delay of response to most stimuli	0	1	3	0	1	1	0

Set 4: Affective Reactions (22-28)

Item							
22. Irritability or restlessness, frequent states of	5	8	11	4	8	7	1
23. Crying states	3	7	12	6	5	2	0
24. Angry screaming, states of	2	5	1	1	3	2	0
25. Sudden, vehement, inexplicable crying, panic	1	0	1	3	1	1	1
26. Proneness to being upset	2	2	4	1	2	3	0
27. Temper	5	6	11	5	4	7	3
28. Facial expression, sad, depressed, or unchangingly sober	1	1	7	3	0	1	0

Table 23 (continued)

Signs		I (27)	II (19)	III (21)	IV (10)	V (21)	VI (15)	VII (5)
					Maternal Types			

Signs	I (27)	II (19)	III (21)	IV (10)	V (21)	VI (15)	VII (5)
Set 5: Object Relations (29-41)							
29. Marked sensitivity to being handled: general (strong fussing, crying)				d.n.a.			
30. Poor accommodation to holding: arching, stiffening, squirming							
31. Poor accommodation to holding: limpness, flaccidity				d.n.a.			
32. Refusal to be fed by mother	1	0	4	3	1	1	0
33. Lack of approach toward mother	1	3	3	4	0	1	1
34. Withdrawal from mother	0	0	1	3	1	0	1
35. Conspicuous demand to be held (by mother or other)	1	2	4	1	3	3	0
36. Rejection of social overture or affectionate approach	0	1	4	0	0	0	0
37. Conspicuously low function pleasure—gross motor	2	3	6	2	7	2	0
38. Conspicuously low function pleasure—fine motor	0	7	8	4	6	4	0
39. Conspicuously low object cathexis—persons	1	3	6	2	5	1	0
40. Conspicuously low object cathexis—inanimate objects	3	4	8	5	7	2	1
41. Transitional object	0	1	0	0	0	1	0

Set 6: Characteristic States of Behavior (42-54)

42. Conspicuously inactive and unresponsive: *general* behavior	0	2	2	1	4	1	0
43. Conspicuously inactive and unresponsive: *motor* behavior	2	3	5	0	3	1	0
44. Chronic irritability on waking, day or night	2	0	2	1	2	1	0
45. Conspicuously inactive and unresponsive: *social* behavior	1	3	7	2	5	1	1
46. Conspicuously inactive and unresponsive: *vocal* behavior	2	2	3	3	4	3	2
47. Conspicuously inactive and unresponsive: *smiling* behavior (none or very rare)	0	4	7	1	5	2	0
48. Apathy, or marked listlessness	0	0	1	2	2	1	0
49. Discomfort difficult to relieve, observed	1	3	3	3	0	1	0
50. Crying during dressing or diaper changes	3	5	1	0	2	5	0
51. Hyperactivity, general	2	2	1	1	2	0	0
52. Restlessness	8	7	4	4	3	2	0
53. Motor inhibition	1	1	4	1	4	1	0
54. Extreme aggressive-destructive behavior	1	1	1	0	0	0	0

Set 7: Character Traits (55-62)

55. Low frustration tolerance, general	6	6	7	3	5	3	2
56. Low frustration tolerance: hunger	0	0	0	0	0	0	0
57. Low frustration tolerance: being alone	6	3	10	2	3	3	1
58. Low frustration tolerance: object stimulation	2	4	6	0	3	3	0
59. Low frustration tolerance: object removal	0	0	0	0	0	0	0

Table 23 (continued)

Signs	Maternal Types						
	I (27)	II (19)	III (21)	IV (10)	V (21)	VI (15)	VII (5)
Set 7: Character Traits (55-62) (continued)							
60. Low frustration tolerance: object inaccessibility or loss	5	5	7	3	8	4	2
61. Conspicuously high demand for food (quantity or rapidity)	1	1	2	1	1	0	0
62. Conspicuous demandingness, general	2	3	3	0	0	3	1
Set 8: Negativistic States (63-70)							
63. Resistance to weaning, any	0	0	1	0	1	0	0
64. Intolerance of prone, supine or sitting positions (severe protest)	1	3	3	3	1	0	0
65. Marked resistance to being changed, dressed				d.n.a.			
66. Marked physical resistance to routines (bath, bed, sitting for meals)	0	1	0	0	0	0	0
67. Marked resistance to being pulled to sitting or to placing weight on feet (becoming limp; flexing knees)	0	0	2	0	2	0	0
68. Demand for night bottle	1	1	2	3	0	1	0
69. Resistance to demonstration (test)	3	4	1	3	2	1	1
70. Negativism, general	6	8	11	7	5	4	2

Set 9: Habits (71-90)

	1	2	1	0	1	2	1
71. Dependence on pacifier	10	6	9	3	7	6	0
72. Thumb-sucking, finger- or fist-sucking, or finger-chewing (not merely associated with teething)	4	5	8	4	7	3	1
73. Excessive mouthing of objects (not merely associated with teething)	7	5	4	3	2	6	1
74. Biting (persons)	6	4	2	0	2	2	0
75. Screaming (prolonged)	5	5	9	5	5	4	2
76. Throwing or tossing (not in play)	3	3	3	1	4	2	0
77. Food throwing, or bottle throwing	1	1	1	0	1	1	0
78. Grabbing	2	1	0	1	3	0	0
79. Chewing inappropriate object	2	6	2	2	3	3	0
80. Blanket holding, sucking, or rubbing	0	1	1	1	0	3	0
81. Breath-holding						0	
82. Strange or unusual posture or means of ambulation (marine crawl; hopping on buttocks; rolling; on all fours, with knees locked)	1	2	4	0	0	1	0
83. Tonguing	1	4	1	0	0	1	0
84. Hitting, pinching, scratching (others)	9	6	5	2	1	0	0
85. Spitting food	0	0	0	0	1	0	0
86. Smearing feces	0	0	1	0	1	0	1
87. Eating feces	0	0	0	0	1	0	1
88. Persistent digging of fingers into objects, e.g., mattress, doll's eyes (as a principal occupation)	0	0	1	1	0	0	0

Table 23 (continued)

Signs	Maternal Types						
	I (27)	II (19)	III (21)	IV (10)	V (21)	VI (15)	VII (5)
Set 9: Habits (71-90) (continued)							
89. Miscellaneous: limb-banging, object-licking, nose-wrinkling or picking, fingering or rubbing nose, ears, hair, blanket	5	5	1	2	4	2	0
90. Habits, other	1	2	0	0	1	1	0
Set 10: Stereotypic Movements (91-95)							
91. Head shaking, rolling	0	1	1	1	0	0	0
92. Body rocking, rolling	4	4	10	5	6	0	2
93. Head banging	3	0	2	2	1	1	2
94. Banging, tossing, thrusting of head or limbs, back, or abdomen; turning, slapping, drumming of hands	4	4	5	0	3	0	0
95. Teeth-grinding	1	0	1	0	1	1	1
Set 11: Fears (96-106)							
96. Separation anxiety; including need for direct physical contact with or proximity to M				d.n.a.			
97. Stranger anxiety	0	3	1	0	2	1	1
98. Stranger anxiety with *withdrawal reactions*	5	2	3	1	1	2	0
99. Stranger anxiety with crying reaction	2	3	2	1	3	1	0

100. Fear of familiar object with some change, i.e., glasses, hair curlers	0	0	0	1	0	1	1
101. Physician; men	1	0	0	0	1	0	0
102. Relative	2	1	2	1	3	0	0
103. Strange places	1	1	0	0	1	1	1
104. Animal	0	0	3	1	1	1	0
105. Miscellaneous: bath; toy animal; sudden movements; toilet; swings; new baby, etc. (any one)	3	5	6	1	6	7	1
106. Miscellaneous (additions to 105)	0	0	0	0	1	0	0
Set 12: Self-Destructive Behavior (107-111)							
107. Scratching, biting, hitting	2	1	3	1	2	1	1
108. Slapping, pulling	3	4	4	1	3	1	0
109. Makes self gag	0	0	2	0	0	0	0
110. Bumps head	0	1	0	0	0	0	0
111. Pica; chewing inappropriate objects	1	0	2	0	0	0	0
Set 13: Cognition (112-113)							
112. Poor concentration, short attention span	3	5	6	5	5	1	1
113. Poor or low interest, exploration of environment	4	3	7	3	7	0	1

TABLE 24

SETS: SIGNS OF DISTURBANCE
SIGNIFICANTLY HIGHEST AND LOWEST FREQUENCIES AMONG INFANTS OF SEVEN MATERNAL TYPES AT THREE INFANT AGES

Set	Six Weeks[a]	Six Months[b]	One Year
1: Physiological Functions			
2: Vital Functions		I*	I*
3: Sensory Responsiveness			
4: Affective Reactions	I* II**		I* III** IV**
5: Object Relations		I* IV**	I* III** IV**
6: Characteristic States of Behavior		I* II* IV**	I*
7: Character Traits			
8: Negativistic States			IV**
9: Habits			
10: Stereotypic Movements			III**
11: Fears			
12: Self-Destructive Behavior			
13: Cognition			

---

[a] At this age, sets 10, 11, 12, and 13 do not apply.
[b] At this age, set 12 does not apply.

*Significantly low frequency for infants of this maternal type.
**Significantly high frequency for infants of this maternal type.

TABLE 25

SIGNS OF DISTURBANCE: INFANTS OF MATERNAL TYPES I, VI, AND REST AT THREE INFANT AGES

Age	Type I/Rest (27) (76)	Type VI/Rest (15) (76)	Type I/Type VI (27) (15)
Six Weeks	23: Crying states[a,b]		23[a,b]

Six Months	23: Crying states[a,b]
	40: Low object cathexis—
	    inanimate objects[b,c]
	42: Inactive, unresponsive—
	    general[a,b]
	112: Poor concentration[c]
		40[d]	

One Year	12: Poor appetite[a,b]
	23: Crying states[a,b,c,e]
	38: Low function pleasure—
	    fine motor[a,b]
	40: Low object cathexis—
	    inanimate objects[f]
	45: Inactive, unresponsive:
	    social[b]
	32, 33, 34: [b,f]
	    Refusal to be fed by mother
	    Lack of approach toward mother
	    Withdrawal from mother
	37, 38: [a,b]
	    Low function pleasure—
	      gross motor
	    Low function pleasure—
	      fine motor
	39, 40: [a,b]
	    Low object cathexis—
	      persons
	    Low object cathexis—
	      inanimate objects
	45, 46, 47: [a,b]
	    Inactive, unresponsive: social
	    Inactive, unresponsive: vocal
	    Inactive, unresponsive: smiling
		39, 40[c]
		
		45, 46, 47[f]
			37, 38[f]
			
			39, 40[a]
			
			45, 46, 47[a]

The following notes apply to Tables 25 and 26 and refer to frequencies found significantly associated with infants of maternal type I, type VI, and the Rest (R: all other infants, i.e., those of maternal types II, III, IV, V, VII).

[a] Significantly fewer among infants of type I mothers; calculations based on entire sample (118).

TABLE 26

SETS: SIGNS OF DISTURBANCE
INFANTS OF MATERNAL TYPES I, VI, AND REST AT
THREE INFANT AGES

Age	Type I/Rest (27) (76)	Type VI/Rest (15) (76)	Type I/Type VI (27) (15)
Six Weeks	Set 1: Physiological Functions[a,b]		Set 1[a]
	Sets 1 and 2:[e,f] Physiological Functions Vital Functions		Sets 1, 2[a,g]
	Set 3: Sensory Responsiveness[a,b]		
	Set 6: Characteristic States of Behavior[b,f]		
	Sets 7 and 8:[a,b] Character Traits Negativistic States		
Six Months	Set 4: Affective Reactions[a,b]		Set 4[a]
	Sets 7 and 8:[a,b] Character Traits Negativistic States		
	Set 13: Cognition[b,c]	Set 13[c,d]	Set 13[h]
One Year	Set 13: Cognition[b,c]	Set 13[a,b]	Set 13[h]

[a,b,c,d,e,f,g,h]See footnotes to Table 25.

[b]Significantly fewer among infants of type I mothers; calculations based on the subset composed of the two groups being here considered.

[c]Significantly more among infants of R mothers; calculations based on entire sample (118).

[d]Significantly fewer among infants of type VI mothers; calculations based on the subset composed of the two groups being here considered.

[e]Significantly more among infants of R mothers; calculations based on the subset of the two groups being here considered.

[f]Calculations based on entire subset.

[g]Significantly more among infants of type VI mothers; calculations based on the subset of the two groups being here considered.

[h]Significantly fewer among infants of type VI mothers; calculations based on entire sample (118).

TABLE 27

SIGNS OF FAVORABLE DEVELOPMENT: SIX WEEKS

Signs	Maternal Types						
	I (27)	II (19)	III (21)	IV (10)	V (21)	VI (15)	VII (5)
Set 1: Physiological and Vital Functions (1-8)							
1. Smooth movement, without undue tension or flaccidity	15	6	6	2	8	4	0
2. Good muscle tone, strength of movement	13	7	8	0	10	8	2
3. Gross coordination very well developed				d.n.a.			
4. Fine coordination very well developed				d.n.a.			
5. Variety of physical postures enjoyed				d.n.a.			
6. Vitality: motoric energy, initiative (not merely repetitive or restless activity)				d.n.a.			
7. Regular sleep patterns (falling and remaining in sound sleep; no need for pacifier, thumb-sucking, rocking, or other special aids)	21	6	9	6	7	6	1
8. Adequate feeding patterns (including appetite, intake, digestion; no conspicuous tension pre- or postprandial)	25	8	5	2	15	6	3
Set 2: Sensory Responsiveness (9-11)							
9. Prompt and intense sensory responsiveness, *including* visual	12	12	10	6	12	9	0

Table 27 (continued)

Signs	Maternal Types						
	I (27)	II (19)	III (21)	IV (10)	V (21)	VI (15)	VII (5)
10. Sustained inspection of new objects, new environment	3	2	2	0	3	1	0
11. Sustained equilibrium in face of strong stimulations, without consequent disruption				d.n.a.			
Set 3: Affective Responsiveness (12-16)							
12. Happy and mobile facial expression	3	1	2	0	3	1	0
13. Ease (readiness) of smiling	9	10	5	3	6	5	1
14. Ease (readiness) of vocalization	11	3	5	3	5	3	2
15. Comfort easily restored	14	2	4	0	3	3	1
16. Rich spontaneous communication, any modality				d.n.a.			
Set 4: Object Relations (17-24)							
17. Social expansiveness: spontaneous	3	1	2	1	0	0	0
18. Social expansiveness: reactive	13	6	4	1	8	9	1
19. High function pleasure: in activity with own body	1	1	6	0	1	2	0
20. High function pleasure: in activity with persons	1	0	1	0	0	1	0
21. High function pleasure: in activity with things				d.n.a.			

22. Capacity to be separated from M for short periods (where cathexis of M is clearly high)				d.n.a.			
23. High and varied forms of intentional imitativeness				d.n.a.			
24. Enjoyment of familiar games with M				d.n.a.			
Set 5: Characteristic States (25-30)							
25. Contentment and/or happiness not easily disrupted	14	4	6	1	5	1	0
26. Peaceful alertness (includes comfortable awareness of environment)	17	10	9	4	10	5	1
27. Activity and responsiveness: social	4	4	3	2	3	3	1
28. Activity and responsiveness: vocal	2	2	2	1	0	1	1
29. Activity and responsiveness: motor	3	7	6	0	4	5	1
30. Smooth variation of moods, mainly positive				d.n.a.			
Set 6: Character Traits (31-36)							
31. Varieties of expressive behavior	0	2	1	0	2	0	0
32. Striving to accomplish difficult tasks (any modality)	2	2	2	0	3	1	0
33. Resourcefulness: capacity to "organize" activity (includes task initiation and task completion, with satisfaction)				d.n.a.			
34. High curiosity: persons, special and non-anxious attentiveness to strangers				d.n.a.			
35. High curiosity: things				d.n.a.			
36. Curiosity: manipulative, genitalia or navel				d.n.a.			

Sets 7, 8, and 9 do not apply

Item							
22. Capacity to be separated from M for short periods (where cathexis of M is clearly high)	18	10	2	4	10	3	1
23. High and varied forms of intentional imitativeness	19	8	5	1	8	4	0
24. Enjoyment of familiar games with M	17	9	6	3	8	7	0

Set 5: Characteristic States (25-30)

25. Contentment and/or happiness not easily disrupted	14	6	4	1	7	4	2
26. Peaceful alertness (includes comfortable awareness of environment)	18	7	5	2	6	5	1
27. Activity and responsiveness: social	21	8	4	4	9	6	1
28. Activity and responsiveness: vocal	14	5	5	1	8	5	2
29. Activity and responsiveness: motor	16	11	9	3	9	5	3
30. Smooth variation of moods, mainly positive	15	3	1	0	4	2	0

Set 6: Character Traits (31-36)

31. Varieties of expressive behavior	17	4	4	1	6	1	1
32. Striving to accomplish difficult tasks (any modality)	17	8	6	1	5	8	3
33. Resourcefulness: capacity to "organize" activity (includes task initiation and task completion, with satisfaction)	12	4	0	0	6	4	0
34. High curiosity: persons, special and non-anxious attentiveness to strangers	18	6	5	1	8	6	1
35. High curiosity: things	20	10	9	4	9	7	3
36. Curiosity: manipulative, genitalia or navel	13	6	5	6	5	4	3

Set 7: Adaptation (37-43)

37. Sustained willingness to follow demonstrations (during testing)	15	7	3	3	8	6	3
38. Capacity to shift from activity to activity smoothly	17	4	1	0	6	3	0
39. Enjoyment, visual and motor exploration, new environment	20	14	5	3	10	7	3
40. Enjoyment, visual and manual exploration, new objects	16	8	6	2	9	5	2
41. Freedom for motor excursion, *with* awareness of and occasional return to mother	16	11	6	2	9	7	2
42. Intentionality of movements, gestures	20	9	4	2	10	8	1
43. Capacity to occupy self alone for short periods, without demands for help, company, physical contact, or rescue	21	14	9	5	15	11	3

Set 8: Cognitive Development (44-46)

44. Prolonged attention span or concentration upon objects	15	6	3	1	9	7	1
45. Persistent examination and varied manipulation of objects	15	4	2	1	6	6	1
46. Independent play with objects: spontaneous activity, *with* good perception of relationships or functions; not merely repetitive handling, or superficial or destructive handling	20	8	4	2	7	6	2

Set 9: Miscellaneous Positive (47-48)

47. Gaiety, humor, or any unusual social grace	6	1	2	0	4	2	0
48. Any special quality or skill (creative manipulation of objects; unusually steady and graceful movement; extraordinary physical agility; superior command of words; etc.)	6	0	0	0	2	1	0

TABLE 28

SIGNS OF FAVORABLE DEVELOPMENT: SIX MONTHS

Signs	Maternal Types						
	I (27)	II (19)	III (21)	IV (10)	V (21)	VI (15)	VII (5)
Set 1: Physiological and Vital Functions (1-8)							
1. Smooth movement, without undue tension or flaccidity	2	0	0	0	1	0	0
2. Good muscle tone, strength of movement	15	12	7	2	7	4	1
3. Gross coordination very well developed	17	8	8	2	9	8	3
4. Fine coordination very well developed	4	3	5	0	6	7	1
5. Variety of physical postures enjoyed	7	2	2	1	4	2	1
6. Vitality: motoric energy, initiative (not merely repetitive or restless activity)	12	3	4	1	7	3	0
7. Regular sleep patterns (falling and remaining in sound sleep: no need for pacifier, thumb-sucking, rocking, or other special aids)	22	8	10	4	9	6	2
8. Adequate feeding patterns (including appetite, intake, digestion: no conspicuous tension pre- or postprandial)	20	11	5	2	14	9	2
Set 2: Sensory Responsiveness (9-11)							
9. Prompt and intense sensory responsiveness, *including visual*	17	6	8	3	9	7	1

Table 28 (continued)

Signs			Maternal Types				
	I (27)	II (19)	III (21)	IV (10)	V (21)	VI (15)	VII (5)
10. Sustained inspection of new objects, new environment	16	6	3	0	6	7	1
11. Sustained equilibrium in face of strong stimulations, without consequent disruption	7	4	0	0	3	1	0
Set 3: Affective Responsiveness (12-16)							
12. Happy and mobile facial expression	11	1	1	0	2	1	0
13. Ease (readiness) of smiling	18	6	4	1	10	5	2
14. Ease (readiness) of vocalization	15	9	7	2	8	6	3
15. Comfort easily restored	15	7	3	1	8	8	0
16. Rich spontaneous communication, any modality	4	1	0	0	2	0	0
Set 4: Object Relations (17-24)							
17. Social expansiveness: spontaneous	11	4	3	1	5	4	1
18. Social expansiveness: reactive	18	11	9	4	12	9	2
19. High function pleasure: in activity with own body	16	8	8	2	8	6	1
20. High function pleasure: in activity with persons	13	3	3	0	5	2	2
21. High function pleasure: in activity with things	10	5	5	2	6	6	0

Item								
22.	Capacity to be separated from M for short periods (where cathexis of M is clearly high)	3	0	0	0	4	0	1
23.	High and varied forms of intentional imitativeness	1	1	0	0	2	0	0
24.	Enjoyment of familiar games with M				d.n.a.			

Set 5: Characteristic States (25-30)

Item								
25.	Contentment and/or happiness not easily disrupted	12	5	4	0	7	4	0
26.	Peaceful alertness (includes comfortable awareness of environment)	15	5	5	1	7	7	1
27.	Activity and responsiveness: social	16	6	3	0	6	3	1
28.	Activity and responsiveness: vocal	8	2	0	1	4	2	1
29.	Activity and responsiveness: motor	15	8	8	2	5	5	2
30.	Smooth variation of moods, mainly positive	10	0	0	0	2	2	0

Set 6: Character Traits (31-36)

Item								
31.	Varieties of expressive behavior	6	1	0	1	2	0	0
32.	Striving to accomplish difficult tasks (any modality)	14	3	4	3	5	6	1
33.	Resourcefulness: capacity to "organize" activity (includes task initiation and task completion, with satisfaction)	4	0	0	0	0	0	0
34.	High curiosity: persons, special and non-anxious attentiveness to strangers	13	7	3	1	10	6	1
35.	High curiosity: things	18	5	7	1	8	8	0
36.	Curiosity: manipulative, genitalia or navel	2	3	0	0	0	0	0

Set 7: Adaptation (37-43)

37. Sustained willingness to follow demonstrations (during testing)				d.n.a.			
38. Capacity to shift from activity to activity smoothly				d.n.a.			
39. Enjoyment, visual and motor exploration, new environment	6	4	2	1	3	3	1
40. Enjoyment, visual and manual exploration, new objects	10	3	3	1	5	6	0
41. Freedom for motor excursion, *with* awareness of and occasional return to mother				d.n.a.			
42. Intentionality of movements, gestures	8	2	2	1	5	2	0
43. Capacity to occupy self alone for short periods, without demands for help, company, physical contact, or rescue	21	6	7	5	11	6	2

Set 8: Cognitive Development (44-46)

44. Prolonged attention span or concentration upon objects	14	8	4	1	7	3	1
45. Persistent examination and varied manipulation of objects	9	0	1	0	4	2	1
46. Independent play with objects: spontaneous activity, *with* good perception of relationships or functions; not merely repetitive handling, or superficial or destructive handling	4	0	0	0	5	1	0

Set 9: does not apply

TABLE 29

SIGNS OF FAVORABLE DEVELOPMENT: ONE YEAR

Signs		Maternal Types						
		I (27)	II (19)	III (21)	IV (10)	V (21)	VI (15)	VII (5)
Set 1: Physiological and Vital Functions (1-8)								
1.	Smooth movement, without undue tension or flaccidity				d.n.a.			
2.	Good muscle tone, strength of movement				d.n.a.			
3.	Gross coordination very well developed	25	13	11	5	11	10	2
4.	Fine coordination very well developed	16	14	7	4	10	8	2
5.	Variety of physical postures enjoyed	17	7	2	2	7	3	1
6.	Vitality: motoric energy, initiative (not merely repetitive or restless activity)	21	6	5	2	8	6	2
7.	Regular sleep patterns (falling and remaining in sound sleep; no need for pacifier, thumb-sucking, rocking, or other special aids)	17	5	6	3	13	6	2
8.	Adequate feeding patterns (including appetite, intake, digestion; no conspicuous tension pre- or postprandial)	23	6	5	2	15	10	1
Set 2: Sensory Responsiveness (9-11)								
9.	Prompt and intense sensory responsiveness, *including* visual				d.n.a.			

Table 29 (continued)

	Maternal Types						
Signs	I (27)	II (19)	III (21)	IV (10)	V (21)	VI (15)	VII (5)
10. Sustained inspection of new objects, new environment	19	7	4	1	9	6	3
11. Sustained equilibrium in face of strong stimulations, without consequent disruption	15	3	3	2	5	4	1
Set 3: Affective Responsiveness (12-16)							
12. Happy and mobile facial expression	16	1	1	0	6	2	0
13. Ease (readiness) of smiling	20	10	7	5	10	4	2
14. Ease (readiness) of vocalization	19	12	11	6	13	9	3
15. Comfort easily restored	20	6	6	0	10	4	2
16. Rich spontaneous communication, any modality	16	5	3	0	6	5	1
Set 4: Object Relations (17-24)							
17. Social expansiveness: spontaneous	21	8	4	2	10	3	1
18. Social expansiveness: reactive	21	8	10	5	11	6	2
19. High function pleasure: in activity with own body	18	10	6	2	10	6	3
20. High function pleasure: in activity with persons	17	5	4	2	6	4	0
21. High function pleasure: in activity with things	17	7	4	2	10	6	2

TABLE 30

SETS: SIGNS OF FAVORABLE DEVELOPMENT
SIGNIFICANTLY HIGHEST AND LOWEST FREQUENCIES
AMONG INFANTS OF SEVEN MATERNAL TYPES AT
THREE INFANT AGES

Set	Six Weeks[a]	Six Months[b]	One Year
1: Physiological and Vital Functions	I*	I* IV**	I* III** IV**
2: Sensory Responsiveness		I*	I* III**
3: Affective Responsiveness		I* III**	I* III** IV**
4: Object Relations		I* IV**	I* III** IV**
5: Characteristic States		I*	I* III** IV**
6: Character Traits		I* III**	I* III**
7: Adaptation		I* III**	I* III** IV**
8: Cognition		I*	I* III**
9: Miscellaneous			

[a] At this age, sets 7, 8, and 9 do not apply.
[b] At this age, set 9 does not apply.
*Significantly high frequency for infants of this maternal type.
**Significantly low frequency for infants of this maternal type.

TABLE 31

SIGNS OF FAVORABLE DEVELOPMENT
INFANTS OF MATERNAL TYPES I, VI, AND REST AT
THREE INFANT AGES

Age	Type I/Rest (27) (76)	Type VI/Rest (15) (76)	Type I/Type VI (27) (15)
Six Weeks	1: Smooth movement[a,b] 7: Regular sleep patterns[a,b] 15: Comfort easily restored[a,b]		7[b]
		18: Social expansiveness: reactive[b]	
	25: Contentment not easily disrupted[a,b]		25[f]
Six Months	6: Vitality: motoric energy[a,b] 7: Regular sleep patterns[a,b]		7[a]

Table 31 (continued)

Age	Type I/Rest (27)	(76)	Type VI/Rest (15)	(76)	Type I/Type VI (27)	(15)
Six Months (cont'd)	10: Sustained inspection, new objects, environment[a,b]		10[e]		10[a]	
	13: Ease of smiling[a,b]				13[a]	
	15: Comfort easily restored[a,b]				15[a]	
	20: High function pleasure: persons[a,b]					
	25: Contentment not easily disrupted[a,b]					
	26: Peaceful alertness[a,b]				26[a]	
	27: Activity, responsiveness: social[a,b]					
	32: Striving, difficult tasks[a,b]					
	35: High curiosity: things[a,b]				35[a]	
	40: Enjoyment, new objects[b,c]					
	43: Capacity to occupy self alone[a,b]				43[a]	
	5, 6:[a,b,e,g]				5, 6[a]	
	Variety physical postures enjoyed					
	Vitality: motoric energy					
	19, 20, 21[a,b]				19, 20, 21[a]	
	High function pleasure: own body					
	High function pleasure: persons					
	High function pleasure: things					
	27, 28, 29:[a,b]				27, 28, 29[a]	
	Activity, responsiveness: social					
	Activity, responsiveness: vocal					
	Activity, responsiveness: motor					
	32, 33:[a,b]		32, 33[e]		32, 33[a]	
	Striving, difficult tasks					
	Resourcefulness					
	39, 40:[b,c]					
	Enjoyment, new environment					
	Enjoyment, new objects					

Table 31 (continued)

Age	Type I/Rest (27) (76)	Type VI/Rest (15) (76)	Type I/Type VI (27) (15)
Six Months (cont'd) One Year	44, 45:[a,b] Prolonged attention span Persistent examination, objects		44, 45[a,f]
	3: Gross coordination[a,b]		
	5: Varieties of postures enjoyed[a,b]		5[a]
	6: Vitality: motoric energy[a,b]		6[a]
	10: Sustained inspection, new objects, environment[a,b]		10[a]
	11: Sustained equilibrium[a,b]		
	12: Happy, mobile facial expression[a,b]		12[d]
			13: Ease of smiling[a]
	16: Rich spontaneous communication[a,b]		
	20: High function pleasure: persons[a,b]		
	21: High function pleasure: things[a,b]		
	22: Capacity to be separated from mother[a,b]		22[a,f]
	24: Enjoyment, familiar games with mother[a,b]		
	25: Contentment not easily disrupted[a,b]		
	26: Peaceful alertness[a,b]		26[a]
	27: Activity: social[a,b]		27[a]
	32: Striving, difficult tasks[a,b]		32[a]
	33: Resourcefulness[a,b]		•
	34: High curiosity: persons[a,b]		34[a]
	42: Intentionality of movements[a,b]		42[a]
	44: Prolonged attention span[a,b]		
	45: Persistent examination, objects[a,b]		
	46: Independent play[a,b]		46[a]
	12, 13, 14:[a,b] Happy, mobile facial expression Ease of smiling Ease of vocalization		12, 13, 14[a,f]

Age	Type I/Rest (27) (76)	Type VI/Rest (15) (76)	Type I/Type VI (27) (15)
One Year (cont'd)	19, 20, 21:[a,b] High function pleasure: body High function pleasure: persons High function pleasure: things		19, 20, 21[a,f]
	25, 26:[a,b] Contentment not easily disrupted Peaceful alertness		25, 26[a,f]
	27, 28, 29:[a,b] Activity: social Activity: vocal Activity: motor		27, 28, 29[a,f]
	32, 33:[a,b] Striving, difficult tasks Resourcefulness	32, 33[e]	32, 33[a]
	44, 45:[a,b] Prolonged attention span Persistent examination, objects	44, 45[e,h]	44, 45[a]
	47, 48:[a,b] Unusual social grace Special quality or skill		

The following notations apply to Tables 31 and 32, and refer to frequencies found significantly associated with infants of maternal type I, type VI, and the Rest (R: all other infants, i.e., those of maternal Types II, III, IV, V, VII).

[a] Significantly more among infants of type I mothers; calculations based on entire sample (118).

[b] Significantly more among infants of type I mothers; calculations based on the subset composed of the two groups being here considered.

[c] Calculations based on entire group.

[d] Calculations based on the subset composed of the two groups being here considered.

[e] Significantly fewer among infants of R mothers; calculations based on entire sample (118).

[f] Significantly fewer among infants of type VI mothers; calculations based on the subset composed of the two groups being here considered.

[g] Significantly fewer among infants of R mothers; calculations based on the subset of the two groups being here considered.

[h] Significantly more among infants of type VI mothers; calculations based on the subset of the two groups being here considered.

TABLE 32

SETS: SIGNS OF FAVORABLE DEVELOPMENT
INFANTS OF MATERNAL TYPES I, VI, AND REST AT
THREE INFANT AGES

Age	Type I/Rest (27) (76)		Type VI/Rest (15) (76)	Type I/Type VI (27) (15)
Six Weeks	Set 3: Affect, Responsiveness[a]			Set 3[a]

[a] See footnote to Table 31.

B. THE SIGNS OF DISTURBANCE

Tables 21, 22, and 23 present, for the infant ages of six weeks, six months, and one year, respectively, the frequencies of SDi found among the infants of each of the seven maternal types.

Signs of Disturbance: Six Weeks

At age six weeks, significantly lower frequency of *Irritability or restlessness* (SDi 22) was found to be associated with infants of type I mothers than with infants of all other maternal types, and the highest frequency occurred in infants of type II mothers.

States of irritability or restlessness are forms of relatively undifferentiated expressive behavior that are most commonly manifested by young infants. They may represent in a most gross manner the young infant's reaction to the quality and quantity of stimulation and deprivation he has been receiving. According to our examinations of the infants at age three days, irritability was randomly distributed. This implies that although a predisposition to irritability may be congenital, such states observed in the neonatal period were not significantly clustered among infants of any one of the maternal types. This behavioral item may therefore be linked to inadequate mothering at age six weeks. Benjamin (1963), as noted above, described a critical period at age three to four weeks in which neurophysiological maturation is rapidly increased and provides a greater susceptibility to internal and external excitations. He postulated that in cases where tension reduction by the mother or her surrogate is inadequate, a major increase in the manifestations of negative affect is to be found. Our findings corroborate this postulate.

The distribution of frequencies in set 4, Affective Reactions (Table 24), belies a common assumption that the young infant is primarily a complex physiological organism. Our finding rather suggests that a six-week-old infant has a discernible affective life, with recognizable emotional states; that these states are signally influenced by the kind of care he receives; and that the greater emotional stability of infants of type I mothers is a direct result of the more adequate and more consistent handling by those mothers. Spitz's statement that "affective discrimination is the earliest of all and breaks the trail for all the rest of development" (1946b) appears to be confirmed by our material, although our findings indicate that both affective and perceptual discrimination set in much earlier than Spitz claimed.

The importance of this finding is not simply that the infants of type I mothers have less disturbed affect, but that the energy otherwise consumed in disturbances of affect and in efforts toward tension reduction are free to flow in more profitable channels, such as perceptual cathexes. To be able to state that manifestations of affect are distinguishable among infants variably mothered, at age six weeks, seems to us to be a sufficiently important finding in itself. It probably should not be expected as well that the *effects* of these variations would be observable at this age, given the limited repertoire of the young infant.

In Table 25, the frequency of *Crying states* (SDi 23) in infants of type I mothers is compared to its frequency in infants of the entire sample (118); in all infants except those of type VI mothers (76); and in those of type VI mothers alone (15). The frequency in infants of type I mothers is shown to be significantly lower than in all other cases. This finding confirms our statements above regarding irritability and affect.

The frequencies of SDi included in the sets (Table 26) show that those of set 1, Physiological Functions, and of set 1 and set 2, Vital Functions, in combination, are significantly lower in infants of type I mothers when compared to all others and when compared only to those of type VI mothers. In addition, the frequencies of SDi included in set 3, Sensory Responsiveness, set 6, Characteristic States of Behavior, and set 7, Character Traits, and set 8, Negativistic States, in combination, are significantly lower in the infants of type I mothers compared to all others, although not compared to those of type VI mothers alone.

In sum, the findings indicate a significantly lower incidence of SDi at age six weeks among the infants of type I mothers in all of the relevant sets except set 5, Object Relations, in which the three relevant SDi refer to reactions to physical handling, and set 9, Habits, in which the single relevant item is *Dependence on pacifier* (SDi 71). Thus, in every germane classification of behavior it is found that adequately mothered infants are at a distinct developmental advantage. They show significantly fewer disturbances of physiological states, sensory responsiveness, states of behavior, and even of behavior which for heuristic purposes we have called character traits and negativistic states, even at age six weeks.

Signs of Disturbance: Six Months

At age six months, the frequencies of SDi in set 2, Vital Functions, set 5, Object Relations, and set 6, Characteristic States of Behavior, are significantly lower in infants of type I mothers than in any others (Table 24).

With regard to set 2 it may be said that the vital functions have lost their initial autonomy; or that although at the infant age of six weeks the cumulative effect of the variable forms of mothering upon vital functions of the infants (i.e., set 2 taken alone) was insufficient to be distinguished significantly in infants of any one type of mother, by the age of six months the effects of the variable mothering upon vital functions were statistically distinguishable across the types.

Of set 5 it may be said that the most adequately mothered infants have at six months achieved a higher degree of socialization and of function pleasure than infants belonging to other maternal types. Assuming an equal potential for these capacities in all of our infants, the indications are that differential types of mothering produce differences in these capacities. Or, to put it more precisely, less adequately mothered infants show greater sensitivity to handling, more disturbed relationships to their mothers, and lower function pleasure.

For set 6 the implication is that at six months, much more clearly than at six weeks (Table 25), the substructures that later on are used in defenses are influenced by the kind of mothering an infant receives. These untoward states of behavior have to do with inhibition, low interaction with other persons (a probable forerunner of faulty identification), and marked absorption in body states.

Sets 5 and 6 concern behavior that is clearly related to emotional states. This suggests that by the age of six months the infant's emotional relationship to the mother is significantly shaped, that certain characteristics of behavior or reactivity have become stabilized, and that a marked degree of socialization has been attained. These statements are in disagreement with those of Gewirtz (1961) regarding the capacity of the young infant to adapt to a variety of "caretakers." Our findings indicate that it is more reasonable to state that the more adequate the mothering of the infant, the less disturbed are his modes of affect and impulse discharge, and the more likely will he be to maintain positive emotional states.

When the frequencies of SDi and of sets of SDi in infants of type I mothers are compared with the frequencies in infants of all other types, we find, as shown in Table 25, that the incidence of *Crying states* (SDi 23) and of *Conspicuously inactive and unresponsive: general behavior* (SDi 42) is significantly lower for the infants of type I mothers compared with that of all other infants; that the incidence of *Conspicuously low object cathexis—inanimate objects* (SDi 40) and of *Poor concentration, short attention span* (SDi 112) is significantly higher for all of the infants (R) except those of type I mothers; that the incidence of *Conspicuously low object cathexis— inanimate objects* (SDi 40) and of *Conspicuously inactive and unresponsive: general behavior* (SDi 42) is significantly lower in infants of type I mothers compared with all others except those of type VI mothers; and that the incidence of *Conspicuously low object cathexis—inanimate objects* (SDi 40) is significantly lower for infants of type VI mothers compared to all others except those of type I mothers.

When comparisons are made among infants of type I, type VI, and R (Table 26), the following sets are found to be significant:

The frequency of SDi included in set 4, Affective Reactions, is significantly lower in infants of type I mothers (27) compared with all others (91), with all others except those of type VI mothers (76), and with only those of type VI mothers (15).

Frequencies of SDi included in set 7, Character Traits, and set 8, Negativistic States, in combination, are found to be significantly lower for infants of type I mothers when compared with all others (91), and with all others (R) excluding those of type VI mothers.

Frequencies of SDi included in set 13, *Cognition*, are significantly higher for all infants excluding those of type I mothers; significantly fewer for infants of type I mothers when compared with all others except those of type VI mothers; significantly lower for infants of type VI mothers and significantly higher for all others excluding those of type I mothers; and significantly lower for infants of type VI mothers when compared with all others except those of type I mothers.

These findings about the comparative incidence of SDi among the infants when grouped as those belonging to the mothers of type I, type VI, and all others (R) reveal that statements made above regarding *Crying states* (SDi 23) are confirmed. In addition, the best and least well-mothered infants have significantly different qualities of inanimate object cathexis, general activity and responsiveness, and attention span. All four behaviors reflect specific deviations from optimal reactivity to internal or external stimuli.

The statements made above regarding the significance of differential mothering for set 4, Affective Reactions, at six weeks, are also confirmed at six months in the relationships found among frequencies for the infants grouped as belonging to mothers of type I, type VI, and R. But there is a marked difference in what set 4 includes at six months: the individual SDi at this age reflect the greater ability of the six-month-old to exhibit gradations of affect discharge, or more specific modes of emotional expression. The six-month-old appears to have established gradients for regression and increased directedness of aggression. All of these, taken negatively, may be regarded as signs of adversely developing ego functions.

Set 7, Character Traits, and set 8, Negativistic States, in combination, are nominally related to low frustration tolerance, intolerance of tension, and varieties of negativism and demandingness, but all of these may be linked manifestations of the failure of early infantile narcissism to be diminished. The narcissism involved in low object cathexis or in low function pleasure differs from the narcissism reflected in sets 7 and 8. We should argue that the object cathexes and the function pleasure of the six-month-old are normally highly narcissistic because the object still tends to exist only for the purpose of need gratification, and because the function pleasure may represent a failure in having experienced sufficient narcissistic gratification rather than its damming up. It may be that the more adequate the mothering, the easier the infant finds it to relinquish his most massive defense against the world, his narcissism.

Set 13, Cognition, really contains the prerequisites for cognitive functioning. The importance of SDi in this set is that at six months behavior crucial for cognitive development is clearly affected by adequacy of mothering.

In sum, at age six months the more adequately mothered

infants showed significantly fewer disturbances in their vital functioning, their object relations, behavioral states and affective states, and in their character traits and early cognitive development.

Signs of Disturbance: One Year

As shown in Table 24, six sets of SDi are found to be significantly differentiable among infants of specific maternal types: set 2, Vital Functions, set 4, Affective Reactions, set 5, Object Relations, set 6, Characteristic States of Behavior, set 8, Negativistic States and set 10, Stereotypic Movements.

As at six months, set 2 achieves significance because of the low frequencies of SDi in infants of type I mothers. These infants have fewer difficulties in eating and sleeping, and probably for that reason fewer conflicts with the environment.[1] Indirectly, this lessened conflict may lead to greater contentment and easier relationships with adults and with the outer world in general. If less energy is consumed in conflict and tension, more is available for channeling into adaptive activities. And it may be that by age one year very adequate mothering has achieved smooth routines of eating and sleeping among the infants, and that less adequate mothering is reflected in the greater difficulty in accommodating to vital routines.

Set 4, at age one, contains a group of easily observable and unequivocal dystonic affective states. The category can be characterized as containing the most visible manifestations of disturbance among the infants. The individual SDi refer to fairly well-organized demonstrations of disequilibrium and protest. Analysis of the distribution of the frequencies shows that set 4 achieves significance because of low incidence in infants of type I mothers and high incidence in those of type III and type IV mothers. The latter are those who are most openly aggressive, and often hostile and punitive, toward their

---

[1]Studies by Blum (1950, 1951) and Carithers (1951) have shown that pediatricians are consulted more often about physical aspects of infant development than about any other problem of infancy.

infants. In these respects they differ from mothers of type II who, although lacking in empathy and often emotionally unyielding, are not unkind; and from mothers of type V, whose affect is markedly inhibited, and who are more likely to withdraw from their infants than to be overtly negativistic toward them. The relative frequencies in set 4 suggest a rather direct reactiveness of the infants to overt behavior of the mothers. Where the infant can copy the mother (identify with her) he does so: he manifests anger in an extreme form. Often he shows, in addition, depression or sadness, which even at this age may be an internalized manifestation of hostility.

Set 5, Object Relations, comprises the infant's reactivity to persons and things. Certainly during the first year of life object relations are directly predicated upon the quality and quantity of the flow of cathexis from the infant to the mother. Some of the SDi contained in this set refer directly to the reciprocal communication between mother and infant. Others, such as function pleasure, are indirect manifestations of their relationship. Set 5 attains significance because of low frequencies of SDi in the infants of type I mothers and high frequencies in those of types III and IV mothers. It appears that where the mother's relationship to the infant is genuinely affectionate, the infant's object relationships flourish relatively undisturbed. Where the relationship is disturbed in particular ways, not only does the infant's direct response to the mother suffer, but the indirect manifestations stemming from the relationship are distorted. In the latter case, the damming up of libidinal cathexis, which at first should be directed toward the mother, seems to arrest the displacement of libidinal and aggressive cathexis toward other objects. In turn, activities which need not require mediation of the mother are inhibited. This extends even to the infant's pleasure in motor activities.

Set 6, Characteristic States of Behavior, refers to general states or moods which characterize the personality of the infant. The set achieves significance because of low frequency in infants of type I mothers. The logical order of sets 5 and 6 might very well have been reversed, as the SDi making up set

6 are almost prerequisites for the object relations referred to in set 5. The thread which runs through set 6 is a preoccupation with the self or the body. The certain statement that can be made is that the high empathy, moderate control, and high efficiency of type I mothers frees their infants from that negative self-preoccupation, or from a dystonic narcissism.

Set 8, Negativistic States, achieves significance because of high frequency in infants of type IV mothers. Normally the one-year-old shows increased motor drive, more skilled and more directed command of his own body, and heightened resistance to passive handling. Optimally, these should be observable in the infants' enjoyment and happy excitement in unaided and independent activity. This joy is frequently recognized when an infant pulls himself erect for the first time, or takes his first few steps, or cruises in an upright position. Bodily mastery is transformed into joy and pride. However, it is *Negativism, general* (SDi 70), comprising varieties of negativistic behaviors rather than resistance to specific routines involving body handling, that shows the highest frequencies in infants of type IV mothers at one year. This is not surprising, since the mothers of type IV are the most clearly hostile and suppressive, and tend to allow their infants least autonomy. An infant's normal striving for mastery, when held down and given insufficient outlet, may make itself manifest in the form of negativism. The activity inherent in motor drives, when dammed up, may find expression in negativism. Aggression is transformed into hostility.

Set 10, Stereotypic Movements, achieves significance because of high frequency in infants of type III mothers. These were infants who were observed to receive high but erratic degrees of stimulation, often both aggressive and exciting. Their proneness to seek bodily gratification from self-stimulating activities would appear to be the result of their own efforts to keep themselves at too high a level of arousal, one to which they had become accustomed and had learned to depend upon. Not being able to obtain this level of arousal from the mother consistently, they may turn to themselves and seek to reach it through repetitious movements of various kinds.

Seven sets of SDi, 1, 3, 7, 9, 11, 12, and 13, fail to achieve significance at age one year when all seven maternal types are taken into account. The following explanations are suggested:

Set 1, Physiological Functions: Only three items are relevant, and their respective frequencies among all 118 cases are only nine, four, and three.

Set 3, Sensory Responsiveness: Two items are relevant, and their respective frequencies are 19 and six.

Set 7, Character Traits: The six relevant items all refer to low frustration tolerance or to demandingness. It is possible that these behaviors should be regarded as normative at age one year, when demandingness may be a partial indication that adequate outlets for aggressive impulse discharge have remained available to the infant. Often it is a prelude to the normal desire of the one-year-old to command the environment.

Set 9, Habits: The full set of 20 items may reflect a transient impulsivity characteristic of all infants at age one, which may not be influenced by types of mothering received by the infants in our study. From one point of view, all of our infants were rather permissively treated. It may be that only an extremely rigid mode of infant rearing can squelch the joy taken by the normal infant in some habitual and repetitive form of impulse discharge.

Set 11, Fears: It is difficult to offer a possible reason why the behaviors included in this set appear to be uninfluenced by types of mothering. One may speculate that the ubiquitousness of ambivalence and of aggression toward the part object, the literal prevalence of primary process in the preverbal period, and the infant's instinctual wishes to eat and to devour, with the reciprocal fear of being eaten and consumed— all these may combine to produce a random distribution of specific fears and of specific anxieties at the end of the first year of life. In other words, many of the observed and reported fears may be both transient and normal.[2] Most of the

---

[2] Our follow-up study is expected to throw light on the vicissitudes or persistence of habits and fears, and of other behaviors that have appeared to be pathognomonic during infancy.

fears cited in set 11 refer to the presence or absence of human objects. These are considered below, in our discussions of separation and stranger anxiety, in Chapter 15.

Set 12, Self-Destructive Behavior: Three of the five SDi have frequencies of three or fewer. The five items have a total frequency of only 33.

Set 13, Cognition: The nonsignificance of the two SDi in this set may be explained by the fact that the behaviors border upon intellectual capacity, and are not discriminable according to maternal behavior at age one.

When the frequencies of SDi in infants of type I mothers are compared with the frequencies in infants of all other types we find, as shown in Table 25, that the incidence of *Poor appetite; refusal liquids or solids* (SDi 12) and of *Conspicuously low function pleasure: fine motor* (SDi 38) is significantly lower for the infants of type I mothers compared with all others (91), and compared with all others except those of type VI mothers (76); that *Crying states* (SDi 23) are present in significantly fewer infants of type I mothers compared to all other infants (91) and significantly more in infants of R mothers. In comparison to all infants except those of type VI mothers, those of type I mothers again show significantly fewer frequencies, and significantly more are shown in infants of all other maternal types.

Certain of the SDi whose individual frequencies were too low to attain significance are clinically related to other SDi with which they have been combined for statistical calculations. Thus, *Refusal to be fed by mother* (SDi 32), *Lack of approach toward mother* (SDi 33), and *Withdrawal from mother* (SDi 34), in combination show significantly low frequencies in infants of type I mothers compared to all others and to all others except those of type VI (Table 25). The same statement holds true for the following combinations of SDi: *Conspicuously low function pleasure: gross motor* (SDi 37), and *fine motor* (SDi 38); *Conspicuously low object cathexis—per-*

sons (SDi 39), and *inanimate objects* (SDi 40); and *Conspicuously inactive and unresponsive: social behavior* (SDi 45), *vocal behavior* (SDi 46), and *smiling behavior* (SDi 47).

For some of the same combinations the incidence is significantly lower for infants of type I mothers in comparison to those of type VI: this is the case for SDi 37 and 38; 39 and 40; and 45, 46, and 47. Finally, for two of these combinations there are significant differences between infants ot type VI mothers and all others except those of type I: this holds for SDi 39 and 40; and for 45, 46, and 47.

Set 13, Cognition, also achieves significance when comparisons are made among infants of maternal type I, type VI, and R, as shown in Table 26. The frequencies for infants of type I mothers are low, and are significantly high for all others. The frequencies in set 13 are also significantly low for infants of type I mothers when compared to all others except those of type VI mothers. For the latter, frequencies are also significantly low when compared to all others and when compared to all others except those of type I mothers.

Reviewing the findings for age one year, we see that the most adequately mothered infants show the fewest frequencies of poor appetite, crying states, low function pleasure, low object cathexis, and low responsiveness. Disturbed relationships to the mother are least present. We find also that infants of types I and VI mothers show least disturbance in capacities commonly regarded as the most pure of the ego functions— cognition, the basis of the later synthetic function of the ego. Type I mothers are, in general, most adequate and most empathic in their mothering. Type VI mothers are, in general, the most competent, and some of their infants appear to achieve independence early; their infants' exploration of the environment and of inanimate objects is often intense and persistent. The influence of these activities upon the development of cognitive aptitudes and attitudes may be considerable.

C. THE SIGNS OF FAVORABLE DEVELOPMENT

Tables 27, 28, and 29 present, for the infant ages of six weeks, six months, and one year, respectively, the frequencies of SFD found among the infants of each of the seven maternal types.

Signs of Favorable Development: Six Weeks

At age six weeks, the frequencies of only one SFD, *Adequate feeding patterns* (SFD 8), and of one set, Physiological and Vital Functions (Table 30) are found to be significantly different among the infants of the seven maternal types. At this age only the first six sets are relevant, as the expressive behavior of the very young infant is visible mainly in physiological states, motor activity, and gross affective states. The SFD included in set 1 may be regarded as forerunners of conditions referred to in the subsequent sets.

The frequencies of SFD and of sets of SFD in infants of type I mothers, compared with the frequencies in infants of all other types, are shown in Tables 31 and 32.

At age six weeks, the frequencies of four SFD, *Smooth movement, without undue tension or flaccidity* (SFD 1), *Regular sleep patterns* (SFD 7), *Comfort easily restored* (SFD 15), and *Contentment and/or happiness not easily disrupted* (SFD 25), are significantly higher for infants of type I mothers compared with all others (91), and compared with all others except those of type VI (76). The frequencies of SFD 7 and SFD 25 are also significantly higher for infants of type I mothers than for those of type VI mothers; and the frequency of *Social expansiveness: reactive* (SFD 18) is significantly higher for infants of type VI mothers compared with all others. In addition, set 3, Affective Responsiveness, is found to be significant (Table 32) in that infants of type I mothers have significantly higher frequencies when compared to all others, to all others except those of type VI mothers, and to those of type VI mothers alone.

The indications are that the most adequately mothered infants are least subject to states of excessive or insufficient tension; that their sleep patterns as well as their feeding patterns are more likely to be well stabilized; that their affective responsiveness is more mature and appropriate; and that their states of contentment are more stable.

A comparison of findings at six weeks for SDi and SFD shows that while *advancements* appear mainly in physiological and vital functions and not in affective reactions, object relations, characteristic states of behavior, or character traits, *disturbances* in affective reactions, characteristic states, character traits, and negativistic states are significantly lower for the most adequately mothered infants. It may be that among normally endowed infants it takes longer for the effects of variable mothering to be reflected in advancements than in disturbances. Possibly the normal infant is more immediately vulnerable to inadequate handling than he is prone to show the immediate effects of adequate handling, for example, in maturational excellence at six weeks. Superior maternal handling during the infants's earliest weeks may lay a groundwork, in a latent fashion, for later manifest advancements in ego development.

Signs of Favorable Development: Six Months

As shown in Table 30, all relevant sets of SFD are statistically significant at six months. Highest and significant frequencies occur in infants of type I mothers; significantly low frequencies occur in infants of type III mothers in set 3, Affective Responsiveness, set 6, Character Traits, and set 7, Adaptation; and significantly low frequencies are found in infants of type IV mothers in set 1, Physiological and Vital Functions, and set 4, Object Relations. The emergence of significant differences in all relevant sets at six months is a striking confirmation of our basic hypothesis concerning relationships between ego development and the mastery of anxiety.

When the further comparisons are made of the frequencies of SFD in infants of maternal type I, type VI, and R, many individual SFD are found to be significant. Inspection of

Table 31 shows that individual SFD and combinations of SFD are distributed among all of the sets. In every instance, the occurrence of the SFD in infants of type I mothers was significantly higher compared to the occurrence in all other infants.

For many of the SFD and combinations of SFD, infants of type I mothers show significantly higher frequencies than infants of type VI mothers; in one instance, SFD 44 and 45, the frequencies in infants of type VI mothers are also significantly low. Finally, for *Sustained inspection of new objects, new environment* (SFD 10), and for *Striving to accomplish difficult tasks* (SFD 32) and *Resourcefulness: capacity to "organize" activity* (SFD 33) combined, frequencies are significantly low for all infants, except those of type I mothers compared with infants of type VI mothers.

At age six weeks, the SFD appeared to be less salient than the presence of SDi in the more adequately mothered infants. At six months, the range of advancements outstrips the range of disturbances. The differences between the poorly mothered and the well-mothered infants are more visible in developmental achievements than in developmental disturbances. The well-mothered infants give the impression of having laid down the basis for more stable physiological, perceptual, and behavioral states, more solid cathexis of animate and inanimate objects, more positive affective responsiveness, and more adequate adaptive and cognitive behavior.

Signs of Favorable Development: One Year

At age one year, four individual SFD showed frequencies significantly different among infants of the seven maternal types: *Adequate feeding patterns* (SFD 8), *Comfort easily restored* (SFD 15), *Social expansiveness: spontaneous* (SFD 17), and *High and varied forms of intentional imitativeness* (SFD 23).

The importance of SFD 8 lies in that at one year, as at six weeks, the infant's response to feeding is a sensitive indicator of the relationship to the mother. SFD 15, 17, and 23 may be regarded as indicating the greater stability of more positive object relations in the more adequately mothered infants; of the capacity of those infants to accept comforting, to initiate social communication, and to show cathexis of human objects by intentional imitating, the last being a visible sign of learning and of identification.

All sets except 9, Miscellaneous Positive, where the expected frequencies for the entire sample are too small to warrant consideration of the set, showed frequencies significantly different among infants of the seven maternal types (Table 30).

When comparisons are made for the frequencies of SFD in infants of the maternal type I, type VI, and R, many individual SFD are again found to be significant. Inspection of Table 31 indicates that the SFD and combinations of SFD are distributed among all of the sets, including set 9. In every instance, the frequencies of SFD in infants of type I mothers are significantly high when compared with all others, and in many cases when compared with those of type VI mothers.

The advanced development observed in the most adequately mothered infants at six months continues in every area of development at one year.

CHAPTER 14

On Certain Special Developmental Signs

In a normal sample of infants it would have been surprising to find certain behaviors appearing with high frequency. One would not, for example, expect many of the infants to be hypertonic (SDi 6) or to have eczema (SDi 9). Some other behaviors that were seen, though with low frequency, were not anticipated at all, for example, *Withdrawal from mother* (SDi 34), or *Strange or unusual posture or means of ambulation* (SDi 82).

On the other hand, high frequency was not unexpected for certain behaviors which, although provisionally classified as SDi, might not be pathogenic either in the first year of life or in the longer span of early childhood: for example, *Thumbsucking* (SDi 72), or some form of *Separation* or *Stranger anxiety* (SDi 96–99). It was also not unexpected that certain favorable behaviors would appear with high frequency; for example, *Regular sleeping patterns* (SFD 7), *Ease of vocalization* (SFD 14), or some form of *Function pleasure* (SFD 19–21).

Some explanations have been offered above for the significance or nonsignificance of most of the single Signs, in contrast to the significance of many sets of Signs. The summary of findings requires amplification, however, with respect to several specific behaviors that have been observed among infants in recent times, and that have been treated in the literature of infant psychology and psychopathology. Although their frequencies in our sample did not achieve statistical significance, their actual incidence deserves attention; and in some cases significant interrelationships did emerge upon further examination of the conditions in which the behaviors occurred. Accordingly, the following Signs are of special interest:

At six weeks: SDi 1: *Tremor, limbs or body (in noncrying states)*

SDi 2: *Tremor, chin (in noncrying states)*

SDi 8: *Colic*

At six weeks, six months, and one year:

SDi 9: *Eczema*

At six months and one year:

SDi 92: *Rocking*

SDi 96: *Separation anxiety*

SDi 97: *Stranger anxiety*

SDi 98: *Stranger anxiety with withdrawal reactions*

SDi 99: *Stranger anxiety with crying reaction*

At one year: SDi 41: *Transitional object*

SDi 86: *Smearing feces*

SDi 87: *Eating feces*

SFD 36: *Genital play*

Each of these Signs is dealt with in this chapter except SDi 96–99, describing separation and stranger anxiety, which are dealt with in Chapter 15.

SIX WEEKS

SDi 1: *Tremor, limbs or body (in noncrying states)*.
Frequency = 14

SDi 2: *Tremor, chin (in noncrying states)*.
Frequency = 21

Six infants showed both kinds of tremor. Therefore the actual number of infants concerned is 29, or almost one fourth of the sample. In all cases this tremor was rapid and the amplitude small.

The trembling of the neonate was counted as a possible

sign of disturbance at age six weeks because it has been assumed to disappear gradually in the first week or two of life. Pediatric texts, if they mention it at all, do so only in reference to organic pathology. Prechtl (Prechtl and Beintema, 1964), who has carried out major neurological studies of neonates, states that normally tremor disappears a few days after birth; that it is "associated with hypermotility, increased resistance to passive movements, low threshold for tendon reflexes and easily elicitable Moro responses"; and that from the fourth day on its occurrence is suspicious except during vigorous crying. In our sample, tremor (chin) was observed only during crying states in only one infant, not included in the given frequencies. For the other 29 infants, the conditions in which tremor was observed were:

only during sleepy states	2
only during auditory or visual stimulation	3
only before feeding	2
only with postural shifts	13
combinations of above	9

Seven of the 29 infants were irritable and tense, six were irritable but not tense, five were tense but not irritable, and 11 were neither tense nor irritable. Five were hard to arouse and showed poor muscle tone; and 19 were alert, responsive, and, with one exception, showed smooth and vigorous movements. No significant relationships were found between the neonatal and the six-week observations of tremor and tension states, either for the 29 infants or for the entire sample of 122 infants.

Tremor similar to that shown by our infants has been observed by Touwen[1] in four infants in a sample of 50 six-week-olds. All four were boys with a rather high activity level. None showed any neurological abnormalities when observed at successive four-week intervals until the time they could walk

[1]B. C. L. Touwen, of the Department of Developmental Neurology, Groningen, Netherlands (personal communication).

without support. In our sample there are 18 males and 11 females; the difference is nonsignificant. A moderately high activity level was observed in 10 infants, seven males and three females. Drorbaugh[2] has found that tremors and hypertonic responses may be present for several months after birth in infants whom he judged to be neurologically normal in childhood.

The relatively high incidence of tremor seen among our infants may be attributed to soft signs of neurological deficit or injury, or to normally greater physiological vulnerability of the infant at six weeks, or to emotional factors assumed to be relevant by Gesell and Amatruda (1949). Further observations of the children in our follow-up study may throw light on the probability that any of these factors was present early in infancy.

SDi 8: *Colic.* Frequency = 12

Colic is one of eight "psychogenic diseases of infancy" for which Spitz (1951b) offered an etiological classification according to wrong or insufficient mother-child relations.[3] His propositions relating colic to congenital hypertonicity and to maternal overpermissiveness are not confirmed by our data.

Of the 12 infants with colic, three were observed to be tense and irritable, two as tense but not irritable, and three as irritable but not tense. None was hypertonic or had been so in the neonatal period. An assumption of congenital hypertonicity in an infant with colic seems to be unparsimonious without specific physiological findings, for if any chronic condition will make a young infant appear to be hypertonic, colic will.

[2]J. E. Drorbaugh, Director, Maternal and Infant Health Study, Children's Hospital Medical Center, Boston, Mass. (personal communication).

[3]Three other disturbances discussed by Spitz (Spitz and Wolf, 1949) are discussed below: eczema, rocking, and fecal play. His hypotheses regarding genital play (1949) are also considered below. Spitz's original investigations have stimulated us to test certain of his theoretical statements.

TABLE 33

COLIC AND MATERNAL PERMISSIVENESS

Case	Maternal Type								
1	I	Overpermissive	Attentive	Anxious	—	—	—	—	—
2	I	Overpermissive	Attentive	Anxious	—	—	—	—	Depressed
3	II	—	Attentive	Anxious	—	—	Restrictive	Controlling	—
4	III	—	Attentive	—	—	—	Restrictive	Controlling	—
5	III	—	—	—	Inattentive	Mechanical	Restrictive	Controlling	—
6	III	—	Attentive	—	—	—	Restrictive	Controlling	—
7	IV	—	—	—	Inattentive	Mechanical	Restrictive	Controlling	—
8	V	—	Attentive	—	—	Mechanical	Restrictive	Controlling	—
9	V	—	—	Anxious	Inattentive	Mechanical	—	Controlling	—
10	V	—	—	—	—	Mechanical	—	Controlling	Depressed
11	VII	Permissive	Attentive	—	—	—	—	—	—
12	VIII	Overpermissive	Attentive	—	—	—	—	Controlling	—

A distribution of the 12 mothers according to type, and in relation to grades of maternal permissiveness noted in direct observation of the mothers as well as in interview data, is shown in Table 33. Three mothers were overpermissive. In one of the three (Case 2) the overpermissiveness was clearly related to depression and bordered on laxity; in another (Case 12), it alternated with an excited and overcontrolling behavior. Only one mother (Case 11) was simply permissive, not excessively. The other eight mothers were controlling or restrictive or both, and often responded to their infants mechanically as well.

Following a hypothesis of Levine and Bell (1950), Spitz assumed that the pacifier, by releasing tension, might serve as a cure for colic. This assumption is not confirmed by our data. Eleven of the 12 infants with colic were pacifier addicts before and during the colic period. The twelfth had never been given a pacifier. The use of a pacifier may in itself be regarded as an index of maternal overpermissiveness, but our interview data do not warrant this conclusion. Many mothers who gave pacifiers to their infants explained that they intended thus to prevent thumb-sucking, and some said in addition that they became too irritated by their babies' crying unless they made use of the pacifier. At best, these reasons reflect an ambivalent permissiveness. Besides, an infant who is often supplied with a pacifier may experience overstimulation of the oral zone, with resultant heightening instead of lessening of oral tension. Our material suggests, in agreement with Spitz, that colic is accompanied by a disturbed mother-infant relationship, though not by the specific form of maternal disturbance that Spitz proposed.

Six Weeks, Six Months, One Year

SDi 9: *Eczema.*   Frequency at six weeks = 2
Frequency at six months = 2
Frequency at one year = 3

Five infants are represented here, as one of them had eczema at all three ages. Spitz (1951b) linked the appearance of eczema to "maternal hostility garbed as manifest anxiety," and cited the anxiety-ridden mother who avoids touching her baby because of her repressed aggression. The second part of his proposition finds support in our data. All five mothers of the infants with eczema did handle their infants minimally and without evidence of pleasure, and all but one did appear to have strongly repressed aggression toward the babies, but in none of the five mothers was anxiety manifest.

Six Months, One Year

SDi 92: *Rocking.* Frequency at six months $= 33$

Frequency at one year $= 31$

The number of infants represented here is 54, as 10 rocked at both ages. The given frequencies naturally excluded cases in which the rocking was considered to be normative, i.e., when it was occasional or transitory, or occurred mainly in states of contentment or cheerfulness.

Spitz (Spitz and Wolf, 1949; Spitz, 1951b) linked rocking to poor control of impulses in the mother, and to rapid oscillations of maternal behavior, from pampering to hostility. This hypothesis appears valid only for the mother of one of the infants, whose rocking was most severe and protracted. His mother told of being criticized for holding the baby all day long in his first weeks, but she felt she needed to show him love that way. By the time he was six months old she left him alone for hours at a time, and was openly resentful of his needs.

Among the 64 infants at both ages whose rocking occurred repeatedly and in dystonic states were 15 for whom the intensity and duration of the rocking could not be ascertained either because the behavior was not observed or because the mother's reports were inconclusive. In the other 49 cases the rocking was clearly stereotypic or agitated, and was provisionally regarded as pathogenic. Table 34 shows that significantly less stereotypic rocking was observed among infants of type I mothers than among infants of all other maternal types. Table 35 shows that significantly less stereotypic rocking was also seen among infants of both type I and type VI mothers than among the rest of the infants.

TABLE 34

STEREOTYPIC ROCKING: INFANTS OF MATERNAL TYPE I VERSUS ALL OTHERS

	Rocking	Nonrocking	
Type I	2	25	27
All Others	47	48	95
	49	73	122

Chi square = 15.97.

TABLE 35

STEREOTYPIC ROCKING: INFANTS OF MATERNAL TYPES I AND VI, AND REST

	Rocking	Nonrocking	
Types I and VI	5	37	42
Rest	44	32	76
	49	69	118

Chi square = 16.28.

Stereotypic rocking in the gravest form seen in our study was thus found to be significantly associated with inadequate mothering, characterized by aloofness, aggressiveness, ambivalence, and hostile attitudes.[4] Thus restated, the relationship between rocking and a disturbed mother-infant relationship, as implied by Spitz, is more clearly defined.

ONE YEAR

SDi 41: *Transitional Object.*   Frequency = 2

This refers to an excessive need to hold to an inanimate object other than a bottle or a pacifier, and at periods unrelated to falling asleep. The low frequency is explained by the distinction of this behavior from two other SDi, *Needs special comfort to fall asleep* (SDi 18) and *Dependence on pacifier* (SDi 71). For one infant the object was a fuzzy toy animal, for the other, a blanket. In both cases, the mother was restrictive and emotionally remote from her infant. This behavior is noted here because we consider that *dependence* upon a transitional object at age one year may be an indicator of an infant's premature relinquishment of gratification from the mother.

SDi 86: *Smearing feces.*   Frequency = 3

SDi 87: *Eating feces.*   Frequency = 2

Four infants are represented, as one infant showed both behaviors.

Spitz (Spitz and Wolf, 1949; Spitz, 1951b) linked fecal play to maternal depression and long-term mood swings, e.g., from oversolicitousness to extreme rejection. This description appears fitting, though not in its extreme form, in only one of the four cases, that of the single infant who both smeared and ate her feces. During her early months her mother was tender, attentive, and very solicitous. As her marital situation deteriorated, the mother withdrew from the baby, became increas-

---

[4]This finding bears upon an earlier hypothesis (Brody, 1961) regarding the genesis of pathological rocking, which is to be tested independently.

ingly irritated by her, and expressed reluctance to answer to the baby's demands.

SFD 36: *Curiosity: manipulative, genitalia or navel.*
Frequency = 45

This behavior was considered as a possible sign of favorable development in view of Spitz's several hypotheses (Spitz and Wolf, 1949): that genital play in the first year of life has normative significance and is associated with a close and balanced mother-infant relationship; that because of the latter relationship, genital play is associated with high DQs; and that genital play and rocking infrequently occur together.

At the infant age of six months, genital manipulation was observed or reported in four male infants and one female. At age one year, it was recorded for 41 infants, and navel manipulation was recorded for four (all female) infants. The genital manipulation usually was reported to have been observed for the first time between five and 10 months of age. Information about its appearance was supplied upon inquiry about the infant's curiosity about any part of his body. In many cases the mother told of the genital play with apologetic explanations that it occurred only when the baby's nakedness could not prevent it, for example, during a bath, and often the play was alluded to with euphemism. The reported incidence may therefore be less than the actual incidence.

Our data do not confirm the first hypothesis of Spitz, which relates genital play to a close and balanced mother-infant relationship. Such a relationship was observed in only 11 of the 41 cases, with no significant differences in frequency among infants of the seven maternal types (Table 36). The total frequency of genital play, which includes only one third of our entire infant sample, indicates as well that the behavior is not normative. We suspect that its appearance is related to a variety of constitutional and experiential factors, and that high among the latter are the varieties of physical and emotional stimulation or deprivation provided by the mother, the father, and the siblings; the encouragement or discouragement of the infant's tactile and kinesthetic gratifications; and the general high intensity of the mother-infant relationship.

TABLE 36

GENITAL MANIPULATION AND MOTHER-INFANT
RELATIONSHIP AT ONE YEAR[a]

	I	II	III	IV	V	VI	VII	VIII	Total
Close, balanced	10						1		11
Close, uneven	2				1	2		1	6
Affect inhibited		5	1		2	2			10
Timid, erratic		1	1					1	3
Aggressive			3	1					4
Aggressive, awkward					1				1
Close, highly ambivalent				5				1	6
	12	6	5	6	4	4	1	3	41

[a]The quality of the mother-infant relationship was judged from film and interview data.

Our data do not support Spitz's second hypothesis, to the effect that genital play is associated with high DQ. The mean DQ for our total sample of infants is 107.07; for those showing genital play, 107.83; and for those not showing genital play, 106.69. These differences are not statistically significant.

The third hypothesis, that genital play and rocking infrequently occur together, is difficult to test as stated by Spitz because of the term "infrequently." However, our data indicate that infants who show genital play show significantly less stereotypic rocking than those who do not show genital play (Table 37). If Spitz's hypothesis is thus reformulated, it can be considered verified.

The literature of psychoanalysis consistently states that it is more difficult for females than for males to discover their genitals, and that female masturbation occurs later than male

TABLE 37

GENITAL PLAY AND STEREOTYPIC ROCKING

	Genital Play	No Genital Play	
Stereotypic Rocking	7	42	49
No Stereotypic Rocking	34	39	73
	41	81	122

Chi square = 13.7.

masturbation. Our data indicate that the incidence of genital play at one year is significantly higher among male infants than among females (Table 38).

TABLE 38

GENITAL PLAY AT ONE YEAR

	Genital Play	No Genital Play	
Male	31	33	64
Female	10	48	58
	41	81	122

Chi square = 13.29.
Significant at .01 level.

Roughly three times as many males played with their genitalia as did females; 50 percent of the males did so in contrast to 16 percent of the females. A related finding by Goldberg and Lewis (1969) of significant differences in play activities of male and female infants at one year, males being more active, more independent, more vigorous, and playing more with nontoys, adds to the idea that genital play may be a specific hand-eye function that, by contributing to the building of body image, influences activity choice.

When tested for significance for social class and sex, the SDi and the SFD, with very few exceptions at age one, were found not to be ascribable to class or sex factors. The exceptions were, *for sex only,* 3: *General tension;*[5] SDi 33: *Lack of approach toward mother;*[6] SDi 46: *Conspicuously inactive and unresponsive: vocal behavior;*[6] SDi 50: *Crying during dressing or diaper changes.*[5] For the SFD, the exceptions were SFD 28: *Activity and responsiveness, vocal;*[5] SFD 36: *Curiosity, manipulative, genitalia.*[6]

[5]Higher for females.
[6]Higher for males.

CHAPTER 15

Separation Anxiety and Stranger Anxiety

This chapter deals with ramifications of our findings about separation anxiety and stranger anxiety at the ages of six months and one year.

SEPARATION ANXIETY

The study of separation anxiety was not a part of our original research design. At the six-month interview no specific inquiry about it was made, on the assumption that the infant's natural physical dependence upon the mother for a variety of need satisfactions at that age made it appropriate for him to feel threatened by her absence or disappearance. However, if in response to inquiry about the infant's affective states a mother spontaneously reported severe distress when she left the infant and went out, the distress was scored as a possible sign of disturbance. This occurred in nine cases, in several of which the mother emphasized that the babies showed anger rather than fear. It is pertinent to note here that *Low Frustration tolerance: being alone* (SDi 57) also was not scored as a disturbance at six months. Very frequently the mothers reported, and we observed, that the six-month-old objected much less to the mother's leaving his presence than to termination of direct physical contact with her. The infants protested most when put down after being held, and less when left alone in a room while the mother was audible or visible; but being alone was not in itself seen to arouse distress.

At the infant age of one year, fear upon separation or threat of separation from the mother also was not originally scored as a disturbance, on the assumption that these reactions would be normative. The assumption rested upon findings of other investigators that have appeared in the last decades. A general awareness of the ill effects of *prolonged* separation of infants and young children from their mothers grew largely after Anna Freud and Burlingham (1943) drew attention to its disastrous effects among evacuated children in nurseries during World War II; and Spitz (Spitz and Wolf, 1949) drew attention to the condition he described as anaclitic depression, in which he linked early maternal deprivation to infant psychopathology as well as to problems of social maldevelopment. Bowlby (1951) then reviewed comprehensively a very large variety of studies bearing upon effects of early separation. More recently, the phenomenon of anxiety arising in the infant during *brief* separations from the mother has been studied by Schaffer and Callender (1959), Robertson (1958, 1962), Benjamin (1961), Schaffer and Emerson (1964), Tennes and Lampl (1964, 1966), Heinicke and Westheimer (1965), Ainsworth and Bell (1970a), Ainsworth, Bell, and Stayton (in press), Ainsworth and Wittig (1969), and others. Mahler's studies (1963, 1965, 1966) of the normal separation-individuation process have highlighted the developmental significance of the normal infant's increasing capacity to bear separation from the mother, and his need to practice the experiences of leaving and returning to her, once locomotion has been achieved. The relevance of the capacity for this practice in the building of postambivalent object relations, and in the development of ego functions, is obvious.

Separation and stranger anxiety would appear to have a common basis: a reaction to the loss of the mother, temporarily or permanently. The two phenomena may be separate, and the difference may be blurred by the fact that most experimenters, as part of their experimental design, create the situation in which the stranger is introduced after the mother has withdrawn. The findings of Stevens (in press) of attachment behavior, separation anxiety, and stranger anxiety in polymatrically reared infants in the Metera Babies Centre suggest that the phenomena are distinct, although the two forms of anxiety are sharper for infants who were more attached (to mother surrogates).

At the one-year interview, we did inquire of each mother how the baby acted when she went away, while she was away, and when she came home again. The mothers' responses can be grouped as follows:

1. No reaction at all observed.

2. Prolonged distress at sight of mother's leaving, in the form of crying, screaming, or whimpering.

3. Crying at sight of the mother's leaving, with quick recovery within minutes, or even moments, after her departure.

4. Sadness and/or reduced activity after her departure.

5. Searching behavior during the mother's absence.

6. Vigilance maintained during the mother's absence.

7. No reaction upon mother's departure or during her absence, but excitement or happiness upon her return.

8. No reaction upon mother's departure or during her absence, but following and clinging to her upon her return.

9. No reaction upon mother's departure or during her absence, but acute crying and tenacious clinging upon her return.

Although our inquiry alluded to what happened before, during, and after the mother's absences, the replies of most mothers were inexact and referred to the infants' behavior in a generalizing manner. They said, for example, "He doesn't care at all," or "He screams when I put my coat on, but then he's fine. He stops crying right after I'm gone." Some explained that the baby's reaction depended entirely upon whether he actually saw the mother leaving the house, or upon who stayed with him. Often the mothers' answers appeared to be influenced strongly by defensive attitudes; for instance, some seemed glad to say that their absence made no difference to the baby, implying with pride that he adapted easily to all other persons; others seemed glad to say that the baby screamed when the mother went away and clung to her fiercely when she came home; still others denied that there was any cause for the baby to be concerned because he was used to the mother's going out often. And one said of her baby, "When he's taken out to the park by his grandmother, *he's* leaving *me*, so he has no reason to complain."

TABLE 39

INFANT REACTIONS TO SEPARATION AT ONE YEAR:
MATERNAL REPORTS

	Main Reaction	Additional Reaction
1. No reaction at all	21	0
2. Prolonged distress	39	0
3. Crying with quick recovery	16	0
4. Sadness and/or reduced activity	3	4
5. Searching	2	2
6. Vigilance	0	2
7. No reaction but pleasure on mother's return	35	7
8. No reaction but clinging on mother's return	5	10
9. No reaction but crying and clinging on mother's return	1	4

According to the maternal reports, as shown in Table 39, at one year 21 infants showed no reaction at all to the mother's going out of the house, and 55 reacted with overt distress. Six reacted to her return with increased demandingness, and 35 with relief or pleasure. The mothers did of course have to depend upon relatives or baby-sitters or household helpers to provide information about the infants' behavior in their absence, yet it is of interest that only five mothers had information of this kind. The great majority indicated that sooner or later the baby was all right, even if he had cried a lot at first, implying that as long as the crying was brief it was of little consequence. It was an unusual mother who said, "I've learned to open the front door very slowly when I come back because the baby waits near it, and the second she hears my footsteps she crawls over and sits down right at the door, waiting for me." Only 39 mothers were able to elaborate upon their main reply with additional information about the infants' reactions after their own return.

TABLE 40

SEPARATION ANXIETY AT ONE YEAR

	Observed	Reported	Agreement
1. No reaction	9	21	7
2. Prolonged distress	12	39	8
3. Crying with quick recovery	3	16	3
4. Sadness and/or reduced activity	6	3	2
5. Searching	0	2	0
6. Vigilance	1	1	1
7. No reaction but pleasure on mother's return	4	35	3
8. No reaction but clinging on mother's return	0	5	0
9. No reaction but crying and clinging on mother's return	0	1	0

The opportunity to observe directly the reactions of some of the one-year-olds to the mother's leaving the room, during visits to our research offices, was neglected until after many of the infants had already been seen at age one. Thereafter, if no natural event led to the mother's going out of the room briefly, she was asked to do so for about half a minute. This was at best an informal procedure, carried out in the hope of acquiring some information that might be useful clinically, although it would not allow for formal evaluation. Observations were thus made in 35 cases, of which 24 were in agreement with the maternal reports. The distribution of the reactions among the infants of the seven maternal types was not significant (Table 40).

Although observations of separation anxiety at age one were far fewer than reports, both threw light upon the variety of factors involved in the study of separation anxiety. It became clear that an infant's reactions to separation from the mother depended first of all upon his immediate physical and emotional state at the time of her leaving him, and on whether he actually saw her go or only noticed her disappearance after the fact. Other relevant factors were the frequency and duration of her usual absences, from the baby's room as well as from home itself; the frequency with which he saw other family members come and go from the home; the quality of the mother-infant relationship (which Tennes and Lampl, 1966, have tried to explore); the infant's locomotor ability, as it affected his freedom to follow the mother or to initiate a greeting upon her return; the persons with whom he was customarily left; his capacity to occupy himself in the mother's presence, and when alone; the length of time necessary for recovery of good humor after her return, and the stability of his recovery.

The short space of time during which staff observations of the infants' reactions could be made precluded opportunities to witness sadness, searching, or vigilance. Judging from the frequency with which infants watched the door out of which the mother went before they broke into a cry, or before they broke out with smiles upon her reappearance, we could surmise that a longer separation might well have provided many observations of subdued activity or of anxious watching and waiting. In fact, it has seemed possible that the infant's behavior during and following the mother's absence may be more telling than his behavior upon seeing her depart, unless he is in a state of acute need at the time of her departure.

We are inclined to believe that appropriate reactions to brief separations from the mother, say for a few hours, at age one, should include some evidence of watchfulness or uneasiness while she is away, and some evidence of relief or pleasure upon her return; and that these emotional reactions should occur even if the infant's other object relations are satisfactory, even if he is accustomed to absences of the mother, and even if locomotor and language development are advanced. Actually, both positive and negative reactions of these kinds appear to be appropriate well before age one and well after it, and to reflect the vicissitudes inherent in learning to tolerate the state of being alone. For these reasons we regard these reactions as normative, and not as indications of anxiety, *unless we are referring explicitly to signal anxiety.*

STRANGER ANXIETY

In view of findings of other investigators[1] to the effect that stranger anxiety normally rises from the fifth month on and ends in the latter months of the first year, we originally scored overt fear in the presence of strangers as a sign of disturbance only at age one year, and found the following frequencies among the 118 infants of the seven maternal types:

SDi 97: *Stranger anxiety.*   Frequency = 8
SDi 98: *Stranger anxiety with withdrawal reactions.* = 14
SDi 99: *Stranger anxiety with crying reaction.*   = 12

Further inspection, however, of the behavior of all 122 infants

[1]Shirley (1933) observed it beginning in the sixth month. Gesell and Amatruda (1949) placed at 24 weeks the normative capacity to recognize the mother. Griffiths (1954) placed at eight months the capacity to distinguish the stranger from familiar persons. Spitz (1950, 1959) referred to the "eight-months anxiety" as a critical organizer of development, its appearance spanning the seventh to the tenth month; Benjamin (1961) and Tennes and Lampl (1964, 1966) placed stranger anxiety between the fifth and ninth months. Piaget (Flavell, 1963) had in 1937 also placed the development of object constancy between the fifth and ninth months.

with strangers at both six months and one year revealed a variety of observed and reported responses that warranted more detailed analysis.

Logically and actually, there are three possible main responses to strangers: to be positively outgoing, either spontaneously or reactively; to respond negatively, either spontaneously or reactively; or to show no visible response. These coarse groupings did not contain all of the observations of behavior shown by the infants to strangers. They showed eight kinds of responses, within two main general categories: Positive Responsiveness and Apprehensiveness. The former category includes all infants who were Spontaneously or Reactively Outgoing, as shown by smiling and/or vocalizing (reactions 1 and 2, below). The latter category includes all those who were neither Spontaneously nor Reactively Outgoing. All infants (in both categories) could in addition have shown Customs Inspection, Unchanging Soberness, Mild General Anxiety, and Strong General Anxiety (reactions 3, 4, 5, and 6, below). Infants who showed no differentiation in behavior at sight of the stranger were classified in the Apprehensive group. Tables 41 through 45 deal only with reactions that could be directly observed in the research setting. Tables 46 and 47 deal with the category of Specific Avoidance, which could not be checked in the research setting, and is treated separately.

The primary classification of infants was either Positively Responsive or Apprehensive. All of the infants could in addition show other reactions, such as Soberness and Mild General Anxiety. When this occurred, the infant was classified under the more or most fearful of his reactions, and his other reactions were eliminated from immediate consideration. Thus there are no overlaps in the categories cited in the following tables. The eight reactions are defined as follows:

1.   Spontaneous Outgoingness. The infant initiates social overtures, often coyly or flirtatiously at first, and later with ease.

2.   Responsive Smiling or Vocalizing. The infant does not

initiate social communication but responds to overtures by the stranger. This includes mechanical smiling, observed in nine infants at six months and in five at 12 months. Probably the latter behavior is equivalent to the "propitiating smile" described by Benjamin (1961).

3. Customs Inspection. The infant quietly and steadily regards the stranger, "sizes him up," with no loss of composure but with temporarily reduced activity; he may then smile, or return to a previous activity, or continue to watch the stranger, yet with no sign of uneasiness.

4. Unchanging Soberness. The infant maintains an apprehensive watch of the stranger, and his facial expression is uneasy. His activity is sharply reduced, and there is no return to good humor or to other objects as long as the stranger is present.

5. Mild General Anxiety. The infant reacts with mild but pervasive distress in the form of whimpering, turning away, or restlessness; and the distress is rekindled by eye contact, by physical proximity to the stranger, or by touch. Cautiousness is maintained and activity is minimal as long as the stranger is present.

6. Strong General Anxiety. The infant reacts with acute and prolonged distress in the form of fearful clinging, crying, or panic, and with avoidance of sighting the stranger. He can hardly be comforted as long as the stranger remains present.

7. Specific Avoidance. The infant freezes or withdraws physically at sight of specific persons (the doctor, an elderly neighbor), or of familiar persons with unusual appearance (grandmother when she puts on her glasses), or when suddenly approached (a visiting relative). This behavior was only reported.

8. No differentiation. The stranger (staff observer) seems to go unnoticed or is responded to as if perceived to be no different from the mother.

Table 41 shows that at age six months 95 infants were either Spontaneously Outgoing and/or Responsive to the stranger and 27 were neither. At 12 months, 90 were Outgoing and/or Responsive and 32 were neither. The number of infants who were Positively Responsive only (no other reactions observed) falls from 51 at six months to 31 at 12 months, and the number showing Customs Inspection rises at 12 months correspondingly. It appears that at 12 months fewer infants were indiscriminately social, and more showed capacity for calm visual appraisal of the stranger. The greater frequency of Soberness at six months may reflect a wariness that in succeeding months matures to Customs Inspection.

TABLE 41

POSITIVE RESPONSIVENESS AND APPREHENSIVENESS AT SIX MONTHS AND ONE YEAR

	Six Months		One Year	
	Positively Responsive	Apprehensive	Positively Responsive	Apprehensive
Positively Responsive (no other reaction)	51	0	31	0
Apprehensive (no other reaction)	0	4	0	3
Customs Inspection	25	6	47	7
Soberness	12	9	3	7
Mild Anxiety	6	5	7	11
Strong Anxiety	1	3	2	4
	95	27	90	32

Chi squares are significant at .001 level for both ages.

Of the 27 infants observed to be Apprehensive at six months, 11 were reported by their mothers to be Positively Responsive, but in four of the latter cases neither the mother nor we observed any additional degree of awareness of the stranger as such. Of the 32 infants observed to be Apprehensive at 12 months, six were reported to be Positively Responsive; but all six were also reported, and four were observed, to show some additional degree of awareness of the stranger. The maternal reports about Apprehensive infants were thus less broadly positive at one year than at six months.

While Positive Responsiveness may be construed as showing positive capacity to accept the stranger, Apprehensiveness need not in itself be construed as absence of the capacity, or as evidence of anxiety. Depending upon the context in which the infant is neither spontaneously Outgoing nor Responsive, his behavior may signify a capacity for cautiousness, or a passing mood, or a temporary indisposition. Customs Inspection, however, does appear to us to signify that effort is being made to work through a normally anxious reaction to the stranger. It indicates that the infant recognizes the stranger as different, and is working visually toward a judgment of the stranger's acceptability. Since this act of judgment is a result of major infantile advances in ego development, we feel it would be confusing to describe it solely as a reaction of anxiety *unless one explicitly means signal anxiety*. We therefore prefer to retain the name *stranger anxiety* only for instances where the infant reacts with overt fear visible in prolonged stillness or soberness, or prolonged restlessness, or turning away or clinging, or audible in whimpering, crying or screaming.

Accordingly, we regard Positive Responsiveness and Customs Inspection as normative and benign reactions to strangers; nondifferentiation as an absence of positive reaction but of equivocal import without knowledge of its context; and Soberness, Mild Anxiety, and Strong Anxiety as indicative of stranger anxiety. Statements about stranger anxiety following here refer only to the latter three reactions, unless otherwise noted.

Thus, a re-examination of Table 41 shows that in the Positively Responsive group of 95 infants at six months, 76 reacted to the stranger with equanimity and 19 with anxiety. In contrast, in the Apprehensive group of 27 infants, only six reacted with equanimity (Customs Inspection) and 17 with anxiety. Four did not differentiate the stranger in any way. The difference between the two groups is significant at the .001 level.

The same relationship obtains at age 12 months (Table 41): of 90 infants in the Positively Responsive group, 78 reacted to the stranger with equanimity, and 12 with anxiety. In contrast, in the Apprehensive group of 32 infants, only seven reacted with equanimity (Customs Inspection) and 22 with anxiety. Three did not differentiate the stranger in any way. The difference between the Positively Responsive and Apprehensive groups is again significant at the .001 level.

TABLE 42

REACTIONS TO STRANGERS
POSITIVE RESPONSIVENESS AND CUSTOMS INSPECTION
VERSUS OVERT ANXIETY AT SIX MONTHS

	Positive Responsiveness and Customs Inspection	Overt Anxiety	Total
Positively Responsive	76	19	95
Apprehensive	6	17	23[a]
Total	82	36	118

Chi square = 25.505.
[a]Four of the 27 infants in the Apprehensive group showed no differentiated reactions.

At both six months and 12 months, stranger anxiety was significantly more frequent among infants who were neither Positively Responsive nor showed Customs Inspection (Tables 42 and 43).

Of 66 infants who reacted with Customs Inspection and no stranger anxiety at both six months and one year, 60 were in the Positively Responsive group and six in the Apprehensive group, a significantly smaller proportion (Table 44).

Of 14 infants who showed stranger anxiety at both six months and one year, eight were in the Positively Responsive

TABLE 43

REACTIONS TO STRANGERS
POSITIVE RESPONSIVENESS AND CUSTOMS INSPECTION
VERSUS OVERT ANXIETY AT ONE YEAR

	Positive Responsive-ness and Customs Inspection	Overt Anxiety	Total
Positively Responsive	78	12	90
Apprehensive	7	22	29[a]
Total	85	34	119

Chi square = 44.43
[a]Three of the 32 infants in the Apprehensive group showed no differentiated reactions.

TABLE 44

CUSTOMS INSPECTION AND NO STRANGER ANXIETY IN
POSITIVELY RESPONSIVE AND APPREHENSIVE GROUPS:
SIX MONTHS AND ONE YEAR

	Customs Inspection and No Stranger Anxiety	Stranger Anxiety	Total
Positively Responsive	60	35	95
Apprehensive	6	21	27
Total	66	56	122

Chi square = 14.3.
Significant at .001 level.

group and six in the Apprehensive group, a significantly
higher proportion (Table 45). This reaffirms the greater tendency of Apprehensive infants to show stranger anxiety over
a prolonged period of time, and to fail to experience, through
Customs Inspection, signal anxiety in an adequate degree.

TABLE 45

STRANGER ANXIETY ONLY IN POSITIVELY RESPONSIVE AND
APPREHENSIVE GROUPS: SIX MONTHS AND ONE YEAR

	Stranger Anxiety Alone	Other	Total
Positively Responsive	8	87	95
Apprehensive	6	21	27
Total	14	108	122

Chi square = 3.84.

At six months, 28 infants were reported to show fear of
specific persons. Of these, 23 were in the Positively Responsive group and five in the Apprehensive group (Table 46). As
seen above (Table 42), in the Positively Responsive group as
a whole at age six months, 19 infants showed stranger anxiety,
and in the Apprehensive group as a whole 17 did so. Thus, of
six-month-olds reported or observed to show fear of strangers
of any kind or degree (Table 46), a significantly higher proportion of the Positively Responsive group showed Specific
Avoidance than showed stranger anxiety. That is, of 42 infants
in the Positively Responsive group, in whom fear of the stranger was evident at six months, in 23 the fear was limited to
specific persons. In contrast, of 22 infants in the Apprehensive group in whom fear of the stranger at that age was evident, in only five was the fear limited to specific persons.

TABLE 46

SPECIFIC AVOIDANCE AND STRANGER ANXIETY IN
POSITIVELY RESPONSIVE AND APPREHENSIVE GROUPS:
SIX MONTHS

	Specific Avoidance	Stranger Anxiety	Total
Positively Responsive	23	19	42
Apprehensive	5	17	22
Total	28	36	64

Chi square = 7.01.

At one year, 53 infants were reported to show Specific Avoidance. Of these, 44 were in the Positively Responsive group and nine in the Apprehensive group (Table 47). As seen above (Table 43), 11 infants in the Positively Responsive group showed overt stranger anxiety at one year, and in the Apprehensive group 22 did so. Thus, among one-year-olds reported or observed to show stranger anxiety of any kind or degree, again in the Positively Responsive group a significantly higher proportion of infants showed Specific Avoidance. That is, of 55 infants in the Positively Responsive group in whom fear of the stranger was evident, 44 showed Specific Avoidance. In contrast, of 31 infants in the Apprehensive group in whom fear of the stranger was evident, nine were reported to show Specific Avoidance.

To the extent that the maternal reports are accepted as reliable, the indications are that infants who are spontaneously or reactively outgoing show fear of discrete aspects of strangers more than apprehensive infants do so. This may imply that positively responsive infants perceive *Gestalten* earlier or better, or achieve a higher degree of visual discrimination, than do infants who are negatively responsive. For the latter, stranger anxiety may take a more general or more inchoate form.

TABLE 47

SPECIFIC AVOIDANCE AND STRANGER ANXIETY IN POSITIVELY RESPONSIVE AND APPREHENSIVE GROUPS: ONE YEAR

	Specific Avoidance	Stranger Anxiety	Total
Positively Responsive	44	11	55
Apprehensive	9	22	31
Total	53	33	86

Chi square = 21.7.
Significant at .001 level.

Since our data regarding infants' reactions to strangers include observations made and reports cited only at ages six months and one year, and referring only to current or to recently observed behavior, no inferences can be made regarding the normative peaks of Custom Inspection or of Stranger Anxiety. It is noteworthy, however, that if we differentiate the benign inspecting behavior from patently fearful behavior, we see that at six months 82 infants (Table 42) and at one year 85 infants (Table 43) showed no stranger anxiety. The distinction between the two kinds of reaction is important because Customs Inspection implies early ego functioning of a more mature nature, and the emergence of a preparedness for signal anxiety.

It appears that, at any period of infancy, understanding of stranger anxiety requires consideration of a large number of variables in addition to infant age, and of such complex factors as drive endowment and maternal behavior and attitudes. To the latter material, information needs to be added regarding a variety of data: the infant's state when the stranger is sighted; whether in the presence of the mother or of another familiar person, or when alone; where the stranger is seen; the manner of the stranger's approach; the frequency with which the infant has been in the presence of strangers; the behavior of the mother in the stranger's presence; the quality and quantity of external stimulations usually available to the infant; the length of time necessary for the infant to recover a positive mood if he has been disconcerted by the stranger; and the stability of his recovery.

The development of tolerance of brief separations from the mother, of social responsiveness, and of the readiness to carry out Customs Inspection, all signify that a reduction of infantile narcissism and a concomitant increase of positive object cathexes are proceeding. The infant who has developed a capacity to respond alertly and positively to new persons, who tries to locate them in the real external world, obviously will be less prone to be threatened by unfamiliar situations. If this is so, then separation anxiety, that is, the failure to experience and to utilize signal anxiety (by watching and waiting) when the mother is missing, may derive in part from an earlier-appearing failure to experience and to utilize signal anxiety (gazing and searching) in the presence of a stranger. While fear of the strange is not equivalent to fear of object loss, as discussed at length by Benjamin (1961), the chronological interval between awareness of the stranger as such, often before six months, and awareness that object loss is possible, often after six months, is in actuality so short that the state of the infant's object cathexes in the midst of his first year would appear to influence his reactions to both the stranger's presence and the mother's absence.

CHAPTER 16

The Balance of Development

When all 118 infants in the seven maternal types are ranked according to both the number of SDi and the number of SFD (Rank 1 is assigned to the case with the fewest SDi and again to the case with the most SFD), and the rank-order correlation rho is computed, an increasingly strong relationship between the absence of SDi and the presence of SFD is found. The converse is also true. Rho increases from .442 at age six weeks to .675 at age one year, and is in every case significant at the .01 level. When this relationship is examined separately for the infants of the seven maternal types, those of types III, V, and VI yield results very similar to those obtained from the total sample. Infants of maternal types I, II, and IV show rank-order correlations that are, for the most part, of similar magnitude, but whose age-to-age changes are not unidirectional.

It has become evident that for all three infant ages the significance of Signs and sets of Signs is based upon high frequencies of favorable signs and low frequencies of unfavorable signs in the infants of type I mothers. When the 118 infants of the seven maternal types were ranked according to fewest number of SDi, and also according to greatest number of SFD, the top 25 in rank were to a large degree made up of infants of type I mothers, as shown in Table 48. Other infants represented in the top 25 in rank were almost entirely those of mothers of types II, V, and VI.

The 25 infants in the bottom rank, i.e., those with most SDi and fewest SFD belonged to mothers of all types, but with notably few from type I. The exact numbers belonging to type I mothers at the three ages are shown in Table 49. For infants of the other six types of mothers, the numbers of both kinds of Signs appeared to vary randomly.

TABLE 48

INFANTS OF TYPE I MOTHERS IN TOP 25
RANK OF SIGNS

Age	Lowest Number of Signs of Disturbance	Highest Number of Signs of Favorable Development
Six Weeks	13	7
Six Months	10	12
One Year	13	14

TABLE 49

INFANTS OF TYPE I MOTHERS IN BOTTOM 25
RANK OF SIGNS

Age	Highest Number of Signs of Disturbance	Lowest Number of Signs of Favorable Development
Six Weeks	0	1
Six Months	2	2
One Year	2	1

The foregoing findings have a clear relationship to early ego development and to maternal influences upon it. The steady increase in rho from six weeks to one year implies that the greater and longer the exposure of the infant to the maternal environment, the more clearly does the negative relationship between SDi and SFD emerge.

If the findings are evaluated from the viewpoint of ego development, the following summary statements may be offered:

1. There are no infants without some SDi. One cannot speak of neurosis in the infant, but our findings may mean that normal ego development does not proceed without psychic disturbance, and that infantile disturbance may serve as an initial organizing point for later neurotic conflict.

2. In general, the more SFD, the fewer the SDi, and conversely, the more SDi, the fewer the SFD. This suggests that, at least during infancy, compensations for unfavorable aspects of development are rare.

3. In general, it does not appear that large amounts of anxiety in the infant makes for precocious ego development, although it may push him into a defensive acquisition of compensatory skills. If there is a relationship between anxiety and precocious ego development, it must appear at a later period of childhood.

Although we have been able to delineate seven types[1] of maternal behavior on a clinical basis through the first year of the infant's life, and to substantiate the types behaviorally at the infant age of six weeks, in many instances single Signs and sets of Signs, and DQs, are not discriminable (statistically significant) for infants of each of the maternal types at age one year. When the statistically significant Signs and DQs are analyzed for contribution of maternal type to the statistical significance, the differences are in the expected direction for all but two SDi at one year, both with low frequencies. We are still left, however, with the question of why the distributions

[1]The relation between these seven types and four types discriminated in the earlier study of maternal behavior with infants (Brody, 1956) will be presented in a separate publication.

were not statistically distinguishable for the infants of each of the maternal types.

A number of answers can be suggested. The most probable is that 118 is too small a number for discrimination among seven groups. If we had had triple the number of cases the distributions might very well have been statistically significant for the infants of each of the seven maternal types. Another possibility is that although seven types of maternal behavior have been firmly established, the effects of the maternal behavior upon the infant behavior and development may have been too fine to be ascertained at the infant age of one year.[2] This point is supported by the fact that when Signs, sets of Signs, and DQs were reanalyzed on the basis of only three maternal types, I, VI, and all others (II, III, IV, V, VII) in combination— or, to put it in more popular language, most adequate, next most adequate, and inadequate mothers— many more Signs and sets of Signs achieved significance, and always in the expected direction.

Finally, it is possible that in the selection of Signs we failed to recognize important behaviors, states, or conditions, as no really refined theory of emotional and cognitive development of the infant yet exists. We proceeded empirically, in the pejorative sense of the word, for lack of a truly systematic theory and of exact specifications of favorable and unfavorable signs of behavior and development.

To summarize the research of the Infant Development Research Project as described in Parts II and III of this book:

Seven types of maternal behavior with infants were discriminated and found to remain stable throughout the infant's first year of life. Infants of one year with high Developmental Quotients, advanced behavior and development, and moderate or few signs of disturbed behavior and development, were found to belong to mothers of certain types. Conversely, in-

[2]We do not yet know whether our longitudinal study of the infants will bear out, during their childhood, the usefulness of establishing as many as seven types.

fants of one year with low Developmental Quotients, no advanced behavior and development, and many signs of disturbance, were found to belong to mothers of certain other types. We have demonstrated an empirical relationship between types of mothering and aspects of infant development at the end of the first year of life. In general, for our population, the more adequate the mothering, the better the development of the infant; the less adequate the mothering, the poorer the development of the infant. These findings indicate that a dynamic process of mother-infant interaction has been tapped, and that its effects at the end of the infant's first year can be distinguished.

The significance of this interaction and its relationship to ego development are dealt with in Part V.

Part IV
MOTHERS AND INFANTS: THE TYPES ILLUSTRATED

Introduction

Seven mother-infant pairs have been selected to exemplify the seven types of behavior observed among the mothers and their infants through the first year of life. Mothers with many kinds of experience and many kinds and degrees of conscious and unconscious conflicts may show similarities of expressive and defensive behavior, and many mothers with overtly different expressive and defensive behavior may have similar conflicts. Our aim is limited here to illustrating briefly some varieties of maternal behavior and infant development, in order to illuminate processes of interaction that appear to contribute to essential aspects of ego formation in the young child.

The case material necessarily includes many details. Infant behavior normally undergoes changes in all aspects of growth, at variable rates, with plateaus, regressions, and accelerations of many forms. The mutual adaptation of mother and infant may be expected to undergo alterations as well, and the forms of activity and the attitudes aroused or reinforced in the mother may be protean. Too sharp summarization of behavior therefore would do injustice to the significance of (objectively) small units of experience.

Variations in the formal content of the case material are to be understood as resulting directly from variations in the actual experiences of the mother or in her reports. For example, only one mother made both frequent and consistently positive references to her husband, and only one breast fed her baby beyond the first three weeks. All the mothers' statements have been kept as close as possible to the verbatim records and set in their true contexts. The very abbreviated descriptions of the infants that have been drawn from clinical and behavioral observations are meant to be compared with the maternal statements. It will become evident that the latter were often self-contradictory or contrary to fact, but it has seemed to us unnecessary to spell out the agreements and disagreements between reports and observations.

Manifold relationships between maternal behavior and attitudes and infant experiences and capacities can be construed at every age in every case. We shall highlight chiefly those which have most direct bearing upon anxiety and ego formation, at the successive observations of the infants.

For each case, data are selected from the following:

1. The Prenatal Interview:[1] statements by the mother about her childhood relationship to her own parents, particularly regarding degrees of affective support and of controls given by them; her education, aspirations, and present use of leisure time; child-rearing attitudes; anticipated (or imagined) strengths and weaknesses as a mother; experiences she considers important for an infant during infancy; and attitudes toward her husband, his work, and his possible care of the infant.

2. The Neonatal Examination: the infant's appearance; degree of activity, muscle tone, and turgor; the balance observed between relaxation and tension; sensorimotor responses; irritability; mouthing behavior; and adequacy of feeding.

3. The Confinement Visit: the mother's comments about the baby, the delivery, and hospital care.

4. Interviews and observations carried out during the subjects' visits at the ages of six weeks, six months, and one year:[2] descriptions of the mother's appearance, behavior, and

---

[1] See Appendices for interview forms.

[2] To allow for practical difficulties of scheduling visits by the mother and infant to the project quarters (bad weather, illness, etc.), the research design was to observe the infant at the stated ages, plus or minus two weeks, with less latitude at the earlier ages. This plan was, of course, not regularly practicable or feasible. For example, Mrs. E came for her last visit when the baby was only 47.2 weeks old,

attitudes; observations of the infant's behavior and general development; maternal reports about the infant's behavior and development, and about her own attitudes and infant care.

5. Clinical Impressions of the Mother: observations of and comments about the mother's self-evaluations as a mother, her enjoyment of mothering, her capacity to report objectively, and her emotional responsiveness to the infant's demands and to the infant as a person.

6. Clinical Comments about the Infant: for each of the infant-age levels, the comments are related to the following:

SIX WEEKS

1. Anxiety preparedness. As defined above (p. 56), an adaptive reaction occurring in active and passive accommodation to stimuli; and an emerging tendency to appeal for help, operative when stimuli become excessive.

2. The first phase of socialization. As described above (p. 78), we have hypothesized that it is characterized by imprinting of the mother as a species-specific object, and that it begins during the first six weeks of life.

SIX MONTHS

1. The emergence of signal anxiety. This is to be seen in evidence that physiological stress has been converted to psychological stress, and in the capacity of the infant to marshal inner resources, or to appeal in a directed fashion for external help, to relieve the stress.

2. The completion of the first phase of socialization, and the progress in the second phase of socialization. As indicated above (p. 81), our hypotheses are that the first phase encompasses the attainment of consciousness, and ends in the third

---

because the family was to move to the Midwest two days later. Mrs. G asked to be allowed to come for her first visit when the baby was only 4.3 weeks old because she felt housebound and was longing to go out.

or fourth month with the imprinting of the mother as a species-specific object; and that the second phase is marked by the discrimination of the mother as an individual: she becomes the specific imprinting object. Accordingly, the infant's capacity to differentiate the mother from nonmothers, to demand gratifications from her specifically and primarily, and to seek gratifications from inanimate objects *in addition*, may be regarded as milestones to pass in moving toward completion of the second phase of socialization, at approximately six months.

ONE YEAR

1. The stability of the signal anxiety so far achieved.
2. Object relations.
3. The level of ego functions.

These combined developments are to be seen in the balance of cathexes of the infant's body, people, and objects; his ability to tolerate frustration, his social responsiveness, his freedom in converting his earlier narcissism into an encounter with the world in which he can be positively affected, and his cognitive abilities.

CHAPTER 17

Type I: Mrs. A and Amy

Mrs. A was relaxed and tidy. Her smile and her attentiveness were encouraging to the interviewer. She listened to be sure she understood the questions put to her, answered as fully as she could, and was pleased to speak about herself and her family. Her choice of words was excellent, although occasional mispronunciations suggested a limited education. Varying facial expressions told the extent of her emotional mobility as humor, reflectiveness, sadness, shame, joy, poise, all appeared in appropriate contexts. Her sixth child was soon to be born, and she felt happy because her whole family was as eager as she for another member of the family.

She is the fifth and youngest child of poor parents. Her father died when she was seventeen. As a child she had felt deeply ashamed of him because he was alcoholic, and she has no specific memories of what he was like or of any activity with him, even talking to him; yet she carries about a tormenting idea that he was brutal to her mother. The idea has been entirely denied by a brother whom she trusts and who has tried to revive for her the memory of the father as a sad immigrant aching to regain a lost dignity. Her mother had loved him deeply and always remained loyal to him, taking over his tasks in the building he superintended and never complaining. Mrs. A describes her mother, who has also since died, with intense admiration and affection. Then she weeps with shame and guilt, because of the persistent vague memories of her father shouting at and wanting to hit her mother, "memories" which she now believes must have been only fantasies. She does

255

recall that when her father was not drunk he was kindly and tender; that he had agreed with his wife's attitudes about the importance of education and had been very strict about his children's school attendance.

Mrs. A had wished to study English or biology in college, but had to work as a stenographer before her marriage. Mr. A, a chauffeur, also was not able to afford college education. He has no intellectual interests, and feels unable to be involved in the children's school life, although he wants to know everything about it. Mrs. A is very sorry that he misses the direct pleasure of knowing about their school activities. He loves to help her with the children in every other way and to take the family on outings.

Mrs. A and her husband both wish she could nurse the new baby, though probably she will not because the home is so crowded and their 14-year-old son might be too embarrassed by it. She is sorry, because breast feeding is a wonderful experience. She breast fed her first baby for nine months, the next two a shorter time, and the latest two not at all, because of the needs of the rest of the family.

Mrs. A says she is lenient with babies. She tries to do what's convenient, maybe too much so ... The feeding schedule will be flexible. It may depend on whether Mrs. A can get some help from the other children, but she won't require them to take over obligations that belong to her or her husband. She will hold the baby for his feedings for the first month and prop the bottle afterward if necessary, but always within her sight. She has no use for pacifiers ... She can't imagine any habit that she might be concerned about during the baby's early years ... She doesn't believe in slapping a child although she might be impelled to if, for example, an 18-month-old touched a hot radiator. If he touched a lamp she herself might push it over to show what might happen ... Her children were a little difficult when they learned to walk and crawl and to scream "No!," but on the whole they have presented no problems. Mrs. A may be quick to raise her hand, but neither she nor her husband make a practice of swatting the children. Mr. A is helpful because he speaks to them in a proper, strict way when necessary. The best punishment Mrs. A has ever thought of or needed was to deprive the children the privilege of going outdoors on a summer day ... The children's happiness is more important than the state of the furniture. Neither she nor her husband like destructiveness, but they find scolding sufficient to deal with it. They would never shame a child ... For toilet training Mrs. A uses a potty chair, and then always has a step for the child to get up onto the real toilet; at the moment, for her youngest child (age three), she is using an old milk case. Learning to use the toilet is such a big thing in itself that all the other aspects of it should be made as easy as possible. Mr. A is the one who usually initiates the toilet training of the children, kindly and firmly. He is wonderfully sensitive with the children, which Mrs. A marvels at because *his* father so lacked this quality.

Babies need most of all a great deal of loving. They need to be played with and talked to even if just brothers and sisters do this when the parents have no time . . . Her hope for all the children's future is that they will have the warmth from a father that she never received . . . Children never should be left alone—though of course they must be, sometimes. She herself may have to go to work in the future. A little baby is easiest to leave with someone because "They sort of stay put—but you can't help looking in on them, anyway."
. . . There never was a day in her childhood when she came home from school and was alone. Her mother was always there with a greeting, and that was wonderful . . . Mrs. A's strength as a mother, stated somewhat apologetically, as if too simple," . . . is that I'm there." Her weakness lies in being lenient, maybe not demanding enough. It is so fortunate that her husband can demand enough, and consistently. With reference to child rearing in general, Mrs. A reflects, "It's so easy to be critical of other people's children."

THE CONFINEMENT VISIT

Mrs. A spoke with joy of having pleased her husband with another daughter, in whom she already saw individual and charming qualities. At first Amy had looked just like all the other children, cut from the same pattern, but now she was taking on her own shape.

Mrs. A had no preanesthesia for the delivery, which took six-and-a-half hours. That, said Mrs. A, seemed short to everybody *else*. On inquiry, she expressed several complaints about the nonchalance of doctors and nurses in the delivery room; in contrast, the care of the ward nurses seemed to her entirely satisfactory. She was not yet eager to go home, but knew she would be in a few days. She gave the impression of being warm and confident. The nurses described her as "radiant all the time."

The Neonatal Examination

Amy was a very fair, pink-skinned baby, very quiet, with a normal degree of activity. Her movements were smooth, narrow in range, and a little less diffuse than that of most neonates. Now and then she extended her legs smoothly and with a quality of relaxation. Muscle tone was good, turgor intermediate. She adapted easily to all physical handling. Slight tension rose when she was pulled to sitting. In the prone, she turned her head to a side readily. No irritability and no crying were observed, and very little mouthing occurred.

Auditory reactions were excellent. She listened persistently to both the rattle and the bell.[1] Visual fixation was good, as horizontal pursuit of the red light was questionably present. Response to tactile stimulation was also adequate, as Amy made movements of head and mouth at the touch of the gauze upon her face. The persistence and vigor of her responsiveness was, in general, moderate.

Before feeding Amy was entirely peaceful. She required a little stimulation to begin sucking, and took three ounces of formula adequately. Gradually she lost interest, hiccoughed slightly, and fell asleep. She was described by both the mother and nurses as never fussing at feeding times, and usually being a bit sleepy.

The Six-Week Visit: Infant Age 6.3 Weeks

Mrs. A looked less neat than she had two months earlier. Her once-fancy dress fit poorly, her hair needed combing, her grooming was very plain. She was at ease nevertheless, and retained a very warm and appealing quality. Speech, action, and feeling were well integrated and she provided information very smoothly.

Amy was a fair, alert-looking, moderately active baby. During most of the time when she was not handled by Mrs. A, she lay supine in the crib, occasionally flexing her limbs. Her

[1]See Appendix 6.

movements were smooth and well coordinated, though not vigorous. She accommodated well to being held, cried when pulled to sitting, and made uneasy sounds when placed in the prone. Tension states fluctuated often, though mildly, and irritability was frequent, especially during testing and feeding.

Auditory responses were strong. Amy smiled at the sound of the bell and of her mother's voice, and frowned "inquisitively" when Mrs. A made clicking sounds to her. Visual responses to both the mother and test objects were strong and steady. She smiled again at sight of the dangling red ring. She paid no attention to the face or voice of the examiner. By error, tactile stimulation was omitted. Mild to moderate throaty vocalizations were heard almost constantly both before and during feeding. Little mouthing was seen. She brought her hand to her mouth only once or twice during the entire visit.

Impatience and irritability were conspicuous early in the feeding, for no discernible reason. She lay cuddled and relaxed in her mother's arms, with her eyes open throughout, but after 10 or 15 minutes she fussed considerably, and continued to do so until she fell asleep. Nevertheless she sucked steadily and finished four-and-a-half ounces of milk in half an hour.

> Amy is still fed mainly on formula, which she takes very well. She made a face when first offered cereal so Mrs. A put just a bit of it in her milk. A few days ago Mrs. A gave her some banana for the first time. Semisolids aren't necessary yet—Mrs. A hopes she is not mistaken about this. She holds Amy for all the feedings and often during the afternoon as well, the only exception being when busyness in the late afternoon makes it impossible. But then her 10-year-old daughter is often eager to hold and feed Amy, and does . . . Amy falls asleep easily, sleeps soundly, and on waking is easily comforted by being fed. The only change in regime Mrs. A looks forward to is Amy's sleeping through the night . . . Amy is so easy to please. Her greatest pleasure is being talked to. She isn't too restless or cranky without a good reason, like hunger, but even then Mrs. A's voice always consoles her. In fact, all members of the family enjoy talking to Amy and everyone except the smallest boys wants to hold her. "She has blended right into the house."

Years ago Mrs. A had feared she might not have love enough for her first two babies because they were so close in age. Now she realizes that her uneasiness came from her own need to go back to school, which she plans to do when Amy is old enough. She is so grateful to her husband for his unfailing help with the children.

Mrs. A's behavior toward Amy harmonized very closely with her expressed attitudes. She carried out all procedures with a quiet facility and often praised the baby's development. In spite of Amy's frequent fussing, especially after feeding, Mrs. A was never impatient. In fact, she explained that Amy was not restless or cranky without a reason. There were few moments when she did not sustain contact with Amy, vocally or tactually, and always she did so in a fond, gentle, and sensual manner that was pleasant to watch. She addressed the baby softly, used many pet names, and remained attentive and unruffled while Amy was cranky on her lap.

The Six-Month Visit: Infant Age 25.6 Weeks

Mrs. A. came poorly dressed, especially for the very bad weather. Her clothes were cheap, inadequate, and beaten. She entered with a smile, was cordial throughout the visit, and at the end looked forward to coming again. She looked happy and well.

In every way Amy was impressively robust. Her dress was old and only fairly neat. She was not big, but her body was extremely firm. Her movements were mild in range, not overly rapid, but strong and definite. Physical activity was prominent and there was a considerable variety to the positions she took as she moved about in the crib. Her facial expression was mature, her skin was rosy and tanned, and lots of blond hair gave a finished quality to her rounded face.

She responded to all test objects immediately, smoothly, enthusiastically. At sight of each she breathed fast, grew excited, beat her legs up and down when supine and kicked them when sitting, and many times sighed happily. She sat alone for the first time, leaned forward for a toy, and re-erected herself easily. Attention was consistently excellent. She never lost interest in any object, yet she remained good-humored as each one was removed. She explored them by mouthing, licking, biting, and scratching. She maturely divided her attention between the objects and the examiner, at intervals smiling to the latter and also turning to smile to her mother, who sat out of the baby's line of vision. Amy's vocalizations were very mature. Several consonants were clearly audible amid the bubble blowing and excited breath sounds, during testing. Her laughing responses to the mirror and the examiner alternately were a joy to watch. All test procedures were tolerated excellently in spite of Amy's having been expected to be hungry an hour earlier.

She showed abundant social vitality, eliciting responses from her mother and the examiner, and maintaining her attention to them even when her serious gaze temporarily traveled around the room. Many grades of smiling were observed, as well as crooked grins and smirks. Some mild thumb-sucking was seen, and more of a gentle tongue rolling. She held her bottle with very unusual adeptness. Her only mild objection was to being placed in the prone position, and she did not cry at all. Everything that Amy did had a steady, concentrated quality.

> Routines continue to go smoothly. Spontaneously and with much emotion Mrs. A says she regrets not having listened to her husband and breast fed Amy in spite of the given reasons because Amy is so good, she really deserved it . . . Everyone in the family plays with her a great deal except the youngest boy. She prefers people to things, by far. When she is alone during the day she loves to lie in her crib and bang her legs, so Mrs. A places her in a position where she can do so easily. Though Amy is physically quiet she has lots of leg power and can be resourceful in finding new positions. . . . It is hard to say what makes her cry, she so rarely does. On the contrary, she has been making such charming sounds, except for occasional screeches, that Mrs. A wishes she could record them. . . . Mrs. A feels happy to see that Amy loves people so much and is almost always in such a good mood. She has been taken with the family to many places with new people and she adapts readily to all of them. She loves being in the park, and loves

best of all to look up at the trees. "She thinks it's one big rattle."
... She minds only sudden loud noises, or rough handling. She
looks a little frightened if the other children get too active in their
play, so everyone tries to be gentle with her. ... The only thing
Mrs. A has been trying to teach her is to say dada and to wave
goodbye, both in vain. ... Mrs. A no longer attempts to hide her
pride in Amy's goodness and lovability, she says, but talks about
it openly. Amy irritated the family just one time, when during a
recent visit to a drive-in movie she may have felt overwhelmed by
having too many people about. Ordinarily she smiles abundantly
to everyone. ... The whole family likes to be together. Each child
has a pet name, a made-up, affectionate nickname that has no
relation to the real one. It is used until outsiders begin to pick it
up. ... Only the youngest boy doesn't like Amy so much. Maybe
all the troubles at his birth (mother's phlebitis) made her own
feelings toward him more complicated. She concludes, "But he is
jealous of Amy, and my heart goes out to him. I wish I knew how
to help him."

Mrs. A handled Amy most adeptly and lovingly, spoke to
her a great deal, and allowed her a great deal of initiative in
physical and playful activities. She laid no stress on the baby's
intellectual progress. Her emotional investment in Amy's general development and the pleasure she derived from her were
obvious and immense. She also had something positive and of
an individual nature to say about each of her children.

The One-Year Visit: Infant Age 52.1 Weeks

Mrs. A's dress was old, torn, and worn, yet as before her
bright and wholesome facial expression dominated her appearance. She enjoyed the interview and showed a remarkable capacity for attending to the baby and to the interviewer
simultaneously.

Amy's physical and perceptual development were superior, but because of a recently developed severe stranger
anxiety she stayed close to her mother and restricted her activity. Her small body size combined with this physical withdrawal gave her an appearance of immaturity except for her
shock of platinum hair, her striking brown eyes, and her very
serious regard.

Gross and fine motor coordination were very advanced. Although Amy did not feel free to cruise about the room, she was continuously and ably active, getting on and off her mother's lap, climbing onto her mother's shoulders, kissing and biting Mrs. A on the neck, twisting and turning, and eagerly pulling on Mrs. A's necklace until it broke. Her perception of relationships between objects was very superior. She matched, fitted, and handled all objects with ease, competently, and with obvious pleasure. She mouthed only one cube, which she kept in her mouth during testing until halfway through, when it dropped because she fussed. Her attention to objects was several times interrupted suddenly when in the midst of play she looked up and caught sight of the examiner. At once she closed her eyes, averted her head, and held her arms out to her mother.

She forgot her anxiety completely when shown the mirror, patted and kissed it many times gleefully, until she spied the examiner holding it, whereupon her smile vanished instantly and she buried her face in Mrs. A's shoulder.[2] She directed many specific sounds to Mrs. A and responded appropriately to all of Mrs. A's requests.

> Amy is taking table foods well and is now content to drink from a cup during the day. But there's no need to hurry weaning because of that. . . . She sleeps soundly and always awakens cheerfully. . . . She was fussy when teething, but otherwise everything has gone smoothly. She is more active and noisier than she used to be. She knows many games, plays with everybody in the family, loves to watch her brothers at play and to play with their toys, and loves to explore around the house. She does like to have people in the room with her, and screams to express this when alone for a while. . . . In restful moods, though, she plays by herself with pots and pans or magazines, enjoying her curiosity and often stopping

[2]Five months later, when Mrs. A came to hear our report on Amy's development in the first year, she reported that at about 14 months Amy had recovered from all of her shyness and fear of strangers. She could then be left by her mother without any difficulty. In all other respects as well Amy's behavior and development were very satisfactory.

to smile at whomever happens by. She has never been in a play-pen. . . . She makes her wants known by reaching or by uttering a little cry, but she has good capacity to wait for things. Crying occurs almost only when she falls, and her comfort is restored as soon as someone gives her some loving. . . . She gets stubborn only about dressing and undressing, which she fights like a tiger. Other-wise she hollers only if her face is washed. But Mrs. A has learned that if she uses smaller strokes Amy doesn't get as upset. . . . She may get into a bad mood if her schedule is upset. The children usually help to get her over it. They can't stand to see her unhappy and they do something immediately. . . . Amy is more cautious than any of the siblings were. She approaches new objects after some delay. For example, two weeks ago she seemed frightened by the Christmas tree. Mrs. A surmises that the cautiousness and the stranger anxiety, which set in about two months ago, may be a result of Amy's having been urged too much by her siblings to walk early, which she did at 10 months, and to perform too many tricks for guests.

Although Amy, on her mother's lap, looks as if she is biting hard, actually she has bitten her mother only once. . . . Her habits are swinging her legs to music, or bouncing up and down to the music. . . . She knows how to blow her nose. . . . Rarely has any scolding been called for—once during dressing, and once for pulling all the shoes and socks from a drawer. Mrs. A has never felt any provocation to hit Amy. Showing her some anger has always been enough. Mrs. A would be upset if Amy started to rip books, which Mrs. A loves so much, but then it would be her own responsibility to keep them out of Amy's reach. . . . Amy is quite undemanding except in the late afternoons. Actually she isn't demanding more, but Mrs. A just feels as if she is because there are so many things to attend to at that hour. . . . Amy is a greater source of pleasure to her than all her previous babies, maybe because she is so bright and cute, and reminds Mrs. A so much of her husband. He is so calm, pleasant, and consistent, whereas Mrs. A has her ups and downs. . . . Mrs. A beams in describing how "congenial" Amy is, and how much pleasure she has brought to the whole family. After her fear of strangers is over, Amy will probably be a calm, warm, and pleasant person. . . . Mrs. A is very happy about her husband's new job, and so glad and thankful to him for all his kindness.

Mrs. A seemed to adore the baby. She was modestly toler-ant of the baby's continuous activity in her lap, which was of a kind that upsets most mothers. Even when Amy broke her necklace, Mrs. A looked at her, called her a pet name, and told her that she had been trying to do that for months and finally had done it. Mrs. A initiated none of the physical activities which were so prominent in the baby's behavior. She did at times encourage the baby to explore about the room but accepted the fact that Amy was frightened and let her cling whenever she wished. At no time did Mrs. A prohibit anything, and her only discomfort with Amy lay in her mild helpless distress at the severity of the baby's avoidance of looking at strangers.

CLINICAL IMPRESSIONS: MRS. A

Mrs. A shows signs of strong identification with her mother's intense loyalty, tolerance, interest in education, and capacity to maintain the family integrity in spite of her husband's maladjustments.

Mrs. A decides to give up her wish to breast feed the baby so as to avoid disconcerting her adolescent son, thus denying herself (and by identifying the baby with herself, also denying the baby) a pleasure in favor of saving her son from displeasure. She seeks always to find a balance between satisfying the baby without dissatisfying the rest of the family, and securely emphasizes the primary significance of a baby's emotional satisfactions.

At the six-week visit Mrs. A's handling of the baby is unfailingly tender. She is free to enjoy sensual contact and to recognize and calmly respond to the baby's irritability. Perhaps there is overacceptance of it. The reports do not say whether the baby's fussiness might have been relieved by more action on Mrs. A's part, but this idea is supported by her description of the more active play with Amy that is offered by other members of the family. Mrs. A presents herself as the protective but quieter figure, who allows activity to others and is pleased enough when they find pleasure.

At the six-month visit Mrs. A is engrossed in all the positive aspects of Amy's development. Again her loving attitudes are conspicuous, as shown in her description of the private names, her tolerance of her youngest boy's aggressive feelings toward the baby and her wish to do more for him. She regrets not having breast fed the baby because the baby *deserved* it —a very atypical comment, as most mothers in a similar position find relief in showing that the baby obviously has done well without breast feeding.

At the one-year visit Mrs. A is remarkably tolerant of the baby's aggression, sees it as related to Amy's immediate stress, and maintains a good humor toward the baby. The habits which she cites are, except for the stranger anxiety, positive ones. She sees it as her own responsibility to teach the baby to avoid dangers and to find ways to make necessary experiences tolerable (face washing). She gladly allows her husband joint active responsibility for all of the children's care.

CLINICAL COMMENTS: AMY

Six Weeks

Amy shows a capacity for bodily relaxation. Although she appears mildly disturbed by inner stimuli she indicates discomfort mildly, and can be comforted. Alertness to external stimuli and tension tolerance are present. The development of anxiety preparedness appears to be close to optimal.

Imprinting to the mother as species-specific object may be inferred from her accommodation to Mrs. A and from her differential and positive responses to the mother in contrast to the absence of visual and auditory response to the examiner. Observations and reports indicate that she may already have attained a first level, or phase, of socialization.

Six Months

Evidence that signal anxiety has developed appears in Amy's reactions to harsh or strong external stimuli. Her general well-being, her freedom from internal and external stress, and her high level of performance, especially in the social area, are such that the capacity for signal anxiety is inferred.

Amy appears to have reached the end of the second phase of socialization. The mother may be regarded as the specific imprinting object, and receives the infant's primary object cathexis. Moreover, Amy's sensorimotor explorations are intense, that is, she seeks gratification from inanimate objects as well as from the mother, which implies that she is not solely dependent upon the mother for external stimulation. The mother is a primary *object*, separate, a person whose absence is not in itself a threat. In Mahler's terms (1966), a hatching process has been well under way.

One Year

Amy's capacity for signal anxiety is seen in her readiness to avert her eyes from the stranger and to appeal directly to the mother for help and safety, and to be comforted gradually, without reaching a state of panic. Except in relation to strangers, Amy responds actively and joyously to persons and things. She makes her wants known in sounds and gestures, and tolerates stimulation from a variety of persons. Conflict with the environment is minimal. Ego functions are advanced, as shown in her freedom of motor activities, her skill and joy in handling objects, her capacity to play alone, and her ability to wait for her needs to be fulfilled. There is an unusual balance of motor, perceptual, and social interests and activities. Frustration tolerance is high. She is so equable and emotionally accessible, and, if one may use the term for a one-year old, so reality oriented, and yet so able to insist that her appropriate needs be met, that her narcissism appears to be optimally distributed. Her cognitive abilities are high but obviously are interfered with by a current severe stranger anxiety. When the latter is not operative, function pleasure is keen. DQ: 114[3].

---

[3]As explained above (p. 143), calculated on a Binet type of scale.

CHAPTER 18

Type II: Mrs. B and Beth

Mrs. B is a chic, poised young woman, with a pleasant though restrained manner. She accepted some questions and did not answer others, with unchanging affect. She gave opinions with more ease than she gave facts about her life, and the attitudes she expressed about her childhood contradicted one another.

She is the elder of two siblings, both on good terms with their parents. She described her mother as an extrovert, a tense, nervous woman who was always busy and loved fussing over people, and who worked from the time Mrs. B began elementary school; and as she had grown up in Europe, she did not understand American children, and Mrs. B never felt close to her. Mrs. B's father is a postal clerk, quiet, retiring, and sensitive. Mrs. B has little to say about her childhood. Her life at home was average, pleasant, and she did well in school. She felt isolated from her parents and now believes that organization was lacking in her home. She feels that she was not disciplined sufficiently and became selfish. Apparently at the wish of her mother she attended a high school in another city, where she lived with relatives; she implies that her mother had hoped to improve Mrs. B's social status. As a result of her absence from home, general family friction grew in a home where formerly ties had been close. Her father had resented her going away and he never overcame his sense of loss. And whereas Mrs. B before leaving home had felt secure, with lots of friends, afterward she felt estranged. She did gradually become more sophisticated and intellectual. After a year at college she decided it was more important to work in a business office, and did so. Once she aspired to a career in fashions; now she thinks ahead of starting a small business. Mr. and Mrs. B have an active social life together and read a good deal.

Mrs. B has seen a 1936 copy of *Infant Care* and to her surprise found it rather enjoyable. She had thought she would breast feed until someone told her it was up to her to decide, and as her pediatrician says it isn't necessary unless she feels an emotional need to do it, she will not. She has read that weaning from the bottle is all right at six or eight months, but that you can also do it at three months or as soon as the baby can grasp something small. She expects not to use a bottle prop except in emergencies. She has no ideas for or against the use of a pacifier but would use one to prevent thumb-sucking. As the coming baby is Mrs. B's first, and she doesn't know what it's all about, she will rely upon her pediatrician for advice.

Toilet training should begin at about six months or sooner, when the baby is able to sit up without constant support. Mrs. A would start by using a potty or training seat. She doesn't know what happens after that but hopes that complete control, night and day, would be established by age two ... Discipline should begin as soon as the baby can see and understand and take any sort of direction—between the third and fifth month. Mrs. B imagines that she will not let the baby poke around on the cold floor much but will keep him in a playpen even if he begins to walk ... Habits begin in the third or fourth month and to prevent their development infants should be treated firmly, should be given limits right away. She wonders if she will spank a child. A good spanking now and then is useful because talk sometimes doesn't get one anywhere.

Mrs. B thinks her strength as a mother will lie in her being well adjusted and organized, and in her being able to give a child a sense of security and purpose. She could not stand a harried household. Her weakness may lie in excessive objectivity toward her child, in her being too much of a disciplinarian ... She hopes that if the baby is a boy, he will become professional ... Toys are important in infancy, especially cuddly ones; and a sense of security—being able to go to one's parents for comfort ... Mrs. B hasn't thought about delivery and anesthesia. If it is painful or unpleasant she will just put it out of her mind and think about the lovely aspects of having a baby.

The Confinement Visit

Mrs. B had wanted a boy, but said that as a baby's health is the most important thing, she was quite happy to have a girl. Her main comment about the baby was that she had no birthmarks, fortunately.

As she had wished, Mrs. B received preanesthesia medication at the beginning of labor (six-and-a-half hours), and experienced hardly any pain at all. She volunteered that she had had no anxiety at all because of her physician's reassuring explanations beforehand as to all that would happen. "I didn't need the experience of labor," she said. She was entirely satisfied with all aspects of her hospital care, but was eager to go home in order to see more of the baby. She was composed, poised, and emotionally reserved.

The Neonatal Examination

Beth was a relaxed, drowsy, inactive baby, who barely moved at all. Muscle tone was poor and turgor moderate. Her limbs were floppy and lacked resistance to pressure. She did not move her head when placed in the prone position. No irritability or crying occurred, and hardly any mouthing was seen.

Responsiveness was generally low. At the sound of the bell she only startled and blinked. Visual response could not be elicited. To the touch of gauze upon her face she reacted with only slight head movement.

Before feeding she was neither tense nor irritable. She sucked spontaneously, with increased alertness and moderate vigor. After she had taken two ounces in 15 minutes, she released the nipple with a grunt, a grimace, and a small vocalization. She then gagged, hiccoughed and spat up a little, and soon fell asleep.

The Six-Week Visit: Infant Age 7.4 Weeks

Mrs. B was self-possessed and good-humored. Her observations were told precisely and in general accorded well with the examiner's. She appeared to enjoy the interview and the visit.

Beth was a tall, thin baby, very appealing because of her mop of black hair. She was markedly active, kicking her legs repetitively and rapidly in both supine and prone positions, flailing her arms jerkily, and often startling. Occasionally her movements were very smooth. She responded to physical handling with increased activity and accommodated to being held by the examiner by slumping at her shoulder as if tired. Body tension appeared to be normal. When she was pulled to sitting, at first some head lag occurred but then she held her head erect, without bobbing.

Auditory responses were prompt, adequate, and well sustained. Visual responses were hard to elicit and short-lived. She did fixate upon the mother when Mrs. B stood at a distance of a few feet, and now and then fixated for minutes at a time on objects about equally distant, such as the brightly colored curtains. She was hardly aware of the examiner. She tried with moderate vigor to get rid of the cloth on her face; this tactile response elicited her strongest and most persistent effort. The test performance was interfered with by frequent states of irritability. It took much patience to arouse any personal responses, no smiling was observed, and most vocalizations were of a fussy nature. No mouthing or hand-to-mouth activity was seen.

Beth took her bottle with noisy and vigorous sucking, but when she gradually lost interest in it, Mrs. B continued to stimulate sucking and appeared to be forcing the feeding. It ended with fussing, which mounted when Beth was placed in the crib. Not until her sobbing reached a throbbing quality did Mrs. B decide to pick her up and offer some physical comfort.

The baby's feeding and sleeping are good. The evening schedule is not quite regular though, and sleep during the day is fitful. Often Beth cries out in her (night) sleep as if from a bad dream, and in the late mornings she is usually fretful. There are times when Mrs. B simply has to let her cry . . . The only thing that makes Beth unhappy is hunger. She may occasionally fuss if her diaper is soiled . . . In the daytime she is placed where Mrs. B can watch her and Mrs. B often talks to and fondles her. Typically the baby's mood is pleasant. She is happiest when held and talked to. She is not a crying baby (Beth was very irritable during this part of the interview), she can wait for things that she wants. But once she reaches beyond the point of tolerance she has a screaming, enraged cry that almost borders on a tantrum (observed when Mrs. B dressed her in outdoor clothing) . . . She has lots of gas and sometimes seems to be in agony.

Mrs. B handled the baby with obvious care, lovingly, and with assurance when specific tasks were to be accomplished. This was noticed especially during the very prolonged feeding. At other times she remained comfortably at ease while Beth lay restless in the crib. She mentioned with satisfaction that she had more patience in handling Beth than her husband did, especially with regard to feeding. She "loved having the baby around." Otherwise she alluded spontaneously to Beth only once.

THE SIX-MONTH VISIT: INFANT AGE 24.3 WEEKS

Mrs. B came smartly dressed, friendly, and was at ease. She spoke simply, directly, with light involvement, no digression, and much emphasis on orderliness of routines. She had all the facts in hand but showed no urgency to tell them. It seemed more important for her to show composure about her personal relationships, quiet control of her feelings, and satisfaction in taking all direction from her pediatrician.

Beth was a small, very neatly dressed little girl, well built, and strikingly beautiful. She had an alert, intense gaze. In the supine position she moved her limbs vigorously, extensively, and rapidly. She was placed in a sitting position for the first time during testing, could not sit erect, and appeared to be trying to orient herself to it, with silence and stillness and inhibition of arm movement. She responded visually to the few objects placed before her and tried to reach them only with her mouth. Even in the supine, however, she made no attempt to reach for them and when they were placed in her hand she took them to her mouth.

Most of the time she was left in the infant seat in a half-reclining position, from where she looked around a great deal, vocalized strongly and almost continuously, and took long, penetrating looks at the observer. She sucked her finger, but poor coordination made it hard for her to do so persistently. She also tried to mouth the side of the seat.

Socially she was very responsive, often waggling her arms as she smiled, and babbling loudly and clearly. She spied the observer at once, initiated and always responded to smiles, and objected to being left in a place where no person was in view. Occasional sounds of complaint changed to coos when she was picked up and cuddled by Mrs. B. No signs of negativism or anger or withdrawal appeared at any time.

Beth takes food well. When occasionally relatives feed her they let her spurn some foods because they are afraid she'll gag or some harm would come if they forced her to eat, but Mrs. B insists that Beth eat what she is given ... Beth falls asleep easily and sleeps soundly ... Mrs. B spends more time with her than anybody else does, playing with her mainly during meal times and when outdoors. She talks and sings to her, sometimes teaches her to play with toys or to imitate sounds ... Beth is most attracted to objects that have color and pattern but she also is glad to play with her own hands and feet and likes to feel for her ears ... Mr. B spends a little time with her and now and then may give her the bottle. He isn't very patient and doesn't care to teach her anything.

Beth prefers her mother, likes being held by anyone, and loves people. She has been somewhat demanding at times when Mrs. B has lots of other things to do in the household. "She's not that bad. I don't mind taking care of her because she is not a cranky or pesty baby." ... Mrs. B supposes that soon Beth will start crawling into cabinets and closets and will make a nuisance of herself in general but that just means Mrs. B will have to watch her ... She is trying to have Beth hold her bottle and also to use a cup, but has given up the latter on the advice of her pediatrician ... She is not trying to teach the baby anything.

Mrs. B made few attempts to communicate with Beth during the visit, but she protracted the feeding into a long engagement. After saying that Beth had had enough potatoes and was about to gag, she persisted in feeding them long after the baby was satisfied, and then she did the same with the fruit. It seemed extremely important to her that Beth finish all of the food and she kept urging it upon her, increasing the speed of the feeding as she neared the end of the supply. She expressed no pride in the baby, showed no pleasure in handling her, had no questions about her development, but appeared to be satisfied and approving of her. Her manner of stating that she did not teach the baby anything implied that she had no wish to "push" the baby, and that "teaching" was something she would definitely not endorse.

Mrs. B had consulted several doctors because of tiredness and dizzy spells and had been found to be slightly anemic. She attributed the fatigue to responding to so many demands of the baby. Mr. and Mrs. B were soon to go for a week's vacation, leaving Beth with a relative.

The One-Year Visit: Infant Age 55.0 Weeks

Mrs. B was elegantly dressed and overtly relaxed. She was easy to interview. Her very winning smile conveyed warmth and a capacity to show affection, but she mainly showed an over-all need to present herself as calm, secure, able to deal with all eventualities. There were no visible alterations of affect as she related pleasing or displeasing facts.

Beth was of average size but her facial expression and her attire were certainly those of an older child. Gross coordination was now excellent. She walked slowly but very steadily. She could stoop, play in the stooped position, and get up on her feet again. She went about the room investigating and bringing objects to the observer as if encouraging the latter to play with her, and otherwise giving much attention to big objects like wastebaskets, pieces of furniture, and doors. Many times she had to be rescued from pulling at and trying to bite electric wires. She accommodated well to handling.

Fine coordination was excellent. Hand motions were slow and confined in space, easy and economical. Her responses to test objects were usually delayed, and although intermittently she took great pleasure in handling them her attentiveness was moderate and had a lethargic quality very unlike the typical eagerness for objects of a lively one-year-old. She perceived relationships and could follow demonstrations, yet seemed not to enjoy the test situation. Her primary attention was given to the examiner.

Vocalizations were moderate in intensity but frequent, and they had an easygoing cheerfulness. She could say about 10 words. Mouthing activity was conspicuous in her biting of many objects.

Beth now takes table foods well, finishes them fairly quickly, and has no feeding difficulties at all. Occasionally she takes sips from a cup and she is trying to use a spoon. Again Mrs. B reports that her pediatrician has told her not to push cup feeding. But for some reason which Mrs. B can't understand, Beth gets very restless in the middle of her feedings, runs her hand through her hair, leans over her food, fusses, etc. Mrs. B tries to distract her with toys but that doesn't help much . . . When she is put in her crib for the night she yells a few times, "Just to let me know she doesn't like it," but gets over that quickly . . . Sleep is light and restless. After being awakened by little sounds she falls back asleep easily . . . She had had great difficulty teething: crying, vomiting, bleeding a little, getting constipated . . . Beth has been put on the toilet seat for the past week. She was very frightened after she urinated in it—maybe because of the sound. Mrs. B hopes to get her into a regular system soon. Beth has moved her bowels into the potty just once, and Mrs. B is soon going to place her on the toilet for 30 minutes after breakfast and dinner.

Beth is active, likes to walk about the apartment, exploring quietly and endlessly, that is, for as long as an hour. Sometimes she sits and plays with a doll or a book in the playpen, but she hates being put in it and screeches and whines for long periods of times, which makes Mrs. B very angry. (From Mrs. B's report it appears that Beth is kept in her crib or the playpen a great deal and probably most of the time when she is not fed, bathed, or taken out of doors.) . . . She screams during the entire time she is diapered. If something is taken away from her she also screams "bloody murder," flushes, and holds her breath. The best way to get her out of a bad mood is to talk to her, play little games or distract her. But she rarely stays in a bad mood long . . . On the whole, she doesn't

cry easily. After a recent fall off the toilet seat she didn't cry at all
—she did vomit and was pale, but she fell asleep and was all right.

Mrs. B plays little games with Beth, like hiding things in her
hand or showing Beth how to put on a scarf, which the baby
imitates, but doesn't try to teach her much, just a few words. She
doesn't really talk to the baby a great deal, but keeps the radio
on during much of the day so that Beth can listen to music
... Beth's greatest excitement occurs when she sees her Daddy,
who has little time to play with her—only about 10 minutes in
the evening, and just a little on weekends ... The baby prefers
to do things by herself rather than to watch people. She is very
independent. She can play alone, talking, singing, teasing the
dog, for an hour and a half ... If Mrs. B leaves her she cries
briefly, so Mr. B's mother says, but Mrs. B doesn't believe it. She
doesn't think Beth really cares. When Mrs. B returns, Beth
screams and laughs and wants to be picked up right away ...
Beth has never been afraid of anyone, but she does get frightened at the sound of the clock chimes.

Beth has several habits: finger-sucking, tonguing, pulling the
dog's hair, grabbing at people's faces, biting—twice her bites
have caused Mrs. B to bleed—playing with her navel and
scratching her belly, and sometimes rocking on all fours or
bouncing up and down on her feet. Mrs. B has had to be very
careful when holding her because of the grabbing and biting
... Beth has been slapped a number of times for picking up
things she shouldn't, or for whining for a long time. Mr. B slaps
her hands so hard they get red, yet Beth always laughs back
when slapped. Mrs. B has almost given up. Probably Beth is too
young to be disciplined. When she gets into trouble and Mrs. B
can't stop her, she just puts Beth into the playpen ... Mrs. B
continues to be troubled by anemia and dizziness, and attributes
all her physical distress to exhaustion from taking care of Beth,
who has become so heavy ... However, Beth is a very even-
tempered little girl, and easygoing. She is very friendly, loves
children, and is quite bright. Mrs. B imagines that Beth will be
a holy terror by age five, very outgoing and into everything, and
needing to be controlled.

Although Mrs. B seemed to be relaxed when speaking to
the interviewer, tension was immediately visible in her neck
and arm muscles whenever she spoke to the baby. During
much of the visit she yelled at the baby resentfully for touching things or she jumped up and grabbed them away. At other

times she looked at Beth fondly and seemed pleased with her play. It seemed that she feared the baby's getting into mischief or trouble. On the whole she kept a considerable distance from the baby. Most of her reactions were critical and complaintive. No particular aspects of Beth's personality appeared to give her particular pleasure except the ability to play independently. She asked no questions about Beth's progress or development and showed no interest in any observations that were made.

CLINICAL IMPRESSIONS: MRS. B

Mrs. B places high value on being well controlled and on her ability to discount emotional needs. One result appears to be an unawareness of inconsistencies in her statements. She sees her father as her less active and aggressive parent, regards him with a mild sympathy, and appears to have identified with her mother in seeking activities outside the home and in aspiring to social mobility upward. She anticipates being a competent and organized mother, a more objective caretaker than her own mother was. She gives no hint of expecting to enjoy her baby.

At the six-week visit her global positive reports are readily contradicted, as it is clear that the baby has unsatisfied needs that Mrs. B cannot acknowledge. Her responsiveness to the baby is restricted. She feels sure of exercising good judgment and is proud of her tolerance and imperturbability.

At the six-month visit Mrs. B is a little more accessible and attributes her better feeling to the baby's not demanding too much. She has conviction that her own demands are appropriate, as seen in her feeding and in her eagerness to accelerate the baby's independence. She is well in command and appears to have no awareness that the baby might benefit from more emotional overtures. She shows no eagerness or no knowledge of how to extend herself to the baby as long as there is no patent cause.

At the one-year visit she once more shows many signs of

wishing to hasten the baby's maturing and stresses as highly positive the baby's capacity to occupy herself independently. She seems sure that the baby does not need her as much as others might think, she does not take the baby's emotions seriously, and is angered by those demands of the baby that she cannot fathom. She shows tenderness to the baby only during routines, readily assumes a punitive attitude, and is not free to enjoy the baby. She anticipates more difficulties when Beth grows older (too independent?) and needs more supervision.

Mrs. B appears to have made a brittle identification with the active qualities of her mother, an identification which is threatened by any evocation of a passive position in relation to the baby. She denies a need to experience feminine body feelings and even a need to be protected from painful ideas. Similarly, she disparages the baby's emotional needs, the more as they become more manifest. She isolates affect regarding her maternal position and tries hard to remain impersonal. Despite her assumed neutrality, anxiety breaks through in the form of somatic symptoms.

CLINICAL COMMENTS: BETH

Six Weeks

Beth is almost eight weeks old when seen for this visit. Her sensorimotor responsiveness is moderate and uneven. States of irritability are frequent and disruptive, and may be interfering with a more balanced accommodation to stimuli and to anxiety preparedness. Imprinting to the mother as a species-specific object lags.

Six Months

Beth can make complaints known, and responds well to comforting, so that a measure of signal anxiety is present. However, when alone she resorts chiefly to motor activity and to mouthing. She responds to human objects much better than to inanimate ones, possibly because persons make overtures to her. Left to her own devices or not appealed to, Beth appears to become inhibited and bound up by her own body states. She is in the second phase of socialization, yet lacks a zestful response to the mother as a specific object.

One Year

Beth has achieved the capacity for signal anxiety, but we note that it is called up with high frequency. Feeding and sleeping evoke restlessness, premature toilet training has aroused fear, and numerous habits indicate the conversion of anxiety into regressive body preoccupations. Cathexis of inanimate objects is superior to cathexis of persons, including the mother: this is a partial reversal of the condition at six months. Frustration tolerance seems inadequate. To a marked extent, there has not been a sufficient progression of narcissism from her own body to investment in the world about her, and her cognitive style is hampered. DQ: 110.

CHAPTER 19

Type III: Mrs. C and Clem

Mrs. C was lithe and attractive. She sat forward, resting her chin in her palm, and kept tapping her feet impatiently. Now and then she smiled though mainly she seemed annoyed at having to talk. Her speech was abrupt and aggressive. She remarked that the interviewer's job must be very boring.

Mrs. C's father is a retired policeman, "a real man's man," rough and outspoken, yet quieter than her active and gregarious mother. As far back as Mrs. C can recall she wanted to be a nurse. She received her training right after high school, and likes best to work in hospitals where there is plenty of activity. She admires her husband's being able to work hard and play hard, too. They have few outside interests, are not readers, and spend leisure hours together watching TV.

Mrs. C plans to breast feed because it is good for the baby's health and to get a feeling of closeness with him, but probably she won't do so for more than a month as the summer is coming and it will be uncomfortable. She will feed on a demand schedule but at intervals of at least three hours. A baby should be held for feedings until he can hold his own bottle. Anyway, bottle propping is dangerous. She expects to wean to a cup at seven or eight months ... A pacifier is said to be harmless but it looks terrible, and a baby shouldn't need it ... Babies can learn to cry for attention in the first months and should not be treated leniently as they must learn to accept discipline early. She would allow a little fun but would be very firm yet probably less so than her parents were with her . . . A little slap on the hand is often necessary because children cannot be reasoned with, especially with regard to dangers, and they deserve to be spanked. As a child she was spanked but not beaten: "It was not brutal." . . . She will start toilet training at nine or 10 months, to avoid the resistance encountered with her first child (now age 18 months) whom she can neither toilet train nor wean from the bottle . . . Mrs. C sees her possible strength as a mother as doing what she thinks is right when she does it, though really she is not sure she has any strength. Her weakness is being easily made impatient. She has to work very hard to force herself to think before she acts . . . She has no ideas about her children's future except that she'd like them to go to college. As to important experiences in infancy, she considers that babies should be around lots of people and other babies even if they don't play together, so they won't shy away from strangers.

Mrs. C's responses were quite without elaboration, she had little facility in offering opinions, and often she had to be prodded for any reply. She treated the interview as a chore. Many times she asked how many more questions were to be asked.

THE CONFINEMENT VISIT

Mrs. C's first impression of the baby was that he was very big; her husband thought the baby looked like a football player, and was very happy to have a son. Mrs. C indicated no preference. She withheld comments about her feelings and thoughts, and in one-word replies said that labor (two hours, 20 minutes) and delivery had been fine because she had preanesthesia medication. Hospital care had been entirely satisfactory, and Mrs. C was eager to go home. She offered no reasons for her eagerness. Her breast feeding was also satisfactory, she said.

THE NEONATAL EXAMINATION

Clem was a full-cheeked, healthy-looking boy, with good pink color. He was markedly active, showed strong crawling movements, and carried out wide, sweeping arm movements as well. Muscle tone and turgor were good. Body tension was observed often, in rigid leg extension, in very strong resistance to pressure against his feet, and in a quick lifting of his head high when he was placed in the prone. When he was pulled to sitting, he held his head erect briefly.

Auditory response was excellent, as he listened to both the bell and the rattle persistently. No visual fixation could be aroused. He reacted to the tactile stimulus alertly, with specific head and mouth movements more than 50 percent of the time. Except visually, the vigor of his responsiveness was good.

Prior to feeding Clem was highly irritable and cried furiously. He quieted gradually while being fed. Sucking was spontaneous, eager, and rhythmic, and he maintained an alert appearance throughout. Mrs. C was observed to hold him very tightly and awkwardly. He took three ounces, hiccoughed slightly, and fell asleep.

The Six-Week Visit: Infant Age 6.2 Weeks

Mrs. C was dressed in a quite feminine way. Her manner, in contrast, was brusque, businesslike, and left no room for either frivolity or reflectiveness. She was entirely uninquisitive and was eager to leave as soon as the baby was fed.

Clem was a big, robust, attractive boy, alert to many kinds of stimuli in spite of continuous irritability. Physical movement was conspicuous in both supine and prone positions. He flexed and extended his limbs well, with good range, and had good head control although he did not hold his head erect when he was pulled to sitting. Because of tension and chronic fussing which seemed to be related to inner discomfort, he was not picked up by the examiner, who estimated that he would not accommodate well to extra handling.

The quality of his sensorimotor responses seemed to vary with his changing and uneven physiological states. Although his auditory response was at first delayed, his attention to the sound of the bell, once engaged, was quite good. His visual response was superior, as he sighted the dangling ring at the mid-line, and also followed it through an arc of 180°. He regarded both his mother and the examiner alertly. Mrs. C reported his having smiled at her, but this was not observed. Clem made vigorous and sustained efforts to remove the cloth from his face, tossing his head from side to side and flailing both his arms for almost 20 seconds. Vocalizations were mainly fussy. As reported and observed, Clem brought his fingers to his mouth only when hungry.

He cried intensely before feeding, gobbled his cereal rapidly, but lost appetite for his bottle very quickly. At Mrs. C's request, the test was carried out before she made another attempt to bottle feed: he then took barely an ounce, and the feeding ended with much crying and irritation on his part.

> Mrs. C gave up breast feeding and began feeding Clem cereals at age three weeks because he seemed hungry. Now he takes cereals and all fruits. His appetite, though, is unpredictable. He can seem hungry and then accept little food. The irritable feeding observed (several attempts) is typical. Mrs. C cannot tell if his crankiness is from still unrelieved hunger or from cramps ... It used to take over two hours to feed him a little bit of food because he fell asleep so much, but now he stays awake during feedings ... He falls asleep easily and sleeps soundly through the night with no night feeding ... He is made most unhappy by hunger, a soiled diaper, or an uncomfortable position. He always stops crying as soon as he is picked up ... He is fussy often ... He likes to see the rattle at the side of his bed ... Mrs. C can elicit a smile by just touching his face (not observed). She may talk to him a bit in the evening when she has time. Actually she takes pains not to spend much time with him because his sister Lucy is so jealous. Lucy was a good first baby; Clem is harder to understand. Lucy pays little attention to Clem. Mr. C talks to him a bit at times, or may feed him sometimes ... Mrs. C is not very good at routines but is managing quite well, her secret being to get both children outdoors as soon as possible every day.

Mrs. C's handling of Clem was definite, economical, and confident. She felt bothered at not knowing whether or not he was content or what might be wrong when he fussed; she was disinclined to elaborate upon these remarks. When he did not respond immediately to the cotton placed under his nose (test) she suddenly blurted out to him, "Well, do something!" She mentioned her husband only in reference to his occasional help, and the sibling only in reference to envy of Clem.

THE SIX-MONTH VISIT: INFANT AGE 26.3 WEEKS

Mrs. C's friendliness was superficial, her replies fast and curt. Her movements were also abrupt, sharp, well-defined, and unusually rapid. She whizzed across the room on entrance, hardly acknowledging the presence of the interviewer, dumped Clem into the crib, and immediately set about fixing his lunch.

Clem was big, extremely sturdy, and unusually active. In contrast, his face was pale, expressionless, and sober. He was much pleased to be held in standing position. In the crib he crawled well and banged his legs. In the supine, he pulled the cloth off his face with one swift, well-coordinated grasp. His activity decreased when he was changed or dressed by Mrs. C, at which time he gazed steadfastly at the interviewer (the only time) with a puzzled expression. At the test table he picked up, inspected, mouthed, and transferred objects from one hand to the other with great rapidity, facility, and smoothness. In fact, he lunged toward them, banged them with a fierce persistence, and strove with all his body to get at those beyond his reach. His reactions were exaggeratedly fast, excited, determined, and strong. For example, the moment he failed to grasp the pellet between his fingers he swept it off the table with an annoyed arm gesture. He tolerated the test as long as he had a continual stream of objects offered to him. When lapses occurred he twisted and turned and fussed. At no time did he look at the examiner if a toy was at hand.

He showed attention to persons only when he wished to get something or to be lifted out of the crib. After considerable verbal stimulation he did smile once to the examiner. Fretful sounds were frequent, and when he was in the crib after feeding his cry turned to angry yelling and then to sobbing. He made few other sounds. For the most part he was emotionally inaccessible.

Clem eats well. He dislikes fluids but will take some from a cup. . . . He falls asleep well by himself, sucking his thumb. He doesn't sleep soundly, especially at night. He cries loudly as soon as he wakes in the morning and until he's taken from his crib, which may be an hour later. . . . He is very quiet but extremely active, crawling about and playing with toys and determined to get things. He cries when he can't, but only briefly. . . . Mr. and Mrs. C play with him, showing him toys, holding him some, or letting him crawl on the floor. Clem prefers rough play and favors his father, who bounces him around. He cries when people leave the room if he is left when awake—though this is usually not more than an hour during the day. Mrs. C just lets him cry it out. He also cries when he doesn't sleep unless he has a toy. . . . He can wait for food if he sees Mrs. C fixing it. Occasionally he chews on his hands when hungry . . . But otherwise he is constantly on the move, in a hurry to get places—walking in his walker or rocking in his crib with such vigor that it moves from one side of the room to the other. . . . Yet he likes to be held and to be handled. If he gets hurt he screams but stops as soon as he is held.

He does not smile readily to strangers. . . . The only thing that makes him frightened is being moved very suddenly. Mrs. C herself moves very rapidly; so sometimes when she has been holding Clem and has moved suddenly and fast she has felt him become very tight and rigid and hold on to her with a viselike grip. . . . Generally, he's a happy baby—a bit demanding, but patient. He used to cry a lot, but not any more. . . . The only thing she has tried to teach him is that he won't be picked up every time he cries; and she is trying to teach him to use a cup.

Mrs. C's handling of the baby was very mechanical. She rushed through his feeding as soon as she could, put him back in the crib immediately after, and was eager to be done with the interview. When Clem in the crib sobbed for a long time she showed no reaction. Only after the interviewer paused and silently looked at the baby did Mrs. C comment that probably Clem didn't care for the strange crib. When asked about any needs she might have for help with Clem she brushed the question aside, saying he was easy. She appeared to regard him as a nuisance to be managed and set aside. There was no evidence that she found any pleasure in caring for him. She made no references to family members.

THE ONE-YEAR VISIT: INFANT AGE 51.2 WEEKS

Mrs. C's appearance and manner were a little more feminine and softer than at previous times, and she seemed more at ease in that she showed pride in the baby's development. She was also a little less businesslike and rough although she maintained the same emotional distance observed before. Often she seemed to be preoccupied with faraway thoughts.

Clem was very active, strong, and bright-eyed. He roamed about the room holding on to furniture with one hand or scurrying on all fours, always with intensity, and mostly in a fairly equable mood. Now and then during his rapid crawling he returned to Mrs. C for some contact and then left again for longer periods. Satisfaction with continuous activity seemed present until the latter part of the visit, when he became irritable and restless, presumably because he had missed his nap. His comfort was always restored quickly when he was held and he accommodated very well to handling.

He performed extremely well and quickly on all test items involving fine motor coordination. Curiosity, initiative, and persistence were high. He could busy himself with an object for several minutes, turn to something else, and turn back to the original one for further handling, inspection, and mouthing. Much less energy went into social activity. Vocalizations consisted mainly of immature babbling, and were strikingly immature. Attention to the examiner was only occasional and transitional, and even less attention was paid to Mrs. C. He seldom smiled.

Clem has been well, and save for fussiness during teething, a few colds and a few hurts, he has been in good spirits. Feeding is entirely satisfactory . . . Sometimes he can wait quietly for breakfast. He manages a cup pretty well and Mrs. C has been trying to get him to feed himself in spite of his sloppiness. She has no ideas about when to wean . . . His sleep is sound—except for waking every night at about 2 a.m. for another bottle, after which he sleeps lightly. He always falls asleep with a bottle or his thumb in his mouth. Mrs. C is in conflict about the night bottle but she gives in, not knowing what to do about his demanding crying at night. She is similarly perplexed about bowel training because of persistent failures with her older child (now 2.6) . . . Clem is active, playful, good-humored, and friendly. Sometimes he's destructive, as when he tears paper. He can sit still if he has something to watch or do, otherwise he's impatient. He makes his wants known by gestures only, like knocking on the refrigerator door when he's hungry . . . He used to prefer his mother but now he turns to his father for good times because Mr. C roughhouses with him . . . He doesn't cry except if tired, bored, or hungry, nor if Mrs. C leaves him unless she leaves him alone. When he was younger he would become less active when she went away, but not now. All she has ever had to do to get him over his crankiness has been to feed or hold him . . . He is a bit of a thumb-sucker . . . If something is denied him he gets very angry, flushes, screams, and bangs his head on the floor. If his sister is the one who has crossed him he bites her. The only thing Mrs. C can think of that makes him happy is eating crayons. He knows he's not supposed to, so when he sees Mrs. C coming he pretends to be writing with them, like his sister.

It takes him about five minutes to warm up to strangers. At first he lowers his head and sits quietly. This shyness began a few months ago. He will smile to a child, though . . . Mrs. C has no idea of his having been frightened by anything . . . She tries to discourage his temper, so that he'll know there are certain things he can't have or can't do. He is demanding only at night—spoiled, really, because he complains so much if his demands aren't met right away . . . Mrs. C feels he should be corrected for touching things he shouldn't. If he doesn't listen to her "No, no," she slaps his hands. But he is pretty stubborn, and her methods are not working . . . He has a wonderful personality. "His happiness and good nature overpower his stubbornness. Probably he'll be a happy child, determined to do anything he wants to do. He might become pretty wild and difficult to keep from doing dangerous things."

Mrs. C was very proud of Clem's motor skills. On arrival she was so eager to demonstrate his ability to walk alone (he could not) that she set him down upon his feet without any assistance at all, almost as if she could get him to do so by decision. He fell, became upset, and cried, which did not seem to bother her at all. She allowed him to explore the room at large, but sometimes prohibited his touching objects which realistically he could have had, and neither removed them nor offered him substitutes. At other times she let him take anything he wanted. Her interest in his test performance varied from being proud to being amused to ignoring him. Now and then she talked to him affectionately and smiled at him. When at the end of the visit he was irritable and wanted to be taken from the crib and held, she tried instead to have him take the bottle and go to sleep, in vain. Not until he fell and hit his head against the crib bars did she pick him up, whereupon he quieted almost at once. At no time was she directly unfriendly or harsh to him. She expressed no concerns about his development and asked no questions.

CLINICAL IMPRESSIONS: MRS. C

Mrs. C's only remarks about her parents refer to their degrees of activity and their discipline. She gives no information about their relationships to each other or to her. She herself appears to find relief from inner tension mainly through rapid activity, which she admires and seeks. Her harshness is conspicuous in her physical behavior, and the severity of her brusqueness affirms the impression of severe inhibition of positive affect. The fact that she hopes her children will not be troubled with shyness suggests that she may have some insight into her own anxieties about feeling or acting with tenderness. While she is aware that her impulsiveness may make for difficulties she denies this with an asserted satisfaction with her ability to act according to her convictions.

At the six-week visit her observations of the baby refer almost entirely to his physical needs. There is scarce evidence of freedom to offer him affective comfort at any time, to appreciate his alertness, or to sympathize with him when he is irritable. At the six-month visit she is excessively rough with him, glosses over his feeding and sleeping difficulties, and describes his daily life with no sign of affection or enjoyment. She appears unable to tolerate the idea that she might take cues from the baby to guide her responses to him. She treats him almost like an inanimate object. The degree of physical stillness necessary for the interview is barely tolerable to her.

At the one-year visit Mrs. C is frankly troubled about several aspects of the baby's training but gives no sign of wishing to receive help, and rather shows resentment about her difficulties with him. Her actions are on the prohibitive side, communication with the baby is very limited, and friendliness toward him is notably absent. Her warmest reaction to him is seen in her pride in his motor achievements.

She is assailed by contradictory impulses toward approval of his activity and sullen retreat from meeting his active demands upon her; and the conflict appears to be disguised by an overt lack of interest in or a carelessness about mothering. The baby must cope with a great deal of tension unaided. As his active strivings increase, she cannot refrain from admiring and encouraging them. The mother and baby vie for control in more active conflicts related to body management and habit training.

CLINICAL COMMENTS: CLEM

Six Weeks

The infant responds to external stimulation fairly quickly, persistently, and with intensity. In contrast, stress generated by internal stimuli unsettles him and is poorly tolerated. His capacity to appeal for help appears to be good, but his experiences in receiving comfort and in learning that he can be comforted, appear to be uneven. Thus his anxiety preparedness is erratic. The first phase of socialization has clearly set in, as may be judged from his alert regard of persons.

Six Months

Signal anxiety is poorly developed. States of irritability are chronic, crying erupts easily and on slight provocation. Tension is reacted to mostly by high and stereotyped motor activity. Rapid passive locomotion frightens rather than exhilirates him, and he responds to it with tight clinging. At the same time, he prefers rough play (by father). As he differentiates the mother from the examiner, he may be said to have entered the second phase of socialization. However, neither observation nor report suggest that the mother is regarded as a dependable source of gratification or relief.

One Year

Signal anxiety is present but is immaturely expressed, mainly by gesture. Language development is scanty, and Clem's appeals for help are diffuse. He manifests distress by dystonic moods and impulsive acts. He is poorly related to people. Motor activity is his chief pleasure, and interference with it is very poorly tolerated. Tolerance of bodily discomfort also is low. Test performance is on a high level, but function pleasure is restricted. DQ: 113.

CHAPTER 20

Type IV: Mrs. D and Drew

Mrs. D's face and voice are youthful, yet her obesity suggests a matron, and her nervous, guarded smiles an uneasy adolescent. She wore a black taffeta dress which fitted poorly on a woman in the latter stages of pregnancy. She began by giving short answers, explaining as she had at recruitment that she did not like to talk much. She was therefore not pressed for details, especially about feelings. Usually her affect was inappropriately neutral. Now and then she showed a little emotion if a question was put to her in a humorous context. More often she left matters to be understood by implication. She showed extreme discomfort when asked anything about the past. "I live in the present," she said. She had almost no information about her husband's life before their marriage. As she became more easy she talked freely and volunteered information of an intimate and sexual nature.

Her father was a shopkeeper and her mother has worked as a salesclerk since Mrs. D's early childhood, although Mrs. D has two younger siblings. The parents separated from each other many times during their marriage. Her father stayed away from home increasingly from the time Mrs. D was about 12 and he died when she was 20. She never found his absence from home disturbing and when he died there were no difficulties because her mother was working and all three children were grown. Mrs. D's only other reference to her father was that in her childhood he often spanked her hard. She used to threaten to leave home because he did not

291

love her any more. She had thought of being a teacher but had to go to work after high school. She loved working as a telephone operator until she married, loved talking with all the other girls, and still often sees them at lunch. She has no interest in working again. She lives close by her mother and is in continuous contact with her family of origin. Her mother is "crazy about" Mr. D.

Mrs. D isn't much of a reader and doesn't remember what she's read about infant care. She has no memory of helping to take care of her younger siblings ... She never considered breast feeding because her mother had not been able to do it; anyway, her breasts are so tender that her nipples might get sore ... She has no ideas about weaning. She has heard that if you put Pablum in the bottle with the milk it will "shut them up for four or more hours—and I hear you can do it right away." She might use a bottle prop at three months, and sees no reason not to use a pacifier ... Habits start at about a year. If the baby cried incessantly and nothing would be wrong she'd just let him cry. Though probably she'll have a panic first and ask the doctor what to do. If he sucked his thumb she'd stop him but if he bit his nails she'd ignore it as he'd grow out of it. She believes in firmness in the first year, especially about bedtime. The baby should know from the start that she means business, but probably she'll spoil him.

Toilet training can begin at a year, with a potty. Probably it can be completed for bowel and bladder, day and night, at about 18 months ... Discipline can be imposed at about 10 months probably by slapping a baby's hand and repeating "No, no." She adds, "I'm very patient. I'd probably let a baby go on before I stopped it." ... She will not spoil her children as her mother did ... Modern mothers are too neglectful, though, and leave their children alone too much. Asked what she thought were important experiences during infancy she asks in turn, "Important for me or for the baby?" To the suggestion that she reply for both she says, "Babies are so helpless—probably the first thing I'll do is grab it and not leave it alone ... I guess having it, taking care of it, sharing it with the father will be most important. For the baby lots of love and attention are the most important." Her reply to questions about aspirations for her child is that she should have twins. Her strength as a mother is having lots of love. However, her friend just pops the baby into a playpen and he's jolly by himself. Her weakness probably would be to fuss over the baby too much. And she would want her children to be happy and jolly and laughing all the time. She couldn't stand a fresh child ... Mrs. D has no concern about taking care of a baby but she is petrified about the delivery. She gained 30 pounds after marriage and another 30 during pregnancy. Her mother, who had weighed 250 pounds, had very difficult deliveries. Mr. D makes light of her fears. She hopes to convince him how real they are when he is present during delivery.

THE CONFINEMENT VISIT

Mrs. D was disappointed to know she had a son but "tickled pink" when she actually saw him. Her husband felt the same. Labor (14 hours, 58 minutes) had been hard and long, and Mrs. D felt "stitched from head to toe." She was satisfied with all aspects of her hospital care.

Her most spontaneous remarks were about her eagerness to go home because she couldn't hold the baby long enough in the hospital. She had felt anxious when first feeding him. She didn't worry any more about handling him, even though she didn't know how to change diapers, she said. She stated emphatically that he was going to be spoiled.

THE NEONATAL EXAMINATION

Drew was a very plump baby with a puffy face but very good color. Activity was minimal, but movements were smooth. His bodily tension was normal, but his legs were floppy and lacked resistance to pressure. Turgor was moderate. Mild body trembling was seen. His strongest physical reactions were to lift his head well in the prone position, and to keep it erect when he was pulled to sitting.

Responsiveness was, in general, poor. Auditory reaction was best: his initial response to sound was to extend his legs as well as to startle and blink, and subsequently he listened to the rattle persistently. No visual fixation was elicited. Tactile response was mild, as he moved only his head in the direction of the stimulus.

His prefeeding cry was loud and sustained. He sucked (bottle) spontaneously, eagerly and vigorously, with an alert facial expression. When the nipple was withdrawn, after he had taken three ounces in a little more than three minutes, he seemed still interested in sucking. He remained awake and peaceful, however, after the feeding ended.

The Six-Week Visit: Infant Age 6.5 Weeks

Mrs. D was well-groomed, very conscious of looking good for the filming. She chattered freely and seemed happily excited about being involved in the study with her baby.

Drew was big and chubby. Aside from his double chin, he was well-proportioned and attractive. Alertness and vitality were evident. Both asleep and awake, he preferred the prone position, in which he repeatedly lifted his head to Zone 2. When pulled to sitting, he kept his head bobbingly erect. Bodily tension was more often rigid than relaxed. His movements were wide in range but coordination was only fair. His lower limbs were more active than his upper ones. He showed no stress while being dressed or undressed, but became unusually tense when in an undressed state, for reasons which later appeared.

Auditory responses were most immediate and were strongest, as in the neonatal period. He not only listened to the bell and to voices with diminished activity, but was diverted from visual responses by any extraneous sounds in the room. Nevertheless, visual responses were excellent. He followed the dangling ring only 30° beyond the mid-line, but followed the (shiny) bell through an arc of 180°. He seemed visually aware of the examiner. He reacted with intensity to the cloth placed on his face, by flailing his arms, moving his head, and making loud, grunting noises.

Vocalizations were frequent, though less than Mrs. D reported. Smiling, reported by her, was not observed. No mouthing was seen.

> The daily schedule is indefinite. It all depends on when Drew sleeps. The late afternoon is his "baddest" time unless Mrs. D holds him. Sometimes he doesn't sleep at all between six and 10 o'clock ... He has been fed cereal since two-and-a-half weeks, and

a larger quantity than the doctor suggested because Mrs. D felt that otherwise he would starve to death ... She gets him to sleep by holding him at her shoulder with his head under her chin and rubbing his back until he dozes off. During the day he sleeps lightly ... Mrs. D holds and talks to him a great deal. He is made happy by being played with constantly. He starts screaming the moment he's put back in his crib if he hasn't played enough ... He enjoys being caressed when he has no clothes on ... He tries to bite off his thumb when hungry, and that's strange because thumb-sucking results from lack of attention and he gets an enormous amount ... He used not to like his hair washed, but now he doesn't mind when the water is poured over his head. He doesn't like having a hat put on, though; but he stops crying once it is on, because he knows he's going outdoors ... He knows the difference between indoors and outdoors because he always falls asleep when out. He also knows the difference between Mr. and Mrs. D because when his father puts him down and tells him to go to sleep Drew perks up his ears, doesn't fuss, and falls asleep; yet when his mother puts him down he keeps his head high and goes on making noises ... He cries a lot because of gas pain ... Her only worry is that he might catch "this or that." She takes his temperature if he looks the slightest bit sick. (She is unwilling to indicate how often, but gives the impression that it is at least once a day.) She herself isn't feeling well yet. Her episiotomy hasn't healed, and Drew cries a lot. The doctor told her to burp him after every ounce of milk, to avoid the gas, so she's had to hold him so much on some days that she can get nothing else done, her husband doesn't understand why, and she feels bad about that.

Mrs. D had preferred not to feed cereal during the observation because it was messy. Unless Drew was very hungry, he would get it all over his hands and face. She waited until he grew fussy and then did feed it. Afterward she carried out an elaborate diapering change. She removed a diaper that was only wet and turned Drew to the prone to wash his buttocks first with a wet and then with a dry cloth, both times vigorously. As she did so the muscles in his lower back and buttocks became very tight and he crawled up to the side of the crib, pressing his head against the bars and trying to clutch at the sheet. He made no sound but obviously was in a state of excitement. Mrs. D went on caressing his buttocks with her hands and kissed them several times. Then she set to powdering them with more, energetic caresses, at the same time explaining to the observer that it was always difficult to separate the cheeks so that she had a terrible time taking his temperature. To Drew she said, "You'd better not have kookie in there (fresh diaper) or I'll shoot you. I told you not to shame me." When the baby fussed slightly she told him fondly to shut up. His tension increased as she applied powder to every crease in the diaper area, down to the knees. He responded by spreading his legs wide, which she said he also did in his bath. Mrs. D pointed to his muscular rigidity as a sign of pleasure. The doctor has told her not to put oil on the baby's head but she does it anyway; and not to use powder, but cornstarch, on his body, but she does that anyway also.

She was highly affectionate toward Drew and talked to him almost incessantly. She was eager to show that he already held his own bottle, and credited him with awareness of many things which later she spontaneously acknowledged could not be true. She many times referred to the probability of spoiling him by holding him so much. The only time she seemed mildly troubled was when she reported her fatigue from caring for the household as well as for Drew, her husband's criticizing her for it, and her ensuing feelings that she wasn't doing a good job.

THE SIX-MONTH VISIT: INFANT AGE 28.5 WEEKS

Mrs. D was now very round in face and figure, and she walked with a ducklike waddle. She was not at all outgoing or friendly, answered questions sharply, reluctantly, and avoided eye contact.

Drew was very big: his flat face, sagging double chin, large stomach, thick arms, and extremely heavy thighs gave him a most ungainly appearance. He was nevertheless endearing because of a strong and ready smile. When, as he lay supine, anyone approached him, he worked with arms, legs, and buttocks to lift himself forward. A great deal of leg banging occurred; it was rhythmic, repetitive, and very forceful.

Arm movements were milder and fewer. Whenever he was in a sitting position, either in his mother's lap or in the test table, he rocked stereotypically. He rocked more excitedly when approached by the examiner, squealed, and lunged toward her hair. Throughout the testing period he rocked so hard that the heavy table he sat in moved back and forth. He reacted immediately to all objects, persisted in trying to get those out of reach, and explored them mainly orally. Attention was just average but hard to estimate because Mrs. D so often interfered with his performance by talking to him. He mouthed every object, though not his fingers. Although he scored well, his interest in the objects was low, and he was repeatedly quick to return to the intense rocking.

Aside from a few gleeful sounds, vocalizations were minimal. He accommodated well to being held but holding him was difficult because he aggressively smacked the examiner's face and pulled her hair up and down with great tenacity. Wild, rapid kicking also occurred during diapering and dressing. In general, Drew's behavior lacked variety. His vitality had a driven quality.

> Mrs. D is very satisfied with the baby's enjoyment of food, and stressed his ability to chew on zweiback or bagels. She never forces him to eat anything. The only feeding difficulty is that he refuses food if it gets cold halfway during the feeding, so she reheats it. He can't wait when hungry. He used to scream at the top of his lungs even when she went to reheat the food, but she stopped that in a hurry by beating him every time he did that, and now he keeps quiet while she rewarms the food. He has taken milk from a glass since the age of four months. The observed feeding is not typical because usually she lets him play around more ... He sleeps easily and soundly, a little better at night than during the day. He usually takes his Teddy bear under his cheek when he falls asleep. Mrs. D rocks him to sleep.
>
> Mr. and Mrs. D play with him a lot. Mrs. D throws him around, plays peekaboo, crawls on the floor with him, and talks to him. When she holds him he giggles, smiles, and rocks back and forth. Mr. D is very rough when he plays. He likes to "chew" on the baby's feet and hands. Drew gets very excited when his Daddy just enters the room. He makes sounds and "throws up a storm"

until he is picked up . . . He is a very active baby though he likes best to be held and fed. He has a few toys that he likes but isn't interested enough to go after them much and he can easily be distracted from them. He doesn't get upset if he can't reach them . . . The only thing he doesn't like is a load in his pants . . . He does cry at loud sounds, like rattling paper or coughing, or at sight of people with glasses. He chews on his blanket. He has no habits . . . He has only two moods: either happy-go-lucky or cranky. He is never furious and has no temper. A rare bad mood, such as occurred during teething, is easily ended if he is held. He is easy and not demanding at all. . . . Now and then he takes a lot of Mrs. D's time and interferes with her housework . . . She has tried to teach him to say words, to play tug of war, to make clicking sounds, to drink from a cup, and to feed himself.

Mrs. D. handled the baby with extreme roughness, tossing him, biting and chewing on his feet in play, and rocking him vigorously in her lap whenever she held him if he did not do so spontaneously. She kept him in her lap most of the time, continuously changed his positions, mauling him, pinning his arms down, saying hostile or flippant things to him about his bad behavior, scolding and threatening. The observed feeding was almost forced. She was thoroughly controlling and disrupting, she reproved him for looking at the interviewer instead of at her; and facetiously said she would kill him if he got any food on her dress, and was going to tell his Daddy that he had misbehaved—he hadn't eaten enough. At one point in the feeding she became annoyed and spanked him on the buttocks with several hard, well-directed swats. She brushed his hair at least eight times, washed his face three times, and again made a major ordeal of a diaper change. She went to great pains to rub large amounts of Desitin into all areas, telling him to be ashamed of having a bowel movement, admonishing him not to kick his diaper off when she covered his penis. Her stimulation of his genital and anal parts had absolutely nothing to do with cleaning, and was carried out in spite of her report that she became nauseated and vomited when changing his diaper because she was expecting another baby in six months.

Aside from her continuous stimulating activity she was indifferent to the baby. She showed no sensitive or perceptive reaction to him at any time and no curiosity about his test performance or any aspect of his development. The degree of her domination combined with her extraordinary seductiveness was baffling.

The One-Year Visit: Infant Age 53.1 Weeks

Mrs. D was superficially friendly but at all times kept herself at a physical and emotional distance, and seemed irritated by the interview or resentful of the time she was giving. She volunteered little, answered questions hastily and abruptly, and avoided eye contact. Her sulky behavior may have been related in part to the presence of her husband, who had come with her, for in contrast to her, he was agreeable, outgoing, and glad to provide information.

Drew was a husky boy, nattily dressed in a navy sailor suit. His physical activity was extreme. He scrambled about the room on all fours, trying to walk, but on his toes and too fast, so that he kept toppling. In the crib he rocked on hands and knees, and jumped up and down with extraordinary force and rapidity, rising several inches from the mattress each time. Sitting in the baby tenda, he banged his legs forcefully. These movements were continuous, restless, aimless, and had an agitated quality. His investment in objects was, in contrast, very low.

During testing he was cheerful and immediately responsive once his attention was aroused, but many times it was difficult to arouse it. At best his responses were swift, his distractibility great. Fine motor coordination was excellent but he had little interest in perceiving relationships between objects. He merely picked them up quickly and tossed them away as quickly. He was not interested in demonstrations, and was seldom persistent at any task whether or not he succeeded in it.

He was not shy of the examiner. Social responsiveness was strong for his mother and father. Their main stimulation was vocal. Drew often ignored his mother's talking and he engaged in no play with either parent. He did vocalize a great deal, made many gleeful polysyllabic sounds and said a few words. He did not accommodate to handling.

Drew eats amply, has no feeding difficulties, and holds a training cup well ... He resists sleep during the day and yells stubbornly and loudly when put into his crib at night. He doesn't like to be told what to do. He must hold a blanket to fall asleep. He doesn't sleep soundly at night. He is restless, bangs his head, thrashes about, and makes fussy sounds. But he always wakes in a good mood, and always is "ready to go." ... Mrs. D has put him on the toilet once and plans to get a potty for him in the next weeks.

Drew likes to crawl around and look out of the window at children playing. Best of all he loves to be played with by Mr. and Mrs. D—he laughs and laughs. He'd much rather be around people than do things. He gets bored by things and throws them away. He likes to watch TV ... He always gets into more mischief if Mrs. D is not in the room with him. Whenever he gets into things he shouldn't, he gets smacked on the behind and then told, "No." He cries for a minute and gets over it ... When things go wrong he goes to his father more than to his mother. She has no special games with him, but she often gets down and crawls and chases with him on the floor even in the eighth month of pregnancy ... He has a few habits: he jumps up and down in his crib while holding on the bars, he throws everything he can from his high-chair or crib, he has bitten his mother and father—which Mrs. D particularly disapproves of—and for giving in to these habits he is beaten each time. He has learned what "No" means and Mrs. D feels her methods have worked very well ... When he's scolded he yells back but doesn't show a temper, like kicking or arching. Often though, he obeys Mrs. D's frowns, and stops himself from touching things ...

When left by Mrs. D with anyone except his father or grandmother he screams the whole time ... He has never shied away from strangers (in the presence of the mother) nor even sized them up. He's always immediately friendly ... He's terrified of the ocean. He shrieked at the top of his lungs when Mr. D tried to put him into the water ... He's very easy to get out of a bad mood, and a few kind words can always make him happy. He even gets over a big slap easily. His only fear is of the drainage in the sink where he is bathed.

Mrs. D interpreted the question of whether she tries to teach him anything in only a negative sense: she tries to stop him from pulling at her earrings or people's hair, which he does at every opportunity. Finally she says that Drew is a good, happy baby; a devil, because he likes to explore everything. By age five he'll be a little monster. Even now if she lets him loose in the park he goes right up to children and hits them.

Mrs. D was extremely tired and was suffering from a great deal of back pain during her pregnancy. She could take entire care of Drew except for diapering, which Mr. D helped her with, because the smell so sickened her. She was preoccupied with cleanliness and insisted that everything that fell on the floor had to be washed before the baby could handle it. As during previous visits she ran through a long ritual in changing his diaper, with soap, water, and washcloth, reminded him to be ashamed, scrubbed his genital and anal parts, pulled back his foreskin and applied Desitin most assiduously. She also frequently looked at herself in the mirror, commented about her dress, and combed Drew's hair and her own several times before the filming. Often she picked him up very tightly and smothered him with kisses. Sometimes she engaged him intensely, then suddenly placed him in the crib, not picking him up again until he complained for 10 or 15 minutes but then insisting on holding his hand wherever he roamed. Actually, she chose to keep him in the crib or infant table most of the time until the interviewer asked to see how he crawled. Mrs. D objected to putting him on the floor but did so.

There was great and continual inconsistency in her handling of him. She alternated between permissiveness and indulgence, and between withholding and punishing. She volunteered that he would have a fit when the new baby came, but he would have to toughen up and adjust. She seemed proud of his aggressiveness, his walking, his voracious appetite, and also seemed greatly to enjoy controlling all of these activities. Both parents said they thought Drew was precocious.

CLINICAL IMPRESSIONS: MRS. D

All meetings with Mrs. D bring evidence of her regressive and crude narcissistic demands upon her infant. Her own infantile activity, her own tolerances and intolerances, are at the heart of all of her ideas about the prospective care of the baby. She is in a steady state of generalized excitement as she anticipates handling him. Her only comment indicative of understanding of a baby's emotional states refers to the tendency she attributes to modern mothers to leave their children alone too much. This opinion contains an obvious denial of her own being left as a young child with her younger siblings when her own mother went to work.

The six-week visit shows that Mrs. D has predicted well. She overfeeds, overtalks, overhandles, overplays with, overexcites her son, and she overestimates his understanding as well. She has some realization of being inwardly compelled to have him serve needs of her own, but she sees nothing untoward in this. Her intense preoccupation with his body functions, and especially the anal zone, tells the strength of her regressive indulgence in him as an anal masturbatory object. At the six-month visit Mrs. D's aggression toward her infant is much increased. She cannot keep her hands off him. At the one-year visit her infantile behavior with him is even more conspicuous. She sees nothing amiss in his development except his "badness," i.e., his insistence upon doing things that she does not want him to do. At the same time she seems to be gratified by his exceeding impulsiveness. A contest brews as to which of the two partners will be able to force the other into submission.

CLINICAL COMMENTS: DREW

Six Weeks

This infant is very reactive to external stimulation, and appropriately so. Lacking that stimulation, however, he grows restless, and is reported to become irritable easily and to scream, especially when inner stress rises. Passive states unsettle him. Anxiety preparedness appears to be unbalanced. Awareness of persons is present, although Mrs. D's report that he smiles at her is not substantiated. The first phase of socialization has barely begun.

Six Months

Stress from whatever source throws the infant into a state of disequilibrium. He is restored to an equable mood by quantities of stimulation which the observer considers would be overwhelming to the average infant. When left to himself, Drew resorts to self-exciting motor activity of various kinds. Stereotypic rocking is marked, and seems to have absorbed a good part of the baby's capacity for signal anxiety. Activity with persons, except for aggression and hilarity, seems to be diffuse. While Drew may have entered the second phase of socialization, he only partially sees the mother as a separate person. His behavior with her, perhaps because she is so overstimulating and seductive, is not adequately differentiated from his behavior with other persons.[1] He is observed to seek excitement from all persons indiscriminately, or from his own body.

One Year

An "aging" process, rather than development, seems to have taken place in Drew. Paniclike states are aroused when he is alone, and at bedtime, that is, in periods of appropriate separation and passivity. When left with anyone but parents or grandparents, he screams constantly and cannot be comforted. On the other hand, if he is punished (slapped) by his parents or frightened in their presence, his comfort can be restored almost immediately; at least they so report. All of these behaviors point to an uneven development of signal anx-

[1]Overstimulation and seduction are, of course, not activities unique to a mothering figure and can be sought from others. Such activities tend to leave an infant unsatiated.

iety, and to an insufficient degree of that differentiation of self from others which is necessary to make stable development of signal anxiety possible.

Object relations are also uneven. The infant clamors for attention from human objects, and has an incapacity to use inanimate objects with discrimination. The need for a transitional object has already set in. Age-adequate reflectiveness is absent. His response to the world is globally motoric.

Body cathexis is inordinately high. Stereotypic rocking persists in severe form. Cathexis of exciting persons is also persistently high, while investment in quiet persons is low. Normally relaxed states, which imply a latency of anxiety, and scanning of the environment, are rarely seen. In contrast, demands for immediate gratification from external objects appear to be continuous. Drew is intolerant of almost any situation in which he cannot be active. One has the impression that bodily stillness, or the quietude necessary for sustained attention, evoke instant anxiety, and that much of his intense activity is a flight from stress.

Good capacity for cognitive skills appears to be present, but performance of age-adequate tasks is impoverished by poor concentration, narcissistic investment of body activity, and low function pleasure with objects. DQ: 100.

CHAPTER 21

Type V: Mrs. E and Emily

The Prenatal Interview

Mrs. E seemed self-conscious of her manners, yet open and friendly and extremely eager to talk. Her facial expressions were very mobile, her affect unduly cordial. Clearly, she was trying to subdue tension.

Mrs. E grew up in a rural area without much companionship, as her siblings were much older and no other children lived nearby. Her relationship to her mother, probably the closest she had, was marred by the frustration and helplessness she used to feel as a result of the many quarrels between her parents. Her father, a skilled worker, never enjoyed his wife or children, and Mrs. E never felt him to be "a real father." In childhood she had feared him especially because her mother built up the fear by continual threats of his punishments. Actually he yelled a lot but did not spank much. The parents did not divorce until after Mrs. E had completed her teacher's training because it was obvious that her father would not support his family once the divorce was final. Mrs. E did not much mind rarely seeing him after he left the home. Her mother was thoroughly devoted to her children. Now that all of them are married she is lonely and unhappy, with no interests of her own.

Mrs. E plans to breast feed for about three months, depending on how convenient it is. She will not hurry weaning because it is good to go along with nature. Besides, the idea that it is an advantage or a sign of brightness for babies to do things early is foolish ... Toilet training should depend upon the baby's understanding. The training of her son, Tom, was fraught with difficulties until Mrs. E suddenly became very strict (at his age 3.3). Sometimes talk

305

gets you nowhere. You have to be strict and make a child "shape up." Discipline can begin as soon as a child can walk ... Probably Mrs. E would be more prone to reason or to scold than to spank, although spanking is better. Discipline is really much easier if one lives in the country, where a child can run free, as she did when young ... Habits begin early in life. Each needs its own method of handling, but Mrs. E has no idea of any methods she may use with the baby because she is always at a loss to control her son. He constantly gets into dangerous situations because of his hyperactivity. Mrs. E has felt a real need for another child in order to teach Tom that he has to share her attention. He has been terribly hard to manage. ... Mrs. E's strength lies in her capacity to love; her weakness, in getting too tired to exert proper discipline ... One of the most important experiences during infancy is freedom to explore ... She hopes that her children will have good professional training for anything they want to do, and that they will have ambition.

Throughout the interview Mrs. E's replies about probable methods of caring for the baby were in terms of her experiences with her son. Repeatedly she stressed the various problems arising from his impulsivity. Her interest in acquiring knowledge about children appeared to derive mainly from a wish to be able to deal with crises.

THE CONFINEMENT VISIT

Mrs. E stated no preference of her own, but hoped her husband was not disappointed about having a daughter. Actually, she added, daughters are marvelous, and "just get through to their dads," so she wasn't really worried. Once the baby developed a real personality, Mr. E would probably "turn to jelly with her" anyway.

Labor had been brief (three hours, 45 minutes), without preanesthesia medication. Mrs. E was entirely satisfied with all aspects of her hospital care and looked forward to going home to see her son, of whom she spoke with great pleasure.

Emily was being breast fed. Mrs. E's milk supply was not yet adequate, but as the baby was very big the nurses

were already letting her sleep through the night without
the two o'clock feeding.

THE NEONATAL EXAMINATION

Emily was a very big, healthy-looking, alert baby. Except
for slight facial bruises and a mottled pink skin, her appearance was very good. She was normally active and relaxed.
Muscle tone was very good, turgor was good, and her movements were moderately smooth. In the supine, she occasionally flexed her limbs, and in the prone she readily turned her
head to the side. When pulled to sitting, she erected her head
slightly, and her shoulders became adequately tense.

All sensorimotor responses were very superior and well
maintained. She listened to both the rattle and bell during
several consecutive trials. Visually, she achieved horizontal
pursuit movements through an arc of 90° and vertical pursuit
movements through an arc of more than 30°. To the touch of
the gauze upon her face she responded with head, mouth, and
coordinated arm movements.

Irritability and mouthing were first observed just before
feeding. Emily was assumed to be quite hungry because of the
effort to restrict her to breast feedings. She sucked spontaneously, with moderate eagerness and strength, but received
only one ounce in 14 minutes. The feeding ended with some
tension and irritability, and much mouthing.

THE SIX-WEEK VISIT: INFANT AGE 5.2 WEEKS

Mrs. E was very simply but prettily dressed, and came
with eagerness to talk about the baby. She said she had felt
very well since the birth, but she did not sound convincing.

Emily was a very big, wide-awake baby, with a fair and
mottled skin. Her appearance was rather relaxed, her facial
expressions mobile. She showed high degrees of activity and
responsiveness, frowning, pouting, and often smiling. Her
movements were moderately vigorous and well coordinated.
In the prone position, which was most habitual and preferred,

she often raised her head and chest so high that she rested her weight on her forearms. When brought to sitting, she held her head bobbingly erect. She accommodated well to being held.

All test procedures were carried out with ease. Auditory response was quick and very good: the sound of the bell elicited facial as well as bodily reactions. Visual response was excellent, as she followed the dangling ring through an arc of 150° several consecutive times. Visual attention was prolonged and steady not only to test objects but to both her mother and the examiner, to whom she smiled often. She also vocalized in response to social stimulation. She reacted to the cloth over her face by turning her head this way and that in efforts to get rid of it.

At no time did she appear to be tired or irritable. No mouthing or hand-to-mouth activity was observed.

> Breast feeding lasted eight days. Mrs. E didn't have much milk, Emily was rejecting the supplements, and the two methods didn't work together. Emily now takes bottle feedings well . . . Her sleep is sound. That is, she falls asleep most easily if rocked or patted, but often she is allowed to cry herself to sleep . . . When Mrs. E is free to play with her, which is mainly in the evenings, she keeps Emily in an infant seat or on the couch because she believes it is not good to hold her so much. "If you spoil them you allow them to make your life miserable." If Mr. E has a little time in the evening he may play with Emily but he does not pick her up.
>
> The baby's greatest pleasure is to be fed, or to be held and talked to; then she can be attentive for long periods. Most of all she dislikes having her face and head washed. She howls until the washing is over . . . She cries for long periods if she is tired or has gas pains. There is nothing Mrs. E can do about it . . . Usually she is quiet and pleasant. When she doesn't get what she wants she cries, but Mrs. E will not let her cry long because babies should be kept happy. Mrs. E feels very guilty about having left Emily with a sitter a few days ago, with a bottle that had a stopped-up nipple. The baby screamed for hours. But a mother has to get out often and do things for herself that she enjoys, or else she can't be a good mother . . . When Mrs. E was in confinement Tommy behaved like a little man, but then he got terribly upset because the nurse with whom he was left, and who had been hired from an agency after

Mrs. E's departure, had a fuss with him and hit him. Mrs. E felt sick about it; she explained that it is quite different if she or her husband spank Tommy because they do so with love. She is always getting upset about Tommy's rash behavior, but "looks the other way" and tries not to worry.

Mrs. E was pleased with Emily's progress and was warm and attentive to her at all times. However, she was far more interested in talking about her husband and son. She was distressed about her husband's driven attitude toward his work, and in considerable conflict about controlling her "roughneck" son for fear of inhibiting him and hurting him in some way.

THE SIX-MONTH VISIT: INFANT AGE 27.6 WEEKS

Mrs. E was much less at ease than in earlier meetings. She was entirely cooperative but there was a forced emotionality in her speech. She answered simply and adequately, volunteered few details, and showed no curiosity about Emily's development.

Emily looked immature. She was small, pale, and had very delicate features. All of her gross movements were gentle and small in range and she was at ease almost only when held on her mother's lap. She cried at first sight of the interviewer, cried any time her mother was not directly in view, and hardly ever smiled. Her handling of test objects was superior. She reached for them eagerly, examined and manipulated them, and breathed excitedly as she did so. Her finger movements were immediate, precise, well directed, and persistent although they did not have the strength, range, rapidity, and force that usually are associated with vigor. In spite of this good performance she was often irritable, especially at sight of the examiner, whom she took pains to avoid looking at. Her curiosity led her to touch the ring on the examiner's hand once, but as soon as she glanced up and saw the latter's face she began to cry. Vocalizations were very few except for unhappy fussing sounds which were heard during most of the visit. Few mouth movements were seen.

When Emily was placed in the crib she became extremely distressed and sobbed and rocked until Mrs. E finally lifted her out and rocked her to sleep in her arms. She accommodated well to her mother's handling and to loving overtures from the mother. At no time did she respond to the social approach of the interviewer.

> Emily takes all foods well and Mrs. E hopes she will continue to do so for a long time so that no special foods will have to be prepared. Mr. E is rarely home for dinner, so Mrs. E fixes "dreadful meals" for Tom and is disinclined to do more . . . Emily sleeps well but sometimes is awakened by noises . . . Mrs. E plays with Emily by holding, talking to, and nuzzling her. Mrs. E's play is especially gentle and, to Mrs. E's surprise, so is Tom's. Emily loves to play with toys while sitting in her tenda, or just likes to slap the table over and over again. Her greatest pleasure is eating and next best is to have the company of her parents . . . She does not wait for things easily. She cries for food while she sees Mrs. E preparing it . . . She's finicky, and fusses whenever her diaper needs changing . . . Her only fear is of unfamiliar loud noises. Recently she screamed in terror at sight of a cat . . . Typically she is happy and easily comforted. Mrs. E does hold her a great deal but doesn't think she's spoiled. Emily's only habit is sucking the pacifier. Mrs. E feels Emily is demanding, not overly, and "admits" she has encouraged this because she has never made Emily wait too long for anything . . . She doesn't try to teach Emily anything, but does do some physical exercises with her . . . Mrs. E has been studying interior design. She realizes she must acquire another skill not only for new stimulation but for her future security. So many men die young, and she should have some way to support herself. Because of her evening classes her household now is neglected, she sorely lacks sleep, and she feels quite exhausted.

Mrs. E addressed Emily endearingly and described her with pleasure. Her observations were meager, however. The alertness with which she reacted to the baby's cries, combined with a mild withdrawal at other times, and her worries about her son's excessive activity, all produced an impression of chronic uneasiness in her. This impression was reinforced when she explained how busy she was, preparing for self-support if necessary.

The One-Year Visit: Infant Age 47.2 Weeks

Mrs. E was agreeable and tactful but rapport was lacking. She sat very still and was under great pressure to speak, mainly about her son and husband. Many times her attention had to be drawn back to considerations about Emily.

Emily was tall and slender. Her pale, listless facial expression was attributed to her having just gotten over a virus infection. But she was also tense and kept in close physical touch with Mrs. E all the time. Often she demanded to be on Mrs. E's lap, and her most spontaneous activity was to sit with her back to her mother, handling toys on an adjacent table. She never remained sitting there for more than a few minutes at a time.

Her skills were good. Concentration and persistence were excellent with some test items. A quickness of response combined with poor attention, which became poorer as tasks grew more complex, reflected a restlessness or an appetite to get at one thing after another with no sustained curiosity for any one. She turned away from objects just as quickly as she had turned toward them. She had no interest in repeating new accomplishments. It was clear that she perceived relationships, like that of a round block to its round hole, but she could not be persuaded to fit the one into the other. She enjoyed most doing something familiar, like tossing a ball. She tossed well but almost reflexly, for hardly did her fingers close on it before she threw it *away* rather than back toward the examiner or her mother. She picked up no cues for reciprocal play.

All expressive behavior was sharply restricted and unvarying. She was remarkably still physically and made almost no sounds. Even her crying was of low intensity. For long periods she stared at the interviewer with wide-open mouth and frozen expression. She did show a forceful quality in a large variety of irritable habits, however: throwing, slapping, pushing, whimpering. She smiled not more than two or three times, twice spontaneously to the interviewer, although she tended to shrink from the latter's direct approach. Perceptual exploration was thus her best activity even though motor restlessness and avoidance of the examiner restricted her test performance considerably. Mouthing of objects was rare. When in mild distress she was observed to shake her wrists rapidly, a gesture which Mrs. E had noted. Emily's lack of spirit might be ascribed to her recent illness. Her inhibitedness could not.

The daily schedule is not rigid. Mrs. E keeps trying to accommodate to Emily's playtime and naps, to no avail, as Emily is restless all of the time. She does take foods well and sometimes even holds her bottle, though Mrs. E doesn't expect her to and really prefers to hold her for the bottle feedings. Now and then she offers the baby milk from a cup but Emily does a poor job and so Mrs. E doesn't really bother her about it. Babies should suck as long as they want to . . . Emily is a very light sleeper both day and night. Only at night can Mrs. E get her back to sleep, by holding or patting her for a while. During the day the restlessness does not get relieved. Even outdoors, instead of sleeping Emily gets overalert, tries desperately to get out of her stroller, and then gets overtired.

She is extremely active, gets into cabinets, drawers, closets, grabbing and chewing her brother's toys, and always is in motion. She'd rather crawl and cruise than be held. She has no favorite toys and isn't interested in little tricks or games. Nor is Mrs. E. Mrs. E doesn't like to play with her much and feels it isn't necessary because Tom is there for Emily before and after school, and that is enough. Mr. E has little time to play with or take any care of Emily . . . Emily gets stubborn when she wants things. She yells, she slaps her hands, she grabs at anything until she gets what she wants or a substitute. She does have a temper . . . She likes new things but gets tired of them quickly. Best of all she loves to watch her brother and his friends and to play with their toys. She is most displeased if he is too rough with her—but mainly it's her feelings that are hurt. Mrs. E can always distract her with something new. She really is always happy as long as she gets her way.

Not much discipline has been necessary. Emily has to be controlled only from getting into dangerous places . . . Then again, she balks at having to lie down at night or to be dressed and Mrs. E has had to spank her lightly on the leg. "Her lips puckered up a little but she got the point." . . . She gets the pacifier for Mrs. E's sake as Mrs. E would go mad without it. "There are times when nothing else will keep them content, and you feel awful if you can't give them something." . . . Emily has been shy of strangers since six or seven months. She always howls when sitters come. She has also been somewhat afraid of dogs ... She has a few habits. The biggest is pushing things away (observed). She screams, throws, rubs and pulls at her ears, and likes to nestle in the corner of her crib with her face snuggled into something. She doesn't care for her playpen, for which Mrs. E blames herself. She should have forced it. But babies should be allowed lots of freedom to roam about. The family is moving to a new home where Emily will have an outdoor yard to play in, and Mrs. E will have household help. She neither expects nor wishes to have more time to play with Emily herself, though. It isn't necessary ... Emily is happy because she is indulged so much. "They grow up so soon, and soon they're going to miss all the little things they enjoy when they're babies." According to the same reasoning, Mrs. E explained that she had felt it right to let Tom keep the pacifier until he was past three. She couldn't bear to take it away and finally did so by telling him that Santa Claus needed it for another baby. "Children have so few pleasures during babyhood," she said, "and babyhood passes so quickly."

On the first day in the city to which the family is moving Emily and Tom will be left with relatives while Mr. and Mrs. E spend the time finding a house. That done, the family will spend two weeks with another relative in another city. Then both parents will leave for a six-week vacation from the children before finally settling into the new house. Though Mrs. E seems to consider that the children may be affected by the series of changes she justifies them casually in terms of her own fatigue.

Despite many hours given to the interview, information gathered about the baby was meager and scattered. Mrs. E gave her attention primarily to the interviewer, allowing Emily to sit near her or on her lap but ignoring her activity as long as Emily was occupied. When the baby was irritable and slight fond comments had no effect, Mrs. E gave her the pacifier which hung on a ribbon around the baby's neck. After very much increased fussing for a long time, Mrs. E looked tense, but she showed no reaction at all when the interviewer offered the baby some playthings. When for similar reasons the interviewer offered to get a cookie to comfort the baby Mrs. E said yes, but as the cookie was not immediately at hand she said not to bother.

Although Mrs. E's remarks implied that she was very much influenced by Emily's needs, she seemed barely observant of the baby's emotional states. What she referred to as allowing freedom looked more like inertia. For example, when the table, which had on it an object that Emily reached for, rolled away, Mrs. E never put out her hand to roll it back, and each time this happened Emily's restlessness increased. She seemed not to enjoy holding the baby. The only time she evinced interest in Emily's skills or development was when she urged Emily to stand alone. Again and again she stressed the degree of Emily's activity, though in fact the baby was inactive except when she was restless. Mrs. E showed her strongest emotion toward Emily when she rocked the sleepy baby in her arms at the end of the visit. When Emily fell asleep the two appeared to cling to each other.

All questions about Emily elicited responses about Tommy, and particularly about his usually getting the best of his mother in their tangles. Mrs. E made numerous and ambivalent comparisons between her two children, stressing that Tom was more active, yet that he was easier as a baby, at other times saying that Emily was easier because Tom was so fantastically active. He was described—with a mixture of pride and anxiety—as defiant, bored, and needing challenge. Mrs. E again spoke at great length about her husband's overinvolvement in his work and about his demands upon her as well. She kept telling him that she didn't want to be a widow too early but he always said that he couldn't help himself.

CLINICAL IMPRESSIONS: MRS. E

Mrs. E's most positive comment about her childhood refers to her mother's devotedness, which was excessive, and led to a dependence upon her husband and children. It appears that Mrs. E imagines that, like her mother, she may become similarly isolated with her children. During confinement she reassures herself with a cliché about the closeness of fathers and daughters, so denying her own experience. She has a moderate degree of empathy, wishes to extend herself kindly to her children, but is very unsure of the demands that she may legitimately make of *them*.

At the six-week visit Mrs. E seems preoccupied with the question of how attentive she should be to the baby, as against how much freedom she herself should have. She seems unable to find a proper measure of frustration and gratification for her children, is openly distressed by anxieties about her husband and son, and directly reports that she tries to ward off anxiety by denial. At the six-month visit she again shows a capacity to be loving and tender, yet feels obliged to restrict herself from indulging the baby's demands. Now she looks forward to finding stimulation outside the home and feels vaguely troubled about her failure to enjoy being a mother. At the one-year visit her attempts to accommodate to an unsettled infant are more fragmentary. She withdraws emotional contact with ready rationalizations about the baby's not needing her, and sees as acceptable various characteristics of the baby that do not bode well, such as the ability to be briefly distracted by new things. She oscillates between self-accusations and complaints about the children. Her relationship to the baby seems inhibited and restricted. Her main absorption is in the problems generated by her husband and son. Fantasies of losing her husband add to her conflicts about being more active in her own right. She fears that tenderness may too easily slide into overindulgence and that discipline may be injurious.

CLINICAL COMMENTS: EMILY

Six Weeks

This infant is highly responsive to external stimuli and seems to be remarkably undisturbed by inner stress other than "gas pains" or unusual hunger. Anxiety preparedness would appear to be optimal. Imprinting to the mother as species-specific object has been achieved. Emily's social response is reliable.

Six Months

The capacity for signal anxiety has diminished surprisingly. Emily appears to lack inner resources to comfort herself, and depends more on stimulation and solace from others. She is usually dismayed by the stranger and by losing sight of her mother, and is found to be comforted mainly by physical measures. Although Mrs. E reports that Emily cries easily and is easily frightened, she also reports that the baby has some ability to play alone. The capacity for signal anxiety is established, but it is overexercised.

Imprinting to the mother as specific object has been achieved, but nonmothers apparently are threatening and anxiety provoking.

One Year

Emily is restless, tense, and irritable. She loses equilibrium easily. In states of discomfort she resorts to screaming, or to aimless and maladaptive gestures, or she avoids contact. It appears that she does not directly signal for help, perhaps because Mrs. E readily relies upon ways of distracting the baby. Practice in signal anxiety may not have been sufficiently reinforced.

Object relations are restricted. Emily clings to her mother and shies away from direct friendly approaches from strangers. Responsiveness to inanimate objects and to unfamiliar tasks is poor. Although Emily is active and has good perceptual ability, her activity tends to be undirected and poorly sustained, and restlessness disturbs her task completion. Body cathexis is uneven, and bodily activity is curtailed. How much the latter is related to Emily's addiction to the pacifier can only be guessed at. Frustration tolerance is low. All of these conditions betoken an insufficient tempering of narcissism.

Cognitive ability is high but erratic, as Emily's curiosity is fleeting and hard to arouse, and she wards off practice of new skills. DQ: 108.

CHAPTER 22

Type VI: Mrs. F and Frank

THE PRENATAL INTERVIEW

Mrs. F was a tall, strikingly erect, and large-limbed woman, impressive at sight because of the sharp look in her eyes and her stern expression. She spoke directly, using intellectual language and seldom pausing for reflection. At times she expressed a skepticism about the relevance of questions put to her. Her reporting was precise and bare of detail, her show of emotion very limited.

Mrs. F's father died when she was three years old, and during the rest of her childhood and adolescence a paternal aunt lived with Mrs. F's mother and her brothers. Her father was said to have been strict and undemonstrative. Her mother was much too lenient, and spent lots of time with her four children instead of keeping her house in order. Her casualness was in strong contrast to the excessive demandingness and continuous criticism of the paternal aunt. Mrs. F was educated in upper-class schools, and plans to return to her work in one of the healing professions when all of her children are of school age. She describes her husband, a biochemist, as dedicated to his work but chronically dissatisfied with his achievements. She blames her husband's poor opinion of himself on his parents, who were always too critical. Mr. and Mrs. F attend the theatre a great deal, and love sports.

Mrs. F will breast feed because it is easier than bottle feeding and because she knows it is best for the infant's immunity to disease. She will let the baby decide when to be weaned from the breast; that is, she will not insist that the baby stay at the breast more than seven or eight months, and she hopes to wean directly to the cup. She would never prop a bottle . . . The baby will have

317

a pacifier available in his first months, as did her elder daughter, though now she gets it only if she goes to bed ... Mrs. F offers clearly stated principles about proper toilet training but shows a current indecisiveness about implementing them with her daughter. Mrs. F should have been more firm. But there's no sense in pressing a child to be trained ...

Habits begin when there is no real need for activities but they continue anyway. Mrs. F would try to fight them, and try to understand the motives for them, and seek substitutes. One should be lenient, but children should not be catered to ... Babies should be left alone and not held too much, and surely she will not hold this baby as much as she did Jane ... Discipline can begin at nine months, when babies understand the meaning of *"No."* They can be dealt with firmly at one year by reproofs and slaps. They should also be given substitutes for things denied them and they should have physical exercise to expend energy. When the child is destructive the mother should let him know she loves him but that what he's doing is inconvenient ... It is also important for parents to spend as much time with their children as they can. She is glad that parents are more permissive now ... Children should have educational toys according to their age level, and lots of athletic equipment. They should be held when very tiny and later encouraged to develop skills ... She hopes her children will have a college education. Certainly they will have to choose for themselves what they are to do. She hopes they will not just be average ... Her strength as a mother lies in her easygoing nature and her ability to take things as they are. She is hard put to think of a weakness and finally offers that she is too lenient.

THE CONFINEMENT VISIT

Mrs. F and her husband were both pleased to have a son. He had seemed very jaundiced at first and Mrs. F had worried about it, but all was well. She said spontaneously that she hoped to have at least three more children, indicating that childbirth and child care were no problem for her.

Labor (10 hours, 36 minutes) and delivery had been easy, with only minor preanesthesia medication, and all of her hospital care had been good. Mrs. F looked forward to going home to see her daughter's reaction to the baby. She spoke at length about difficulties that can be aroused by sibling rivalry, and didactically emphasized the needs of young children for attention to physical as well as emotional needs. She expressed much intellectual concern with the attention that she hoped the research staff would be giving to observations of physical development, and raised many questions about the significance of observations that were already planned.

THE NEONATAL EXAMINATION

Frank was a big, heavy baby, with bright pink skin and a sturdy appearance. Spontaneous physical activity was low. Muscle tone seemed to be good except when, in the supine, he extended his legs and kept them rigidly elevated. Head movements in the prone were strong.

The examination of this infant proceeded with much difficulty, and in unusual circumstances. When first seen in the nursery, he was sleepy and peaceful. Mrs. F insisted that he be brought to her room for the examination, and that it should be carried out before she fed the baby, even though she believed he was hungry. His vehement cries shortly persuaded her that she should feed him without more delay.

Frank had a hard time grasping the nipple because by the time the feeding began he was making frantic rooting movements. Soon his sucking was eager and strong. During the six-minute feeding, kept brief so that the mother's nipples not become sore, Mrs. F continuously stroked the baby's hair and jiggled his body. She withdrew the nipple when he was still bent on sucking, whereupon he hiccoughed slightly and then grew irritable. The mother then explained that he had been placid until the past two feedings. When his distress and cries became acute, Mrs. F gave him a pacifier, explaining at the same time that it really was too big for the baby's mouth. She then so firmly insisted that the test should go on, in spite of the baby's state, that to have refused would have amounted to a direct affront to her.

Yet every time the examiner approached Frank, Mrs. F interfered by snatching him up in her arms, rocking him or putting him down in another place, and in a few minutes picking him up again. The infant, with pacifier in mouth, rooted wildly and with little pause except in a few brief moments when he was held by his mother's arms and swung from side to side by her. Eventually it was difficult to end the examination because Mrs. F repeatedly asked that more test items be tried.

Responsiveness to external stimuli was found to be excellent. Frank listened persistently to both the rattle and the bell. Though horizontal pursuit movements were only questionably present, vertical pursuit movements were obtained. He reacted well to the tactile stimulation upon his face, moving his head about. The auditory and visual responses were elicited while he had the pacifier in his mouth.

The examiner's impression was that this infant basically was not irritable and could have been soothed readily, but that his initial and intermittent quietness was repeatedly upset by the delay of feeding, the too-brief nursing, and the extra activities of the mother.

THE SIX-WEEK VISIT: INFANT AGE 6.3 WEEKS

Mrs. F's plain attire, stiff movements, and worried facial expression all lent a gracelessness to her manner. As the interview progressed she became more relaxed and showed slight humor, but she was never really at ease. She was perceptive and articulate, offered opinions liberally, and seemed well satisfied with her maternal competence. She was highly critical of the placement of equipment in the observation room.

Frank was a small, well-proportioned, and uncommonly beautiful infant. His complexion was pink and fair, and an abundance of blonde hair added to his attractiveness. He was very active and very alert. In the supine, the TNR position was predominant but a few times he held his head in midposition. He flexed and extended his legs often. All of these movements were moderately vigorous; they were also tense, restless, and rather jerky. In the prone, he rotated his head frequently, and although he could barely lift his head to Zone 1, he tried again and again to do so. When he was pulled to sitting his head lagged markedly. When held in arms by the examiner, he squirmed uneasily, but he accommodated well to other forms of handling, and was not made irritable thereby.

All of Frank's sensorimotor reactions to test stimuli were mature, well sustained, and accompanied by definite facial expressions. The sound of the bell brought a decrease in his activity and aroused an immediate facial response. His visual responses to persons were stronger than to test objects, yet he did also follow the dangling ring through a horizontal arc of 180°. The tactile stimulus evoked a surprised sound, along with aversive head movements. No other vocalizations were heard. During much of the visit Frank sucked on a pacifier that Mrs. F had provided on the assumption that he needed extra sucking experience. She reported that he had smiled at her a few days before the visit, but no smiling was observed.

> Breast feeding continues satisfactorily. Mrs. F hopes to breast feed for about eight months, and she is vague and casual as to when she may begin to offer semisolids. She recalls that when Jane was born she wanted to do something for her that nobody else could, implying that this reasoning still obtains; and breast feeding is easier than fixing formulas. At home she usually does other things while breast feeding, such as fixing breakfast for the family or reading to Jane. It feels strange, now, to be doing nothing but feeding the baby ... His sleep is induced with the help of a pacifier. He wakes at about 4:30 a.m., and after his pacifier is restored to him he sleeps until 7:30 a.m. ... He prefers sucking on the pacifier to sucking at the breast. The word "pacifier" is not correct, really—it implies that the object is only a substitute rather than something good in itself, something that fulfills an actual need.
>
> Mr. F plays with Frank more actively than Mrs. F, who just holds him or moves his hands. In the evenings the whole family has a social time: Mr. F plays a guitar, and Mrs. F and Jane sing. During waking hours, Frank can be ignored. He spends hours alone, placid and happy ... He is more interested in people than in things. Jane got more attention, perhaps too much ... Frank knows the difference between his mother and father, because he moves more

when he is in his mother's arms; and as he likes being in the infant seat more than in the crib, she is sure he distinguishes between the two.

Mrs. F's activities with Frank were, overtly, of a different quality during feeding and nonfeeding periods. When she fed she was relatively inattentive, stroking and fondling him mechanically from time to time, and she carried out the feeding as if she had delegated her maternal responsibility to her breast. When not feeding she kept her eyes on the baby, was quick to inspect him at the slightest sound and to change his diapers, or to take him on her lap. These responses were devoid of any sign of emotion.

Mrs. F spoke of Frank as being very good, easy to care for, and "able to endure things." She spontaneously criticized her husband for being too casual about various aspects of the children's health. She asked no questions about the baby's development.

The Six-Month Visit: Infant Age 27.0 Weeks

Mrs. F was superficially at ease. In word and act she emphasized her casual attitudes toward the baby and toward child care generally. It seemed to be a matter of self-esteem for her to show that nothing in the baby's behavior or development disconcerted her in the least. She showed some scorn of the interviewer's admiration of the baby's romper, explaining that it was a gift but she was using it anyway.

Frank was excellently built, slender, very mature-looking, and highly attractive. He was steadily alert, attentive, and observant. His facial expression was sober, reflective, cautious. His physical movements had a quiet, relaxed quality and were well executed though moderate in range. He sustained his weight excellently when held to a standing position, but spontaneously brought himself only to put his weight on his knees.

Test scores were excellent. Fine coordination was superior, he explored objects visually, banged and mouthed them actively, yet there was no evidence whatsoever that he derived any emotional pleasure from his use of them. His first response to the examiner was a spontaneous smile. Gradually he became more cautious and appeared to prefer dealing with objects than with persons. Nevertheless, during testing he grew restless, and as objects were withdrawn, more and more irritable until half of the testing had to be postponed.

He accommodated well to his mother's handling, with no visible pleasure or displeasure. He immediately squirmed and fretted when Mrs. F touched him during the feeding (she said her hands were cold). Except for occasional coos and laughing aloud, few vocalizations were heard. Throughout the visit the infant was unusually subdued, quick to frown and to cry, difficult to comfort. He needed to be handled most tactfully to remain in an equable mood. His behavior was highly efficient in all respects, but his responsiveness was guarded at all times. Rocking and banging movements appeared to bring him most pleasure.

Frank is still breast feeding well, though he vomits frequently (not observed). "He's such a pig, he eats too much and then throws it up." Mrs. F never breast feeds away from home (observed feeding was from a bottle) because she herself is not relaxed enough, Frank seems aware of it, and then bites her nipple. And this feeding is less relaxed than usual probably because the baby fell on his head in the morning ... Mrs. F began to offer semisolids early because she feels babies should learn that not all foods are liquid. Frank will be weaned to the cup at nine months. By that time he'll be able to hold his bottle well, although by then Mrs. F will expect him to be using the cup more. .... Sleep is all right because Mrs. F waits until Frank is tired before she puts him to bed. He sleeps less well in unfamiliar places than he did formerly. Probably this is the result of curiosity rather than uneasiness.

Everyone in the family plays with Frank a great deal. He loves to be jiggled on somebody's knee, and is pleased by everything that has to do with physical exercise. He's never alone much, because he's placed where he can watch people. Besides, the dog is just like a person to him, and keeps him company all the time. Jane is quite rough with him but she is swiftly punished. Mrs. F makes no reference to any play of her own with the baby but describes play equipment she has set up for the children—slides and ladders for Jane, and a swing for Frank ... Frank accepts physical discomforts and hurts without complaint and only whimpers a little if distressed about anything ... When denied something he's easily distracted by substitutes. Actually, he's more contented if Mrs. F simply removes from sight anything he should not have—although at sight of food being prepared he does "have a fit" and demands to be fed at once ... He can be comforted by being jiggled or given a toy, or by being held very tightly in his mother's arms ... He isn't uneasy with strangers except for baby-sitters, so Mrs. F is careful to introduce him to new sitters by having them hold him for a few minutes ... Frank did become frightened once and screamed when a blanket fell on his head momentarily; he screamed after the fall in the morning; was very frightened after a fall caused by a slide on a little rug; and is very frightened when tossed in air—so Mr. F waits until he is ready before starting that kind of play ... On the whole, the baby doesn't show many emotions ... He is undemanding, self-sufficient, and usually busy in a relaxed way ... Asked if she tries to teach the baby anything, Mrs. F replies firmly that she certainly does not. She says assertively that naturally there is no competition between her two children because they are of different sexes.

When Frank was four months old the family went on a skiing vacation. Mrs. F believed it important for the baby to have the experience with the family rather than be left with strangers in the lodge, and so on several days she carried him along in a sling on her back. Usually, after a short time in the carrier he would slump down and probably wasn't very comfortable, but even after two hours or so he didn't complain. He did catch cold, but Mrs. F hopes the family will take a similar vacation next year.

Mrs. F's reports were thin and lacked sensitivity. She had not observed the baby well nor did she seem interested in doing so. She made no effort to communicate with him in any way, was neither affectionate with nor critical of him at any time. She seemed to take it for granted that Frank was impervious to distress. For example, several times in order to demonstrate how he loved to be jiggled on someone's knee, she awakened the near-sleeping baby to do so; before feeding, she not only draped a diaper all around the baby's neck but under it placed a scratchy paper towel as well.

She directed strong criticism against her parents-in-law for their questioning of Mrs. F's ways of caring for the children. And there was implied criticism in her asking the interviewer a number of times whether the interviewer was sure there weren't more questions to ask or more things to have the baby do.

THE ONE-YEAR VISIT: INFANT AGE 53.2 WEEKS

Mrs. F was overtly friendly and self-assured. Her attitude was more instructive than curious. She was quite disconcerted by some of the baby's behavior.

Frank was sturdy and most attractive. He restricted himself physically to being in Mrs. F's lap or at her side almost all of the time. He moved about only on his knees and showed no interest in exploring about the room. He was more limp when held in arms than most one-year-olds. Testing was poorly tolerated. His initial responses were delayed, his attention span was short, his curiosity moderate, and he was disinclined to follow demonstrations or complete tasks. He watched the examiner more than he looked at objects. As at six months, the test procedures had to be interrupted because of his increasing irritability and wariness. His capacity to handle objects was actually superior, as shown by his successful completion of tasks at moments when he picked them up from the table independently, in nontest periods.

He made many cheerful sounds, babbled a great deal, and had a repertoire of six or seven words. Many times at unexpected moments he looked up at the examiner, raised his hand, grinned, and said, "Hi!" The grin was so exaggerated and mechanical that Mrs. F spontaneously explained, with an apology, that she had taught Frank to make this sort of a grin in order to show his teeth, and then could not unteach him. A number of times in the midst of apparent contentment Frank suddenly and inexplicably seemed to become overwhelmed with irritability: he arched, kicked, flailed, and screamed. Each time, he was gradually comforted when Mrs. F picked him up and talked to him, gave him the pacifier, or put him down in a new place. Except for these mood swings his behavior was entirely subdued. He took no natural pleasure in social engagements. He banged one leg rhythmically a great deal during feeding.

The baby was weaned from the breast by nine months. He takes foods well and eats more than anybody else in the family (during this visit he ate very little). Occasionally he won't eat a meal or a specific food, probably if it hasn't been prepared in the usual way ... He falls asleep with the help of the pacifier and sleeps soundly. Several months ago, however, he got into a bad habit of waking up and crying during the night, even four times a night. It wasn't his problem, but hers, because she had to pick him up and rock him to sleep on account of the neighbors. Mrs. F herself would have let him shriek away and get out of the habit.

Frank began to walk on his feet "months ago" but gave it up after discovering suddenly that he could kneel and get about on his knees ... He can sit and play for long periods with toys, putting them inside one another, or just looking out of the window. There is so much to see that he can occupy himself for long periods of time. He is a great watcher ... He is fun all the time though Mrs. F may play with him only in the evenings ... It is very important for a baby not to need to be entertained by others ... Frank waits well for things he wants because he is still so easy to distract. Mainly he shows discomfort by whimpering. He never pouts, is always cheerful, and best of all loves to play games and to rough-house with his sister. They know they're going to get hurt, and if it's worth it to them Mrs. F will let them do it ... Frank is rarely stubborn. He does often get very angry and screams if clothing is pulled over his head or if he's taken out of his bath. He is stoic. When he fell off a chair he hardly whimpered. When his sister hits him he doesn't cry, but if he realizes she has hurt him deliberately he has a temper tantrum.

There is very little to discipline a one-year-old for, except danger. Anyway, Mrs. F tries to reason with Frank or looks at him crossly and scolds. Frank usually bursts into tears even if there is no scolding. Mrs. F has never hit him ... He has a habit of biting which Mrs. F tries to interfere with only if people are being bitten. No success yet. He also occasionally bangs his leg and he rocks ... He is very independent ... The only thing that upsets him is to be placed in an unfamiliar surrounding where he can't see Mrs. F. He gets frightened if new people pick him up. And he's rather cautious of strangers. A few times Mrs. F has left Frank with friends and he hasn't fussed at all, nor even paid attention to Mrs. F on her return, because he's been having such a good time. Frank hasn't changed in any basic ways over the year. He has remained unusually patient, endures hunger well, and probably will be an easygoing and sensible type of person.

Mrs. F's attitude toward Frank was hard to estimate. She kept trying to keep him busy with toys, urging them upon him mechanically. She talked to him now and then, but not in response to him, and without inviting any responses from him. Rather, she made remarks to quiet him and showed no interest in his condition. She appeared to be proud of not having tried to teach him much, just to play pat-a-cake and to keep away from dangers. Otherwise, she just lets him pick up whatever (knowledge) he's exposed to. When Frank succeeded in carrying out a task with blocks on an advanced level, Mrs. F immediately interjected that the test was not fair because he already had experience with blocks.

She was distinctly embarrassed, however, by the baby's sudden bursts of irritability, and said impatiently that she just didn't know *what* the baby wanted. Something seemed awry with their communication all of the time. This impression may have resulted from Mrs. F's repeated emphasis on how amazingly easy, contented, and undemanding Frank was, in spite of his manifest distress and his generally restricted behavior. Mrs. F's meager investment in observing his activity was suggested yet again by her reference to Frank's having suddenly discovered, after having started to walk, that he could kneel. Actually, the preference for kneeling had been visible during the six-month visit. Mrs. F asked no questions about the baby's development. She remarked with satisfaction that she used to worry that he was brighter than his sister, but she no longer did.

CLINICAL IMPRESSIONS: MRS. F

Mrs. F's ideas of child rearing show her high degree of self-reliance and her unshakable confidence that she can carry many responsibilities with equanimity and objectivity. Her attentiveness to the baby is rote and affectless. She is identified with the two parent figures of her childhood, at least in respect to those qualities in them which consciously she repudiates: excessive casualness and excessive demandingness. During the neonatal examination she dramatizes her inability or unwillingness to accept any role assigned to her by another. At the six-week visit she is impersonal and, as before, has many rationalizations to justify the correctness of her procedures. The baby is praised for enduring things, which here may be translated as bearing pain or displeasure without complaint and without loss of composure.

At the six-month visit Mrs. F's reports are again singularly lacking in empathy or sympathy. They reflect an overweening confidence in her efficiency and judgment, and no awareness of their many contradictions. She is extremely insensitive to the baby's emotional needs and seems quite untouched by the advances in his behavior, or even by his unusual beauty. The baby is expected to accommodate to high degrees of physical stimulation and to tolerate physical hardship. The mother's total emphasis is on the baby's capacity to get along with minimal personal contact.

At the one-year-visit the reports include signs of tension in the infant which again are rationalized as insignificant (the night crying was really Mrs. F's problem), or as positive developments (Frank is stoic). Mrs. F has no idea that there may have been some relationships between the baby's earlier screaming during the night and the more recent panic states. Toward the baby no affection, no appreciation, and no spontaneity are to be seen. The emotional energy of this mother appears to be consumed in maintaining an inner security against any social or affective overtures that might emanate from herself or from others. It appears that she sees herself primarily as a neutral caretaker.

CLINICAL COMMENTS: FRANK

Six Weeks

The vitality and responsiveness of this infant are marred by his tension and restlessness. He is active, but his movements lack smoothness. As he accomodates much better to external stimuli than to stress arising, apparently, from internal sources, his anxiety preparedness is hard to appraise. However, the degree of effort he summons up to master the internal stress is auspicious. His visual response to persons suggests that he has entered the first phase of socialization.

Six Months

Frank's regard of the environment is cautious, and the cautiousness grows during testing, as if cumulative interaction with the examiner gradually disconcerts him. Even the mother's overtures arouse stress and withdrawal. Mrs. F reports, on the one hand, that the baby manifests distress easily but lightly, and can be distracted easily. On the other hand, she tells of a number of experiences that have made him scream with fright. The indications are that he tends to be overcome with anxiety by incidents which many other infants might tolerate adequately. He does appeal for help, but his appeals are restricted and leave him in states of chronic uneasiness. The signal anxiety so far developed appears to be too unstable, even for a six-month-old.

He is in the second phase of socialization in that he differentiates the mother from nonmothers, yet one gets the impression that he does not perceive her as an outstanding source of gratification or of relief from distress. Mrs. F's behavior and attitudes may engender an affectlessness in their relationship; this could help to explain how a defensive emotional quality has become characteristic of Frank.

One Year

Frank appears to inhibit physical responsiveness to persons as well as to inanimate objects. Premature defenses may have set in, but they are disrupted from time to time by sudden and inexplicable raids of irritability, which are best relieved by physical comforting. As at six months, he is on the one hand described as stoic and cheerful, and on the other hand as screaming, bursting into tears, and having tantrums for insufficient reasons. Signal anxiety is unstable.

Language development suggests that the infant is striving to relate to persons, but no real joy is visible in his contacts with people. He watches them more than he engages with them. He is more comfortable with inanimate objects, which evoke his maturest cathexis, in spite of his inhibition of function pleasure. Frustration tolerance is very erratic, as shown in his oscillations from "stoicism" to fury. Narcissism is unduly heightened by chronic and unrelieved bodily distress and emotional isolation. He seeks release in numerous aggressive habits: banging, biting, rocking, screaming. Cognitive ability, as observed during testing, is superior but cannot be exercised appropriately. DQ: 116.

CHAPTER 23

Type VII: Mrs. G and Gena

THE PRENATAL INTERVIEW

Mrs. G was a well-rounded, pleasantly smiling young woman. She moved easily and quietly, with a childlike modesty. Her speech was well modulated, her affect always composed. She told of her experiences and gave opinions smoothly and thoughtfully, and stressed her desire to learn the best ways to bring up a baby. She gladly accepted an offer of lunch, after having mentioned that she had come a long distance and had not had much breakfast.

> Her mother had died after a long, debilitating illness, when Mrs. G was nine years old. As an only child, Mrs. G had found her mother's companionship very important, and recalls playing games with her. She regrets that sometimes she took advantage of her mother's illness to get her way, and remembers the mother's threats to report Mrs. G's bad behavior to her father, who did occasionally spank her. Mrs. G had been afraid of him, especially of his voice. After his wife's death he did not remarry, and Mrs. G lived with him alone ... Following her high-school graduation Mrs. G studied art and worked as a free-lance designer until she married. Her father has never accepted her husband, who is of a different religion, and since the beginning of Mrs. G's pregnancy her father's jealousy has been so keen that he has refused even to see her. Mr. and Mrs. G are both avid readers on many subjects, ranging from history and philosophy to avant-garde literature. Their social life is very limited, partly for financial reasons and partly because Mr. G does not get on well with people. It is for the latter reason that he also does not hold on to any job, Mrs. G adds, ruefully. She is the stronger partner in the marriage.

Mrs. G expects to bottle feed, for no particular reason. Probably she will keep the baby to a flexible demand schedule, but is not sure. She has no idea about when to wean. Her reading about infant care has convinced her that babies should be held for feeding, and that bottles should not be propped . . . She doesn't know when to begin toilet training, but assumes that some sort of control should begin at about a year. She would try sitting the baby on the potty, and if that didn't work she'd probably wait . . . Habits could develop early, so babies should be given substitute satisfactions. For example, if he began to suck his thumb, Mrs. G would use a pacifier; but if he started to chew the pacifier, Mrs. G would take it away. If he bit his nails she would simply cut them short . . . It is important to give a child affection, yet not so much that he loses independence, or gets spoiled. If a baby were crying only to get attention, she would "let it scream, or turn it on its stomach, and give it a slap." Methods of discipline would depend upon the child but, definitely, children should be treated firmly. One could begin by saying "No" when the baby is crawling, and could already understand the "no." "Mainly I would talk, and then hit." . . .

A mother's attitude toward the child's play is very important. She should provide simple toys, because a baby should learn how to create, and how to improvise. She hoped her child would be intelligent and intellectual . . . It is also extremely important for a child to have someone to go to with his problems. She would try to be as affectionate and positive as possible toward her child, so he would have freedom to express himself. So far, she has chosen only a boy's name—for girls she has only been able to think of ridiculous names.

THE CONFINEMENT VISIT

Although Mrs. G had wanted a son, she had found her little girl cute at first sight, and "now wouldn't change her for anything."

Labor (12 hours, 35 minutes) and delivery were difficult, much more painful than Mrs. G had expected, in spite of her getting preanesthesia medication. The doctors just hadn't seemed to know what to do for her. She was not especially eager to go home as she was very comfortable in the hospital, and very satisfied with the care she was currently receiving. Her husband was very lonesome, however. In fact, he was observed to spend an unusual amount of time in the hospital, reading, talking with Mrs. G, and sharing her meals.

THE NEONATAL EXAMINATION

This was a gentle-looking, moderately active little girl. Skin color, muscle tone, and turgor were good. In the supine, Gena flexed and occasionally extended her limbs, quietly and with moderate smoothness. Resistance to limb pressure was low. In the prone, she did not lift or move her head at all. Slight fussiness was often present.

Her responsiveness was quite varied. She failed entirely to react to auditory stimuli but did very well visually. Horizontal pursuit movements through an arc of 30° were easily obtained. To the tactile stimulus she reacted with head, mouth, and coordinated arm movements.

Mild crying before feeding was easily relieved when Gena was held and patted by her mother. She sucked spontaneously, with moderate eagerness and energy. Her states during feeding fluctuated between alertness and drowsiness. She took three-and-a-half ounces, coughed and gagged slightly, and seemed satisfied and sleepy at the end.

THE SIX-WEEK VISIT: INFANT AGE 4.3 WEEKS[1]

Mrs. G's dress was very worn and drab. Most of her abundant hair hung loose below her shoulders, and some was held

[1]This mother arranged for her visit with the baby as early as she could because of her own gladness at an opportunity to be out of her house for a few hours, and so Gena was seen at a younger age than other infants. Once arrived, Mrs. G told us that she had to go out to do some little errands, and would feed Gena on her return. During her absence the baby became fretful, and as her test tolerance was poor the tactile stimulation could not be presented adequately. After the feeding, Gena fell into a deep sleep. It was decided not to awaken her for either the tactile stimulus or the response to being held by the examiner; therefore these two items were omitted. Subsequently, technical difficulties with the camera showed that the

up in a bun, which gave her a somewhat disheveled appearance. Her skin was very clean. She was cordial, appealing, and would have stayed for many hours and asked many questions about the research and about babies. She treated the session as a social engagement, and spent much time drinking coffee. It transpired that she was hungry and expected to be given lunch and cigarettes, and to stay as long as she found convenient.

Gena, a healthy-looking, very fair-skinned baby, was active and alert. Muscle tone appeared to be normal. In the supine, the TNR position predominated. In the prone, she lifted her head high recurrently, and rested her upper body on her forearms. When pulled to sitting, she held her head well and slightly forward. When pulled to standing, she held a small fraction of her weight briefly. Occasionally the movements of her extremities were tremulous.

As at three days, she did not respond at all to the sound of the bell, but her visual response was very adequate in pursuit of persons as well as of test objects. Mrs. G reported that sometimes Gena reacted to Mrs. G's voice, but not to noises in the room. Gena was not observed to smile. She uttered a few vowel sounds. A moderate amount of hand-to-mouth activity was seen, but it was not well enough coordinated for her to get much satisfaction from it.

According to the written record, the feeding was easy and satisfying. Gena was very alert, had an excellent grasp of the nipple as she sucked, took six ounces steadily, and ended the feeding peacefully.

---

feeding had not been filmed. Mrs. G's eagerness to come to the project offices made it easy to invite her to come again so that we might film another feeding, and the latter was carried out when Gena was 6.4 weeks old. Unless otherwise noted, all observations of the infant reported here have been drawn from the main session, at the age of 4.3 weeks. In order to avoid duplication or confusion, staff observations of Mrs. G and reports by Mrs. G in both sessions have been combined, except where the information varies, in which case it is given separately for each infant age.

Gena feeds well but takes longer than Mrs. G had expected, and likes to be held after her feedings as well. If not, she will cry and cry. Cereal was added to her diet in the third week because she did not sleep well after her feedings during the day ... She began to sleep through the night in her fourth week. She needs to be full (satiated) and tired in order to fall asleep, but then sleeps soundly. When she wakes, she's so cute. She brings her arms up and stretches, and looks like—"I almost said—looks like a human being," said Mrs. G with mild humor.

Gena is very strong. She has such a loud cry; when her diaper is being changed, she stiffens her legs so much that Mrs. G can't bend them; she "flings" her bottle (pushes it away) and her pacifier (spits it out); and she can lift her head high and turn it from side to side ... She recognizes her bassinet, Mrs. G thinks, because when placed in it she screams ... If a baby of this age can be considered spoiled, Gena is, because of the way she cries after being well fed.

Mrs. G is having difficulty finding time to hold Gena and also do household chores. The first day and night were the hardest—Mrs. G thought the baby might die unless she was watched every minute. Now she worries that Gena may not hear.

SECOND VISIT: INFANT AGE 6.4 WEEKS[2]

Gena was chubby, had good body tone, but was not lively. She sat well, with her head forward. When she lay supine, her movements showed increased maturity. She attained symmetrical positions often and kicked her legs rhythmically. She cooed and vocalized softly a number of times.

Mrs. G expressed pleasure in having overcome her initial anxieties about handling the baby. Nevertheless, all of her movements of Gena were extremely gentle and extremely halting. When it was time to feed, she asked if she might have a cigarette first, and she relaxed with it in a leisurely way. Gena became fretful, Mrs. G said she would start the feeding, yet she neither took the bottle from the warmer nor asked for it. As the hour was growing late it occurred to the interviewer that Mrs. G might be waiting for the bottle to be brought to

[2]See footnote 1, this chapter.

her, and accordingly gave it to the mother, who then offered it to the baby. During the slow and awkward feeding Gena seemed less alert and active than the notes of the previous observer had implied. Mrs. G was exceedingly cautious about her smallest movements, trying again and again to keep Gena and herself comfortable, in vain.

Afterward she stood about, asking thoughtful questions ("Do babies have any memory?" "What does hiccoughing mean?" "When do babies become conscious?"), reporting her own hunger, describing her cold and cramped apartment, and her husband's search for work, all with subdued affect. As she chatted and moved about amiably and languidly, she left Gena unsupervised in the crib, though the side bars were down, asked for more coffee and cookies, and delayed her departure unduly. Final dressing of the baby was inept and dilatory. The absence of overt tension in this mother was very marked.

THE SIX-MONTH VISIT: INFANT AGE 25.5 WEEKS

Mrs. G came half an hour late and, as at the previous visit, immediately left the baby with the interviewer, this time in order to go out for cigarettes. She was dressed in very poor but clean clothing, except for dirty old sneakers. She was placid and her movements lacked tone; she seemed glad to talk.

Gena captured attention at once with her spontaneous, intense smile and her feminine grace. She enjoyed large body movements. In the prone position she raised herself high and rolled around in many positions, kicked, pivoted, rocked, and often threw her body down and let all her limbs go upward in an exciting manner. She held herself well in a standing position. She seemed particularly delighted when held in arms, and gazed idly around the room, yet her interest in the environment was low. The only specific object she was seen to regard spontaneously and prolongedly was the wall surface next to the crib.

Test scatter was wide. Attention to objects was much delayed and had to be aroused by the examiner's bringing them into Gena's line of vision or making sounds with them. Once she caught sight of an object she showed no eagerness, and only reached for it with her mouth. Even then, she preferred to mouth the edge of the table in a way that resulted in her looking mainly into her own lap. For almost every test item, manual approach had to be elicited by the examiner's lifting the baby's hands onto the table and putting the object very close to them. Then, unless Gena could bring the object directly to her mouth, she looked away, as if for something more familiar to rest her eyes upon, though not necessarily her mother or the examiner.

During the testing of her responses to objects, Gena showed vigor solely in repetitive mouthing and in frequent, strong vocalizations. A persistent restlessness and an increase of fussing suggested to Mrs. G that the baby might be hungry ahead of schedule, and tired, but Gena stayed awake during the feeding of 45 minutes, and for a full hour thereafter. Actually, her fussing decreased markedly as soon as she was removed from the test table.

Except when hungry, tired, or when the mother was absent from the room, Gena's social vitality was very superior, in contrast to her poor performance with inanimate objects. She glowed as she made personal overtures and reacted to the overtures of others with happy excitement. Her vocalizations were mature and clear, she could mix consonants and utter them on different levels and with different intensities. But her social grace and her physical adeptness had limits. In neither was there much range. She repeated the same movements and the same sounds over and over, and in spite of the maturity of these actions in themselves, one had the impression of their not bringing satisfaction to her. Possibly this was because she maintained just the same excited activity for nearly three hours, without any interest in the nonhuman environment. In general, her behavior reflected a lack of resourcefulness and a lack of curiosity.

Gena takes all foods well. Mrs. G has started to use a training cup, but will not hurry weaning. She tries to please Gena, offering just one new vegetable at a time, and making sure the baby digests it well before introducing the next. She expects the baby to vomit a lot, because when she sucks, Gena swallows a lot of air. (The observed feeding, reported to be typical, was very uneasy: the baby slumped, squirmed, fretted, yet Mrs. G kept on feeding a great deal, even after Gena vomited.) ... Gena has slept through the night since she was three weeks old, but much less during the day ...

Actually, the day's program has become more and more hectic, and how any day goes depends entirely on the baby's mood. Mrs. G gets up in the morning a little while .after Gena does. Then she tries to postpone feeding Gena for another half hour. After a long bottle feeding, of about 45 minutes, Gena gets egg, cereal, and more milk, and ends her breakfast in a very cranky state. She is put down "any place," restless, yelling; if she has been put into her infant seat she may fall off it. Giving her a cracker or a toy may not help at all. If she takes a short nap, she's "not so bad" after it ... She may drink some juice and sleep again until lunch time. She can wait pretty well for food, though she doesn't respond to smiles while she's waiting ... After lunch, in her crib, she rolls about, whimpers, fusses, calls, wants attention. Holding or cuddling her helps, or giving her a cracker; these failing, she will be comforted by the pacifier ... yet she often pulls out the pacifier, and when she reinserts it into her mouth she can't release it, so she pulls it out again without intending to; this brings on screaming again, and Mrs. G has to help her again ... Maybe she's teething ... She may scream for about 15 minutes, though now and then she may stop and look around. If she's in a bad mood when she's picked up, she still twists and turns and Mrs. G can hardly hold her ...

When Mrs. G takes her outdoors Gena becomes very good, enjoying responses from every passer-by. When Gena is put into her crib for the night, she becomes very insulted—once she cried for half an hour—so she's taken to the living room for an hour or two. Sometimes she continues to scream there until she is finally put to bed ... Once, after she had diarrhea, Mrs. G gave her only liquids on the next day. Gena screamed all that day. A day later Mrs. G realized that the baby must have been hungry; she felt terrible for having let her scream until she was quite hoarse and could hardly make an audible sound ...

Gena is very active, loves attention, loves to watch Mrs. G moving fast around the house, and loves to sit with Mrs. G, watching television. Mrs. G plays with her most, interrupting her housework occasionally to hold the baby, kiss her body, toss her

in the air, and make noises with her. If Gena gets tired of being
in one place Mrs. G just changes her position ... Mr. G plays the
same way, but much less ... Mrs. G hasn't been interested in
offering toys to Gena, and doesn't really know what toys to give,
except a rattle. And Gena would rather play with Mrs. G than
with toys. Gena doesn't retain interest in any playthings. She
likes to put everything into her mouth. When she wants something she grunts and growls and screams, but after a while she
may just give up. Sometimes, in excitement or anger, she hits her
own thighs repeatedly, and seems unable to stop this once she
gets started. Or she bangs her heel into her crotch. She pulls on
her ears. She likes to suck her hand, or forearm, or upper arm—
she bites on it, really, but she doesn't suck her thumb ... The
first time she was frightened was when someone who was holding her slipped on a rug and came down heavily. Gena at first
was still with shock, then she screamed her head off. She also
was frightened by the rusty sounds of her crib before it was oiled
... Sometimes she startles at sight of a stranger ... The only
specific cause of displeasure for Gena is lumpy egg yolk.

Mrs. G felt well until the last several weeks, that is, since the
baby has been "a pain in the neck." Sometimes, when Gena is so
demanding for attention, it helps to rock her in arms; other
times, Mrs. G has just left her alone to cry, lest Mrs. G herself get
too impatient and angry. She gets so irritated at the fretful
sounds Gena makes ... She feels dejected and helpless. All her
reading about babies hasn't helped her. In the beginning everything seemed easier than people had predicted, and of course it
would be easier if Mrs. G had some help in the house. Since
Gena's birth Mr. and Mrs. G have been out for dinner just once.
Mr. G doesn't like to be left alone with the baby, so Mrs. G is
stuck in the house all day. She supposes things will stay this way
all through the summer, which has just begun.

Mrs. G was quite unusually careless of the baby's being in
the crib while the side bars were down. Because of the infant's big and rapid movements, many times she might have
rolled off the bed had the interviewer not been close to steady
her. At these times Mrs. G never approached the baby. She
went about the large room, talking, smoking, looking at objects, eating all of the cookies available, or using the telephone. At one point when she had carried out a very long

telephone conversation with a friend, the interviewer had to leave the room for a minute or two, and decided it was safest to carry Gena along with her. Mrs. G took no notice of their leaving or returning. She also showed no reaction at all when, more than an hour after feeding, Gena's mouth was obviously full of curdled milk, which she spat out from time to time. On the other hand, Mrs. G was highly interested in the baby's test performance and showed great pride in any signs of progress, and especially in the baby's social maturity. She was also extremely curious about methods of teaching a child to read at 18 months, and eager to have our opinion of those methods. Mrs. G's main attitude toward the baby was summed up by the interviewer to be, "If she's going to drive me nuts I put her in the bedroom."

The One-Year Visit: Infant Age 50.3 Weeks

Mrs. G had a youthful, bohemian appearance, but seemed heavy with fatigue. Her clothes were seedy and rumpled. Her skin was, as usual, very clean. Her behavior was subdued, her affect constricted; she told of having been depressed in the last few months. She had taken an afternoon and evening job, and was having great difficulty getting up in the mornings.

Gena was physically well developed, very feminine in appearance, and nicely dressed. Her motor development was somewhat advanced, though she could not yet walk alone. She cruised about, exploring the room actively and with interest, but not stopping to examine any objects in particular. When she was in the playpen, she occupied herself with the inspection of all its parts: the bars, the texture of the net, the mattress, the metal, etc., but gradually turned most of her efforts toward eliciting attention from her mother or the interviewer, calling to them and showing objects to them. She made no other demands.

Although Gena was curious to reach out for test objects, her attention to them was only moderate and gradually decreased. Her perception of what could be done with them appeared to be good, and fine motor coordination was adequate; nevertheless, her efforts to execute tasks were very superficial. Alertness to sounds from outside the room often pre-empted her attention. The infant's tolerance of frustration was very low. She was quick to dismiss objects which presented any difficulty, and was content with them only if she could bring them to her mouth. The only thing she took into her mouth was the cup, from which she pretended to drink. Boredom appeared, and soon she tossed each object off the table and looked to her mother to pick them up. Or she simply turned to Mrs. G and tried to involve her in play. She was somewhat wary of the examiner, scrutinizing her for long periods, and a few times responding with a smile. Throughout the visit she was active in an undirected way, rarely able to concentrate her attention upon any one object or activity. She babbled constantly. She fed herself semisolids with unusual skill.

Gena has no regular daily schedule, as the family life now revolves around a single definite event: the hour at which Mrs. G must go out to work. Mrs. G gets up in the morning after she hears the baby cry, gives her a bottle, and then Gena feeds herself the other foods in a high chair. Mrs. G began teaching her to use the spoon at seven and a half months. Gena eats without any clothes on, so Mrs. G needn't mind the mess . . . Mr. G puts Gena to bed at night. Often she protests, so after about 15 minutes he takes her out of her crib for a while; probably she's not tired enough to fall asleep . . . She usually rocks herself to sleep. She is a light sleeper, and wakes if Mrs. G even puts a blanket on her. In fact she wakes several times a night, and may stay awake for as long as two hours, playing.

She much prefers to watch people than to do things herself. She is never really alone in their tiny apartment, but she can play by herself for an hour and a half, "talking" to things while she handles them . . . She doesn't cry so much now. She is more active, crawling, climbing, picking things up, but not much interested in toys unless they're new . . . If she wants something that she can't reach, she'll persist for a while, then give up and turn to something else, but if Mrs. G denies her something specific, Gena gets fiercely angry and has a temper tantrum. All Mrs. G can do then is to put her on the floor and leave her alone, or offer her a biscuit.

Sometimes picking her up won't help, as Gena, in anger, throws things, and keeps on screaming. Then Mrs. G just leaves her alone ... She cries when she has to wait for food. Her main habits, though, are throwing and rocking. She rocks in a rapid, excited way, with great pleasure, mainly when alone; she rocks slowly, rhythmically, without pleasure, when she is tired, and then she also bangs her head on the crib bars ...

Mrs. G has not had to impose much discipline. She has just to speak to Gena firmly, telling her not to touch electrical outlets, or tear paper, and Gena minds ... When she was five months old, and two or three times lately, Gena has taken off her diaper after having a bowel movement, and has smeared the feces over the crib, and eaten it ... Gena used to be afraid of her father. Now she likes him better, perhaps because he is at home with her more. Sometimes he doesn't let her cry at all, and sometimes he leaves her to cry alone. She is not shy of anybody, but may be a little cautious of strangers. About three months ago she was frightened by a cat, and once she was frightened when she was left by Mrs. G in a strange room. Now she doesn't mind if Mrs. G leaves. She acts just the same as when Mrs. G remains present. Her typical mood is one of happy contentment.

Mrs. G. feels quite unable to care for Gena properly, and as a result she tends to curtail the baby's freedom. She worries about Gena's choking when Gena keeps large amounts of food in her mouth (here Mrs. G pointed to a wad of semisolids the baby had been keeping in her mouth), about when to begin toilet training, when to wean to table foods, even though she doesn't really feel up to preparing foods herself. She worries about how Gena is reacting to the tension between her and her husband, and wishes she had some place to go to where there would be people who knew about children, such as psychiatrists, social workers, or psychologists, whom she could ask questions. She has been trying to teach Gena sounds and words, and again speaks of her wish to begin teaching Gena to read at 18 months ... On the whole, she lets Gena do what she wants, and only discourages her when she gets into dangerous places ... Gena is very easy to take care of because she doesn't cry so much anymore ... If she stays as she is, she'll be independent and well adjusted, a happy child who likes to try new things.

Mrs. G appeared to be unconcerned about the baby's rocking, head banging, fecal smearing, and generally restless activity. She expressed nothing proud or positive about Gena, save that she was easy to take care of. She was passive toward the baby, watching her when the examiner did, not doing so when the examiner did not. She neither prohibited nor admonished. Although her comments implied that she felt affection for the baby, she did not show it except in fondness and patience when she encouraged Gena to feed herself. Physical contact between mother and infant was rare.

CLINICAL IMPRESSIONS: MRS. G

Mrs. G's life has been lonely, and her pregnancy has brought about an increased withdrawal of her father. The quiet tolerance of his disapproval and of her husband's difficulties, shown during her pregnancy, makes one wonder if she will be able to acquiesce similarly to the demands of a baby. She expresses her wish to be competent as a mother, but her ideas about infant care are vague and undeveloped. Even in the confinement period, she is confronted with the problem of her husband's dependence upon her and is sympathetic to him in his loneliness.

At the six-week visit, her reports show that she is at a loss to set up routines or to cope with the baby's demands. She takes pride in the baby and can be affectionate to her, but even her tenderness has an exceeding, fearful quality. Lapses in her attention to the baby's needs suggest mild depression. At the six-month visit, her lack of organization and her helplessness are pronounced. She is highly irritated by the infant's chronic fussiness and barely mindful of Gena's regressive and anxious behavior. While some of the mother's difficulties clearly seem to be attributable to her husband's dependence and withdrawal, she blames only the baby for upsetting her. Possibly she is embarrassed by her marital conflicts. Positive developments in the infant relieve her worry and sadness but meagerly. At the one-year visit, Mrs. G's sadness has become chronic. She has become less observant, less tender, less interested, and even less concerned with the obvious signs of distress in Gena. Her efforts to encourage age-adequate activities in the infant are sporadic at best. Contact and communication between mother and infant are irregular, erratic, and unsatisfying.

Mrs. G's initial aspirations toward competence in mothering have gradually receded, and she has become more and more oppressed by her own unsatisfied longing for affective support. The concomitant wish to depend passively upon others for practical satisfactions as well appears to aggravate her maternal insufficiency. None of this is surprising, in view of her early loss of her mother, the current disturbances in her relationships to her husband and her father, and the constriction of her own emotional resources.

Clinical Comments: Gena

Six Weeks

Upon the first observation (4.3 weeks), reactivity in all modalities except auditory is good to superior. Upon the second observation (6.4 weeks), physical maturity is increased and vocalizations are more frequent. Responsiveness to external stimuli is direct, appropriate, and strong. The infant accommodates less well to inner stimuli, as shown in the difficulty in being comforted after feeding, and in falling asleep. Alertness seen during waking states seems to diminish during feeding, almost as if some regression sets in; possibly this is related to the mother's manifest and verbalized insecurity about the adequacy of her feeding methods. Anxiety preparedness in the infant appears to be conspicuously uneven.

Imprinting to the mother as species-specific object is not observed. The maturest sign of social response at six weeks occurs in frequent vocalizations, but there are few indications of any distinct responses to persons.

Six Months

Inner stress is observable on numerous occasions: during testing, after feeding, in insufficient daytime sleep, frequent screaming, excessive need for comforting, restlessness, and tantrums. The infant's demands are best relieved by being held and by passive locomotion. Inanimate objects provide little or no relief. Gena seems unable to avail herself of inner resources against distress. She can appeal directly for help. Signal anxiety is present, although when the signal is not responded to very quickly, she is flooded with anxiety.

Social responsiveness is strong. Gena's capacity to be comforted by the mother shows movement toward completion of the second phase of socialization, but differentiation between the mother and other persons appears to be meager.

One Year

Anxiety is not confined to its signal manifestation. There appear to be few periods when the infant shows the capacity to appeal directly for help and to wait for it. Stress rises rapidly at bedtime, during sleep and on waking, and when food and other objects are not immediately accessible. When distress sets in from whatever source, severe disequilibrium ensues.

Object relations are clearly disturbed. Gena appears to depend excessively on the mother for comfort. Despite her interest in people she does not respond to them with age-adequate curiosity. Interest in inanimate objects is quickly spent. The balance of cathexis is tilted sharply in favor of investment in the body and in immediate satisfactions. Agitated rocking, head banging, fecal smearing and eating are resorted to frequently. Frustration tolerance is low. According to the mother's report, not contradicted by observation, Gena is less prone to get upset than she was when previously seen, despite the many "habits" that she currently shows. Conceivably, this lowered sensitivity signifies an early onset of depressive states. The normal reduction of narcissism at the end of the first year of life has hardly occurred.

Good cognitive ability is impaired by insufficiently developed avenues for tension discharge ("boredom"), restlessness, and poor maintenance of curiosity about any specific objects. DQ: 108.

Part V
MOTHER-INFANT INTERACTION AND NARCISSISM

CHAPTER 24

On Some Issues in the Study of Mother-Infant Interaction

An investigation of how mothers affect infants can hardly be satisfactory without knowledge yet to come from genetics and biochemistry, as far as the infants are concerned. For the mothers, we need more knowledge of the conscious but unstated feelings and ideas they have about their infants, of their unconscious strivings, and of their marital lives.

As to the biological determinants of the infants' behavior, neither we nor to our knowledge anyone else at present know how to assess, shortly after birth and before the newborn's behavior has been influenced by the mother's attitudes and handling, what the individual infant brings to bear upon their relationship. But we recognize that it is the interplay between the maternal personality and the specific biological constitution of the infant which moulds the behavior of the normal infant. We have stressed biological determinants less than some other investigators, first, because we could not define them nor study them operationally, and second, because in all but one of the maternal types, the infants were usually at their best at the six-week observation. In general, the curve of disturbance increased after that. This phenomenon cannot be explained parsimoniously in terms of constitutional factors, but it can be if greater weight is given to the influence of the mother.

In spite of the manifest disturbances that have been described and implied among the infants, at six months all of them had attained the second phase of socialization, and at the end of the first year all had developed signal anxiety. Psychological test performances (DQs) at one year were adequate in all cases. All of the mothers expressed pleasure about their infants' development, except in those instances where they considered the infants too demanding. Consciously they were satisfied. Whether the expression of satisfaction stemmed from an unwillingness to confess disappointment or worry, from a form of denial, or from a lack of knowledge about infant development, or whether it is a tribute to maternal tolerance, we do not know. On the other hand, many of the mothers were also unable to appreciate favorable developmental signs in their infants' behavior. One can say that infancy, unlike adolescence, tends to be taken for granted.

We made no direct effort to gather knowledge of the mothers' conflicts, defenses, and fantasies because to obtain these in depth would have reduced our sample to only a few cases. Of the mothers, it may be said that they were probably as "normal" as is the general population. Closer scrutiny might have shown more indications of health as well as more pathology in them, just as close psychological probing of an individual brings evidence of mastered and of remaining anxieties and conflicts. Even in the relatively superficial material at our disposal, it was obvious that the mothers' mental health varied greatly. The reader may be struck by the degree of pathology found in both mothers and infants in six of the seven illustrative cases, especially as these few cases reflect conditions found among the larger sample. Many strengths are also present. Nevertheless, the total picture yielded by the mothers and infants is far from the one frequently assumed, of the happy and smiling mother and infant pair typical of an intact home and family.

Thus we end the first chapter of reporting our longitudinal investigation with no more than pertinent clues about the interplay between specific maternal behaviors and specific infant personality and development. Our material does allow us, however, to express certain convictions.

The first refers to a common assumption that mothers can and often do show different maternal behavior when their children enter new phases of maturation. An example is the mother who is described as a person who finds little babies dull but reacts with lively pleasure to the toddler because she feels more comfortable with the child when his personality has become more distinct. Our finding that types of maternal behavior remain internally consistent does not support this belief, at least not for the infant's first year. Our mothers did not change their basic modes of response in spite of the changing needs and demands of their infants. Ainsworth and Bell (1970), too, have found that maternal behavior with infants ($N=26$) was consistent through the first year of life and was clearly related to differences in the infants' attachment and exploratory behavior in the last quarter of the year.

While we have always held an assumption (Brody, 1956) that, by and large, the fundamental behavior pattern of a mother is sustained over long time spans, although in ways that may not be visible to the untrained eye, it was still expected that individual differences among 122 infants would accordingly dispose some mothers to show alterations in their responsiveness during the first year. Yet by a statistical analysis of, in most cases, as many as 36 variables, only four mothers in the sample remained unclassified; that is, only four failed to show a consistent pattern of behavior. It is to be noted that these four were among the most erratic in the sample. Their behavior showed mixtures of confusion, infantilism, and excitement, and instability was a common characteristic among them. We have yet to see to what extent maternal behavior will change in keeping with the maturation and development of our infants as they grow into children. Nevertheless, our view of an inner continuity of maternal behavior is reinforced.

We are of the opinion that the observed continuity only reflects the essential consistency of the usual adult character. With the probable exception of cases in which the condition of motherhood in itself arouses or relieves the force of the

superego, we should expect that a mother's character structure is not likely to undergo basic alteration as the child grows
older. We believe that the typology revealed relatively unchanging behavior because the criteria used for its construction were conjoint measures of the mother's actual response to
current and observable needs of her particular infant, during
a significant and very familiar joint task, and did not isolate
the behavior of either partner. The scoring of Empathy, Control, and Efficiency centered on the mother's behavioral responses to whatever thoughts or feelings the needs of her own
infant appeared to evoke in her. It is regrettable that the
criteria do not provide a simple formula for evaluating the
adequacy of maternal behavior. They provide guides for its
evaluation, and in doing so they probably are no more inexact
than many diagnostic criteria in psychiatric usage.

A second common assumption which, interestingly
enough, is made about specific infants or children by parents
or other close relatives, though not usually about children in
general, is that certain characteristics have been present from
birth or almost from birth, e.g., an alert glance, an irritable
temper, a loud cry. Some of our infants did maintain specific
qualities of behavior from the time of our earliest observations,
such as sluggishness, or a form of hypersensitivity, or imperturbability. Certainly neonates show innate dispositions toward varying patterns of sensorimotor activity and of state,
and different intensities of instinctual demand, which are
more or less enduring, subject to all sorts of "complementary
series." Early behavioral and response patterns among some of
our infants appeared to remain fairly stable or to change
smoothly and gradually. The behavior and responsiveness of
many other infants, however, changed dramatically, and more
often for the worse than for the better. As indicated above,
consistency in patterns of infant behavior, even with relatively
crude measures, was not found between three days and six
weeks, nor between six weeks and six months or one year.
Judging from many findings related to the behavior and attitudes of the mothers in our sample (to be published sepa-

rately), we are convinced that just as the anxious worries of some mothers became self-fulfilling prophecies, so habituation to patterns that were instituted in the first weeks of life became perpetuated as time went on, and retrospectively were considered to have been present from the beginning. Certainly, many statements—both positive and negative— about behavior in older infants having been seen from birth were contradicted by our records. Although we do not really know under what conditions neonatal patterns persist in spite of maternal efforts to sustain or alleviate them, we so often saw sharp changes in infants' behavior between six weeks and six months that, without very detailed material about the accommodation of mother and infant to each other in the first weeks of life, we should wish to suspend judgment about early and permanent patterning of infant behavior.

There is a remarkable contradiction between the two frequent assumptions to which we have alluded. The one implies that mothers change under certain conditions, the other that infants remain the same under obviously changing conditions of growth. Logic suggests that both assumptions may rest upon a need to seize upon general explanations of behavior and to obscure the possibility that in many cases it is not the kind of baby a mother has that counts so much in the quality of his development as the extent to which the mother's conscious ideas about him, and her actual behavior toward him, are in conflict with her unconscious ideas about him.

Our findings also convince us that in the quest for determinants of mental health or illness it is idle to seek reassurance in the idea that we do not know just what infants are born with, or to make use of this fact to delay recognizing what does happen to them at the hands of well-meaning but troubled or uninformed mothers. While our data cannot offer essential proofs of how particular forms of maternal behavior have particular effects upon infant development, we have ample grounds for postulating that a relationship between the two is operative from the first weeks of life, and may become less and less reversible with the passage of time. No reader will have failed to note the high frequency of disturbed maternal behavior in our "normal" sample. The most adequate behavior (type I) and the least adequate (type IV) are the easiest to recognize. On the whole, the former mothers (27) showed fewest disturbances of behavior; the latter (10) not only showed severe disturbances and apparently extreme defensiveness, but were governed by anxieties that interfered severely with good infant care. In between these two types was a large group of mothers (85) who showed varying kinds and degrees of disturbances, and apparently frequently unsuccessful defenses against anxiety. Their infant care was amiss, though less obviously than that of the openly aggressive or seductive mothers of type IV. They were usually conscientious, but also fearful, inhibited, resentful, overactive, rough, depressed, or withdrawn. Although we do not extrapolate from our sample to the general population, we feel it is reasonable to consider that very many mothers with similar varieties of inadequacy exist in our culture.

CHAPTER 25

Narcissism and Early Development

The process by which physiological anxiety is changed to psychological anxiety is not directly observable. Until such time as it may be detected by techniques of physiological measurement, we can try to discern effects of the change in altered states of behavior. No doubt the more gradual the process of change, the more difficult it is to see the behavioral indices of its having occurred, or its occurring. For example, the SFD (encompassing changes of a wholesome nature) that were culled from our data are fewer than the SDi, more apt to be integrated into the total behavior and personality of the normal infant, and more pleasing to the mother. The presence of SDi, on the other hand, is more likely to indicate that the process of change from physiological to psychological anxiety has *not* been taking place in a favorable manner or at a favorable rate.

What, then, can we consider to be behavioral signs that psychological anxiety has come into being? We might expect the signs to show in the infant's awareness of changes in tension states. The nature of the signs obviously would depend upon the infant's age, but at any age we should look for repeated strivings toward tension reduction, and repeated attainments of that reduction.

At the three ages at which our infants were studied, signs that the work of bridging from states of physiological tension to states of awareness of sensation is proceeding might be visible in a variety of ways. For example:

At six weeks: by a rise of alert attention to comforts offered gently and in good time and a rise of crankiness when the comforts are lacking; by repeated regard of proximal objects, especially if offered for the purpose of distraction; by reduction of physical activity at the approach of "new" sights, sounds, or tactile stimulation; by reactive sounds, facial expressions, directed head movements, or bursts of physical activity in direct response to stimulation by the human face or voice; and by rise and fall of tension with the advent of routine care such as occur before and after feeding, with position changes, and with relief at the removal of cold, wet diapers.

At six months: according to hypotheses explicated above (p. 88), consciousness should be present, and efforts to give voluntary attention to, and to control, sensations should denote the establishment of the infantile ego. With this accomplishment, the capacity for signal anxiety, and thus the maturation from physiological to psychological anxiety, should be visible. Optimally, the accomplishment would be registered by alert attention to events in the immediate environment; by reactive sounds, gestures, and movements indicating changing moods, feelings, and wishes; by spontaneous movements or sounds toward external objects, animate and inanimate, as in reaching, mouthing, banging, listening; by physical activities sought and enjoyed, and missed when interfered with; by tolerance of being alone for short periods, especially if the mother is audible or visible; by signaling satisfactions or dissatisfactions with specific and appropriate affective behavior and with few gross signs of distress; and by cessation of crying when help becomes available or is seen to be nearly available.

At one year: by capacity to communicate feelings intentionally and to make independent effort to avoid stress. Both the communications and the avoidances would be specific and controlled, i.e., object cathexis would remain intact.

These processes of change have been described previously (Brody, 1956, pp. 340–342), as encompassing the normative movement from autoerotism and primary narcissism to secondary narcissism and the cathexis of objects in the external world.

The concept of narcissism generally has been used to clarify the nature of the object in which instinctual energy is invested. Perhaps it is superfluous to speak of narcissism in the neonate, whose energy, psychologically speaking, still operates within a closed circuit. It seems more useful to think of an instinctual energy which in the neonate is objectless, and of a perceptual threshold in the neonate which will facilitate the development of object cathexis. The threshold would rest upon the anaclitic relationship of the instinctual drives to vital functions in the infant's own body. The importance of our recent learning about sensory responsiveness in the neonate is that very early in life some objects appear in the infant's perceptual field which are external and entirely novel. When their appearance comes smoothly, without disrupting the state of the infant, we might say that the protective shield, as a container of narcissism, has been penetrated smoothly. The oceanic feeling imputed to the infant may be startlingly brief, as the indications are that from the very beginning his responses are not random, and that learning takes place through miniscule repetitions of experiences that alter physiological states. It may well be that where experiences of sensory arousal, learning, and reinforcement are low or erratic, reactions normative to a critical period of development may be especially subject to early extinction.

Normally, from the neonatal period onward, and according to degrees and forms of sensorimotor arousal and response, we expect that the infant is bound to invest instinctual energy in perceptions of the external world. As he does this, he feels an "inner reward" in the sense of rising —and surprising—"feelings of pleasure." Typically, the three-day-olds not only turned their heads in the direction of sound but also froze, "staring at the sound" (Winnicott, 1953). When put down in their beds they might cry, but then also followed with a short period of restless head or limb activity. When covering and clothing were removed, they stretched or flexed their limbs, or sometimes became more wakeful or fretful. These immediate responses were not self-limiting. They ushered in states of further activity, alertness, or fussiness.

Those of our infants who at six weeks reacted often or intensely to external stimuli were usually those who had been receiving mild and frequent stimulation. Practice in sensorimotor activities seemed to be prized, to be seized upon, by those infants. In cases where appropriate stimulations continued to be provided in the larger span of the first year of life, it was possible to observe the infant's continued syntonic excitability and pleasure, and a steady increase of object cathexis. We assume that to the extent that pleasure is sustained and dystonic sensations are relieved by expenditures of energy directed outward, more and more the infant can "dare" to invest the external world. Pleasure deriving from external stimulations and from phase-specific activities then supersede narcissistic absorption in the body alone. For pleasure derived from the body alone has natural limits: alimentary satisfaction, the good feeling of movement, the absence of pain, all these are necessary but not sufficient ingredients of continued pleasure. Pleasures wrested from external reality, and experienced in a rhythmic rise and fall of displeasure, are essential to the maturation of object relations.

On the other hand, excessive stimulation, or high degrees of stimulation *prematurely withdrawn,* would appear to harm object cathexis. Many infants in our sample who showed their most age-adequate behavior at six weeks and poorer development at subsequent observations had mothers who were very active, even exuberant, in the handling of their very young infants, and later quite clearly lacked tenderness or empathy. Perhaps the naturally high dependence of the young infant facilitates the bold behavior of such mothers, for when their infants' ability to initiate activity increased, the mothers acted as if they felt abandoned, and reacted with resentment. One might say that the primary narcissism of the (overstimulated) infants had been reduced unevenly in the first weeks of life, and that subsequently the infants failed to achieve those normal increments of object cathexis that could have promoted secondary narcissism. Or one might say that their narcissism had been left dangling.

Under conditions which severely blunt or discourage the infant's approach to the external world, a more fluid and partial return to primary narcissism and autoerotism would be expected. Indications of such regressive movement may not be observed until the neuromuscular maturation of the infant permits him the expression of narcissism in more protean forms. The one-year-old who often makes excessive demands for objects, only to discard each in turn, may be no more narcissistic than the six-week-old who immediately screams when he is hungry; but the more coordinated and complex expressions of need in the older infant may make him appear more narcissistic.

Possibly two extreme kinds of treatment of the young infant may increase narcissism: one in which there is too little reduction of narcissism by appropriate dosage of relief and of stimulation, the other in which stimulation is so high that the infant gets too little or too erratic experience in tension tolerance.[1] In any case, narcissistic lability may be highest during the period of infancy when differentiation between the self and the external world is least perceived.

Direct and clinical observations suggest that infantile narcissism excessively nourished very early in life in turn nourishes modes of tension discharge that contribute to aberrant character development. During infancy the excessive narcissism may be visible in hypercathexis of states of extreme activity or extreme inactivity, both of which lead to develop-

[1]The psychic effects of inappropriate relief and stimulation have been described in detail (Kaplan, 1964), in the case of a well-endowed infant whose mother was aloof and left the infant to manage high degrees of tension unaided. Kaplan attributes the severe unresponsiveness of the infant to her inability to divest herself sufficiently of narcissism and to cathect objects. The relation between inappropriate maternal handling and aggravations of narcissism is seen in several of the cases presented in Part Four of this book, and in several other brief illustrations from our sample (Brody, 1967).

ment of a stimulus-bound infant or child. The form of hyper-cathexis may very well depend upon as yet unknown physiological or constitutional factors, as well as upon the individual infant's stimulation history. Thus degrees of stimulation, internal and external, positive and negative, which have been greater than the individual infant can absorb in a given time span would be likely to further narcissistic investment of defensive functions, and to nourish infantile roots of pathological character. Similar ideas have been presented by M. James (1960).

Character, in this context, refers to a basic organization of attitudes on the basis of which the valuational aspects of perception are formed. It involves fundamental expectations that an individual cultivates, for example, optimism versus pessimism, trust versus distrust. Character is always highly personal. As the ego is a precipitate of the id, a formulation we prefer to keep, so one may say that character is a precipitate of pregenital drives and their derivatives and of the defenses erected against both. To the extent that infantile character takes form through narcissistic investments rather than through object investments, it would be reasonable to expect intrapsychic conflict in the prephallic phase.

The SDi are in themselves composite indications of the presence of anxiety states and of primitive defensive maneuvers against anxiety. Our central proposition is that when clusters of disturbances are not reduced before the end of infancy, then the reduction of primary narcissism which is necessary to sound object cathexis and ego development in the first year of life is not achieved. The hypertrophy of secondary narcissism, and the alternative flourishing of derivatives of primary narcissism, essentially influence the nature of controls that become characteristic of an infant's behavior and of his concomitant apperception of himself and the outer world. By virtue of these characteristic controls, the infantile ego takes shape; and built into the infantile ego we may find a bedrock of pathological character formation.

Faulty shifts in the location of cathexis of instinctual energies can be summarized as follows:

1. An infant excessively absorbed in dealing with dystonic *internal* sensations, as in colic, is prone to endure frequent states of irritability and discomfort, to have few waking intervals entirely free of spasms, and to have insufficient time to experience pleasurable play with his mother or pleasurable attention to playthings, much less to food. So much energy is taken up in the struggle to maintain internal equilibrium that opportunities to attend, experience, and respond to outer stimuli, and to practice mastery of impulses toward or against those stimuli, are too sporadic.

2. An infant excessively absorbed in dealing with *external* stimuli may either develop a chronic stimulus hunger or be prone to show chronic restlessness or hyperactivity. Or, according to factors of endowment or modes of stimuli, he may develop forms of withdrawal: He may perceive the approach of external stimuli as a series of tiny assaults upon his senses, and almost reflexly protect himself by generalized restriction of responsiveness. His energy then becomes used mainly to stave off new experiences emanating from the outer world, and to try to maintain an island of equilibrium.

3. An infant whose tension states have been insufficiently or erratically aroused or relieved, because he has experienced partial forms of neglect (handled and talked to only during routines, or unpredictably, or harshly; rarely played with; physically isolated in a crib or playpen; strongly excited for short periods and suddenly left alone), may develop uneven investments in external objects and events. He may, for example, accustom himself too exclusively to activity which allows for the exercise of small muscles only, or too exclusively to silent observation of distant objects only, or too exclusively to noncommunicative vocalizations. In such an infant, uneven distribution of energy inward and outward may eventuate in the development of special skills—for good or ill—early in the second year of

life, such as may be seen in atypical varieties of locomotion, speech, or play, and such as persist in the form of personality and character.

Several assumptions underlie the foregoing propositions:

1. Sensorimotor arousals in small degrees evoke the exercise of the very young infant's mental equipment agreeably to receive new stimuli as they continue to be made available, agreeably to respond to them, and rhythmically to sustain alertness to internal and external stimuli. In these ways the narcissism of the neonate may be tapped and optimal preparedness for anxiety may become possible.

2. The greater the need to invest energy in maintaining homeostatic balance as a barrier against the assaults of too sudden, too much, too frequent, too rough, or too unpredictable stimuli, the less energy will be available for use in "energizing" control operations, that is to say, energy drawn into excessive struggles for a preparedness for anxiety becomes less available for the control of perception and sensation.

3. Even if we regard infancy as one broad critical period, habitual experience in needing to ward off stimuli results in insufficient or excessive internal scanning, with consequent defective knowledge of the source of sensations. The probable result would seem to be the growth of sets of distorted attitudes, anticipations, and expectations about stimuli from many sources. It seems possible that if such sets become entrenched during critical periods of mental development, irreversible judgments may be made. Those made in preverbal phases of development would be expected to be most subject to repression, and to become a fixed basis for evaluations of stimuli throughout life. We know that the core of every neurosis, operationally speaking, is a series of misperceptions.

We have assumed that the greater the narcissistic investment, the more liable will the infant be to fail in the mastery of conflicts inherent in psychosexual development. We are proposing that this failure of mastery sets in during early infancy and in itself exaggerates feelings of narcissistic injury.

Given such increments of narcissistic cathexes, the defenses arising therefrom are narcissistically charged as well, with the cumulative effect that later attempts to diminish such neurotic defenses may invoke unbearable psychic pain. In this way ineradicable elements of neurosis can sustain disturbances of character or can continue to deform character, and in turn place heavy barriers against approaches to sublimation.

Sublimation may be regarded as an end product of a psychic process that promotes a level of ego development farthest removed from primary narcissism. The process requires the development of capacities that are instituted very early, in normal defensive operations against internal uneasiness, and against loss of external libidinal objects. The internal loss of pleasure has to be compensated for by a hypercathexis of mental attention which leads to a capacity to isolate.

One of the nascent functions of the infantile ego is to externalize sensations. This done, the infant can summon help from the maturer ego of his mother, or later can take up the task of mastering dystonic stimuli by himself. The accomplishment of delay, the achievement of a state in which sensations are held at bay and in which attention can be given to both tension and signal, comes about when both are followed by attention to the means by which, or the object through whom, the tension will be diminished. This is the infantile model of abstract thinking, in which more of the cathexis is upon an object than upon the sensations impinging upon the self.

It follows from our discussion of the necessity of the infant to proceed from awareness of sensation to awareness of affect, and then to sufficient mastery of that affect to convert sensation to a sign, that for proper ego development even a very young infant needs to become capable of perceptual cathexis and of a rudimentary form of isolation. The early use of isolation by the infant seems to us to be one of the first appearances of normal defense against anxiety: one of the first adaptive acts of the ego. Isolation accomplishes the task of permitting selective attention to the stimulus. Unless affect is to some extent isolated, selective attention cannot be given freely to ways of reducing unpleasant stimuli or of taking action signaled by a slight quantum of signal anxiety. In the presence of the gross affect of anxiety, attention is rather forced back upon the inner state from which flight is not possible, and where the signal produces ever greater waves of anxiety a paniclike state results. There is, so to speak, a regression from the external signal to internal sensations, against which the protective shield is not operative. For eventual sublimation, the infantile isolation should attain a level of development that would safeguard it from being significantly encroached upon by unanticipated alterations of psychic balance. The loss of the external libidinal object has to be compensated for by a hypercathexis of perceptions of the object such that object constancy can be maintained and can provide for identification—one of the preconditions of sublimation.

The prototype of sublimation, the exercise of abstraction, may be visible initially when an infant, in a situation where stimuli are overpowering, masters the dystonic physiological effects by efforts to bear them, to be conscious of them as separable from himself. By means of this consciousness he seems to find energy to convert the dystonic experiences into signals, and he calls for aid or looks toward the mother. When the crying infant accepts comfort from a smiling mother and begins to smile too, we see an isolation of affect, a reaction formation, an identification, and a proper reinforcement of secondary narcissism—essential developmental exercises necessary for eventual sublimation. A bit of work has been accomplished in the transformation of pain into pleasure.

APPENDICES

APPENDIX 1

FACE SHEET

Interviewer: **Code:**

Date:

(SURNAME)   (FIRST NAME)   (MAIDEN NAME)   HUSBAND'S NAME

(ADDRESS)

Obstetrician's name, or Dispensary #:

E.D.C. Date:

Age: Marriage Date:

Birth Date: Occupation:

Birthplace: Salary:

Educational Level: Religion:

HOUSEHOLD MEMBERS:

A. Husband

    Age: Occupation:

    Birthplace: Salary:

    Educational Level: Religion:

B. Children:

    Name   Sex   Birth Date

C. Others in household:

HOUSING ACCOMMODATIONS:

Number of rooms: Remarks:

Private house:

Apartment:

APPENDIX 1 *(continued)*

FINANCES:

Insurance (medical):   Total (current)
Rent per month: family income:

ADMINISTRATIVE NOTES:

Mother advised of filming:

Prenatal Interview date set:

Babysitter reimbursement:

APPENDIX 2

MOTHER'S MEDICAL HISTORY

Data collected by: Code:

Date: Name:

I. General

    A. Menstruation

        Age of onset: Days of pain:

        Usual duration: Flow:

        Regular   Irregular

    B. Major illnesses:

    C. Childhood illnesses:

II. Obstetric

    Number pregnancies:

    Number children:

        Dates:

        Type delivery:

        Feeding methods:

        Other data available:

III. Current Pregnancy

    First date visited Clinic: or M.D.'s office:

    Special symptoms, first
        trimester:

    Special symptoms, second
        trimester:

    E.D.C. Date:

    Actual delivery date:

APPENDIX 3

PRENATAL INTERVIEW

Interviewer: Code:

Date: Name:

I. Description of Mother

   A.   At recruitment interview

   B.   At prenatal interview

      1. General physical appearance; dress; grooming.

      2. Carriage; facial expression.

      3. Movement: tempo, quantity, ease.

      4. Speech: vocabulary, rate, tone, fluidity; any physical accompaniments.

II. Personal-Social History

   A.   Re self

      1. Place of birth and growing up?

      2. Family of origin, constellation; marital status of parents; current occupations, parents and siblings; current degree of association with family members? (For major illness, death, divorce, etc., inquire mother's age at the time, or date.)

      3. Education: highest level achieved? More study or training ever desired?

      4. Work experience after education? Degree of satisfaction?

      5. Aspirations toward any other kind of work now? When younger? During childhood? Husband's attitude toward mother's work aspiration?

      6. Any events during childhood or adolescence that seemed important? Any particular persons admired? or influenced by? or from whom mother sought advice?

   B.   Re husband

      1-6. All questions above (A), as far as applicable.

APPENDIX 3 (*continued*)

    C. Relationship to husband

        1. Circumstances of meeting him? At what age?

        2. What interests are shared? Any special qualities about marriage that makes it different from marriages of relatives or friends?

        3. Any aspect of relationship of particular importance to mother?

    D. Relationship to own mother

        1. Frequency of visits or other contact with her? What kinds of activities shared with her?

        2. Does mother often share opinions of her mother? Seek her mother's advice? About what? (If not, why not?)

        3. What about own mother is admired? Disliked? Or wished were different?

        4. In what ways does mother think she is like her own mother? Unlike?

    E. Children

        1. Ordinal position of expected infant?

        2. General description of other children in family?

III. Current Activities

    A. How time spent during pregnancy? Changes from past?

    B. Usual leisure activities? What kinds of entertainment sought? Vacations?

    C. What kinds of reading material preferred? Any particular subjects? Are latter shared by husband? What about articles or books on child rearing?

    D. Extent of social involvement with friends? Family? How is time together spent?

IV. Plans and Attitudes re Child Rearing

    A. Any experiences in child or infant care prior to birth of first child? If experience has been professional, how satisfying?

    B. Prior to marriage, did mother have any ideas about whether

APPENDIX 3 (*continued*)

to have children? How many? Any particular reasons?

C. Feeding and weaning

1. Breast or bottle feeding planned? Why? Previous experience with older children?

2. When does mother think a baby is ready to be weaned to bottle (if breast fed)? To cup? How does she think she would go about it?

3. What kind of feeding routine does mother expect to follow? Regular intervals? Or when baby seems hungry? How will mother judge?

4. Does mother expect to use a bottle prop? Why? When begin? (or) Under what circumstances might mother use it?

5. Does mother think she will make use of a pacifier? Why? Under what circumstances might mother use one?

D. Habit formation

1. How early does mother think habits can begin to develop? What kind? In what ways might a habit be harmful? How handle?

2. How would mother react to thumbsucking? How handle?

3. Does mother think infants need firm or lenient handling of habits?

4. If habit were persistent night crying, how does mother think she would handle it?

E. Bowel and bladder control

1. When begin? Which first?

2. What method does mother think she might use?

3. At what age should bladder control be established? Bowel? Night? Day? If it is not established by then, does mother have any idea as to how she would handle the problem?

F. Discipline

1. How early can one start to correct a baby's behavior? What sort of behavior is important to correct early?

2. Any ideas about preferred methods? (Urge for specific choice, as re spanking, shaming, depriving, giving extra security, etc.)

APPENDIX 3 (*continued*)

        3. Does mother recall what method of discipline worked for her in childhood? To what extent would same methods seem desirable or appropriate now?

        4. What are husband's opinions about discipline? What differences from mother's?

    G. Educational attitudes

        1. Are playthings necessary for babies during their first year? When? What kind?

        2. How much of the day should a baby be left by himself? When would it seem all right to leave him overnight with someone outside the family?

        3. What are important experiences for a baby in his first year?

        4. Does mother have any aspirations for child in future? How much education would she wish them to have? Any sort of career imagined?

        5. Can mother think of any experiences in her own life that she would wish child to have? to avoid?

V. Current Pregnancy

    A. Has mother had ample time to prepare for this baby (implied question as to whether pregnancy is well-timed)? Has mother felt well?

    B. Attitude of family members toward pregnancy? Have children been told? Did they react as mother anticipated? (or, How does she think they will react?)

    C. Practical arrangements

        1. Is husband's presence desired during labor? delivery?

        2. Any concern about anesthesia? delivery? Or is natural childbirth planned?

        3. Name chosen for baby? Explanation?

        4. Any plans for help with new baby after return from hospital?

        5. Sleeping arrangements after baby is born? (Where will baby sleep?)

APPENDIX 3 *(continued)*

     6. Does mother expect husband will try to help care for baby? If so, in what ways? Any other help to be expected from family or others (after first weeks)?

VI. General Attitudes and Opinions

    A. Has mother had any thoughts about ideal size family for her?

    B. Does mother think that experiences during infancy affect a child's personality when he gets to school?

    C. Does mother think a child's development has more to do with the way he is at birth, or the way he is brought up?

    D. What does mother see as her own strengths as a mother? Weaknesses?

    E. What traits are most valued in mother herself? In her children?

    F. If we could offer help in care of baby during his first year, would mother want it?

VII. Relation to Interviewer

    A. Adequacy of information; reactions to being questioned; facility in expressing opinions and telling facts.

    B. Manner of reporting: detailed, tangential, associative, concise, etc.

    C. Attitude: intellectual, animated, suspicious, nonchalant, condescending, etc.

    D. Affect: degree of freedom, quality of rapport, appropriateness; degree of pleasure in being interviewed, and in speaking of expected baby.

    E. Impression of self-confidence in mothering (past and/or future).

    F. Degree of interest shown in learning more about child rearing.

APPENDIX 4

OBSTETRIC AND PEDIATRIC RECORD

I. Mother

    A.   Admission

        Date:

        Time:

        Pains:

        Weeks of gestation:

    B.   Labor (indicate date and time)

        1st stage began: duration: hr.   min.

        2nd stage began: duration: hr.   min.

        Membranes ruptured:

        Delivery at:

        Duration total labor:

    C.   Last fetal heart rate recorded on labor room record:

    D.   Preanesthesia medication:

    E.   Anesthesia

        Agent:

        Duration (actual time):

    F.   Presentation:

    G.   Position:

    H.   Delivery:

    I.   Remarks re mother's condition:

II. Infant

    A.   At birth

APPENDIX 4 (*continued*)

      1. Sex:

      2. Length:

      3. Weight:

B. 72-96 hours

      1. Amount of formula (or breast milk) consumed: oz.

             No. of formula:

      2. Weight:

C. Apgar rating

      1. At 1 min:

      2. At 5 min:

D. Remarks on condition at birth:

E. Remarks in nursery record:

F. Type of feeding:

G. Neonatal examination set for:

APPENDIX 5

CONFINEMENT VISIT

Interviewer: Code:

Date: Name:

   I. Delivery date:

  II. Description of delivery:

     A. Was it as mother expected? easier? harder? (Record running account, if given.)

     B. Is mother glad she chose natural childbirth? (or not?)

     C. Was husband present during labor? delivery?

 III. Initial response to baby

     A. How did he look?

     B. Mother's reaction to sex?

     C. Any concerns about baby?

     D. Any other remarks about impression baby made on mother.

 IV. Husband's reaction to baby's sex:

  V. Satisfaction with hospital care:

 VI. Feelings about going home (eager? reluctant? ambivalent?) Why? (husband? other children? fatigue? wish to see baby more?):

VII. Is baby feeding well? Is feeding (breast or bottle) proceeding as planned?

VIII. Impression of mother's emotional state, appearance, and attitude toward being visited:

 IX. Date set for six-week observation:

Appendix 6

Neonatal Examination

Examiner: Code:

Date: Name:

                                                  Sex:

                                                  B's Name:

A. General Description

   1. Appearance: (size, skin, color, blemishes; over-all degree of alertness and activity; persistence and vigor of movement)

   2. Turgor: Poor _____ Intermediate _____ Good _____

      Circumcised:

      Date:

      Time:

   3. Degree of prefeeding irritability: 0   1   2   3

   4. Cry: degree of prefeeding intensity: 0   1   2   3

   5. Trembling: none _____ mild _____ moderate _____ severe _____ areas:

B. Description of Feeding

   1. Initial response to nipple: Sucks spontaneously _____

                                Requires stimulation _____

   2. Continued response: Eagerness: 0   1   2   3
                           Vigor: 0   1   2   3

      Is sucking rhythm regular? _____ Does tension decrease? _____

   3. Response to nipple removal _____

   4. Response to burping procedures _____

   5. Degree of alertness throughout: 0   1   2   3

   6. At end of feeding, B: loses interest _____ still interested _____

      sleeps _____

   7. Degree of regurgitation: 0   1   2   3

APPENDIX 6 (*continued*)

8. Degree of hiccough: 0   1   2   3

9. Degree of gagging: 0   1   2   3

10. Degree of cough: 0   1   2   3

11. No. of formula _____   Amount consumed: _____

12. Sucking time: _____   Total feeding time: _____

13. Postfeeding condition: _____
_____

14. Comments on feeding by M or nurses: _____
_____

C. Examination

1. Visual scale[1]

   Credit 0:   No response of fixation or pursuit *and* one of the
                 following abnormal features is observed:

                 a. wandering, uncoordinated movements   _____
                 b. immobilization or staring   _____
                 c. pinpoint pupils   _____

   Item 1:   No fixation or pursuit but none of the above
              abnormalities is observed   _____

   Item 2:   Fixation is brief or obtained with difficulty_____

   Item 3:   Fixation is clearly present and easily elicited,
              i.e., occurs in a majority of the trials   _____

   Item 4:   Horizontal pursuit is questionably present _____

   Item 5:   Horizontal pursuit movements through an arc
              of 30° are obtained with difficulty   _____

   Item 6:   Horizontal pursuit movements through an arc
              of 30° are easily obtained   _____

   Item 7:   Vertical pursuit movements are obtained   _____

   Item 8:   Horizontal pursuit movements through an arc
              of 90° are obtained   _____

   Item 9:   Vertical pursuit is obtained through an arc
              of more than 30°   _____

   Item 10:   Horizontal pursuit movements through an arc
              of more than 90° are obtained   _____

APPENDIX 6 (*continued*)

2. Auditory reaction (supine) —5" stimulus periods[1]

   a. Response to bell (startle, blink)   ———

   b. Response to rattle (as above)   ———

   c. Listening to rattle (opening eyes, decreased movement, head turning) ———

   d. Persistent listening to rattle (3 or 4 presentations), or listening also to bell ———

   e. Persistent listening to both rattle and bell ———

3. Cotton (supine) 20"[1]

   a. Any movement within 2" ———

   b. Specific movements of either head or mouth (back and forth movements or sustained head retraction or movements of mouth in direction of stimulus) ———

   c. Both specific head and mouth movements present more than 50% of response time. ———

   d. Head, mouth, and coordinated arm movements all present ———

4. Pull-to-sitting[1]

   a. No change in tone, marked droop ———

   b. Slight compensation of head; shoulders tense, not floppy ———

   c. Tone improves, slight assistance given; sitting, head erect briefly ———

   d. Already tense and no change in tone; head lags ———

   e. Already tense and no change in tone; no head lag ———

5. Head Reaction (prone position) 60"[1]

   a. Turns head to side in 20" ———

   b. Head clears bed in 60" ———

6. Tension rating[1]

Flaccid (−2) ——— Poor Tone (−1) ——— Normal (0) ———

Tense (+1) ——— Marked Tension (+2) ———

APPENDIX 6 (*continued*)

7. Spontaneous movements[1]

   a. Virtually absent _____

   b. Minimal   _____

   c. Normally active _____ ,

   d. Markedly active _____

8. Nonhunger Cry: Observed Cause: _____

     Relieved by: _____

9. Irritability rating: 0   1   2   3

    How shown? _____

10. Degree of Mouthing: 0   1   2   3

    Specify kind: _____

11. Subjective impression of infant: _____

_____

12. Any maternal comments about infant: _____

_____

[1] From the tests of Graham, Matarazzo, and Caldwell (1956), with permission of the American Psychological Association.

APPENDIX 7

SIX-WEEK VISIT

Observer: Code:

Date: Name:

I. Infant Examination

    A. Gesell Schedules: Chron. Age: Developmental Age:

                        weeks_____days_____   Motor

                                                        Adaptive

                                                        Language

                                                        Personal-Social

    B. Qualitative description

        1. Test state (physiological; at what point of interview):

        2. Immediacy vs. delay of response (specify items):

        3. Attention span:

        4. Vigor and persistence:

        5. Test tolerance; fatigability:

        6. Awareness of examiner:

    C. Supplementary observations

        1. Physical qualities (size, proportion, form, skin):

        2. Reactions to tactile stimulation

            a. Diaper on face:

            b. Dressing and undressing:

            c. Other:

        3. Mouthing and hand-to-mouth activity (kind, intensity, duration):

        4. Typical body positions

            a. Awake:

            b. Asleep:

APPENDIX 7 (*continued*)

     5. General impression of muscular tension (flaccidity vs. rigidity):

     6. General impression of movement (smoothness vs. jerkiness; range; integration; coordination):

     7. Bodily accommodation to being held:

     8. Other:

II. History

  A. Baby's typical day

     1. Schedule of feeding and sleeping (include specific foods for each meal, manner of feeding):

  B. Feeding

     1. Variety offered up to present:

     2. Persons who feed B, beside M (effectively?):

     3. Anticipation of change:

       a. Diet

       b. Weaning to whole milk?   bottle?   cup?

     4. Methods used, not originally anticipated:

     5. Difficulties (since when? how handled? effect?):

     6. Does M use prop? If not, why not? If yes, since when? Regularly? Under what conditions would M use (not use) a prop? Does M think it makes a difference to B?

     7. Mother's rationale, if any: or any comments re procedures:

     8. This feeding, describe. At what point of interview? What? How taken? Typical?

  C. Sleeping history

     1. How induced; soundness; effects of light and noise:

     2. Difficulties? How handled?

  D. Stimulation (play)

     1. Persons who play with B (when? how?):

APPENDIX 7 (*continued*)

    2. Playthings available to B (if none, when to be introduced):

E. Response to bath

F. General health

    1. Weight:

    2. Elimination (regularity, quality):

    3. Skin (color, vascular changes, rash):

    4. Illnesses:

       Age or Date

       Problem

       Treatment and Sequel

G. Affective development

    1. Manifestations of pleasure (What seems to make him most contented? How can you tell?):

    2. Manifestations of displeasure (What seems to make him most unhappy? Does he only cry? How easy is it to comfort him when he is distressed?):

    3. Typical mood when awake (Does he make any sounds yet? Kind? Situation?):

    4. Frustration tolerance; capacity for delay (How does he act when he can't get what he wants? What can he wait for best?):

    5. Self-comforting (How does he try to comfort himself? Finger- or thumb-sucking? Holding on to anything?):

    6. Use of pacifier. Reasons? If yes, since when? Will M use (not use) it under any conditions? How long? Mother's attitude?

H. Object cathexis

    1. Signs of awareness to people? places? objects? (Does B notice anything yet?):

    2. Has M felt it important to encourage these kinds of awareness?

APPENDIX 7 (*continued*)

III. Maternal Behavior and Attitudes

    A.   Self-judgment of adequacy and competence. (How have you been feeling?):

    B.   F's participation: amount and kind of care? play?

    C.   Sources of help and advice (specify nature and usefulness):

    D.   Questions re B's development. Aspects of infant behavior for which M wishes she had been better prepared?

    E.   Anticipation of any difficulties?

IV. Major Family Events since Last Interview

    A.   Illnesses, separations, household changes:

    B.   Sleeping arrangements (Where does B sleep now? nap?):

V. General Impressions of Mother

    A.   Physical appearance. Emotional expression and intellectual qualities:

    B.   Spontaneous reference to family members other than B:

    C.   Extent and quality of M's observations and reports of B's behavior, maturity, moods:

    D.   Emotional responses and intellectual attitudes toward B's behavior and development:

    E.   Areas of special enjoyment and of special anxiety re B:

    F.   M's expressed wishes to encourage or discourage B's activity:

VI. General Impressions of Infant

    A.   Physical appearance. Attractiveness. Nourishment:

    B.   Typical motor patterns. Limb and head involvements. Tension phenomena:

APPENDIX 7 (*continued*)

    C.   Degree of vitality and responsiveness. Sensory alertness. Facial expressions. Emotional expression. Degree of irritability:

    D.   Degree of effort necessary to ease discomfort or restore comfort:

    E.   Any other individual characteristics:

APPENDIX 8

SIX-MONTH VISIT

Observer: Code:

Date: Name:

I. Infant Examination

    A. Gesell Schedules: Chron. Age: Developmental Age:

           weeks_____ days_____   Gross motor

                                  Fine motor

                                  Adaptive

                                  Language

                                  Personal-Social

    B. Vienna and Cattell test items

        1. E places diaper on head and face of B.

            In supine, B makes flight movements:_____ (5th month)

                    B removes it with hands: _____ (6th month)

            In prone, B removes it with hands: _____ (7th month)

        2. Attains rattle at shoulder level,

                    with one hand: _____ (5th month)

                       two hands:_____ (5th month)

      • 3. E smiles and frowns at B successively.

                    B reflects mimic:_____ (6th month)

        4. E takes away play object from B's hands.

                    B holds fast:_____ (6th month)

        5. E looks at B without moving or speaking.

                    B creates contact:_____ (7th month)

    C. Miscellaneous observations

        1. B smiles to E spontaneously: on arrival _____

APPENDIX 8 (*continued*)

        frequently_____ occasionally_____ rarely_____ never_____

        during play with test objects _____

        during other play _____

    2. B's mood at departure:

    3. During tests M remains in background_____hovers

    near_____ helpfully_____watches silently_____interferes

    physically_____ interested _____only superficially inter-

    ested _____occupies self otherwise _____

D. Qualitative description (*specify stimuli whenever possible*)

    1. Test state (physiological; at what point of interview):

    2. Immediacy vs. delay:

    3. Attention span:

    4. Explorative interest:

    5. Vigor:

    6. Persistence:

    7. Test tolerance; fatigability:

    8. Attention to examiner:

E. Supplementary observations (*note any disagreement with M's reports*)

    1. Physical qualities (size, proportion, form, skin):

    2. Mouthing and hand-to-mouth activity (kind, intensity, duration):

    3. Vocalizations (variety, clarity, quantity):

    4. Preferred body positions (awake, asleep):

    5. General impression of muscular tension (flaccidity vs. rigidity):

    6. General impression of movement (range, integration, coordination, rapidity):

    7. Bodily accommodation to being held: to being dressed and undressed:

    8. Other:

APPENDIX 8 (*continued*)

II. History

  A. Baby's typical day

    1. Schedule of feeding and sleeping (include specific foods for each meal, manner of feeding):

  B. Feeding history

    1. Variety offered at present. Preferences or dislikes? Usual duration of meals:

    2. Persons who feed B, beside M (effectively?):

    3. Methods at present:

      a. Usual positions for solids, for liquids (lap? high chair?): Propping (when? why?):

      b. Weaning (to bottle? to cup? when? how?):

      c. Anticipated changes of method (when? why?):

    4. Difficulties (since when? how handled? effect?):

    5. M's rationale, if any, or comments re procedures):

    6. This feeding. At what point of interview? what? how taken? typical?

  C. Sleeping

    1. Amount; how induced; soundness; mood on waking; differences day and night?

    2. Difficulties (since when? how handled? effect?):

  D. Stimulation (play)

    1. Persons who play with B (when? how?):

    2. Playthings available:

    3. Amount of time B all alone; reactions:

    4. Response to bath (in what is he bathed?):

  E. General health

    1. Weight:

APPENDIX 8 (*continued*)

2. Elimination:

3. Skin (color, rashes, blemishes):

4. Illnesses

   Problem:

   Age or date:

   Treatment and sequel:

5. Reactions to pain (teething? accidents?):

F. Instinctual drive development

   1. Balance of active and passive aims

      a. Spontaneity, resourcefulness, reflectiveness, alternation between rest and activity (Do you think of him as active or as quiet most of the time? Is he the kind of B who is in a hurry to do things, or the kind who rather likes to take his time? Does he give up easily when he is after something?):

      b. Response to frustration. Capacity for delay (Can he wait for things he wants? What does he do while he waits? What does he do when he doesn't get what he wants? besides cry?):

      c. Efforts to communicate (Can you usually tell when he wants something? How?):

   2. Affective development

      a. Manifestations of pleasure (What does he enjoy most? What is the clearest way he shows happiness? Can you play little games of any sort with him yet?):

      b. Manifestations of displeasure (What makes him especially unhappy? Clearest way he shows unhappiness?):

      c. Repertoire of emotions, from tears to laughter (What are all the different ways he has of showing you how he feels?):

      d. Signs of anxiety (What has he been afraid of? When first noticed?):

      e. Typical moods when awake; activities preferred:

      f. Distractability from dystonic states (How do you get him out of a bad mood?):

APPENDIX 8 (*continued*)

      3. Self-comforting (How does he help himself out of a bad mood? Habits—pacifier? rocking? finger- or thumb-sucking? holding on to things? other?):

      4. Object cathexis

         a. Preferred persons (How can you tell? Does he like to be kissed? handled?):

         b. Tolerance of unfamiliar persons, places:

         c. Curiosity re objects (Any things he likes especially to watch? touch?):

         d. Curiosity re own body parts:

         e. Other interests noted:

III. Maternal Behavior and Attitudes

    A. Self-judgment of adequacy and competence:

    B. Father's participation: amount and kind of care? Play? attempts to teach B? discipline?

    C. Sources of help and advice (specify nature or usefulness)? Questions or concerns re B's development:

    D. Anticipation of any difficulties (before next visit with us)?

    E. M's efforts to teach anything to B?

IV. Family Events Since Last Interview

    A. Illnesses, separations, household changes:

    B. Sleeping arrangements (Where does B sleep now? nap?):

V. General Impressions of Mother

    A. Physical appearance. Emotional expression and intellectual qualities:

    B. Spontaneous references to family members other than B:

    C. Extent and quality of M's reports of B's behavior, maturity, moods:

    D. Manner of addressing and handling B. Permissiveness? Degree of control?

APPENDIX 8 (*continued*)

    E.   Emotional responses and intellectual attitudes toward B's behavior and development (manifest pleasure, pride, approval, or opposites):

    F.   Areas of special enjoyment and of special anxiety re B:

VI. General Impressions of Infant

    A.   Appearance, with respect to general maturity. Nourishment. Attractiveness:

    B.   Degree of vitality. Motor patterns. Tension phenomena:

    C.   Responsiveness. Expansiveness versus withdrawal. Negativism:

    D.   Variety and quality of expressive behavior (motor, perceptual, social, vocal):

    E.   Varieties of manifest emotional levels and nuances (anger, smiling, crying, coyness, irritation, frowning, etc.):

    F.   Degree of effort necessary to ease discomfort or restore comfort:

    G.   Any unique feature of B:

APPENDIX 9

ONE-YEAR VISIT

Observer: Code:

Date: Name:

I. Infant Examination

   A. Gesell Schedules: Chron. Age: Developmental Age:

        weeks ___ days ___   Gross Motor

                             Fine Motor

                             Adaptive

                             Language

                             Personal-Social

   B. Vienna and Cattell test items

      1. Uncovers object under diaper: ___   (10th month)

      2. Peg board, fingers holes: ___   (10th month)

      3. Cube under cup: ___   (11th month)

      4. Takes objects from behind screen: ___   (12th month)

      5. Pencil, makes marks: ___   (12th month)

      6. Spoon, imitates beating: ___   (12th month)

      7. Cube, unwraps: ___   (13th-14th months)

      8. Peg board, peg out: ___ peg in: ___   (13th-14th months)

      9. Glass, frustration: ___   (13th-14th months)

     10. Round box, closes: ___   (15th-16th months)

     11. Peg board: urged, number in: ___   (16th month)

   C. Miscellaneous observations

      1. B smiles to E spontaneously: on arrival ___

      frequently ___ occasionally ___ rarely ___ never ___

APPENDIX 9 (*continued*)

during play with test objects ＿＿＿ during other play ＿＿＿

2. B's mood at departure:

3. During tests M remains in background ＿＿＿ hovers near ＿＿＿
helpfully＿＿＿ watches silently ＿＿＿ interferes physically ＿＿＿
interested ＿＿＿ only superficially interested ＿＿＿
occupies self otherwise ＿＿＿

D. Qualitative description (specify stimuli)

1. Test state (physiological; at what point of interview):

2. Immediacy vs. delay in response to E; to objects:

3. Attention span:

4.' Intensity of curiosity and activity:

5. Perception of relationships:

6. Test tolerance:

7. Balance of attention to examiner, to M, and to test objects:

8. Balance between motor, perceptual, and social activity:

E. Supplementary observations

1. Physical qualities (size, proportion, form, skin):

2. General impression of muscular tension (specify body area involved or situation where observed, when possible):

3. Coordination and control of movement; range; tempo:

4. Any preferred or habitual body positions:

5. Accommodation to physical handling:

6. Mouthing activities (kind, intensity, duration):

7. Vocalizations: variety, intensity, frequency:

8. Any typical gestures?

II. History

A. Baby's typical day

1. Schedule of feeding and sleeping:

APPENDIX 9 *(continued)*

B. Feeding

1. Variety offered at present. Usual durations of meals? Preferences or dislikes?

2. Persons who feed B, beside M (effectively?):

3. Methods at present

   a. Usual positions (lap? high chair?):

   b. Propping (when? why?):

4. Difficulties (since when? how handled? effect?):

5. M's rationale, if any, or comments re procedures:

6. This feeding (what? how taken? typical?):

C. Sleeping history

1. Amount; how induced; soundness; mood on waking; difference day and night?

2. Difficulties (since when? how handled? effect?):

D. General health

1. Weight:

2. Teething (any difficulties? how handled?):

3. Illness

   Age or date:

   Problem:

   Treatment and sequel:

4. Reactions to pain (falls, shocks, accidents, others' aggression, teething):

5. Elimination

   a. Any difficulties? When? How handled?

   b. Does B show any understanding of, or interest in use of toilet?

   c. Does he let you know in any way that he is wet or soiled?

   d. Plans regarding training?

APPENDIX 9 (*continued*)

   E. Instinctual drive development

      1. Balance of active and passive aims

         a. Spontaneity, initiative, resourcefulness, reflectiveness (Do you think of B as more active or more quiet than when he was younger? What sort of activity absorbs him most? Can he keep busy all by himself?):

            (What does he like you to do for him? How does he let you know what he wants?):

         b. Capacity for delay (How quickly does he get frustrated? How does he show it? Can he wait for things he wants? What does he do while he waits):

         c. Persistence and vigor (What sort of things does he get stubborn about? When he wants something can he get distracted without fussing?):

      2. Affects

         a. Manifestations of pleasure (What does he do when he's happy or pleased?):

         b. Manifestations of displeasure (What does he do when he's cross? How angry does he get? What makes him have a tantrum?):

         c. Reciprocal affective signs and signals (Can you have conversations with him just by looks? gestures? words?):

         d. Distractibility from dystonic states (How do you get him out of a bad mood? Can other people help him in the same way?):

         e. Signs of anxiety (What sort of things has he been afraid of? When first noticed?):

         f. Repertoire of emotions (How does he show greatest degree of joy? distress? in-between moods?):

         g. Response to mother's absence (How does he act when you go away? Do you know if he acts differently while you're away? and when you return?):

      3. Habits

         a. Kind (biting? throwing? screaming? sucking? rocking? repetitive behavior?):

APPENDIX 9 (*continued*)

      b. When most indulged in?

      c. M's attitude?

   4. Discipline

      a. Reasons (necessary for what sort of behavior?):

      b. Kind (How have you tried to correct him?):

      c. Effects (Do you think he has understood what you want?):

      d. M's attitude (Satisfied with this method?):

   5. Object Cathexis

      a. Preferred persons and preferred activities with them (Games? Tricks? Does he imitate anybody?):

      b. Differential responses to persons; Familiars? Strangers? (From whom does he shy away?):

      c. Curiosity re objects (How does he explore new things? What does he try to do with them? Favorite toys or other prized objects?):

      d. Curiosity re own body parts. Kind and degree (At what times does he do it most? Since when? How long did that last?):

      e. Awareness of surroundings. (Do you think he likes to watch people more or to do things by himself? Any special things he likes to watch? to do?):

      f. Independent behavior (How does B amuse himself when alone? How long can he do that? Do you think he plays in a different way when he's alone or when someone else is in the same room with him?):

III. Maternal Behavior and Attitudes

   A. Self-judgment of adequacy and competence:

   B. Father's participation: amount and kind of care? play? attempts teach B? discipline?

   C. Sources of help and advice (specify nature and usefulness). Questions or concerns re B's development:

APPENDIX 9 (*continued*)

    D. M's efforts to teach anything to B (Note behavior knowingly encouraged or discouraged):

    E. M's impression of changes in B's personality over year span. (Any ideas about kind of personality he is apt to develop in next years?):

IV. Family Events

    A. Illnesses, separations, household changes since last interview:

    B. Sleeping arrangements. (Where does B sleep now? nap?):

V. General Impressions of Mother

    A. Physical appearance. Emotional expression and intellectual qualities:

    B. Spontaneous references to family members other than B:

    C. Extent and quality of M's reports of B's behavior, maturity, moods:

    D. Manner of addressing and handling B. Permissiveness? Degree of control:

    E. Emotional responses and intellectual attitudes toward B's behavior and development (manifest pleasure, pride, approval; or opposites):

    F. Areas of special enjoyment and of special anxiety re B:

    G. M's questions about B's progress. Interest in poststudy interview?

VI. General Impressions of Infant

    A. Appearance, with respect to general maturity. Nourishment. Attractiveness:

    B. Degree of vitality. Motor patterns. Tension phenomena:

    C. Responsiveness. Expansiveness versus withdrawal. Negativism:

APPENDIX 9 *(continued)*

D. Variety and quality of expressive behavior (motor, perceptual, social, vocal):

E. Varieties of manifest emotional levels and nuances (anger, smiling, crying, coyness, irritation, frowning, etc.):

F. Degree of effort necessary to ease discomfort or restore comfort:

G. Stimulation: Sought?   Tolerated?   Avoided?   (specify):

H. Any unique features of B or of his behavior:

References

Ainsworth, M. D. S. (1962a), Reversible and Irreversible Effects of Maternal Deprivation on Intellectual Development. In: *Maternal Deprivation*. New York: Child Welfare League of America, pp. 42–62.

———(1962b), The Effects of Maternal Deprivation: A Review of Findings and Controversy in the Context of Research Strategy. In: *Deprivation of Maternal Care: A Reassessment of its Effects.* Public Health Papers, 14. Geneva: World Health Organization, pp. 97–163.

———(1967), *Infancy in Uganda.* Baltimore: Johns Hopkins Press.

———(1969), Maternal Behavior and Infant Initiative. Paper presented at symposium, Maternal Behavior in Mammals, Internat. Union Biol. Sci., London.

———& Bell, S. M. (1970a), Attachment, Exploration, and Separation: Illustrated by the Behavior of One-Year Olds in a Strange Situation. *Child Devel.*, 41:49–62.

——— ———(1970b) Some Contemporary Patterns of Mother-Infant Interaction in the Feeding Situation. In: *The Functions of Early Post-natal Stimulation*, ed. J. A. Ambrose. London: Academic Press.

——— ———& Stayton, D. J. (in press), Individual Differences in Strange-Situation Behavior of One-Year-Olds. In: *Origins of Human Social Relations*, ed. H. R. Schaffer. London: Academic Press.

———& Wittig, B. A. (1969), Attachment and Exploratory Behavior of One-Year-Olds in a Strange Situation. In: *Determinants of Infant Behaviour*, IV, ed. B. M. Foss. New York: Wiley, pp. 111–136.

Ambrose, J. A. (1961), The Development of the Smiling Response in Early Infancy. In: *Determinants of Infant Behaviour*, Vol. 1, ed.

B. M. Foss. New York: Wiley, pp. 179–195.

———(1963a), The Concept of a Critical Period for the Development of Social Responsiveness in Early Human Infancy. In: *Determinants of Infant Behaviour*, Vol. 2, ed. B. M. Foss. New York: Wiley, pp. 201–226.

———(1963b), The Age of Onset of Ambivalence in Early Infancy: Indications from the Study of Laughing. *J. Child Psychol. Psychiat.*, 4: 167–181.

Arlow, J. A. (1963), Conflict, Regression, and Symptom Formation. *Internat. J. Psycho-Anal.*, 44: 12–22.

Axelrad, S. (1962), Infant Care and Personality Reconsidered: A Rejoinder to Orlansky. In: *The Psychoanalytic Study of Society*, Vol. 2, ed. W. Muensterberger & S. Axelrad. New York: International Universities Press, pp. 75–132.

Bayley, N. (1932), A Study of the Crying of Infants during Mental and Physical Tests. *J. Genet. Psychol.*, 40: 306–329.

Benjamin, J. D. (1961), Some Developmental Observations Relating to the Theory of Anxiety. *J. Amer. Psychoanal. Assn.*, 9: 652–668.

———(1963), Further Comments of Some Developmental Aspects of Anxiety. In: *Counterpoint: Libidinal Object and Subject*, ed. H. S. Gaskill. New York: International Universities Press, pp. 121–153.

——— (1965), Developmental Biology and Psychoanalysis. In: *Psychoanalysis and Current Biological Thought*, ed. N. C. Greenfield & W. C. Lewis. Madison & Milwaukee: University of Wisconsin Press, pp. 57–80.

Bennett, E. L., Diamond, M. C., Krech, D., & Rosenzweig, M. R. (1964), Chemical and Anatomical Plasticity of Brain. *Science*, 146:610–619.

Bergman, P., & Escalona, S. (1949), Unusual Sensitivities in Young Children. *The Psychoanalytic Study of the Child*, 3/4:333–352. New York: International Universities Press.

Bernstein, L. (1957), The Effects of Variations in Handling upon Learning and Retention. *J. Comp. Physiol. Psychol.*, 50: 162–167.

———Blank, M., Bridger, W. H., & Escalona, S. K. (1965), Behavioral Inhibition in Neonates Produced by Auditory Stimuli. *Child Devel.*, 36:639–646.

Birns, B. (1965), Individual Differences in Human Neonates' Responses to Stimulation. *Child Devel.*, 36:249–256.

———— Blank, M., Bridger, W. H., & Escalona, S. K. (1965), Behavioral Inhibition in Neonates Produced by Auditory Stimuli. *Child Devel.*, 36:639–646.

Blum, L. H. (1950), Some Psychological and Educational Aspects of Pediatric Practice: A Study of Well-Baby Clinics. *Genet. Psychol. Monogr.*, 41:3–97.

————(1951), The Pediatrician in the Role of Psychologist and Educator. *Amer. J. Dis. Child.*, 80:238–244.

Bowlby, J. (1951), *Maternal Care and Mental Health.* Geneva: World Health Organization Monogr. Series, No. 2.

————(1960a), Separation Anxiety. *Internat. J. Psycho-Anal.*, 41:89–113.

————(1960b), Separation Anxiety: A Critical Review of the Literature. *J. Child Psychol. Psychiat.*, 1:251–269.

Brazelton, T. B. (1962), Observations of the Neonate. *J. Amer. Acad. Child Psychiat.*, 1:38–58.

————(1963), The Early Mother-Infant Adjustment. *Pediat.*, 32: 931-937.

————Scholl, M. L., & Robey, J. S. (1966), Visual Responses of the Newborn. *Pediat.*, 37:284–291.

Brenner, C. (1953), An Addendum to Freud's Theory of Anxiety. *Internat. J. Psycho-Anal.*, 34:18–24.

————(1955), *An Elementary Textbook of Psychoanalysis.* New York: International Universities Press.

Brody, S. (1956), *Patterns of Mothering.* New York: International Universities Press.

————(1961), Self-Rocking in Infancy. *J. Amer. Psychoanal. Assn.*, 8:464–491.

————(1964), *Passivity: A Study of Its Development and Expression in Boys.* New York: International Universities Press.

————(1966), The Developing Infant. Essay review, R. A. Spitz, *The First Year of Life. Children*, 13:158–160.

————(1967), Some Infantile Sources of Childhood Disturbance. *J. Amer. Acad. Child Psychiat.*, 6:615–643.

————(1970), A Mother Is Being Beaten. In: *Parenthood: Its Psychology and Psychopathology*, ed. A. J. Anthony & T. Benedek. Boston: Little, Brown.

Bronson, G. W (1968a), The Development of Fear in Man and Other Animals. *Child Devel.*, 39:409–432.

_____(1968b), The Fear of Novelty. *Psychol. Bull.*, 69:350–358.

Bronson, W. C. (1966), Early Antecedents of Emotional Expressiveness and Reactivity-Control. *Child Devel.*, 37:793–810.

_____(1967), Adult Derivatives of Emotional Expressiveness and Reactivity-Control: Developmental Continuities from Childhood to Adulthood. *Child Devel.* 38:801–818.

Brown, J. L. (1964), States in Newborn Infants. *Merrill-Palmer Quart.*, 10:313–327.

Caldwell, B. M., Hersher, L., Lipton, E. L., Richmond, J. B., Stern, G. A., Eddy, E., Drachman, R., & Rothman, A. (1963), Mother-Infant Interaction in Monomatric and Polymatric Families. *Amer. J Orthopsychiat.*, 4:653–664.

Carithers, H. A (1951), Mother-Pediatrician Relationship in the Neonatal Period. *J. Pediat.*, 38:654–660.

Carmichael, L. (1946), The Onset and Early Development of Behavior. In: *Manual of Child Psychology*, ed. L. Carmichael. New York: Wiley, pp. 60–185.

_____(1951), Ontogenetic Development. In: *Handbook of Experimental Psychology*, ed. S. S. Stevens. New York: Wiley, pp. 281–303.

Caudill, W., & Weinstein, H. (1969), Maternal Care and Infant Behavior in Japan and America. *Psychiatry*, 32:12–43.

Collins, T. B., Jr. (1965), Strength of the Following Response in the Chick in Relation to Degree of "Parent" Contact. *J. Comp. Physiol. Psychol.*, 60:192–195.

Dayton, G. O., & Jones, M. H. (1963), Developmental Study of Coordinated Eye Movements in the Human Infant. *Arch. Ophthalmol.*, 71:871–875.

DeNelsky, G. Y., & Denenberg, V. H. (1967), Infantile Stimulation and Adult Exploratory Behavior: Effects of Handling upon Tactual Variation Seeking. *J. Comp. Physiol. Psychol.*, 63:309–312.

Denenberg, V. H. & Karas, G. G. (1960), Interactive Effects of Age and Duration of Infantile Experience on Adult Learning. *Psychol. Rep.*, 7:313–322.

Elliot, O., & Scott, J. P. (1961), The Development of Emotional Distress Reactions to Separation in Puppies. *J. Genet. Psychol.*, 99:3–22.

Erikson, E. H. (1950), *Childhood and Society.* New York: Norton.

Escalona, S. K. (1950), The Use of Infant Tests for Prediction Purposes. *Bull. Menninger Clin.*, 14:117–128.

_____(1962), The Study of Individual Differences and the Problem of

State. *J. Amer. Acad. Child Psychiat.*, 1:11–37.

———— & Heider, G. N. (1959), *Prediction and Outcome*. New York: Basic Books.

Fantz, R. L. (1958), Pattern Vision in Young Infants. *Psychol. Rec.*, 8:43–47.

———— (1961), The Origin of Form Perception. *Sci. Amer.*, 204 (5):66–72.

———— (1963), Pattern Vision in Newborn Infants. *Science*, 140:1–2.

———— (1964), Visual Experience in Infants: Decreased Attention to Familiar Patterns Relative to Novel Ones. *Science*, 146:668–670.

———— (1966), Pattern Discrimination and Selective Attention as Determinants of Perceptual Development from Birth. In: *Perceptual Development in Children*, ed. A. H. Kidd & J. L. Rivoire. New York: International Universities Press, pp. 143–173.

———— (1967), Visual Perception and Experience in Early Infancy: A Look at the Hidden Side of Behavior Development. In: *Early Behavior: Comparative and Developmental Approaches*, ed. H. W. Stevenson. New York: Wiley, pp. 181–224.

———— & Nevis, S. (1967a), The Predictive Value of Changes in Visual Preferences in Early Infancy. In: *The Exceptional Infant*, Vol. 1, ed. J. Hellmuth. Seattle: Special Child Publications, pp. 349–414.

———— ———— (1967b), Pattern Preferences and Perceptual-Cognitive Development in Early Infancy. *Merrill-Palmer Quart.*, 13: 77–108.

———— Ordy, J. M., & Udelf, M. S. (1962), Maturation of Pattern Vision in Infants during the First Six Months. *J. Comp. Physiol. Psychol.*, 55:907–917.

Fish, B. (1963), The Maturation of Arousal and Attention in the First Months of Life: A Study of Variations in Ego Development. *J. Amer. Acad. Child Psychiat.*, 2:253–270.

Fisher, C. (1964), Psychoanalytic Implications of Recent Research on Sleep and Dreaming. I: Empirical Findings. *J. Amer. Psychoanal. Assn.*, 13:197–270.

Flavell, J. (1963), *The Developmental Psychology of Jean Piaget*. Princeton: Van Nostrand.

Flint, B. M. (1959), *The Security of Infants*. Toronto: University of Toronto Press.

Freedman, D. G., King, J. A., & Elliot, O. (1961), Critical Period in the Social Development of Dogs. *Science*, 133: 1016–1017.

Freud, A. (1953), Some Remarks on Infant Observation. *The Psychoanalytic Study of the Child*, 8:9–19. New York: International Universities Press.

_____(1965), *Normality and Pathology in Childhood. The Writings of Anna Freud*, 6. New York: International Universities Press.

_____& Burlingham, D. (1943), *War and Children*. New York: Medical War Books.

_____(1944) *Infants Without Families*. New York: International Universities Press.

Freud, S. (1900), The Interpretation of Dreams. *Standard Edition*, 4 & 5. London: Hogarth Press, 1953.

_____(1911), Formulations regarding the Two Principles of Mental Functioning. *Standard Edition*, 12:213–226. London: Hogarth Press, 1958.

_____(1914), On Narcissism: An Introduction, *Standard Edition*, 14:-69–102. London: Hogarth Press, 1957.

_____(1915), Instincts and Their Vicissitudes. *Standard Edition*, 14:109–140. London: Hogarth Press, 1957.

_____(1920), Beyond the Pleasure Principle. *Standard Edition*, 18:1–64. London: Hogarth Press, 1955.

_____(1923), The Ego and the Id. *Standard Edition*, 19:1–66. London: Hogarth Press, 1961.

_____(1925), A Note upon the "Mystic Writing-Pad." *Standard Edition*, 19:227–232. London: Hogarth Press, 1961.

_____(1926), Inhibitions, Symptoms and Anxiety. *Standard Edition*, 20:75–175. London: Hogarth Press, 1959.

_____(1940), An Outline of Psychoanalysis. *Standard Edition*, 23:141–207. London: Hogarth Press, 1964.

Fries, M. E. (1944), Psychosomatic Relations between Mother and Infant. *Psychosom. Med.*, 6:159–162.

Fuller, J. L., & Waller, M. B. (1962), Is Early Experience Different? In: *Roots of Behavior*, ed. E. L. Bliss. New York: Hoeber-Harper, pp. 234–245.

Geldard, F. A. (1960), Some Neglected Possibilities of Communication. *Science*, 131:1583–1588.

Gesell, A. (1954), The Ontogenesis of Infant Behavior. In: *Manual of Child Psychology*. ed. L. Carmichael. New York: Wiley, pp. 335–373.

_____& Amatruda, C. S. (1949), *Developmental Diagnosis*. New York: Hoeber.

Gewirtz, J. L. (1961), A Learning Analysis of the Effects of Normal Stimulation, Privation and Deprivation on the Acquisition of Social Motivation and Attachment. In: *Determinants of Infant Behaviour*, Vol. 1, ed. , B. M. Foss. New York: Wiley, pp. 213–289.

Gifford, S. (1960), Sleep, Time and the Early Ego. *J. Amer. Psychoanal. Assn.*, 8:5–42.

Goldberg, S., & Lewis, M. (1969), Play Behavior in the Year Old Infant. Early Sex Differences. *Child Devel.*, 40:21–32.

Gough, D. (1962), The Visual Behavior of Infants in the First Few Weeks of Life. *Proc. Roy. Soc. Med.*, 55:308–310.

Graham, F. K., Matarazzo, R. G., & Caldwell, B. M. (1956), Behavioral Difference between Normal and Traumatized Newborns. *Psychol. Monogr.*, 70.

Gray, P. H. (1958), Theory and Evidence in Imprinting in Human Infants. *J. Psychol.*, 46:155–166.

——(1960), Evidence that Retinal Flicker Is Not a Necessary Condition of Imprinting. *Science*, 132:1834.

Greenacre, P. (1941), The Predisposition to Anxiety. In: *Trauma, Growth and Personality*. New York: International Universities Press, 1969, pp. 27–82.

——(1944), Infant Reactions to Restraint: Problems in the Fate of Infantile Aggression. In: *Trauma, Growth and Personality*. New York: International Universities Press, 1969, pp. 83–105.

——(1945), The Biological Economy of Birth. In: *Trauma, Growth and Personality*. New York: International Universities Press, 1969, pp. 3–26.

——(1958), Toward an Understanding of the Physical Nucleus of Some Defence Reactions. *Internat. J. Psycho-Anal.*, 39:69–78.

Greenman, G. W. (1963), Visual Behavior of Newborn Infants. In: *Modern Perspectives in Child Development*, ed. A. J. Solnit & S. A. Provence. New York: International Universities Press, pp. 71–79.

Griffiths, R. (1954), *The Abilities of Babies: A Study in Mental Measurement*. London: University of London Press.

Group for the Advancement of Psychiatry (1966), *Psychopathological Disorders of Childhood: Theoretical Considerations and a Proposed Classification*. New York: Mental Health Materials Center, pp. 163–343.

Guiton, P. (1961), The Influence of Imprinting on the Agonistic and Courtship Responses of the Brown Leghorn Cock. *Animal Behav.*, 9:167–177.

Guthrie-Smith, H. (1926), *Tutira, The Story of a New Zealand Sheep Station*. Edinburgh: Blackwood, 1953.

Harlow, H. F. & Zimmerman, R. R. (1959), Affectional Responses in the Infant Monkey. *Science*, 130:421–432.

Hartmann, H. (1950), Comments on the Psychoanalytic Theory of the Ego. *The Psychonalytic Study of the Child*, 5:74–96. New York: International Universities Press.

_____ (1952), The Mutual Influences of Ego and Id. *The Psychonalytic Study of the Child*, 7:9–30. New York: International Universities Press.

Haynes, H., White, B. L., & Held, R. (1965), Visual Accommodation in Human Infants. *Science*, 148:528–530.

Heinicke, C. M., & Westheimer, I., (1965), *Brief Separations*. New York: International Universities Press.

Hershenson, M. (1964), Visual Discrimination in the Human Newborn. *J. Comp. Physiol. Psychol.*, 58:270–276.

Hess, E. H. (1959a), Imprinting. *Science*, 130:133–141.

_____(1959b), Two Conditions Limiting Critical Age for Imprinting. *J. Comp. Physiol. Psychol.*, 52:515–518.

_____(1959c), The Relationship between Imprinting and Motivation. In: *Nebraska Symposium on Motivation*, ed. M. J. Jones. Lincoln: University Nebraska Press, pp. 44–77.

_____(1960), Effects of Drugs on Imprinting Behavior. In: *Drugs and Behavior*, ed. L. Uhr & J. G. Miller. New York: Wiley, pp. 268–271.

Hoffer, W. (1952), The Mutual Influences on the Development of Ego and Id: Earliest Stages. *The Psychoanalytic Study of the Child*, 7:31–41. New York: International Universities Press.

Hollingshead, A. B. (1957), *Two Factor Index of Social Position* (mimeographed.)

Hoopes, J. L. (1967), *An Infant Rating Scale: Its Validation and Usefulness*. New York: Child Welfare League of America.

Isakower, O. (1938), A Contribution to the Psychopathology of Falling Asleep. *Internat. J. Psycho-Anal.*, 19:331–345.

Jacobson, E. (1954), The Self and the Object World. *The Psychoanalytic Study of the Child*, 9:75–127. New York: International Universities Press.

James, H. (1959), Flicker: An Unconditioned Stimulus for Imprinting. *Canad. J. Psychol.*, 13:59–67.

James, M. (1960), Premature Ego Development: Some Observations upon Disturbances in the First Three Years of Life. *Internat. J. Psycho-Anal.*, 41:288–294.

Jones, E. (1957), Pai)n. *Internat. J. Psycho-Anal.*, 38:255.

Kagan, J. (1969), Continuity in Cognitive Development During the First Year. *Merrill-Palmer Quart.*, 15:101–120.

Kaplan, S. (1964), A Clinical Contribution to the Study of Narcissism in Infancy. *The Psychoanalytic Study of the Child*, 19:398–420. New York: International Universities Press.

Klatskin, E. H., McGarry, M. E., & Steward, M. S. (1966), Variability in Developmental Test Patterns as a Sequel of Neonatal Stress. *Child Devel.*, 37:819–826.

Klopfer, P. H., & Hailman, J. P. (1964), Perceptual Preferences and Imprinting in Chicks. *Science*, 145:1333–1334.

Korner, A. F., & Grobstein, R. (1966), Visual Alertness as Related to Soothing in Neonates: Implications for Maternal Stimulation and Early Deprivation. *Child Devel.*, 37:867–876.

Kris, E. (1951), Opening Remarks on Psychoanalytic Child Psychology. *The Psychoanalytic Study of the Child*, 6:9–17. New York: International Universities Press.

Kubie, L. S. (1941), A Physiological Approach to the Concept of Anxiety. *Psychosom. Med.*, 3:263–276.

Levine, M. L., & Bell, A. I. (1950), The Treatment of "Colic" in Infancy by Use of the Pacifier. *J. Pediat.*, 37:3–7.

Levy, D. M. (1960), The Infant's Memory of Inoculation. *J. Genet. Psychol.*, 96:3–46.

Lewis, M., Kagan, J., & Kalafat, J. (1966), Patterns of Fixation in Infants. *Child Devel.*, 37:331–341.

Lipsitt, L. P. (1966), Learning Processes of Human Newborns. *Merrill-Palmer Quart.*, 12:45–72.

Loeb, L. (1945), *The Biological Basis of Individuality.* Springfield, Ill. Charles C Thomas.

Lustman, S. (1956), Rudiments of the Ego. *The Psychoanalytic Study of the Child*, 11:89–98. New York: International Universities Press.

Mahler, M. (1952), On Child Psychosis and Schizophrenia: Autistic and

Symbiotic Infantile Psychoses. *The Psychoanalytic Study of the Child*, 7:286–305. New York: International Universities Press.

———(1963), Thoughts about Development and Individuation. *The Psychoanalytic Study of the Child*, 18:307–324. New York: International Universities Press.

———(1965), On the Significance of the Normal Separation-Individuation Phase: With Reference to Research in Symbiotic Child Psychosis. In: *Drives, Affects, Behavior*, Vol. 2, ed. M. Schur. New York: International Universities Press, pp. 161–169.

———(1966), Notes on the Development of Basic Moods: The Depressive Affect. In: *Psychoanalysis—A General Psychology*, ed. R. M. Loewenstein, L. M. Newman, M. Schur, & A. J. Solnit. New York: International Universities Press, pp. 152–168.

———(1967), On Human Symbiosis and the Vicissitudes of Individuation. *J. Amer. Psychoanal. Assn.*, 15:740–763.

Moltz, H., Rosenblum, L., & Halikas, W. (1959), Imprinting and Level of Anxiety. *J. Comp. Physiol. Psychol.*, 52:240–244.

Moss, H. A. (1967), Sex, Age and State as Determinants of Mother-Infant Interaction. *Merrill-Palmer Quart.*, 13:19–36.

Nissen, H. W. (1951), Phylogenetic Comparison. In: *Handbook of Experimental Psychology*, ed. S. S. Stevens. New York: Wiley, pp. 347–386.

Nunberg, H. (1931), The Synthetic Function of the Ego. *Int. J. Psycho-Anal.*, 12:123–140.

Paine, R. S. (1965), The Contribution of Developmental Neurology to Child Psychiatry. *J. Amer. Acad. Child Psychiat.*, 4:353–386.

Pitz, G. F., & Ross, R. B. (1961), Imprinting as a Function of Arousal. *J. Comp. Physiol. Psychol.*, 54:602–604.

Polt, J. M., & Hess, E. H. (1964), Following and Imprinting: Effects of Light and Social Experience. *Science*, 143:1185–1188.

Pratt, K. C. (1954), The Neonate. In: *Manual of Child Psychology*, ed. L. Carmichael. New York: Wiley, pp. 215–291.

Prechtl, H., & Beintema, D. (1964), *The Neurological Examination of the Full-Term Newborn Infant*. London: The Spastics Society Medical Education and Information Unit. Wm. Heinemann Medical Books.

Provence, S. & Lipton, R. (1962), *Infants in Institutions*. New York: International Universities Press.

Rheingold, H. L. (1961), The Effect of Environmental Stimulation upon Social and Exploratory Behaviour in the Human Infant. In:

Determinants of Human Behaviour, Vol. I, ed. B. M. Foss. New York: Wiley, pp. 143–177.

Ribble, M. (1945), Anxiety in Infants. In: *Modern Trends in Child Psychiatry,* ed. N. D. C. Lewis & B. D. Pacella. New York: International Universities Press, pp. 11–26.

Richmond, J. B., & Lipton, E. L. (1959), Some Aspects of the Neurophysiology of the Newborn and Their Implications for Child Development. In: *Dynamic Psychopathology in Childhood,* ed. L. Jessner & E. Pavenstedt. New York: Grune & Stratton, pp. 78–105.

_____& Lustman, S. (1955), Autonomic Function in the Neonate: I. Implications for Psychosomatic Theory. *Psychosomat. Med.,* 17:269–275.

Robertson, J. (1958), *Young Children in Hospitals.* New York: Basic Books.

_____(1962), *Hospitals and Children.* London: Victor Gollancz, Ltd.

Roffwarg, H., Muzio, J., & Dement, W. C. (1963), A Sleep EEG-Rapid Eye Movement Cycle in Newborn Infants Associated with Specific Physiological Variations. *Communication to the Association for the Psychophysiological Study of Sleep.*

Sackett, G. P., Porter, M., & Holmes, H. (1965), Choice Behavior in Rhesus Monkeys: Effect of Stimulation during the First Month of Life. *Science,* 147:304–306.

Schaffer, H. R., & Callender, W. M. (1959), Psychologic Effects of Hospitalization in Infancy. *Pediat.,* 24:518–539.

_____& Emerson, P. (1964), The Development of Social Attachments in Infancy. *Monogr. Soc. Res. Child Dev.,* 29:1–77.

Schur, M. (1953), The Ego in Anxiety. In: *Drives, Affects, Behavior,* ed. R. M. Loewenstein. New York: International Universities Press, pp. 67–103.

_____(1958), The Ego and the Id in Anxiety. *The Psychoanalytic Study of the Child,* 13:190–220. New York: International Universities Press.

_____(1966), *The Id and the Regulatory Principles of Mental Functioning.* New York: International Universities Press.

Scott, J. P. (1958), *Animal Behavior.* Chicago: University of Chicago Press.

_____(1962), Critical Periods in Behavioral Development. *Science,* 138:949–958.

_____(1963), The Process of Primary Socialization in Canine and Human Infants. *Monogr. Soc. Res. Child Dev.*, 28:1–47.

——Deshaies, D., & Morris, D. D. (1961), Effect of Emotional Arousal on Primary Socialization in the Dog. Address to the New York State Branch of the American Psychiatric Association.

Shirley, M. M. (1933), *The First Two Years: A Study of Twenty-five Babies.* Minneapolis: University of Minnesota Press.

Siqueland, E. R., & Lipsitt, L. P. (1966), Conditioned Head-Turning in Human Newborns. *J. Exper. Child Psychol.*, 3:356–376.

Sluckin, W. (1965), *Imprinting and Early Learning.* Chicago: Aldine.

Spitz, R. A. (1945), Hospitalism. *The Psychoanalytic Study of the Child,* 1:53–74. New York: International Universities Press.

——(1946a), Hospitalism, II. *The Psychoanalytic Study of the Child,* 2:113-117. New York: International Universities Press.

——(1946b), The Smiling Response: A Contribution to the Ontogenesis of Social Relations. *Genet. Psychol. Monogr.*, 46:57–125.

——(1950), Anxiety in Infancy. *Int. J. Psycho-Anal.*, 31:138–143.

——(1951a), Purposive Grasping. *Personality.* 1:141–148.

——(1951b), The Psychogenic Diseases in Infancy: An Attempt at Their Etiological Classification. *The Psychoanalytic Study of the Child,* 6:255–275. New York: International Universities Press.

——(1953), Aggression: Its Role in the Establishment of Object Relations. In: *Drives, Affects, Behavior,* ed. R. M. Loewenstein. New York: International Universities Press, pp. 126–138.

——(1955), The Primal Cavity: A Contribution to the Genesis of Perception and Its Role in Early Infancy. *The Psychoanalytic Study of the Child,* 10:215–240. New York: International Universities Press.

——(1957), *No and Yes.* New York: International Universities Press.

——(1959), *A Genetic Field Theory of Ego Formation.* New York: International Universities Press.

——(1961), Some Early Prototypes of Ego Defenses. *J. Amer. Psychoanal. Assn.*, 9:626–651.

——(1963), Life and the Dialogue. In: *Counterpoint: Libidinal Object and Subject,* ed. H. S. Gaskill. New York: International Universities Press, pp. 154–176.

——(1965), *The First Year of Life.* New York: International Universities Press.

——& Wolf, K. M. (1946), Anaclitic depression. *The Psychoanalytic Study of the Child,* 2:313–342. New York: International Universities Press.

———— ————(1949), Autoerotism. *The Psychoanalytic Study of the Child*, 3/4:85–120. New York: International Universities Press.

Stevens, A. (in press), Attachment Behavior, Separation Anxiety and Stranger Anxiety in Polymatrically Reared Infants. In: *Origins of Human Social Relations*, ed. H. R. Schaffer. London: Academic Press.

Tennes, K. H., & Lampl, E. E. (1964), Stranger and Separation Anxiety in Infancy. *J. Nerv. Ment. Dis.*, 139:247–254.

———— ————(1966), Some Aspects of Mother-Child Relationship Pertaining to Infantile Separation Anxiety. *J. Nerv. Ment. Dis.*, 143: 426–437.

Thomas, A., Chess, S., Birch, H. G., Hertzig, M. E., & Korn, S. (1964), *Behavioral Individuality in Early Childhood.* New York: New York University Press.

Thomas, H. (1965), Visual-Fixation Responses of Infants to Stimuli of Varying Complexity. *Child Dev.*, 36:629–638.

Von Senden, M. (1960), *Space and Sight.* London: Methuen.

Waelder, R. (1936), The Principle of Multiple Function: Observations on Over-determination, *Psychoanal. Quart.*, 5:45–62.

Wertheimer, M. (1961), Psychomotor Coordination of Auditory and Visual Space at Birth. *Science*, 13:1692.

White, B. L., & Held, R. (1963), Plasticity in Perceptual Development during the First Six Months of Life. Paper presented to the American Association for the Advancement of Science, Cleveland.

Winnicott, D. W. (1953), Transitional Objects and Transitional Phenomena. *Int. J. Psycho-Anal.*, 34:89–97.

Wolff, P. H. (1959), Observations on Newborn Infants. *Psychosomat. Med.*, 21:110–118.

————(1963), Observations on the Early Development of Smiling. In: *Determinants of Infant Behaviour*, Vol. 2, ed. B. M. Foss. New York: Wiley, pp. 113–133.

————(1966), The Causes, Controls, and Organization of Behavior in the Neonate. *Psychol. Issues*, Monogr. 17. New York: International Universities Press.

Yarrow, L. J. (1962), Maternal Deprivation: Toward an Empirical and Conceptual Reevaluation. In: *Maternal Deprivation*, ed. H. L. Witmer. New York: Child Welfare League of America, pp. 3–41.

INDEX

Abstract thinking, 363, 364
Activity
  level, 13
  and tremor, 216–217
  type, congenital, 13
Adaptation, at 6 months, 211
Affect
  awareness of, 363
  conscious, 56
  definition, 3
  derivatives, 93
  discharge, at 6 months, 201, 203
  emergence of, 40, 82
  first conscious, 51
  isolation of, 364
Affective
  discharge, and mothering, 201
  reactions at 6 weeks, 199
  reactions at 6 months, 202–203
  reactions at 1 year, 204–205
  responsiveness at 6 weeks, 210–211
  responsiveness at 6 months, 211
  states, dystonic, at 1 year, 204–205
Affectomotor storm, 3
Aggression
  and fear, 107
  and negativism, 206
  at 6 months, 203
  cathexis, at 1 year, 205
  impulse discharge, at 1 year, 207
Ainsworth, M. D. S., 99, 101–102,
  103, 148, 228, 351, 400
Allport, G. G.
Amatruda, C. S., *see* Gesell
Ambivalence
  and fear, 207
  maternal, 140
Ambrose, J. A., 10n., 33, 400, 401
Anaclitic
  depression, 98, 148, 288
  gratification, 50–51
  relationship, drives, and vital func-
    tions, 357
Animal infancy, 27–32

Anticipation, capacity for, 92
Anxiety, 10, 93
  affect during infancy, 3
  affect of, 8, 39, 52, 54, 89, 92, 93
  and birth, 7
  and ego development, 5, 8, 37, 211
  and ego formation, 8, 91
  and ego-id conflict, 6
  and fear, distinction between, 6
  and Signs of Disturbance, 360
  and socialization, 92
  as danger signal, 6
  as pre-affect, 6
  as reaction to danger, 38
  definition, 5–6
  development, 54, 88
  "eight-months," 233
  emergence of affect, 8, 78, 91
  physiological, 54–55, 355ff.
  potential, 26, 53–54
  predisposition to, 6, 47, 53
  preparedness, 39, 56–57, 77, 83,
    88–90, 93, 149, 242, 362
  preparedness, examples, 58–77
  primary, 7
  proper, 5, 6, 7
  psychological, 355ff.
  reactions, 53
  rudimentary, 56
  seat of, 7–9
  signal, 7–8, 39, 52, 56, 58–77
    passim, 91, 92, 112, 233, 237,
    240, 243, 356, 364
  and fantasy, 8
  as ego function, 54
  separation, 7, 92
  stranger, 83, 92
Apgar scores, 104–105
Appetite, poor, at 1 year, 208
Apprehensiveness, 234ff.
Arlow, J. A., 54n., 401
Arousal
  and tension states, 13
  of perception, 88–89

413